RECONSTRUCTING OLD TESTAMENT THEOLOGY

OVERTURES TO BIBLICAL THEOLOGY

RECONSTRUCTING
OLD TESTAMENT THEOLOGY

AFTER THE COLLAPSE
OF HISTORY

Leo G. Perdue

FORTRESS PRESS

MINNEAPOLIS

RECONSTRUCTING OLD TESTAMENT THEOLOGY
After the Collapse of History

Cover and book design by Joseph Bonyata
Cover image: One of the city gates of Meggido built during the reign of King Solomon. © Erich Lessing / Art Resource, NY.

Library of Congress Cataloging-in-Publication Data
Perdue, Leo G.
   Reconstructing Old Testament theology : after the collapse of history / Leo G. Perdue.
      p. cm. — (Overtures to biblical theology)
   Includes bibliographical references and index.
   ISBN 0-8006-3716-X (alk. paper)
   1. Bible. O.T.—Theology—History of doctrines—20th century. 2. Bible. O.T.—Theology. I. Title. II. Series.
   BS1192.5.P48 2005
   230'.0411—dc22
                                                                    2005003316

The paper used in this publication meets the minimum requirements of American National Standard for Information Sciences—Permanence of Paper for Printed Library Materials, ANSI Z329.48-1984.

Manufactured in the U.S.A.
10   09   08   07   06   05   1   2   3   4   5   6   7   8   9   10

CONTENTS

EDITOR'S FOREWORD

WITH THE PUBLICATION OF *THE COLLAPSE OF HISTORY: RECON-structing Old Testament Theology* (Overtures to Biblical Theology; Fortress Press, 1994), Leo Perdue established himself as the primary chronicler of contemporary scholarship in Old Testament theology in the English-speaking world. (See also Walter Brueggemann, *Theology of the Old Testament: Testimony, Dispute, Advocacy* [Fortress Press, 1997], 61–114.) Perdue, in that book, traced the demise of the hegemonic influence of Walther Eichrodt and Gerhard von Rad in the mid-twentieth century, and fully understood the uneasy and somewhat uncritical settlement that pertained in the field between faith and history. The significance of Perdue's earlier study, however, concerns developments in the post-von Rad period of scholarship, which was a time of considerable confusion and venturesome diversity in method, perspective, and outcome. A signal mark of that book was the close attention to Jeremiah studies as a case study in new methods, thus giving the dynamism of the field textual particularity. It was evident in Perdue's study that the field would not ever again return to a simple, single model about which there would be consensus.

In the present volume, Perdue now takes up more recent developments in the field, reiterating some earlier points, but also accounting for the surprising and breathtaking advances that are now available. While the lines of development in theological interpretation become clearer, the intense ferment in the field was inchoate at the time of Perdue's earlier study and continues to some extent to be so. This fact leads us to expect, in time to come, another effort from Perdue that will keep the account current.

In the present volume, the move beyond Euro-American domination of Old Testament theology becomes staggeringly apparent. In the latter part of the book we may notice in particular three developments that were only at their beginning at the publication of the earlier volume. First, the entry of Jewish participation into the scholarly work of biblical interpretation is now vigorous and accessible in a way that non-Jewish scholarship may and must take into account. The contribution of Jon Levenson in

ix

this regard is of special significance and the impetus of *Debru Emet* has helped to create an environment for such interaction.

Second, attention to postmodern hermeneutics is of immense importance for the field. The term "postmodern" of course runs the risk of being only a slogan and is remarkably imprecise. Nonetheless it is clear that a reading that is genuinely "post" to modernism makes an immense difference; it is clear that the "hard men" of "modernism" do not yield easily to such requirements. Third, the move beyond the old-fashioned centrist consensus is clear in postcolonial readings as, for example, when Musa Dube can speak of the "villagizing" of scholarship as a challenge to uncritical "globalization" that has passed uncritically as "assured result." These new initiatives currently have remarkable energy, and we are only at the beginning of their importance for the field.

Our common debt to Perdue for this book is very great. His close attention to detail, matched with a capacity to see the larger picture, means that he has in an inventive way formulated something of a "canonical" account of current scholarship. Perdue understands as well as anyone that his judgments and assessments are open to review, because new developments require both time and seasoning for critical appraisal. Nonetheless Perdue's willingness to "put it all together" in this way is a welcome resource. I am delighted to be his cohort in this important contribution to our common work. Perdue has made clear that every scholarly attempt now must take into account voices other than one's own. The point of that awareness is that every interpretive offer is kept open as penultimate, an important awareness in our culture where interpretation too much takes on the shrill tone of absoluteness. Such shrillness is apparent, of course, in church interpretation, but also at times in the hardness of the guild. Perdue reminds us that such shrillness, in guild or in church or synagogue, violates the text we study and the interpretive enterprise that we share.

Walter Brueggemann
Columbia Theological Seminary
March 23, 2005

ABBREVIATIONS

AARAS	American Academy of Religion Academy Series
AARCCS	American Academy of Religion Cultural Criticism Series
AB	Anchor Bible
AGAJU	Arbeiten zur Geschichte des antiken Judentums und des Urchristentums
BASOR	*Bulletin of the American Schools of Oriental Research*
BCR	Blackwell Companions to Religion
BEATAJ	Beiträge zur Erforschung des Alten Testaments und des antiken Judentums
BETL	Bibliotheca ephemeridum theologicarum lovaniensium
BibInt	*Biblical Interpretation*
BibIntSer	Biblical Interpretation Series
BibSem	Biblical Seminar
BJS	Brown Judaic Studies
BLS	Bible and Literature Series
BM	*Beth Miqra*
BSNA	Biblical Scholarship in North America
BZAW	Beihefte zur Zeitschrift für die alttestamentliche Wissenschaft
CJA	Christianity and Judaism in Antiquity
CJT	*Canadian Journal of Theology*
ConBOT	Coniectanea biblica: Old Testament Series
CRBR	*Critical Review of Books in Religion*
CSHJ	Chicago Studies in the History of Judaism
DBAT	*Dielheimer Blätter zum Alten Testament und seiner Rezeption in der Alten Kirche*
DBI	*Dictionary of Biblical Interpretation.*
EBib	Etudes bibliques
EvTh	*Evangelische Theologie*
ExpT	*Expository Times*
FCBS	Fortress Classics in Biblical Studies

FRLANT	Forschungen zur Religion und Literatur des Alten und Neuen Testament
GBS	Guides to Biblical Scholarship
HBT	*Horizons in Biblical Theology*
HSM	Harvard Semitic Monographs
HSS	Harvard Semitic Series
IDB	*Interpreter's Dictionary of the Bible.*
Int	*Interpretation*
ISBL	Indiana Studies in Biblical Literature
JAAR	*Journal of the American Academy of Religion*
JBL	*Journal of Biblical Literature*
JBTh	*Jahrbuch für biblische Theologie*
JCHS	Jewish and Christian Heritage Series
JNES	*Journal of Near Eastern Studies*
JR	*Journal of Religion*
JSJSup	Journal for the Study of Judaism Supplements
JSOT	*Journal for the Study of the Old Testament*
JSOTSup	Journal for the Study of the Old Testament Supplement Series
JTSA	*Journal of Theology for Southern Africa*
LAI	Library of Ancient Israel
MLBS	Mercer Library of Biblical Studies
NIB	*New Interpreter's Bible*
NovTSup	Novum Testamentum Supplements
OBT	Overtures to Biblical Theology
OTL	Old Testament Library
PTMS	Pittsburgh Theological Monograph Series
SABH	Studies in American Biblical Hermeneutics
SBLAM	Society of Biblical Literature Annual Meeting
SBLDS	Society of Biblical Literature Dissertation Series
SBLSymSer	Society of Biblical Literature Symposium Series
SBT	Studies in Biblical Theology
SBTS	Sources for Biblical and Theological Study
SCJ	Studies in Christianity and Judaism
SHANE	Studies in the History of the Ancient Near East
SJOT	*Scandanavian Journal of Old Testament*
SJT	*Scottish Journal of Theology*
SOR	*Studies in Oriental Religions*
SWC	Studies in World Christianity
ThBü	Theologische Bücherei
ThR	*Theologische Rundschau*
TLZ	*Theologische Literaturzeitung*

TS	*Theological Studies*
TynBul	*Tyndale Bulletin*
VF	*Verkündigung und Forschung*
VT	*Vetus Testamentum*
VTSup	Vetus Testamentum Supplements
ZAW	*Zeitschrift für die alttestamentliche Wissenschaft*

PREFACE

THIS VOLUME BEGINS WHERE *THE COLLAPSE OF HISTORY,* PUB-
lished originally in 1994, ends. In the intervening years, other methods
and approaches have gained increased notoriety in the continuing rewriting and reviving of Old Testament theology. These encompass the History
of Religion; ethnic approaches (African American, womanist, Hispanic,
mujerista, and Asian American); global studies, in particular the vast array
of postcolonial approaches; and literary and cultural investigations, especially reader-response, deconstruction, and postmodern explorations. One
of my theses in *The Collapse of History* was that approaches to Old Testament theology reflect the development of new methods and points of view
in interpreting the Bible as well as the context and orientation of the interpreter. This continues to be true, as will become clear in the summaries
and evaluations of the approaches in the present volume. This richness in
diversity of approaches has added much to our comprehension of the
theology of the Old Testament, while at the same time, it has increased
the complexity of understanding both the text's theology or theologies
and those of the interpreters and the social and ideological frameworks
they bring to the task. This volume is a modest attempt to trace the contours of some of these newer methods to assist scholars and students to
make an informed, critical entrée into this most engaging of biblical fields.
Some of the language of the first volume is repeated in order to create a
more integrated approach to the present book. This is especially the case
in the discussion of feminism in the first part of the fifth chapter.

This volume was written during my sabbatical year in 2003 and
2004, spent in residence at the Theological Faculties of Ruprecht-Karls-
Universität Heidelberg and Georg-August-Universität Göttingen, where I
was respectively guest lecturer and guest professor. I am especially grateful
for the warm hospitality of and stimulating conversations with Professors
Manfred Oeming and Michael Welker in the Theologische Facultät at the
University of Heidelberg and Professors Hermann Spieckermann and Reinhard Kratz on the Theological Faculty at the University of Göttingen. These

congenial and courteous hosts not only granted me a conducive environ-ment for research and writing, including an office, library, and computer resources, but also provided me a myriad of insights that enriched im-mensely my own thinking, which has been incorporated into this volume.

Other colleagues also have stimulated my thinking and guided me in seeking out resources that would enable me to understand and evaluate more recent and various approaches to biblical and systematic theology. I thank especially Henning Graf Reventlow, emeritiert at the University of the Ruhr; Erhard Gerstenberger, emeritiert at the University of Marburg; Rudolf Smend, emeritiert at the University of Göttingen; Konrad Schmid at the University of Zurich; and three of my colleagues at Brite Divinity School: Toni Craven, Stephen Sprinkle, and Stacey Floyd-Thomas. Their theological insights into several of the methods I introduce in this volume have been particularly helpful. Finally, one colleague stands out as the one from whom I have learned the most in the area of theology: Walter Brueggemann, now retired from the faculty of Columbia Theological Seminary. He has been not only hugely creative and productive in his own writing and lecturing, but also most gracious and generous in assisting those of us interested in the Bible and theology to continue to engage in the pursuit of understanding and embracing this esteemed parent of all other biblical disciplines. His passion for justice in a world that has experi-enced little of it has affected the lives of many.

Finally, I would like to dedicate this book to my mother, now deceased, who, although an impoverished widow and minority (Chickasaw Nation), somehow still managed to raise my brother and me and to provide us tenderness, warmth, and security. Throughout our youth, she encouraged us in countless ways to discover what it is to be simply human, to find our own place within the world, and to value who and what we are. May the depth of her slumbers, which now are uninterrupted, bring her the peace that she rarely experienced while alive.

1

The Present Status of
Old Testament Theology

[History] above all is a cemetery and field of the dead.
—*K. G. Steck*

God created man, because he loves stories.
—*Elie Wiesel*

The past is not dead; it is not even past.
—*William Faulkner*

If thinking wants to think God, then it must endeavor to tell stories.
—*Eberhard Jüngel*

There is no power relation without the correlative constitution of a field of knowledge, nor any knowledge that does not presuppose and constitute at the same time power relations.
—*Michel Foucault*

Introduction

THESE QUOTATIONS, THE FIRST FOUR OF WHICH I USED TO INTRO-
duce my earlier book, *The Collapse of History*, provide a variety of apt metaphors for the current state of Old Testament theology. These and many others, rich with evocative and compelling insight, lead us into the intellectual and imaginative travels of the human spirit into a past that has long since disappeared, save for the texts produced by its savants, artists, and dreamers.[1] We have been discomfited by the lost of paradigms

---

1. Important surveys of Old Testament theology include Barr, *The Concept of Biblical Theology*; Bruce, "The Theology and Interpretation of the Old Testament"; J. Collins, "Is a

and metanarratives that have shaped our worldview, for we now have encountered new and compelling realities shaped by what is often to many
of us a strange and at times disconcerting discourse. The recovery of meaning for some and the discovery of self-understanding for others are a twin-
pronged essence of the human spirit that must determine something that
means in order to find a restful conclusion to our journeys of the spirit.

For those in the dominant classes in the West, including Europe and
North America, new approaches and discoveries of the intensity and opu-
lence of other cultures and ways of being have challenged the once unrivaled epistemologies and subsequent philosophies and theologies of the
Enlightenment entering into and being sustained by narratives of culture
and superiority. These more recent methods, approaches, and understandings, which have slowly seeped into the hearts of the human character,
have proceeded to create new theological language, leading to fresh and engaging articulations taking shape in novel accounts of the immortals who
have provided their most illustrious creature with human worth and
moral value.[2] Biblical theology has moved from the dominance of historical
positivism, at one time cultivated and honored in the halls of the European
and North American *académie,* into other types of discourse grounded in
different philosophies as varied as structuralism to neo-Marxism to deconstruction.

Different philosophies have led to a diversification of theologies shaped
by an almost unlimited set of global contexts and the multiple varieties of
social communities located in each one. The meaning of the Bible is no
longer buried in the graves of the dead who shaped ancient civilizations

---

Critical Biblical Theology Possible?"; Coats, "Theology of the Hebrew Bible"; Hasel, *Old
Testament Theology;* Hayes and Prussner, *Old Testament Theology;* Høgenhaven, *Problems
and Prospects of Old Testament Theology;* Jeremias, "Neuere Entwürfe zu einer 'Theologie des
Alten Testaments,'"; Kraus, *Die Biblische Theologie;* Ollenburger et al., *Old Testament Theology;*
Reventlow, *Problems of Old Testament Theology in the Twentieth Century; Problems of Biblical
Theology in the Twentieth Century;* "Modern Approaches to Old Testament Theology,"; and
Smart, *The Past, Present, and Future of Biblical Theology.*

2. For a discussion of the premature obituary of the "Biblical Theology Movement," a
largely American phenomenon, see Childs, *Biblical Theology in Crisis.* Criticisms of historical
criticism began especially in the 1970s with the development of literary approaches and have
grown in intensity to the present. The criticisms have targeted many features of this method,
including the longstanding claim of its inability to contribute to systematic theology. For
this criticism, see, e.g., Stuhlmacher, *Historical Criticism and Theological Interpretation of
Scripture.* Of course, historical criticism was never intended to be a theological method for
contemporary faith. Its focal point is history, not modern theology. However, it is capable of
being used to reconstruct historical theology, tracing its multifaceted developments through
time, space, and culture. Its application to contemporary faith makes use of analogical and
not the constructive formulations.

that formed the written texts, but now is to be situated—at least to some extent, if not, as some would argue, completely—within the myriad of interpreters with their vast networks of multiple social, sexual, gender, ethnic, and postcolonial milieus. Uniformity of meaning, once a cherished and nurtured yet highly utopian dream, has been blown by the winds of differentiated and conflicting possibilities into many situations and numerous ways of knowing and being.

As noted in *The Collapse of History*, once-traditional paradigms of biblical studies that produced theologies that largely reflected the philosophies and cultural products spawned by the Enlightenment, idealism, empiricism, and then positivism and the resulting historical method, then and now dominant, have come under serious assault, leading to what I called a decade ago the "collapse of history." By the "collapse of history," I did not intend to suggest that historiography and its resultant views of history, construed largely through epistemologies of thought, experience, and analytical sifting of literary and material data, have become insignificant for biblical scholarship and the Old Testament theology that emerges. I characterize as obscurantist and perhaps even intentionally abstruse those voices that completely negate historical method while contending that we have entered a postmodern world with significantly different epistemologies and sociopolitical arrangements or, better said, unlimited cultural diffusion.[3] To be sure, we have learned what Foucault's initial quote affirms: knowledge and power are inextricably linked, and we have been awakened to the fact that the subjective knower is heavily involved in shaping meaning and subsequently the proposed interpretation. However, once that is said, we do not therefore rush to the precipice of historical nihilism and plunge headlong into the darkened abyss of meaninglessness that rises up from the void of non-"sense." For some postmodernists, history and existence in space and time have lost all meaning, because knowledge in any objective, commonly agreed upon sense of the term cannot be obtained. Indeed, so it is submitted, objectivity is an illusion. In following this line of "thinking," what remains is nothing but the ideology of persons and groups that, operating solely on the basis of self-interest, are incapable of transcending the multiple locations in which they exist. Or so we are told. In some of the forms of postmodernism, the objective is to counteract this self-interest and thus to rescue the biblical text from what may only be described as the

---

3. Important earlier discussions of postmodernism, theology, and biblical theology include: Burnham, *Postmodern Theology;* McKnight, *Postmodern Use of the Bible;* Moore, "The 'Post-'Age Stamp: Does It Stick?"; Olson, "Postmodernity and Faith"; Rascke, "Fire and Roses"; Scharlemann, *Theology at the End of the Century;* and H. Smith, "Postmodernism's Impact on the Study of Religion." See the more detailed bibliography present in chapter 7 on postmodernism in this volume.

arrogance of elitism, enhanced by historical criticism making unproven claims concerning the attainment of objective knowledge. No longer imprisoned by Western elitism, all people, including marginals, are now empowered to pursue their own ideologies, which cannot be criticized from the outside. Indeed, if some postmodernists are "right," the only discourse left to pursue is that of insiders who speak to each other, with the purpose not of discovering objectified truth, but rather of encountering multiple understandings, each tinged with self-interest. Nothing is true that resides outside the self-made world created by private interest. If postmodernism is correct, then this book should be nothing more than the lengthy obituary of a dead and now curious search of unenlightened souls for past understanding that is neither recoverable nor relevant to modern existence.

By the expression "collapse of history," I did not mean to suggest that history is finished. While I find it curious that "new historicism" continues to use the term *history,* the objective is to subvert anything approaching history (i.e., the recovery of the past). In my own work, I have consistently refused to dispense with rational discourse that reaches back to the Enlightenment and the consequential historical-critical method that this epoch of human knowledge created. But I did mean by the phrase that for a quarter century at least, there has been an active revolt against the domination of history (particularly in its positivistic expression) and historical method in accessing the meaning of the Hebrew Bible and the birthing of Old Testament theology. In the decade since the appearance of *The Collapse of History,* even more methodologies have either gained momentum or emerged in biblical studies, increasing significantly the number of approaches, and many seem to have the agenda of subverting past studies before offering their own insights.[4] While I shall suggest that these newer approaches come to us with offertory basins filled with the wine of fresh insight, it is unfortunate that some have sought to devalue previous gifts. With the rise of fresh methods for studying the Bible, nurtured within a variety of newly emerging sociopolitical locations in the contemporary world and the challenging of epistemologies assumed to be true without being subjected to rigorous examination since the Enlightenment, historical method has suffered great duress, buffeted by the winds of unsympathetic change. With the end of colonialism and the emerging of a defiant postcolonialism,

---

4. E.g., as early as 1980, James Luther Mays ("What Is Written") argued, "Currently there is a restlessness in many quarters at the dominance of Biblical interpretation by historical criticism—in newer literary criticism, in structuralism, in the hermeneutics of Paul Ricoeur, to mention only several." What these methods share is a concern primarily with the literary and phenomenological character of the text, rather than with the history behind the text.

new epistemologically informed approaches to biblical study, including the variety of understandings of postcolonialism, liberation theologies, and the pronounced emphasis on fiction and imagination, all largely ahistorical, have led to new ways of understanding the world, including the Bible. These new configurations of biblical study and Old Testament theology have produced a significant degree of diversity that enriches the understanding of human existence and cultures but makes the quest to present the theology or even the theologies of the Old Testament extremely difficult and for some impossible. Thus, they indeed are the "pearl of great price," often requiring the desecration of the memories of the ancestors before moving into our present understandings. Any talk of discovering uniformity in understanding the method, shape, and meaning of Old Testament theology now is submerged in the churning waters of pluralism. My earlier fancy that conversation would lead to some points of convergence has faded into wistful disillusion. Not only is conversation not taking place, the ideological commitments to contradictory approaches are so intense that listening with a view to change does not appear possible. While offering us an unbounded enrichment of understanding the Bible and theology, the pluralism of many methods inevitably rejects the confinement of absolutism. Yet the concern is that relativism is only a short step away. Some interpreters refuse to impose any limits on relativism. I find this especially disturbing in view of the dialogical and ethical consequences.

Regardless of the constant methodological tossings in contemporary biblical study and the larger epistemological framework for knowing and persuading, and in spite of the appearance of many recent descriptions of Old Testament theology, what continues to be surprisingly lacking is a serious representation and then critical analysis of new methods for biblical study and their contributions to discourse.[5] Indeed, on the one hand, those methods that assert they are beyond critical engagement are the most deliberate in assailing the views of others. In making disparaging remarks about other ways of doing biblical theology, some of the practitioners of newer approaches engage in conversation to find commonality, but only among themselves. Either that, or some of the more radical devotees of postmodernism would cast classical history and its methods of analysis into the ash heap of intellectual rubbish that has permitted the misconstruing of theology against the exercise of free discourse and even the oppression of many groups. To be sure, there are important criticisms that should be raised against various historical approaches to Old Testament theology, but these are discussed in books and journals and normally not

5. See Trible, "Five Loaves and Two Fishes."

in face-to-face dialogue. This self-critical perspective is indigenous to Enlightenment epistemologies and constructions of history and theology based on them. As I shall argue, the posture of "beyond criticism" to which some of the devotees of newer methods adhere simply will not do, for it results in a denial of what is central to human thought and discourse and leads to a veritable black hole of inescapable skepticism reflective of the Athenian New Academy that, for its followers for two centuries, led to the eventual loss of any claim to approach the precincts of truth considered either to be plausible or beyond reasonable doubt.

Yet, on the other hand, most contemporary surveys of biblical theology have been content to continue discussing the classical approaches to Old Testament theology and often take little, if any, notice of vital and new ways of getting at the understanding of texts that are grounded in different epistemologies and pose often different, unconventional questions. While occasional summaries of Old Testament theologies are accompanied by evaluations, most of these have sidestepped the larger and more pressing issues. This also will not do.

As I noted in *The Collapse of History*, too many modern scholars since World War II, including those who have written descriptions of ways of doing Old Testament theology and others who actually have produced Old Testament theologies, have ignored the voices of discontent that are directed against Enlightenment strategies for knowing, historical criticism, and traditional biblical theology that builds on this methodology. These critical and, until recently, marginalized voices have continued to expand in numbers and perspectives in order to include liberation and narrative theologians, canon and literary scholars, phenomenologists and linguists, feminists and womanists, postcolonialists and postmodernists, and numerous ethnic interpreters (African American, Hispanic, Hispanic American, Asian, Asian American, and Jewish). Indeed, some biblical scholars continue to write and speak as though the destabilized language of traditional approaches will continue to convince and convict, while hoping that new methods and their impact on theological discourse will somehow simply disappear.[6] Yet some of the practitioners of newer approaches have often become tendentious and immune to examination, so much so that they refuse to permit themselves to be subjected to scrutiny or to be engaged by those who hold different views.

Other scholars have abandoned what usually has been regarded as the subject matter of Old Testament theology, i.e., God, in order to focus their attention on other matters, including the social and anthropological de-

---

6. For example, see Preuss, *Theologie des Alten Testaments;* and Høgenhaven, *Problems and Prospects of Old Testament Theology.*

scription of human beings and avoiding the location of the church.[7] Theology becomes, in this case, a category of social knowledge, even self-serving ideology. It is easier to speak about human nature or the literary character of the text than it is about the transcendent. Still others pursue the existence and interpretation of historical fragments themselves, avoiding larger constructions of meaning, especially theological and ethical ones, as abstract, speculative, abstruse, or outside the domain of legitimate biblical scholarship. This retreat into historical obscurity leaves to contemporary theologians, pastors, and the unlearned, often neophytes in the complicated tools and understandings of historical-critical study, the task of engaging biblical theology in conversation with contemporary hermeneutics and constructive theology. Thus, by failing to valorize matters of faith and ethics in the present, biblical scholars too often have disengaged from contemporary faith and practice and have left to the uninformed and untrained the task of interpreting the biblical texts and deriving contemporary meaning from ancient Scripture.

Even among those who consider themselves to be biblical theologians open to new methodologies and hermeneutical issues that originate in the contemporary world, many have taken leave of dialogue, debate, and argumentation when it comes to the tasks and methods of theology, stressing instead the quality of interpretation, not the method leading to its formation. Thus, in this age of pluralism and diversity, we should celebrate multiculturalism and rejoice over our differences, even when these differences point to significant variations of textual interpretation and human meaning.[8] Yet this makes theology nothing more than a matter of individual preference concerning questions of human import that are at the heart of human existence. Relativism is the inescapable outcome. An open presentation of the contours of an approach and its results that evokes discussion is the necessary objective of theological discourse. Admittedly, the search for, discovery, and application of criteria of evaluation is a rational process, but I know of no other way to engage in conversation and the quest for meaning understood in many different ways. The establishment of a carefully proposed and rigorously applied analysis would not result in only one way of doing Old Testament theology, but it would provide the basis for informed discussion and even occasional consent. Appropriate criteria, carefully applied, could evaluate and assess the quality of an interpretation in important ways and remove it from the realm of subjective preference and what may be even preposterous claims.

---

7. For a survey of this field, see Gottwald, *Social Scientific Criticism of the Hebrew Bible and its Social World.*

8. See J. Sanders, *Canon and Community.*

All this is not to say, then, that the field of biblical theology is stagnant or even declining.[9] Indeed, the reverse is true. But there are multiple approaches, making disparate claims, advocating dissimilar objectives, and applying diverse methods with competing philosophical and theological orientations and assumptions, that are competing for adherents. The variety of expression and the lack of clear ways of proceeding often have silenced those raised in a simpler time to practice a more traditional, often confessional, approach. Now they are in danger of becoming the voices of silence, marginalized outside the boundaries of human community, because they are viewed as either representing or being oppressors of the past continuing to the present. These are the ones too often relegated to the realm of quiet repose.

But for the most part, biblical theology today has not become a mute statue of a deity of a long-dead religion, but rather a panorama of deities seeking adherents who command no consensus, clash with or ignore different approaches, and attract no overwhelming following. Some basic understanding of new approaches and content is essential, if conversation between biblical theologians and ultimately between biblical and contemporary theologians is to occur with considered and engaging vitality.

Reasons for the Collapse of History

Before moving into the discussion of new paradigms, we should remind ourselves of the reasons for the collapse of history. The causes behind the collapse of history as the dominant paradigm for Old Testament theology are many and complex. To simplify, I shall mention only those that I consider to be the most important.

The "Gap" between History and Present

First, the collapse of history has been due in part to a challenge as to whether historical-critical method (normally grounded in philosophical positivism, although other approaches — for example, neo-Marxist — are used) is appropriate for theological discourse. This challenge is true only of a theological approach based on the categories of idealism, but not on history. It also is true of Protestants who move from the Reformation or Enlightenment to the biblical periods, choosing to ignore the theological contributions of the early church fathers and the teachers of the Middle Ages. Consequently, the tracing of theological views through the centuries, noting their changes due to different worldviews and sociopolitical arrangements, is certainly possi-

9. Barr, *The Concept of Biblical Theology.*

ble. Nonetheless, during the past generation, other methods for Old Testament study have developed that have different philosophical underpinnings that eschew the historical enterprise. These include, for example, new criticism, Brevard Childs's canonical approach, History of Religion, literary expressions of feminist and womanist hermeneutics, some approaches to postcolonialism, and numerous types of the ellusive term *postmodernism.*

At times, exponents of more recent paradigms argue that these approaches make more accessible theological meaning that, in their judgment, resides in and is shaped, not by an "objective" history behind ancient texts, but rather by the political implications of liberation, the theological faith of the community of believers, the order and continuation of creation, the context and experience of the interpreter, the narrative world created through the interaction of the implied audience with both the "voice" of the text and the text itself, the imagination of writer or audience, and the particular interests and understandings of different groups, including those who have been marginalized. For example, theologians of imagination and metaphor may argue that theological discourse, including that of biblical theology, does not simply issue from the historian's "reproductive imagination," to use the figure made popular by Paul Ricoeur, but also from the fiction writer's "productive imagination."[10] For proponents of some of the newer approaches, history as the theme, center of interpretation, and frame for theological discourse has lost its once unchallenged position of dominance. Indeed, the resultant interpretations of historical critics have often been censured for being heavily ideological, reflecting a Eurocentric narrative that seeks to legitimize white-male dominance, status, and control of others.

Theological Diversity

The fragmentation of theological discourse resulting from the collapse of history is also due in part to the protean character of contemporary theology that shares a common heuristic world with biblical scholarship. As early as 1981, Lonnie Kliever used the apt metaphor of "the shattered spectrum" to describe the state of contemporary theology, a metaphor that is even more appropriate a generation later.[11] This lost unity of theme and method and its replacement by diversity is obvious in even a cursory

---

10. Ricoeur, "The Metaphorical Process"; and "The Narrative Function."

11. Kliever, *The Shattered Spectrum.* For a cogent and clear survey of American contemporary theology up to 1990, see Ferm, *Contemporary American Theologies.* More recent surveys include Miller and Grenz, *Fortress Introduction to Contemporary Theologies;* and Markham, *A Theology of Engagement.*

reading of contemporary and biblical theology. Liberation, process, hope, creation, feminism, metaphor, story, imagination, power, ideology, oppression/justice, experiences of ethnic and social groups, social location, and the role of the reader in shaping meaning have emerged to reconceive the strategies and questions of theology. No commanding contemporary theology has appeared to form a consensus, as did old liberalism and neo-orthodoxy in the first sixty years of the twentieth century. Subsequently, the disarray of contemporary theology has contributed significantly to the present diversity of ways to approach Old Testament theology.

The Crisis of Epistemology

A third, more existential factor has contributed to the present disarray in biblical theology since the collapse of history. This may be coined the loss of confidence in the epistemological claims of the Enlightenment about objectivity and critical, rational inquiry. Objective truth discernible to the human mind through rational and empirical study is considered an illusion of distorted imagination. Patriarchy, colonialism, the Holocaust, the deterioration of the biosphere, the threat of nuclear war, neocolonialism, organized terrorism, and technology as the weapon of modern pariah nations are the real and potentially destructive by-products of modern civilization, which require a theology that focuses on these threats to existence.

As Foucault, among others, has argued, it is those who control capital and technology who inherit the earth, and the drive for power over nature and nations has brought modern civilization and life close to its own collapse by the threatened use of weapons of mass destruction, not only in the hands of rogue nations, but also in the control of terrorists intent on destroying cultures they find opposed to their own ideologies. We now find ourselves threatened by the very technology we once hailed as our god, savior, and comforter, for it has created weapons that may bring an end to all life, not simply the independence of nations. And it is not only the danger of the threat of terrorists that poses an end to life, but also that of the leaders of nations obsessed by ideologies of self-interest, whether the United States or North Korea. In the G-8's increasingly sophisticated weapons of war and shameful disregard for the environment and global genocide, it is far more likely that they, in the pursuit of things desired by unrestrained greed, will destroy the good earth than will terrorist organizations with their small resources and numbers. Unless we develop a new paradigm for life that values human worth and relationships with peoples and will make creation not an object for human mastery, but rather a sustaining environment for human dwelling, the world will not have to concern itself with the advent of a "big bang" in some unfathomable future. In the cosmos, the death of this planet will make absolutely no difference, but it will mean the obliteration of our own life and environment. A new paradigm is needed that understands and supports history, not as the mastery of the weak by the strong, but rather as the movement toward a viable world in which all nations and people share, celebrate, and live in peace, justice, and a treasured creation.[12]

The alternative is to make biblical study and Old Testament theology no more than a discipline of antiquarian interest removed from the vital interests of contemporary society and its quest not only for meaning and values, but also for the survival of all life. If biblical studies ignores theology and issues of existential concern, it evokes little interest and lacks any utilitarian use in the contemporary world struggling with issues of peace, justice, and even survival, save among nations searching for legitimation or a small number of pedantic scholars who find some satisfaction in the obscure and the irrelevant.

Rejection of the Descriptive Approach

The collapse of history also has resulted from an increasing number of biblical theologians rejecting the descriptive character of positivistic historiography[13] in favor of a reflective, critical, constructive, and/or systematic strategy. A purely descriptive approach is epistemologically questionable in and of itself, because all interpreters approach the text from the locations of their time, place, social position, and even self-interests. Indeed, the descriptive approach may be capable of presenting multiple, historical theologies present in each of the two testaments, but it does not lead to a systematic theology that engages life.

Since a self-described historical, descriptive approach does not attempt to address present culture, it leaves that task to contemporary theologians who see modern culture, philosophy, tradition, and the Bible as important considerations in developing interpretations that lead to theological discourse. Lessing's "ugly ditch" between past and present, separating descriptive analysis from modern application, is impossible to cross by the use of historical criticism without serious reflection and giving credence to the long line of generations and their worlds of meaning. An increasing number of biblical scholars, however, are not satisfied only to describe

---

12. Winter, *Liberating Creation: Foundations of Religious Social Ethics* (New York: Crossroad, 1981).

13. See the classic statement for the descriptive approach by Stendahl, "Biblical Theology, Contemporary."

the contents of Old Testament theology, but rather insist that questions of modern culture must be addressed to the text.[14] If we are to overcome this separation between the past and present, awaken the text to life, and allow the understandings of the faith to move through the various traditions since the closure of the canon and the present, we need to engage in discourse that allows scholars and communities of faith to enter into conversation and continue to articulate new theological understandings. This requires that Old Testament scholars develop an increased theological sophistication or participate in conversation with systematic theologians who are able to interact with the results of biblical theologies.

The World of the Postmodern

Perhaps we might understand the preceding four reasons collectively as the critical questioning of Enlightenment epistemology and the philosophy of positivism that it spawned. In some contemporary circles, we are told that we have entered into a postmodern world that has followed and supplanted the reign of rationalism and empiricism, the twin pillars of scientific method. We now find ourselves in a period when the epistemologies and worldviews issuing from the Age of Reason are contested by numerous rivals, competing for commitment. Postmodernism is an especially amorphous and elusive expression, for it is used to refer to almost any way of knowing or not knowing that differs from or is critical of Enlightenment thinking. Thus, postmodernism may include such diverse entities as postcolonialism, reader-response criticism, speech-act theory, and deconstruction. If there is a unifying factor in postmodernism, it is, ironically, an affirmation of pluralism in ways of knowing and being in the world. Thus, perspectives on reality as well as reality itself (one should say "realities") are a kaleidoscope that is constantly changing.[15] Of course, the *Geist der Aufklärung* (spirit of the Enlightenment), especially rationalism and empiricism, which issued forth in scientific method, provided the epistemological basis for historical criticism. Subsequently, this methodology for critical inquiry and theological analysis, which is grounded in an intellectual age whose culture and cultural products are often criticized, has much more difficulty in making persuasive arguments, especially if some contend that these in principle cannot be made. Whether this represents a

---

14. This is the goal of a new series I am editing, The Library of Biblical Theology, for Abingdon Press. This series brings together systematic, New Testament, and Old Testament theologians to explore fundamental theological themes.

15. The apt metaphor of kaleidoscope is used by H. Smith, "Postmodernism's Impact on the Study of Religion," 660–61.

crisis in epistemology that will lead to an abandonment of historical-critical method remains to be seen, but I predict that the Enlightenment's epistemology will continue long after the demise of its most ardent critics.

The Requirement of Hermeneutics

Finally, the collapse of history, at least theologically speaking, results from the inability of the paradigm to lead us where we hope to journey: the world of meaning, in this case, the meaning of God, human existence, and the creation for human dwelling. We are content only when we are able to comprehend salient theological features implicit and explicit in the biblical text, adequately articulate their engagement of faith, acknowledge and cope with anomalies that defy the logic of a theological system, and construct dynamic theological hypotheses, in all of their variety, which respond to and then correlate with human experience. Historical criticism was never intended to prescribe current theological affirmations. But it can and does trace the development of theological views and values into the present. It is concerned with the interpretation of the past by people long since dead. Biblical scholars have uncovered their views, however, which contemporary theologians should take into consideration, for they have implications for present faith. At least the canon has significance for modern belief and practice. But a different kind of discourse is needed for the realization of this ambition to shape theological meaning in the present. Although historical critics and the early biblical theologians share the major objective of liberating the Bible from the tyranny of church dogma shaped by ecclesiastical officials, they have not sought to replace church dogma with a new biblical theology that ignores tradition and the present.

What is needed is a thick description of the biblical text and its possible contributions to modern theological discourse. A careful and rigorous application of criteriology must weigh the merits of any construal of meaning, whether of biblical, historical, or contemporary theology. I propose the formulation of a biblical theology that enables systematic theology to address and incorporate where deemed important the Scripture in informed ways. A criteriology for assessment of approaches should involve four major areas: the historical, the cultural (past and present), the economic (historical and contemporary), and the theological (the formulation of the faith out of which the interpretation is rendered). All of these occur within a variety of contexts that influence their understandings and are written by people who cannot escape the confinements of their own limited understandings. These criteria allow for a canonical memory to participate in formulations of current faith and also place limits on pluralism that inevitably results in the quagmire of relativity. At the same time, absolutism is dismissed as entirely foreign to the theological quest to articulate both past and present understandings of faith.

In any intellectual inquiry, no theology—or, for that matter, no ideology—should be exempted from the close examination of rational investigation and judicious criticism. And here I speak as an unrepentant rationalist. Simply to argue that all theology is ideology and thus exempt from critical evaluation, since all linguistic and historical constructions are concerned with power and self-interest, leads to deadly consequences, as the catastrophic results of foreign policies of the ideologies of the British Empire, National Socialism, and the recent Bush administration have taught us.[16]

What has occurred is the collapse (though certainly not the demise) of the historical paradigm as the singular approach for doing Old Testament theology in present discussion, but this methodological consensus should also become the cause for new and critical reflection about how we approach and carry out the task. With the current, vigorous debate that has emerged, new paradigms of theological discourse have taken shape. If no compelling consensus has appeared on the horizon and if it is highly unlikely that one will, at least new conversation needs to be under way.[17] What is at stake is nothing less than the vitality of theological interpretation, both biblical and contemporary, and, some would say, the possibility of authentic life in the world.

After the Collapse of History

An important place to begin with the delineation of approaches to biblical theology is definition. One of the major problems confronting contemporary scholarship has been that of clearly defining this discipline and its purposes, methods, and objectives. In his recent volume, *The Concept of Biblical Theology,* James Barr has dealt in detail with the issue of definition, although the approaches he concedes have value as biblical theology are limited to those that came to the fore prior to the 1980s.[18] This is a serious shortcoming, for it limits theological discourse to historicism. Yet his study is a place to begin seeking necessary clarity about the concept of biblical

16. See Forstman, *Christian Faith in Dark Times;* and Rubenstein, *After Auschwitz.*

17. The series, Overtures to Biblical Theology, was specifically conceived to bring together exegesis and contemporary hermeneutics in a variety of ways. I am currently editing a series on biblical theology with James Dunn, Michael Welker, and Walter Brueggemann (consultant). The series, The Library of Biblical Theology, is designed to produce sixteen volumes that combine exegetical, biblical theological, and systematic theological features.

18. Barr, *The Concept of Biblical Theology,* 1–18.

theology. According to Barr, there have been several key ways of defining and understanding biblical theology:

1. "Something that is done by Biblical scholars, whether of Old or New Testament"

2. "Something new, in the sense that it is searching for something that is not already known"—not "something already laid down in a past or ancient tradition," but rather "*something that has still to be discovered*"

3. Something "possessing an *ecumenical* potential," even though the "actual theologies that have emerged have been very different"

4. Something that should be asked "whether [it] is really theology in the proper sense at all," which means biblical theology must have "features and aspects that are *analogous* to the working of theology in the proper sense"

5. Something "having clarity only when it is understood to mean theology as it existed or was thought or believed within the time, languages and cultures of the Bible itself." This implies that the concerns of biblical theology have often come from people of the modern period seeking answers to their questions from the texts of the Bible. Yet these modern questions must pay close attention to the views of the cultures that expressed their faiths in the content of scriptural texts.[19]

For Barr biblical theology is at its essence a "*contrastive* notion." This "notion" assumes a different shape, depending on its contrast with each of the following:

- *Doctrinal (systematic, dogmatic, or constructive) theology.* Normally, biblical theology has been understood as a descriptive, historical discipline in contrast to dogmatic theology (viewed as the articulation of what is to be believed by Christians) in the variety of Christian communities.

- *Nontheological study of the Bible.* Historical criticism largely has concerned itself with textual philology, historical background, older literary criticism, form criticism, and tradition history and not, as is the case with biblical theology, with the "message" of the Bible, its theological themes, and its underlying convictions for the communities of faith.

19. Ibid.

- *History of Religion and corresponding approaches.* The approach of historians of religion tends to speak of the biblical writer's borrowing from earlier and contemporary ancient Near Eastern and Greco-Roman religions. At times the biblical understanding wrongly was thought to have evolved in order to reach a "higher plane." In addition, the biblical references to other cultures and their religions are often obscure. Nevertheless, the study of these religions tends to fill in the gaps in the historian's knowledge to understand the distinctive features of Old Testament religious thought. These distinguishing characteristics of the Hebrew biblical texts and the religion of Israel have been viewed at times as expressive of true faith in contrast to the false views of so-called pagan religions. Of course, this argument largely has been rejected.

- *Philosophical theology and natural theology.* Many modern scholars (including Karl Barth and Krister Stendahl) have argued that biblical thought contrasts with modern, philosophical approaches, including natural reason. This view contends that revelation through biblical writers and their texts contrasts with understandings of God and/or the sacred that may derive from human reason and the understanding of the world.

- *The interpretation of* parts *of the Bible as distinct from the larger complexes taken as* wholes. This argues that individual texts and traditions have their own unique theologies and not a common one running throughout. To write a comprehensive biblical theology is thought to be impossible.

Barr's articulation is especially clear, but it operates on the basis of a dated agenda—that of a strict rationalism, if not in reality a rigid historicism—and it limits itself to theology that follows traditional modes. He leaves out most of the new approaches. It would be interesting to receive from him an answer of why he chooses to do this. His criticism of postmodernism, for example, provides some insight into this reluctance to regard this method as one of biblical theology. But it would be helpful to read a comprehensive statement as to why some more recent approaches apparently are not biblical theology. He ignores so many of the pressing hermeneutical issues and contemporary reconfigurations of doing Old Testament theology that his book, while incisive and trenchant, was an apt analysis for the 1980s and older historical-critical approaches. His major contributions that speak to the present are his assessments of canonical theology and his important discussion of the reemergence of the History of Religion as a way of approaching biblical theology. Barr professes that he sees biblical theology, on the one hand, as a discipline that describes the faith of the biblical periods and, on the other hand, as normative for articulating modern faith and practice. This distinction is significant to maintain in the study of biblical theology, yet it is the second part of the agenda that falls short. I do not think that hermeneutical judgments should be bracketed, but there are contemporary biblical theologians who build bridges between biblical text and contemporary implications that are much more substantial and compelling than his remarks suggest. And he is never clear about contemporary hermeneutical methods for understanding the contribution of biblical theology to modern discourse. The question for me is whether the biblical scholar is competent to move from a biblical text through the traditions of the church over the centuries into the present and thus present his or her own articulation of the faith. This person, to my knowledge, does not exist and never has. The long and winding journey from text to contemporary meaning requires biblical scholars, historical theologians, contemporary theologians, and the faiths of contemporary churches to make this journey together. Then, and only then, will interfaith dialogue be possible.

New Approaches: The Fundamental Assumptions

The issues presented in newer approaches to Old Testament theology are numerous and often conflicting. These polarities include: historical or literary, subjective or objective epistemology and goals, rational or contextual, apolitical or political, absolutism or relativism, unity or diversity, and canonical or inclusion of extracanonical understandings. A judicious assessment would reside somewhere between these various polarities.

Historical or Literary

The first polarity in approaches is the determination of whether a theology engages in a historical interpretation of Old Testament that is largely developmental and seeks to understand texts and their important beliefs within the larger context of Israelite and ancient Near Eastern history, or is more oriented to interpretation that examines the literary character of texts according to one or more methodologies for contemporary culture and modern church. Historical method, while placed within a variety of different philosophical orientations, such as positivism or neo-Marxism, is still concerned with tracing religious beliefs of the sociohistorical communities of ancient and early Judaism. This method is normally accompanied by the results of material culture emerging from excavations in the larger region of the eastern Mediterranean world. While the philosophy of

history contributes significantly to the interpretations of theology and ideology, historians are still engaged in the efforts to locate ideas and beliefs
within the cultural and social contexts that occasioned them. The historical
approach, while under serious criticism by minimalists who doubt the data
support many of the assumptions of biblical critics who seek to reconstruct
the life and society of ancient Israel in the premonarchical and even monarchical periods, and by postmodernists who often consider the epistemologies used by historians to be outmoded and deceptive, has received new
vitality from an unexpected source: theology's typically unsympathetic
critic, the History of Religion, in this case, Israelite religion. Indeed, many
of the new theologies, particularly coming from Germany and German-
speaking countries, have used the History of Religion as the major way of
assessing the theologies of ancient Israel that developed over a thousand-
year period.

Literary methods are even more diverse in terms of questions, interests,
and ways of obtaining information, but in the period since World War II,
these approaches have been either uninterested in or even antagonistic to
history in the sense of interpreting texts to reconstruct Israel's past, including its theology. New Criticism, developing in American literary scholarship in the 1930s, became especially popular in biblical criticism during
the 1970s and following. Now there are numerous approaches borrowed
from literary criticism and ideology practiced in the academy. They include
in particular rhetorical criticism, reader-response, speech-act, structuralism, and poststructuralism. These are not necessarily antipathetic, one to
the other, but their goals and strategies of interpretation are significantly
different. Inherent in these various literary approaches is the view that
meaning, including theological understanding, is not yoked to history.
Texts can be interpreted and assessed with little or no knowledge about
the historical or social context.

Subjective or Objective Epistemology and Goals

A relatively new issue in recent theological discourse among scholars of
the Hebrew Bible is whether the epistemology used to determine views is
objective, as long claimed by historians, or subjective in part or in its entirety. The hallmark of historical criticism that provided the foundation of
most biblical theologies prior to the impact of postmodernism on biblical
studies, beginning especially in the latter part of the 1980s, was the affirmation of objectivity. Methods were developed to keep interpreters from simply reading their own views into the text.

While objectivity is still a definitive goal of most biblical research, the
shift toward an ever-expanding role of subjectivity is clear. Even biblical

scholars of the nineteenth century admitted the difficulties with objectivity due to a variety of factors, philosophical as well as evidential. Increasingly, epistemology has moved to the more generally accepted position that the interpreter of texts unavoidably participates in the process of knowing. This process cannot help but occur, so objectivity is partially compromised. Other considerations have been added, including especially that of context, meaning then that the context of the text, the text itself, and the social location of the interpreter and the text are joined together in obtaining understanding. More recently, some interpreters have assumed a postmodernist position to deny any objectivity is operative and that meaning is a subjective, self-created entity. Thus, ideas like objectivity and truth are abandoned as impossible to determine. If that is true, then theology and all other forms of thought are useless exercises in the circum of the absurd. The debates involving this polarity are the most significant in shaping the discussion of Old Testament theology in the present.

Idealism or Materialism

Old Testament theologians in their approaches to determining or deriving meaning also are divided between idealism and materialism. Is meaning rationally expressed and then later interpreted by the theologian, or is meaning determined by the context, including the context of the text and that of the interpreter? Is it possible to argue that ideas and beliefs transcend the settings of time, space, and people who have a clear, thinking mind to grasp, or are they an intrinsic datum of the material context that gives them shape and meaning? While many current Old Testament theologians have moved away from idealism to embrace an Aristotelian sense of experience coupled with context in order to understand the theology of the Bible, others still seem intent on arguing that the limitations of the data concerning historical and social context are so severe that one is incapable of anything other than a quest for theological meaning obtained through the application of the rational methodology espoused by idealism.

Apolitical or Political Objectives

Another polarity at work in Old Testament theology is whether the objective of writing a theology of the text is apolitical or political. Here, I use the term *political* in a much broader sense than simply a philosophy of ordering common life through the decisions of an empowered ruling group. This term includes to some extent the views of androcentrism, feminism, heterosexuality, homosexuality, race, color, ethnicity, geographical region of the globe, globalism, imperialism, neocolonialism, and postcolonialism.

Most Old Testament theologians have come to recognize the high stakes of interpretation when moving into political arenas. The older notion that scholarship devoid of political agendas is the best way to proceed in interpreting the Bible and its theology is now largely abandoned. Implicitly or explicitly the Bible has become politicized to support one agenda over against another. Indeed, most biblical scholars have traced the ideologies of self-interest that drive the modern interpretation of history, ideas, and institutions to the biblical texts themselves. The Bible is now used by a variety of competing political orientations to support or condemn the very same affirmation. I suggest that the politicization of the biblical text has always been a part of an interpreter's agenda, but now it is often no longer hidden beneath the layers of the protestation of objectivity.

Absolutism or Relativism

The longstanding opposition between absolutism and relativism occasionally is present in theological discourse, but only rarely. Outside of fundamentalists, absolutism has no place in scholarship that pursues the writing of Old Testament theology. However, relativism is a different matter. One could go to the extreme of arguing for the nonexistence of truth or for the position that it is impossible to know if something is true when it comes to theological and ethical attestations. If postmodernists are correct, it seems to me that there is no other recourse than to say that all beliefs and ethical practices are relative. More common, however, is for biblical theologians to draw back from personally affirming a biblical belief is true or false and to set forth views inherent in texts without making an evaluation.

Unity or Diversity

Before the 1980s, interpreters generally sought a way of speaking of the unity of Old Testament theology. This normally was found in a "center" that provided the focal point for a variety of themes that were systematically described. These themes inevitably allowed for a variety of understandings, but the center still served to organize the theological interpretation into a coherent whole. During the past two generations, however, many Old Testament theologians have affirmed and demonstrated the diversity of theologies present in the different texts of the Hebrew Bible. Any semblance of unity, outside of simply naming subjects (God, history, or creation, for example), consequently has been discarded. This said, the hermeneutical task of the contribution of Old Testament theology to contemporary faith has become extraordinarily difficult.

Inclusion or Exclusion of Noncanonical Texts

A final polarity has resulted from the theological implications of canon. Of course, Old Testament theologians are immediately confronted by the existence of several different canons that vary in terms of books included, their order, and their larger categories. In addition, they are faced immediately with having to answer the question "Is theology constrained by the limits of the canon that is admittedly reflective of the beliefs and worldview of late Jewish communities and their teachers, or should noncanonical texts, including even material culture, be a part of the overall equation?" For example, since the Hebrew Bible is decidedly patriarchal, what of evidence of women's theological understandings found in more popular, cultural contexts (for instance, the worship of goddesses)? Thus, some Old Testament theologians have abandoned the constrictions of canon to argue for the inclusion of additional understandings present in or implied by material data and texts, not chosen to be reckoned among Scripture, in the cultures of Israel's historical development. After all, how different is this from systematic theologians of culture, such as Paul Tillich, who bring into view the understandings of modern cultures, philosophies, and sciences in shaping contemporary understanding of faith and morality?

The positions taken on these issues largely determine the nature of the Old Testament theology that is written, together with much of its contents. It would be the epitome of arrogance to argue for the "superiority" of one or the other polarity, but the approach one takes has the responsibility to set forth the positions taken in pursuing interpretation.

Description of the Present Task

The following narrative, over the next eight chapters, is designed to provide a basic introduction to recent and emerging approaches to Old Testament theology. It seeks to offer a more informed entrance into the modern conversation and to provoke both reflection and discussion. Subsumed under this overarching goal are two important, related objectives.

The first objective is to review critically the various ways of doing Old Testament theology since the Second World War, with particular emphasis on the present period. Several recent efforts seek to accomplish this task, but these have failed to explore many contemporary approaches that are blazing new paths for contemporary biblical theology. While there is in general a tendency to trace with great thoroughness European scholarship, not enough consideration has been given to important work done outside of the Western tradition and the domain of history. These histories of research also often fail to be attentive to two important relationships that biblical theology has in common with other interpretative enterprises. One failure is the lack of recognition or explanation of the important connection between methodology in biblical exegesis and the way that the theological task is conceived. Thus, with the continuing developments in exegetical interpretation and hermeneutics, new ways of going about the theological task are continually developed and refined. The other failure is neglect of an explanation that the paradigms for doing biblical theology are normally shaped or at least influenced by interaction with contemporary theology and many other disciplines shaped by and at work in the larger academy. Hence, any historical overview of Old Testament theology should also trace the primary developments in contemporary theology and the academy that dramatically affect biblical theology.

The second objective is to select examples of recent approaches to biblical study that issue forth in Old Testament theology. It is impossible to consider in detail every important contribution to each of these approaches, since this task would be endless. My own criteria for examining some works in detail are that they are representative of a particular approach and also are well conceived, clearly written, and provocative.

The agenda for biblical theology set out in J. P. Gabler's famous inaugural address at the University of Altdorf in 1787 rarely has been carried out by those doing biblical theology.[20] This is partly because the dichotomy he proposed was too precise and not at all capable of being so adroitly articulated. According to Gabler, an important differentiation should be made between dogmatic (systematic) theology and biblical theology. Prior to Gabler, biblical theology had been the handmaiden of dogmatics; the Bible set forth the divine, universal, eternal truths, which dogmatic theology was to arrange in systematic order. In opposing this view, Gabler argued that biblical theology is a historical enterprise that seeks to portray the theology of the biblical authors, and that the appropriate method to follow is historical criticism. For Gabler, the distinction is between true biblical theology that is the limited, conditional theology of the biblical writers (historicism) and pure biblical theology that seeks to discover the eternal theological truths of divine revelation (idealism). Dogmatic or systematic theology was concerned with shaping a coherent theology that applies the theological truths of pure biblical theology to the contemporary world. Thus, Gabler tries to mediate between biblical theology as a historical exercise to reconstruct the history of Israelite religious ideas and biblical theology as a tool of systematic theology that incorporates the salient, universal ideas of the Bible into a systematic form addressing current situations.[21]

---

20. For the text of the speech, see Merk, *Biblische Theologie des Neuen Testaments,* 273–84.
21. For a recent discussion of Gabler's proposal, see Ollenburger, "Biblical Theology."

Gabler's agenda is flawed and not at all realistic for doing Old Testament theology, for it leaves out context, the questions of truth, the possibility of its attainment, diversity, and a more sophisticated epistemology in which the interpreter participates in determining meaning. Heuristically, however, Gabler's dichotomy might be embraced as an operating procedure that allows for the differentiation between ancient belief and modern faith.

This volume seeks to demonstrate that, while there are major tensions between various approaches to Old Testament theology, there are significant points of contact that should allow fruitful discourse. But how to engage Old Testament theology, presented in a variety of ways, in conversation with contemporary hermeneutics is the primary question at hand, since so many biblical theologians cannot talk even to each other, much less to systematic theologians. The concluding chapter will make some suggestions as to how this conversation and, subsequently, Old Testament theology itself may proceed. Finally, for our own heuristic purposes, we shall apply each approach to the book of Jeremiah to discover how each approach seeks to interpret the text theologically.

We begin with chapter 2, "From History as Event to the History of Religion: *Religionsgeschichte* and Biblical Theology," which explores the interaction of the History of Religion and biblical theology in the work of several biblical theologies to demonstrate how the History of Religion may be properly used to understand the development of Old Testament theology. Chapter 3, "From Eurocentric History to Voices from the Margins: Liberation Theology and Ethnic Biblical Interpretation," interprets the work of ethnic scholars who approach the text as historians and several different ethnic theologies that also use historical criticism along with interests specific to their cultures and social locations. Chapter 4, "From Exclusion to Inclusion: Feminist Interpretations of History," articulates the constructions of feminist history by examining not only the interpretation of biblical texts through a historical, feminist lens but also the hermeneutical implications for feminist theology. Chapter 5, "From History to Rhetoric: Feminist, *Mujerista,* and Womanist Theologies," adds to the uses of metaphor, New Criticism, and rhetorical criticism by Western feminists of the racial majority, particularly in North America, other literary approaches by women of color, who interpret the literary text from their own experience as ethnic minorities. Chapter 6, "From Jewish Tradition to Biblical Theology: The Tanakh as a Source for Jewish Theology and Practice," examines the debate between Jewish scholars as to whether there is a Jewish biblical theology or Jewish theology and whether Jews should engage non-Jewish constructions of Old Testament theology. This chapter delineates the reasons some Jewish scholars are strongly critical of biblical theology's adequacy and appropriateness for Judaism and then articulates the viewpoints of other Jewish scholars, who not only advocate the construction of either a Jewish biblical theology or a Jewish theology, but also actually engage in its pursuit. Chapter 7, "From History to Cultural Context: Postmodernism," articulates the major views of postmodernism and highlights the work of biblical scholars who have delved into this area. Of course, it is not clear if postmodernism would even entertain the writing of Old Testament theologies, but if so, this approach would maintain the necessity of constructing limits of any truth claims. Chapter 8, "From the Colonial Bible to the Postcolonial Text: Biblical Theology as Contextual," reviews the work of major postcolonial theologians who point to their own intrinsic traditions as the basis for proceeding that allows them to shape a more distinctive and relevant hermeneutic for their own communities. The concluding chapter, chapter 9, "The Changing Future of Old Testament Theology: A Postscript," offers general observations about the present state of Old Testament theology, sets forth some criteria to use in evaluating various formulations, and suggests a way into the future, particularly in articulating both a biblical and a systematic theology.

I shall argue that in addition to distinctive features of approaches to biblical study and Old Testament theology, there are also important, common features shared by historical criticism and literary analysis that should avoid polarizing the discussion for all but the extreme historicists, especially the minimalists, and the most radical of postmodernists. The extremists are not interested in discussion, in any event. It will be suggested that these many, diverse methods and areas of understanding have their distinctive contributions to make to Old Testament theology, biblical theology, and contemporary hermeneutics. But at the same time, they should be brought together in critical dialogue. The utterance of theological discourse in the present awaits those who not only have ears to hear and eyes to see, but also minds to imagine and tongues to speak.

2

From History as Event to the History of Religion: *Religionsgeschichte* and Biblical Theology

I have heard those songs that are in the tombs of old,
What they tell in extolling life on earth,
in belittling the land of the dead.

— *"A Harper's Song" from the tomb of Neferhoter*

Introduction

Since the 1920s it is clear that the pendulum has continued to swing back and forth between two primary interests and approaches to biblical studies. These are *Religionsgeschichte,* in which emerging methods of the study of religions have been coupled with historical criticism to the reconstruction of plausible understandings of ancient Israelite religion and early Judaism, and the various approaches of Old Testament theology that, until recently, have generally searched for a thematic unity in the midst of diversity in the canon along the lines of themes or traditions. The practitioners of the first area of interest, *Religionsgeschichte,* have normally not been interested either in biblical theology that for Christians would include the New Testament or in contemporary hermeneutics in which the theology of the Hebrew Bible would engage or be engaged by contemporary understandings of faith and practice. Indeed, the multiple literary approaches of more recent Old Testament scholarship, like the foregoing harper's song, has made light of the past and its dead civilizations in the theological quest to focus more on the vitality of the text stripped of historical context. However, in recent years a number of scholars have attempted to meld the two areas together so that a historical reconstruction of Israel's religious understanding and activation in society and life would venture into the realm of contemporary theology and, at the same time, allow the contemporary expressions to enter into critical dialogue with the multiple faiths of the Old Testament. In addition, there has been until now, especially in

North America, a proclivity toward social and anthropological theories that ignore altogether the fields of theology and contemporary ethics. This chapter seeks to trace the development of these lines of difference and understanding and to assess where they have something to offer and where they fall short.

Loss of Interest in Biblical Theology

In place of Old Testament theology,[1] other scholarly disciplines received greater attention during the late 1970s through the early 1990s: the history and phenomenology of religions and ritual studies (e.g., Mircea Eliade, Claude Lévi-Strauss, and Mary Douglas);[2] social scientific approaches (e.g., Max Weber,[3] Karl Marx, and neo-Marxism, notably the Frankfurt School,[4] Émile Durkheim, Antonin Causse,[5] and Gerhard Emmanuel Lenski);[6] cultural anthropological methods (e.g., Victor Turner[7] and Marvin Harris);[8] ethnoarchaeological theory (Charles E. Carter);[9] and a variety of literary methods, including New Criticism (Cleanth Brooks and John Crowe Ran-

1. See Oden, *The Bible without Theology.*

2. For *Religionsgeschichtliche* and phenomenological studies, see especially Eliade, *The Sacred and the Profane;* Eliade and Kitagawa, *The History of Religions;* and Eliade, *Myth and Reality.* For a more recent use of phenomenology in the interpretation of religious literature, see Sawyer, *Sacred Languages and Sacred Texts.* For works by Lévi-Strauss and for Douglas's ritual studies based on cultural anthropology, see the bibliography.

3. For relevant works by Weber and the other scholars named in this chapter, see the bibliography.

4. For an introduction to the Frankfurt School, see O'Neill, *On Critical Theory.* Leading theorists include Theodor W. Adorno, Jürgen Habermas, and Herbert Marcuse. For an application of neo-Marxist theory to ancient Israel, see Gottwald, *The Tribes of Yahweh;* and "Reconstructing the Social History of Early Israel."

5. See Kimbrough, *Israelite Religion in Sociological Perspective.*

6. For an overview of social scientific models, see Carter, "A Discipline in Transition"; "Social Scientific Approaches"; Herion, "The Impact of Modern and Social Science Assumptions"; Benjamin and Matthews, "Social Sciences and Biblical Studies"; and Herion, *Ancient Israel's Faith and History.* For earlier studies, see Kimbrough, "A Non-Weberian Sociological Approach to Israelite Religion"; Malina, "The Social Sciences and Biblical Interpretation"; and Mayes, *The Old Testament in Sociological Perspective.*

7. For applications of Turner's anthropological method to biblical wisdom, see Perdue, "Liminality and the Social Setting of Wisdom Instructions."

8. See Overholt, *Cultural Anthropology and the Old Testament.*

9. Important methodological studies include Kramer, *Ethnoarchaeology;* David and Kramer, *Ethnoarchaeology in Action;* Gould and Watson, "A Dialogue on the Meaning and Use of Analogy in Ethnoarchaeological Reasoning"; and David, "Integrating Ethnoarchaeology." For studies of ancient Israel that make use of this method, see Meyers, *Discovering Eve;* "An Ethnoarchaeological Analysis of Hannah's Sacrifice"; "Early Israel and the Rise of the Israelite Monarchy"; and Finkelstein, "The Emergence of the Monarchy in Israel."

som),[10] Russian Formalism and its critics (Viktor Shklovskii and M. M. Bakhtin),[11] reader-response theory and criticism (David Bleich, Jonathan Culler, and Umberto Eco),[12] and speech-act theory (J. L. Austin).[13]

Among the recent developments in biblical studies is the use of post-modernism, a rather comprehensive term that refers to any approach that questions the philosophical basis of modernism. This potpourri of ideas, insights, and interpretations has sought to open new vistas about the way humans think and go about their philosophical, literary, social, and cultural tasks. Whether or not it has engaged in productive discourse in biblical studies has been subject to debate. Postmodernism is not a method that one applies to various phenomena, including literature and other forms of art, society, politics, and economics, but rather is more of a perspective that attempts to decenter the assumptions of modernism originating in the epistemology (rationalism and empiricism) of the Enlightenment and to legitimate a variety of ways of knowing that are limited in their scope and fallible in their character. Postmodernism began to affect biblical criticism in the 1990s and, as will be argued in chapter 7, has much to say about approaching biblical theology and even doing biblical theology at all. Suffice it to say at this point that postmodernism, which began to appear in the late 1940s, has spurred a debate among scholars especially in the arts and humanities over epistemology. What postmodernists hold in common is a strong skepticism about modern claims to know "objectively" the so-called external world by attempting to negate the cultural and subjective reality of time and place in which the interpreter exists.

New Disciplines in Old Testament Study

In addition to the continuing problems posed by a center or *Mitte* (e.g., covenant, election, salvation history, and redemptive history and creation) and a systematic structure (e.g., thematic, historical, and tradition

10. See especially Alter, *The Art of Biblical Narrative;* and *The Art of Biblical Poetry.* See also Gros Louis, Ackermann, and Warshaw, *The Literary Interpretations of Biblical Narratives;* and Groden and Kreiswirth, *The Johns Hopkins Guide to Literary Theory and Criticism.*

11. See the description and bibliography in McCauley, "Russian Formalism." See also Newsom, "Bakhtin, the Bible, and Dialogic Truth."

12. A solid introduction is Tompkins, *Reader-Response Criticism.* Especially important is the book of essays by Fish, *Is There a Text in This Class?* See also Iser, *The Act of Reading.* In biblical studies, see McKnight, "Reader-Response Criticism"; Exum and Clines, *The New Literary Criticism and the Hebrew Bible;* Clines, "Why Is There a Book of Job?"; and Darr, *Isaiah's Vision and the Family of God.*

13. Among biblical scholars who discuss this approach, see Patte, "Speech Act Theory and Biblical Exegesis"; Hugh C. White, "Introduction," and "The Value of Speech Act Theory for Old Testament Hermeneutics."

complexes) in gaining a strong following, is the recognition that Old Testament theology has now been affected by methods that have poured old wine into new wineskins with a host of questions emerging from the social scientific and literary methods pursued during the past generation that extend theological debate into new arenas of discourse. The articulation of the text's sociocultural context, for example, has been expanded to include the especially perplexing question of the relationship between the multiple contexts of the biblical writers and editors and the very different, various ones of contemporary interpreters. How is it possible, for instance, to move back and forth between the vastly different social worlds and worldviews of an Iron Age social world in a largely agrarian, certainly preindustrial state and the technological societies of modern Europe and North America without affecting the historical understanding of a tradition arising in significantly different social and cultural matrices? In addition, new literary studies have questioned many of the assumptions of historical criticism's efforts to capture the "original" meaning of texts. For example, reader-response criticism has raised anew the questions arising from the role of the interpreter in determining the meaning of the ancient text. This role of the response of the reader and interpreter may well vary from that of earlier readers, even the idealized "original reader and hearer" of the text.

Of course, most of these criticisms directed against historical criticism were known even by its early creators and exponents. They were equally aware that their efforts were affected significantly by their own subjectivity, self-interest, and modern and differing cultures. However, the major difference between historical critics and exponents of new methods that are antihistorical is that the former still attempt to write history while acknowledging their own cultural and ideological assumptions, while the latter reject the effort to write history, according to the procedures of historical criticism even when given a postcolonial, feminist, or neo-Marxist orientation, as an exercise in futility and illusion.

New Questions for Biblical Theology

To shape this complexity facing biblical interpretation into a more specific theological form, interpreters who are located in the cultures influenced by the Reformation, Counter-Reformation, and Enlightenment churches see the Hebrew Bible as the first of a two-volume canon of the Bible. The task of the Old Testament theologian, as envisioned and practiced by these scholars, is to interpret its major theological teachings for the understanding, if not universal acceptance, of the church. These interpreters most often are clergy who teach in theological schools in Europe and North America and are engaged in the education of students for the ministry of the Western church. In addition, these clergy-scholars examine a variety of ways that the two testaments may be related in terms of the proclamation of the Christian Gospel and in the articulation of its important teachings.

In contrast, some Jewish scholars who recently have entered the dialogue concerning the theology of the Hebrew Bible, even if few in numbers, read and interpret the text while situated in Jewish cultures and the synagogue. However, most Jews would reject biblical theology and replace it with Jewish theology that continues this traditioning process through later corpora of texts (Mishnah, Talmud, Midrashim, Commentaries, and later Jewish thinkers). There is no issue of a second volume of the canon with which to wrestle, but there is the obligation for religious Jews to interpret the text through the lens of both Jewish tradition and modern critical methods. Even the arrangements of the books of the canon reflect different religious understanding. For the Jewish Bible, what points to fulfillment is the Chronicler's vision of a restored Jerusalem, while for the Protestant Old Testament, it is the promise of a forerunner to a Messiah who will bring about the culmination of the kingdom of God.

During the past century, many global scholars have joined the voices of dissent who recognize that Europe and North America no longer completely dominate biblical studies, as the more recent outpourings of post-colonial studies of the Bible have demonstrated. The interpreters of the Bible in Latin America, Africa, and Asia, many coming from the "Third World," have pursued their studies from the standpoint of very different cultures and histories than those of the West.

Then there are secular interpreters, especially in many public and even private universities in the United States, whose field of biblical interpretation engages the text in cross-disciplinary activity with those who teach world religions, the various disciplines of the humanities, sociology, and anthropology. Biblical theology in this context may be no more than curiosity about the "history" of the interpretation of the biblical text, not a means through which the Christian and Jewish God addresses contemporary audiences. Thus, many biblical scholars often find their courses and conversation partners in departments of literature, philosophy, anthropology, sociology, and history. The Bible as literature, the sociology of religion, and anthropology are disciplines or departments of study that consider religion to be a part of ancient or modern cultures.

These four idealized types of interpreters (Christian clergy and laity, Jewish scholars including some who are rabbis, postcolonial critics, and university professors) do not even begin to take into worldview consideration the issues of gender, sexuality, and race in affecting interpretation. People engaged in interpretation come from a variety of social contexts and are shaped by their different gender, sexual, and racial identities. They cannot simply put aside the worldviews, understandings of faith and religion, and cultural location formed by their identities when engaging the text. How then is it possible to speak any longer of an objective reading of the text when we have learned, especially in the past generation, that context and reader play a substantial part in determining meaning, including the meaning of the Bible, both past and present?

The complexity of biblical theology is increased by the longstanding recognition of the diversity of the text, due in part to the fact that the text was put together over a period of more than a thousand years. Not only do narrators, prophets, sages, and priests differ in their roles and ideologies, they also compete for power and status that would enable them to claim that they are the sole possessors of authority given and legitimated by divine favor. Further, who is to say that Job's understanding of God, itself rather difficult to derive from his speeches, is superior to that of Proverbs, or that the Zadokites were the true priests, while the Levites were those who held lower positions? Are Haggai and Zechariah discredited prophets for having spoken of Zerubbabel as the chosen king, while Isaiah, who speaks of an ideal king who is to come in the near future, is a true visionary? Scholars are hard pressed to find an interweaving narrative of faith or theological theme that somehow transcends this diversity or overlooks obvious gaffes. Unity in diversity may be a coveted ideal, but is it obtainable, regardless of how clever the argument? I think not.

These weighty questions concerning context, the role of the reader in interpretation, and diversity continue to haunt the restless nights of the contemporary biblical theologian. Ten years ago, I had hoped that we would begin to move toward a consensus concerning these issues. However, today there is far less agreement on the task and purpose, if not the very existence of, biblical theology than only a decade ago. These continue to be heady days when we dream new dreams and create new interpretative worlds. But ever threatening our common work as scholars and intellectuals is fragmentation that opposes any concurrence of meaning. The intellectual wars, based on the drive for power, authority, and domination, have turned malicious.

The danger confronting us all is theological, ethical, and hermeneutical relativity. Are we faced today with a morass of conflicting views that will silence all interchange of discourse? May we no longer affirm that even ethically significant issues may reside on fundamental principles of the value of life of all creatures and the preservation of the environment? These are the questions biblical theologians must strive to address in their scholarship. New approaches have developed that seek to reinvent the work of biblical theology: postmodernism, postcolonialism, feminism, liberation theology, and ethnic studies. But do these provide clues to the engagement of meaning systems, both past and present, or do they represent an ever-expanding pluralism? With the increasing dissatisfaction with history as an approach (historical criticism) and as a theme of Old Testament theology, is there a way of beginning to reconstitute its importance for theological study? Or need we look elsewhere?

One approach to rehabilitate history in order to enhance the doing of biblical theology is in interaction with the methods and content of the history of Israelite religion. These two approaches to the study of the Hebrew Bible have often been in tension for over a century. However, recently there have been efforts to bring the two together in order to shape the discourse of biblical theology. Their success continues to be debated, but then, what important issue is not?

The History of Religion and/or Biblical Theology?

Some theologians recently have returned to modernist interpretations of the History of Religion as a way to approach or at least supplement the task of biblical theology. The general starting point for discussing the birth of biblical theology is the inaugural address of thirty-three-year-old Johann Philipp Gabler at the University of Altdorf (March 30, 1787).[14] It is clear that Gabler in this address wished to give dogmatic theology a firmer grounding in biblical theology. However, what became most significant was his argument that the two should be separated, at least initially. Biblical theology was to be in and of itself a discipline independent of dogmatic theology. The task of biblical ("true") theology would be decidedly historical and formulated in isolation from the dogmatic theology of the church. Biblical theology was to be a comprehensive description and summary of biblical views that would be set forth in chronological order regardless of their innate theological value. "Pure" biblical theology would be a compendium in which biblical theology provides views and understandings that are universal and divinely sanctioned dogmas. Biblical theology thus would provide two foundations: first, the understanding of the faith of ancient Israel and the early church, and second, participation in the formulations of dogmatic theology for the church.

Beginning with this historical understanding of the task of biblical theology, the developments of historical criticism, the history of Israelite

---

14. *Oratio de justo discrimine theologiae biblicae et domaticae regundisque recte utriusque finibus.* See the English translation of Gabler's address, "An Oration on the Proper Distinction between Biblical and Dogmatic Theology." For studies of Gabler, see Merk, *Biblische Theologie des Neuen Testaments in ihrer Anfangszeit;* Morgan, "Gabler's Bicentenary"; Saebø, "Johann Philipp Gablers Bedeutung für die biblische Theologie"; and Sandys-Wunsch and Eldredge, "J. P. Gabler and the Distinction between Biblical and Dogmatic Theology."

religion, and biblical theology assumed a decidedly historical cast that included both Romanticism and positivism as philosophical underpinnings. During the past two centuries, the debate between the task of describing the history of Israelite religion and the writing of biblical theology has continued with one and then the other gaining the upper hand, but rarely achieving a satisfactory compatibility. Until recently, one was thought to exclude the other.[15]

Definition: The History of Religion Approach to Israelite Religion

While representing a variety of topics and methods, the general term *History of Religion* makes use of all elements of the material cultures of different societies.[16] Thus, the History of Religion "is concerned with the forms and aspects of all human religions."[17] Normally, historians of religion operate out of a variety of anthropological and social scientific methods that seek to discover and then explicate the key underlying features of human religions as part of the structure of societies in order to explain their development, social roles in human communities, similarities, and differences.[18] The application of the History of Religion to Israelite religion

15. See the earlier historical surveys of literature by G. Anderson, "Hebrew Religion"; and Zimmerli, "The History of Israelite Religion." Also see North, "Old Testament Theology and the History of Hebrew Religion"; Irwin, "The Study of Israel's Religion"; Barr, "The Problem of Old Testament Theology and the History of Religion"; and Bleeker, "Comparing the Religio-Historical Method and the Theological Method."

16. Among the various studies of the history of the religion of ancient Israel, see Barr, *The Concept of Biblical Theology,* 100ff; P. Miller, "God and the Gods" and "Israelite Religion"; Sandys-Wunsch, "The History of Religion,"; and Toorn, *Family Religion in Babylonia, Syria and Israel.* For the importance of archaeology for Israelite religion, see Dever, "The Contribution of Archaeology" and "Archaeology and the Religions of Israel"; and Nakhai, *Archaeology and the Religions of Canaan and Israel.* The importance of iconography for Israelite religion is convincingly demonstrated in the publications of Othmar Keel and his students. Important works include *Die Welt der altorientalischen Bildsymbolik und das Alte Testament* and, with Christoph Uehlinger, *Gods, Goddesses, and Images of God in Ancient Israel.* For the importance of ancient Near Eastern religions and their impact on Israelite religion, see Stolz, "Probleme westsemitischer und israelitischer Religionsgeschichte." Knauf ("From History to Interpretation") argues along with several other historians that archaeology is more important than the biblical texts in writing a History of Religion. For more general surveys of the History of Religion, see Hvidtfeldt, "History of Religion, Sociology and Sociology of Religion"; Sharma, "An Inquiry into the Nature of the Distinction"; Imen, "The History of Religion as Social Science"; and Leuze, "Möglichkeiten und Grenzen einer Theologie der Religionsgeschichte."

17. Barr, *The Concept of Biblical Theology,* 100–101.

18. See the social scientific and anthropological studies referenced in the chapter's introduction.

is based on a variety of theoretical methods that consist of numerous approaches, interests, and objectives largely found in the areas of cultural and social anthropology. Theology, on the other hand, "tends to be concerned with the truth claims of one religion and especially with its authoritative texts and traditions and their interpretation."[19]

In addition to the use of theoretical models issuing from anthropology, another important feature of the history of the religion of ancient Israel is the influence on and similarity to other religions of the ancient Near East. These influences and comparisons occur in the material culture of architecture, art, utensils, cultic paraphernalia, pottery, and most importantly literature (including myths, laws, narratives, legends, royal chronicles, wisdom texts, psalms, and metaphors), rituals, and social roles and institutions (priesthood, temple, sages, and kingship). These similarities—while some have been extremely remote, to say the least—may be explained in a variety of ways, including cross-cultural borrowing and the sharing of a common cultural context. Some appear to be only tangential to Israelite religion. In addition, even when Israelites appropriated a particular element from the nations and cultures of the ancient Near East, it may have been transformed into an understanding or practice that was acceptable to their own religion. For example, myths, suggests Frank Cross, were historicized,[20] while, on occasions, gods were reduced to servants of Yahweh or demons. However, efforts by conservative theologians to point to distinctive features of Israelite religion as evidence of its superiority have been less than convincing.[21]

Biblical Theology or the History of Religion

Until the 1980s, biblical study had been primarily placed in historical categories that included both method (historical criticism) and themes (especially salvation history). But, many biblical theologians make use of the History of Religion in doing biblical theology. Others have argued these two approaches possess different procedures and goals that exclude each other. As we shall see, *Religionsgeschichte* fell into disrepute in Christian theology especially due to the pervasive influence of Karl Barth. But is Barth's neo-orthodoxy defensible as a proper theological approach that may be used for biblical interpretation?

19. Barr, *The Concept of Biblical Theology*, 101.

20. Cross, *Canaanite Myth and Hebrew Epic*. This betrays a conservative attempt to rescue the Bible from pagan religion by indicating that history, not myth, was the foundation of Israelite religion.

21. See G. Ernest Wright, *The Old Testament against Its Environment*. Wright asserts that Israelite religion was unique in the ancient Near East in arguing that Yahweh was a deity who acted in history. This view has been disproved. See Albrektson, *History and the Gods*.

Biblical Theology and the History of Religion

The History of Religion and biblical theology normally have been considered different disciplines, with distinct approaches and different objectives.[22] Otto Eissfeldt makes one of the clearest differentiations in an early, formative essay in 1926.[23] According to Eissfeldt, the problem of the polarities of absolute/relative and transcendence/immanence is to be addressed in doing Old Testament theology. The question for the Old Testament, raised by the History of Religion approach, is whether Israelite religion is one religion among many or in some way the "true one" as is asserted in Old Testament theology, i.e., the revelation of God. While admittedly a Christian scholar, Eissfeldt announces that "the religion of the Old Testament [must] be investigated by the same means with which historical scholarship otherwise works: linguistic and historical critical mastery of the sources, and analysis of their content on the basis of an empathetic personal reliving."[24] Eissfeldt notes that Old Testament theology requires the interpreter to move beyond the methods of historical criticism to insist that the message of the Old Testament may be accessed only by faith. Arguing from his location within the church, the importance of the contents of the Old Testament is decided on the basis of what is significant for the Christian faith, with Jesus Christ becoming the apex of Christian meaning and faith. Thus, the relationship between the two testaments becomes important in order to carry out the aims of biblical theology. In spite of their differences, Eissfeldt argues that the two methods are a unity and that they both strive to know the same truth "by which faith is grasped."[25]

Carl Steuernagel's essay,[26] which appeared shortly before Eissfeldt's, already asserted, in language reminiscent of Gabler, that if Biblical theology is to be freed from the chains of dogmatic theology, then it must also be unimpeded by the History of Religion. For Steuernagel, Old Testament theology holds an independent position within Old Testament studies. Old Testament theology provides a systematic overview of Old Testament religion. He asserts that biblical studies still require both History of Religion and biblical theology to operate in a liaison of mutuality in order to prevent systematic biblical theology and contemporary theology being discredited by the lack of historical grounding.

Later, in 1929, Walther Eichrodt wrote a significant essay that raises the question of whether or not Old Testament theology is an independent dis-

---

22. Zwickel, "Religionsgeschichte Israels."
23. Eissfeldt, "Israelitisch-jüdische Religionsgeschichte."
24. Ibid. (citing pp. 20–21 from the English translation).
25. Ibid., 29.
26. Steuernagel, "Alttestamentliche Theologie und alttestamentliche Religionsgeschichte."

cipline within Old Testament scholarship.[27] His goal was to defend Old Testament theology as a separate and necessary science for understanding the faith of ancient Israel and for determining what is normative for today's church. As will be discussed in more detail later in this chapter, Eichrodt developed a method that is both thematic (God and Israel, God and Humanity, and God and the World) and unified by a center, specifically the covenant that provides a cross section of the various texts of the Hebrew Bible. Eichrodt reviews the argument that Old Testament theology is a historical discipline related to the history of Israelite religion and different only in terms of the means of analysis and selection of material.[28] According to Eichrodt, Old Testament theology has drawn our attention to both its foundation and its central problem, that of revelation. He concludes that modern believers cannot be content simply with a historical approach. However, he notes that it is not clear how we are to achieve the goal of understanding the religious faith of ancient Israel.

Thus, the place of Old Testament theology within the framework of Old Testament study becomes a major question. Old Testament theology is not a historical quest to discover what happened, but rather a discipline concerning what may be determined to be true. History cannot adjudicate and determine the truth, but only surmise that an event happened and why it happened on the basis of the major elements of material culture. If this understanding is affirmed in too restrictive a fashion, then Old Testament theology falls outside the domain of history and becomes a part of philosophy and dogmatics. However, Eichrodt, working with a cross section of the Old Testament to obtain what it considers to be meaningful and true, sought to discover the essence of beliefs necessary for faith both in ancient Israel and in the modern church. Old Testament theology is a historical enterprise in the sense that historical research cannot dispense with discovering the essence of Old Testament faith, a center (a unifying *Mitte*) that leads to a cross section of the biblical texts.

Eichrodt argues that his *Mitte* (center) and systematic (thematic) approach to Old Testament theology do not stand in opposition to historical method. However, historical research cannot lead to the discovery of what is normative. Only the contemporary church that engages the text with its own faith may determine the normative. There is a subjective moment in historical interpretation when the historian affirms that something happened or when a selection of what is to be studied is made. This means that history does not engage in an undertaking of absolute objectivity. History also involves the "perspectival concept of purpose under which an

---

27. Eichrodt, "Does Old Testament Theology Still Have Independent Significance?"
28. Ibid.

historical development is placed." Even historical research involves the sub-jectivity of the scholar.[29] Each historian approaches his or her discipline with a philosophy of history. In terms of both object and method, Old Testament theology uses the tools of the History of Religion in achieving its own distinctive place within the historical-critical research.[30] However, the normative is the decision of the interpreter operating within the context of the church and not that of the historian. Thus, for Eichrodt, the history of the religion of Israel and Old Testament theology are two different fields. The former deals with knowledge, while the latter focuses on faith.

Preeminence of History of Religion (1870–1914)

Wilhelm Vatke (1806–1882)[31] published in 1835 his *Religion des Alten Testaments,* in which we find the first major historical overview of Israelite religion. Adopting a Hegelian understanding of history and religion, Vatke argues that the history of Israelite religion was a spiritual process in which the absolute spirit dialectically moved through history to reveal itself to the people of Israel. This process witnessed the victory of the spiritual over the natural. Some of his more salient conclusions include the view that Moses was a gifted prophetic leader who rejected natural religion in favor of the worship of Yahweh as the national God of Israel, although he was not the founder of a state theocracy; the prophets represented the high point of Israelite Yahwism in affirming the universal character of God and in the development of a theocracy; and the cultic and legal formulations of ancient Israel were not completed until the postexilic period. Vatke contends it was not until the Hellenistic period after the universalizing of legalistic teaching by wisdom that Jewish religion de-clined, only to be revitalized as the final synthesis in early Christianity. His study of Israelite religion anticipates and formulates a basis for the later history of Julius Wellhausen, an influence Wellhausen himself readily acknowledges.

Julius Wellhausen wrote the prolegomenon to the history of Israel and a major history of Israel, which continue to influence our understanding of First- and Second-Temple Israel and Judah.[32] Especially influenced by

29. Ibid., 34.

30. Ibid., 38.

31. Vatke, *Die biblische Theologie wissenschaftlich dargestellt.* Due to the substantial influence in theological and church circles of the conservative scholar Ernst Wilhelm Heng-stenberg, who was opposed to what Vatke argued, he never finished his project. For a dis-cussion of Vatke's theology and significance, see Perlitt, *Vatke und Wellhausen.*

32. Wellhausen, *Prolegomena zur Geschichte Israels* and *Israelitische und jüdische Ges-chichte.* For important studies of Wellhausen and his influence on Old Testament studies, see

Heinrich Ewald, his teacher, until they later parted company because of political and methodological disputes, Wellhausen also came under the sway of other major Old Testament historians, including De Wette, Vatke, Reuss, Graf, and Kuenen. Perhaps the most important element in Wellhausen's view of the history of Israel was the place of the Torah, which first emerged as significant in Deuteronomy in the late seventh century B.C.E. and then became formative in shaping Judaism in the Second Temple period. Another important feature was his clear formation of the documentary hypothesis to which he gave classic expression. This analysis allowed him to relate the literary documents of the Pentateuch to the history of Israel. As many Old Testament scholars came to do, Wellhausen combined two features to write his history. The first was the methodology of the History of Religion, and the second was the theological polarity consisting of Yahweh, the God of Israel, and Israel, the people of Yahweh. This polarity was the basis for Israel's national consciousness.

Rudolf Smend, in his *Lehrbuch der alttestamentlichen Religionsgeschichte,* argues, "The History of Religion will demonstrate how this religion originated among the people of Israel, how they lived within its structure, how they experienced especially their fortunes through its strongest influences, and how they created and maintained their life through it, how it ruled their life, how it required their subjection, and how it allowed the people of the Jewish community to re-emerge."[33] Smend recognizes the distinction between the history of Israelite religion and the teaching of the church, develops the insight that biblical religion is fundamentally historical, emphasizes the freedom of the interpreter in subscribing to the authority of the Bible, affirms the importance of historical truth for biblical religion, and stresses the freedom of interpretation from dogmatic religion. Yet he also argues that the Hebrew Bible can be understood correctly as something that was both a development from the religion of Israel and Judaism and as something that was new.

The History of Religion School

The early History of Religion School included such notable scholars as Hermann Gunkel,[34] Albert Eichhorn, William Wrede, Wilhelm Bousset,

---

Perlitt, *Vatke und Wellhausen;* Knight, *Julius Wellhausen and his Prolegomena;* and Smend, *Deutsche Alttestamentler in drei Jahrhunderten,* 99–113.

33. Smend, *Lehrbuch der alttestamentlichen Religionsgeschichte,* 7.

34. For important studies of Gunkel, see Klatt, *Hermann Gunkel;* and Smend, *Deutsche Alttestamentler in drei Jahrhunderten.* For a helpful summary, see Scullion, "Gunkel, Johannes Heinrich Hermann."

Sigmund Mowinckel, Hugo Gressmann, and as already noted, Rudolf Smend. During this period, the major tools of research were phenomenological, historical, and comparative. Theological interests are not absent in many of the writings of these scholars, but they do differentiate clearly between the History of Religion and theology. especially in their dissimilar goals.

Hermann Gunkel (1862–1892) was the first scholar of the Hebrew Bible to make systematic use of the textual discoveries of the ancient Near East, in particular, Mesopotamia, in writing his history of Israelite religion. His most important work in the field of the history of Israelite religion, *Schöpfung und Chaos,* argues that the Babylonian creation myth, *Enūma eliš,* influenced the Hebrew understandings of creation. However, by the time of the completion of the priestly document, he argues, Babylonian polytheism had been excised and Israelite understanding was placed squarely within its own system of religious belief. The chronology of Babylonian influence was broken down into three sections: the original Babylonian myth of Marduk's creation, the Hebrew poetic formulation of the creation myth, and the priestly narrative in which mythology was almost totally removed. Gunkel advances two major hypotheses. One hypothesis is that significant religious ideas in human history were articulated by great personalities only after a period of lengthy struggle. The second is that revelation is not opposed to history and does not exist outside of history, but rather occurs within the ascending development of the human spirit. However, Gunkel did not abandon Hebrew theology when engaging in his historical work. For instance, he argues that early Christianity, in the theme of resurrection, brought to light life that is mystically shared with the believers in Jesus Christ.

Karl Albert August Ludwig Eichhorn (1856–1926) studied under such important scholars as Emil Schürer, Wilhelm Baudissin,[35] and Paul de Lagarde. Sometimes known as the head of the *Religionsgeschichtliche Schule,* Eichhorn emphasizes three major features that have continued to characterize the application of the History of Religion methodology to the study of biblical religions: (1) the study of ideas and practices in their sociohistorical context, in contrast to the written formulation of literary source critics; (2) the traditio-historical approach, which notes the changes due to the evolution of the Israelite and Jewish communities and institutions; and (3) the significance of Mandaean writings for understanding the Gospel of John, which, when extended more broadly, points to the

---

35. For the bibliography of Wilhelm Baudissin, see Frankenberg and Küchler, *Abhandlungen zur semitischen Religionskunde und Sprachwissenschaft.*

influence of the cultures of the ancient Near East and the Greco-Roman world on Israelite and Jewish religion.[36]

Sigmund Mowinckel (1884–1985), one of the leading figures of the Scandinavian School, was a prodigious writer whose works proved revolutionary in shaping the discourse and direction of the methodology of the history of Israelite religion. The most influential of his writings were his six volumes on the Psalter,[37] in which he developed his thesis of sacral kingship. Psalms, in his judgment, were written for the national festivals that included mythical-sacramental dramas. The most important was the new year's festival in which the king and queen played a key role in the ongoing experiencing of creation and salvation. In the combat myth that was dramatically performed, the king played the role of the creator defeating chaos, ascending the throne as ruler of heaven and earth, recreating the world, and participating in a *hieros gamos* that empowered once again the forces of fertility of the earth and its inhabitants, thereby providing blessing for the coming year. This festival celebrated the enthronement of Yahweh and his representative, the Israelite king (e.g., Pss 47, 93, 95–100). Most likely, argues Mowinckel, this new year's myth was borrowed from the Babylonians. For Mowinckel, this festival provided the context for the development of Israelite eschatology in which, on the "Day of Yahweh," salvation and creation were repeated into the future.[38]

Hugo Gressman (1877–1927) was a prodigious writer who also appropriated emerging material culture from the ancient Near East for understanding the Bible. He and Gunkel were both instrumental in shaping the methodology of form criticism. His expertise in ancient Near Eastern literature and culture led to his producing the major standard translation of ancient Near Eastern texts in German, *Altorientalischen Texten und Bildern zum Alten Testament*.

Preeminence of Old Testament Theology (1914–1970)

Karl Barth (1886–1968), destined to become the most significant theologian in the twentieth century, broke the strong grip of the History of Religion approach on biblical studies with the appearance of his commentary *Der*

---

36. Rollmann, "Eichhorn, Karl Albert August Ludwig" and "William Wrede, Albert Eichhorn, and the 'Old Quest' of the Historical Jesus." See especially Eichhorn, *Das Abendmahl im Neuen Testament.* Several of the scholars of the *Religionsgeschichtliche Schule* taught at Göttingen (see Lüdemann and Schröder, *Die Religionsgeschichtliche Schule in Göttingen*).

37. Mowinckel, *Psalmenstudien* I–VI; see also *He That Cometh.*

38. For a review of Mowinckel's conceptions, see Barstad and Ottosson, "The Life and Work of Sigmund Mowinckel."

Römerbrief in 1919, only a year following the end of the Great War.[39] While Swiss, Barth was teaching at Bonn when Hitler became Führer of Germany. Barth was expelled from Germany when he refused to take the oath of loyalty to Hitler and chose to join, instead, the Confessing Church in its opposition to National Socialism. He moved to Basel, where he served as a professor of theology.

Barth emphasizes the interpretation of the Bible by arguing that the Word of God is located in Scripture and not in human religious experience or in the social and cultural life of human beings.[40] Barth requires theology to be relevant to the life of the contemporary church, while the Bible is to serve as the foundation for dogmatic theology. The unifying feature of his biblical interpretation, expressed frequently in his *Church Dogmatics,* is the affirmation that the Bible serves as a witness to the Word of God. He interprets Scripture as sacred canon, rather than as a historical text reconstructed by biblical criticism. This Word of God, most fully realized in Jesus Christ, speaks through the Bible in human words that become proclamation. Even so, the Word of God is not to be confused with human words, for God is not comprehended by anyone. It is possible for the church to know the Word of God only through this text and yet, at the same time, it is the Word that allows for the proper interpretation of Scripture. This Word of God does not comprise the words of human beings and their cultures, but rather through it, God addresses them and demands of them the response of either "yes" or "no." This means for Barth that the Word of God is a dialectic, not in the sense given by Hegel, but rather in the address of God to humans and their response.

As a Christian, Barth stresses that all biblical texts are to be understood in their relationship to Jesus Christ. Thus, Barth gives a Christocentric interpretation to both the Old and the New Testaments. Jesus Christ is not only the one to whom biblical texts testify, but also the one who is the active subject of the salvific narratives that constitute the Christian story. Barth's interpretation of Scripture centers on the themes that may be shaped into dogmatic tenets and on the narratives that compose the Christian story for the community of faith. Barth's influence, while not shaping exegetical and historical biblical studies in the generations to come, did rekindle interest in the writing of biblical theology. We need, argues Barth, a new Old Testament theology that cannot be brought about simply by recon-

---

39. Translated as *The Epistle to the Romans,* based on the sixth edition. Important studies of Barth and his work include Bächli, *Das Alte Testament in der Kirchlichen Dogmatik von Karl Barth;* Rau and Busch, *Karl Barth;* Ford, *Barth and God's Story;* and Smend, "Karl Barth als Ausleger der Heiligen Schrift."

40. McGlasson, "Barth, Karl."

structing its History of Religion. This is due to his belief that Christian faith for modern humanity is not primarily historical but more of an encounter with the Word.[41]

Walther Eichrodt (1890–1978), a colleague of Barth's for a time at Basel, published the first fascicle of his theology of the Old Testament at the time Hitler *kam auf der Macht* ("came to power," 1933). His Old Testament theology, completed in the years that followed, came to be heralded as one of the true classics of biblical studies. He sought to overcome the stagnation of Old Testament theology that derived from the proof-texting method of orthodoxy and the historicism of Old Testament research, both of which he thought negated a valid, theological articulation of the Old Testament. Casting aside the ahistorical use of the Old Testament by the dogmatic theology of orthodoxy and rejecting the lack of theological engagement of the text by historical criticism, Eichrodt makes the successful transition from writing an orthodox compilation of themes and from the delineation of a history of Israelite religion to composing a theology of the Old Testament. Eichrodt shapes, not a historical development of Israelite theological ideas, but rather a systematic theology based on a thematic cross section of the Old Testament. For Eichrodt, what was determinative for the theology of the Old Testament was the eruption of the kingship of God into human history. Israelite religion may be divided into national, prophetic, and Jewish-legal elements. However, its theology may be articulated only by delineating a cross section of the Old Testament, that is, its covenantal faith. This cross section leads to a systematic, theological summary. The three circles related by covenant are God and the people of Israel, God and the world, and God and humanity, categories drawn from systematic theology.

Eichrodt does not dismiss the discipline of history and historical research. On the contrary, he regards Old Testament theology as a historical discipline that points to the characteristic features of ancient Israelite faith and ethics. The history of Israel and the faith of Old Testament theology are to cohere closely. Eichrodt accomplishes this coherence by placing each of the major theological themes within the context of the history of Israelite religion. This allows him not only to point out the plurality of understandings, but also to articulate a unity (i.e., covenant as the *Mitte,* center that brings together the other themes and traces their development throughout the periods of the life of ancient Israel). At the same time, Eichrodt

---

41. Brevard Childs is the most prominent example of an Old Testament scholar who incorporates many of the features of dialectical theology into his theology (see his *Biblical Theology of the Old and New Testaments*). Childs rejects as invalid anything that has to do with the History of Religion when applied to formulating and understanding Old Testament theology. Here he follows Barth.

approached his theological description of the Old Testament as a Christian. This meant that he also regarded the New Testament as essential for pointing to the unity of the Bible and to presenting its overarching theology. However, the task of New Testament theology is left to scholars of the Second Testament. Overall, then, Eichrodt points to the legitimacy of Old Testament as a discipline in and of itself, yet it is still tied to history and firmly entrenched within its ancient Near Eastern context. In addition, it is a significant but separate part of biblical theology that includes both testaments for the church. What he achieved was a way of finding unity in diversity, a diversity that results from an evolving Israelite religion and faith that experienced durative change. The unity was the covenant.

As we have already noted in our interpretation of his theological work, *Gerhard von Rad's* two-volume *Old Testament Theology* has surpassed even the significance of Eichrodt's theology and has shaped much of the study of Old Testament theology for half a century. In this monumental work, he asks two substantial questions that, once answered, guide his overall theological interpretation: First, should we study the history that is articulated by the biblical writers themselves or the one that is reconstructed by scholars? Second, if Old Testament faith has to do with the presentation of its theology about God and God's revelation, then where does this revelation reside? Does it reside in the history reconstructed by scholars or in the picture of God that is present in the Old Testament?

These are trenchant questions, for Old Testament theology often does not correspond to this reconstructed history. If one understands by history that which scholars have determined to have happened, then this would be the history that resides at the basis of theological formulation. This is the position of G. Ernest Wright in his introductory text, *The God Who Acts*. For Wright, the events of salvation history encompass divine revelation.[42] Von Rad regarded history, as it functions within Old Testament theology, to be primarily the developing traditions of Israelite faith that are expansions of Israel's creedal beliefs about God. Whether these events actually happened ultimately is not important for faith. What is essential is the "history" of the development of these affirmations that comprise the traditions of faith. Revelation resides within these creedal expressions, not within the ongoing history of the nation. Von Rad argues that Old Testament theology is not to be equated with the History of Religion. Rather, this theology has to do both with the testimonies of faith that reveal God's activities of redemption in history and with divine revelation in the acts and the words of prophets, priests, and sages.[43] The Old Testament, for

---

42. Wright, *The God Who Acts.*
43. Von Rad, *Old Testament Theology.*

von Rad, is a "history book" *(Geschichtsbuch)* primarily in the sense of the developing stories or traditions of Israelite faith, and not in the modernist sense of "what actually happened." Old Testament faith is a history of evolving traditions of faith, not a reconstruction of events that may have transpired. The first is a theology, while the second is a critical history.

In spite of his criticism of the limits of the method of the History of Religion, von Rad nevertheless launches his Old Testament theology with a brief survey of the history of Israel. It is never clear how the theology that follows relates to this historical introduction. Indeed, they exist side by side but do not engage each other. I assume he intends to set forth the historical setting for the development of the traditions of faith within the context of Israelite history, but to accomplish this assumed objective requires some integration that is not clearly provided.

For von Rad, the content of Old Testament theology is not to be found in placing the materials of the Hebrew Bible in the systematic categories derived from the dogmatic theology of the church, but rather consists of what Israel itself has said about God. Thus, in essence, Old Testament theology consists of Israel's own testimonies of faith, and their presentation assumes the forms of confession and retelling. Von Rad writes, not a History of Religion, but rather a history of religious traditions of faith that serve as the locus for divine revelation. These religious traditions develop their own history by continuing to be interpreted and reinterpreted by the successive communities of Israel and by providing the content for new traditions of creation, the covenant, the exodus, and the promise to David. Speaking from the context of the church, von Rad, in a less than convincing move, uses typology to describe the relationship between the two testaments. The typological salvific events foreshadow the final salvation history to which the New Testament witnesses. Thus, when von Rad argues "the Old Testament is a history book," he is speaking of both the subject matter of its texts and the kerygmatic proclamation of the developing traditions of Israel's faith. This history of tradition eventually breaks forth into normative theology for the church, a connection that is made typologically in moving from the acts of salvation in the Old Testament to those of the New.[44] I am puzzled, however, by von Rad's shift to typology when he addresses the issue of the relationship of the New Testament to the Old. Would it not have been more consistent to continue the development of traditions into and through the New Testament on until the present for contemporary theology?

---

44. For important studies of von Rad, see Honecker, "Zum Verständnis der Geschichte in Gerhard von Rad's *Theologie des Alten Testaments*"; Wolf, Rendtorff, and Pannenberg, *Gerhard von Rad*; and Crenshaw, *Gerhard von Rad*.

Alternative Voice: The History of Religion during the
Reign of Neo-Orthodoxy

While not held in the same esteem it had enjoyed prior to the emergence
and thriving of dialectical theology, the History of Religion approach continued to produce important studies in this period of theological dominance. Two groups of scholars, the British Myth-Ritual School and the
Scandinavian School, worked independently, although they both concentrated on the relationship between myth and ritual in the ancient Near
East and in ancient Israel and came to similar conclusions. Especially
important were the nature and relationship of the new year's festival, the
mythology of creation, and the mythic and ritual role of kingship.

The British Myth-Ritual School. The so-called British Myth-Ritual School
continued to articulate the major features of the history of Israelite religion, even though Old Testament theology due to the influence of Karl
Barth did not hold this approach in high regard. In 1933 and again two
years later, S. H. Hooke edited the papers of two symposia.[45] Among the
important scholars who participated in these important collections were
W. O. E. Oesterley, T. H. Robinson, and E. O. James. This collection was
followed a quarter of a century later in 1958 when Hooke produced a third
collection, *Myth, Ritual, and Kingship.* The scholars who worked in this
area and continued to be influential included A. R. Johnson and Hans-
Joachim Kraus.

These scholars, while often differing on specific issues, generally hold
that a common myth and ritual pattern existed in the ancient Near East.
This mythic pattern involved two major elements: a new year's festival
and sacral kingship. This mythic and ritual pattern found its most significant expression in an annual new year's festival that led to the well-being
of the community for the coming year. For example, the Babylonian *akitu*
(new year's) festival consisted of several recurring features, including a
dramatic enactment of the death and resurrection of the god, a reading of
the myth that empowered the event, a ritual combat between the god of
creation and the powers of chaos, the *hieros gamos* (sacred marriage), and
the culminating enthronement of the victorious god, who then recreated
the world and gave it renewed vitality for the coming year. The king, who
was chosen by God to rule as his "son," played the role of the deity and
had a significant cultic place in Israelite religion. The king possessed a sacral
character and, according to some scholars, was even considered to be

---

45. Hooke, *Myth and Ritual* and *The Labyrinth.*

divine by some scholars (cf. Ps 45:7). This school's work rejected the common view of the moral monotheism of a spiritual religion articulated by the prophets who were essentially anticultic and opposed to ancient Near Eastern mythology. Instead, Israel was said to have a significant mythic religion that included an important role for cult and ritual.

The Scandinavian School. The myth-and-ritual approach had its greatest influence on the work of Scandinavian scholars who continued to develop the features of the history of Israelite religion during the reign of neo-orthodoxy on the European continent. Among the most significant Scandinavian scholars were Ivan Engnell, Helmer Ringgren, Alfred Haldar, Sigmund Mowinckel, Johannes Pedersen, and Aage Bentzen. The stimulus for the myth-and-ritual work came from the anthropologist James G. Frazer. The same emphases mentioned above drove the work of these scholars. Engnell even argues that the Israelite king was divine, since he was the embodiment of Yahweh, while Haldar contends that at least some of the prophets (including, for example, Amos) were cultic officials. In addition, he suggests their books may have been cultic liturgies, reflecting their prophecies made during the context of ritual worship.

Not surprisingly, these studies moved readily and quite naturally into later cultural- and social-anthropological, as well as social scientific studies that strongly influenced Old Testament scholarship, beginning especially in the 1970s.[46] The anthropological investigation of the religion of Israel became one of the most important areas of study for at least thirty years, and it has gained enormous attention as interest in the area of Old Testament theology in the United States began to wane in the late 1960s. However, theology was still the chief discipline for the study of the Old Testament in Germany.[47] Continental Old Testament theologians had, to a large extent, not continued their work along the lines of the History of Religion.[48]

A Period of Tension (1970–1990)

Brevard Childs's 1970 book on the crisis of the biblical theology movement in America announced the decline of interest in biblical theology in North

---

46. Of the numerous studies affected by more modern anthropological methods, one may mention Frank Gorman's *Ideology of Ritual,* which uses the theories of Victor Turner, Mary Douglas, and Clifford Geertz in the study of priestly ritual.

47. One of the important collections of ancient Near Eastern texts is Beyerlin, *Religionsgeschichtliches Textbuch zum Alten Testament.*

48. Rendtorff, "Die Entstehung der israelitischen Religion."

America.[49] Scholarly focus here began to shift away from biblical theology to social scientific and literary methods. The History of Religion approach began once again to obtain an ascendancy over biblical theology, especially due to its easy adaptability to social scientific methods. Beginning in the 1960s, Helmer Ringgren, Walther Eichrodt,[50] Georg Fohrer, and Frank Cross wrote significant histories of Israelite religion. However, it would be incorrect to argue that Old Testament theology was largely neglected in this period. A notable exception came from the students of W. F. Albright: Frank Cross, who accessed the Old Testament through the History of Religion approach, and G. Ernest Wright. Their depiction in turn allowed them to speak of Old Testament theology as grounded in history. The Albright school has never abandoned the History of Religion approach and to this day continues its practice as the fundamental avenue to understanding the Old Testament. The series Overtures to Biblical Theology, which began in the late 1970s and has recently passed its thirtieth year, is still edited by one of its founders, Walter Brueggemann, who eschewed doctrinaire approaches and a primary focus on methodology, in order to obtain theological insights into the biblical texts. Most of these volumes also demonstrate little interest in the history of Israelite religion. The series contains numerous volumes on biblical theology covering a wide range of topics. However, the lack of methodological conformity, while enriching, points to the lack of anything approaching a consensus in doing biblical theology.

Search for a Resolution (1990–Present)

Over the past decade, biblical scholars have continued to write important histories of religion that are not theological in purpose or content. These include works by Susan Niditch, Patrick Miller, Karel van der Toorn, and Mark S. Smith. Their absence of concern for theological purpose and content does not, however, prevent biblical theologians from appropriating their insights. Also, a number of important biblical theologies have been written that do not approach their subjects through the interaction of biblical theology with the history of Israelite religion—for example, those of Rolf Rendtorff[51] and Brevard Childs.[52] Even so, others have approached biblical theology through the lens of the History of Religion and have

---

49. It was the approach of G. Ernest Wright and other representatives of "biblical theology" in America that was strongly criticized. This was certainly not the case with other approaches. See Childs, *Biblical Theology in Crisis.*

50. Eichrodt, *Religionsgeschichte Israels.*

51. Rendtorff, *Theologie des Alten Testaments;* and *Der Text in Seiner Endgestalt.*

52. Childs, *Biblical Theology of the Old and New Testaments.*

sought to bring together the two methods, objectives, and bodies of content. This effort to combine the two recognizes the importance of the historical character of Old Testament theology. As Preuss has argued, "On the whole, a 'theology of the Old Testament' still remains an historically oriented as well as a descriptive undertaking."[53]

Historians of religion, even those from the late nineteenth century (e.g., Hermann Gunkel), have often incorporated elements of biblical theology into their reconstructions. This is due, in part, to the use of historical criticism by biblical theologians and to the rich array of comparative data provided by the material cultures and texts of other nations and cultures of the ancient Near East. And it is due, in part, to the fact that most of the scholars who wrote histories of Israelite religion were clergy. Many Old Testament theologians have also written histories of Israelite religion, and consequently, the two undertakings are not always clearly differentiated.

However, there are important differences between the two disciplines:

1. The first is in the context of the writer: Old Testament theology comes from the church, and the History of Religion emerges out of the academy.

2. Another difference is their purpose: Old Testament theology is written for the shaping of the doctrines and instruction of the church, while the History of Religion is written more for the academic reader, whether scholar or student. Old Testament theology seeks to establish a theological relationship with the theologies of the New Testament and the church, while the History of Religion does not move beyond the cultural life of ancient Israel and early Judaism.

3. They also differ in whether judgments are made. Old Testament theology does not refrain from arguing that some the teachings of the Hebrew Bible are normative or at least theologically true, while the History of Religion does not make normative evaluations or designate a belief or practice to be theologically true.

4. The History of Religion regards the biblical text as a human document to be critically investigated in the same way that

---

53. Preuss, *Old Testament Theology*, 20. Preuss combines systematic (thematic) theology, the center for which is divine election and human responsibility, with the historical development of this theology through engagement with ancient Near Eastern and Israelite popular religion intimated by material culture.

other literature is studied, while Old Testament theology in some manner regards the text as inspired revelation for believing communities.

5. Old Testament theology deals exclusively with the biblical text and sets forth its theological affirmations, while the History of Religion examines all features of material culture in Israel and the ancient Near East and has the objective of presenting both the official and the popular expressions of religious life in ancient Israel. Neither is judged superior to the other.

6. The History of Religion is based on a common periodization into which the data, both texts and material culture, are placed,[54] while biblical theology most often is presented systematically and thematically and draws from the doctrinal categories of contemporary theology (e.g., God, community, redemption, sacral leadership, creation, and eschatology).

7. The History of Religion approach eschews any unifying factor, save for noting ongoing themes and ideologies that develop socially (e.g., semi-nomadic, tribal-agrarian, towns, and urban), while biblical theology usually searches for a center *(Mitte)* that provides unity for the articulation of its faith.

8. It is important to recognize that most, if not all, of the Hebrew Bible is written by the elite, especially of Judah, with an ideology supporting their own self-interest and is not the product of social inferiors and the marginalized of ancient Israel.[55]

In spite of these fundamental differences of objectives and methods, important similarities remain between the two undertakings. In more recent years, a number of scholars, while choosing not to blur the distinc-

---

54. See, e. g., Japhet, "Periodization."
55. See Niehr, "Auf dem Weg zu einer Religionsgeschichte Israels und Judas." He adds that two types of religion existed in Israelite culture and history. A primary religion speaks of the order of the cosmos and stresses a hierarchal society in which authority moves from gods to kings to the bureaucracy and ultimately to the lowest social stratum. A secondary religion places in the foreground the personal relationship of humans to God and expresses itself confessionally. He argues that, in contrast to theology, the purpose of the History of Religion is to engage in the reconstruction on the basis of material culture and texts, not in retelling the biblical narrative's depiction of Israelite religion. This same way of approaching ancient Israelite history and religion has been proposed and carried out by Ahlström, *The History of Ancient Palestine.*

tions between the two approaches, have sought to use the history of Israelite religion to help them shape their articulations of the theology of the Hebrew Bible.

Rainer Albertz

The most visible, and at times controversial, of these scholars is Rainer Albertz, whose point of departure is the history of Israelite religion.[56] The appearance of his two-volume history of Israelite religion has brought into sharp focus once again the differences between Old Testament theology and the history of Old Testament religion. Albertz rejects Old Testament theology when done in the context of the church, and this has led to sharp criticism of his work. Instead, he proposes that the objective of Old Testament scientific inquiry is to understand the religious development of ancient Israel. According to Albertz, the two methods, Old Testament theology and the history of Israelite religion, cannot be equated, unless Old Testament theology is understood as the presentation of the religiously diverse ideas of ancient Israel.[57] However, what has provoked significant discussion has been the convoluted argument that the history of Israelite religion is itself a theological undertaking. This position has led to a rather crisp debate between Albertz and his critics.

In an earlier work,[58] Albertz points to several features to which he returns in later writings. These include the pluralism of Israelite religion and the popular piety that rivaled official religion throughout the periods of Israelite history. Part of this popular religion was revealed in the personal names of Israelites and part in the material culture. Thus, another type of religion—that of the village—existed alongside family and state religions. Methodologically, he compares Israelite and Babylonian religions, noting the many similarities between the two.

In the introduction to his two-volume history of the religion of ancient Israel, Albertz articulates his fundamental methodological assumptions

---

56. Albertz, *A History of Israelite Religion in the Old Testament Period.*

57. Rendtorff doubts that a debate concerning the value of one of the two methods over the other is useful or even necessary. Indeed, like many others, he sees them as different methods with divergent objectives ("Die Hermeneutik einer kanonischen Theologie des Alten Testaments"). He notes that Old Testament theology has two major presuppositions. One is that the Old Testament is a theological book (cf. Smend, "Theologie im Alten Testament," *Verifikation*). The second is that the subject matter of Old Testament theology is the final form of the canon (cf. his *Theologie des Alten Testaments*). By contrast, he argues that the History of Religion is concerned with reconstructing the life and religious thought of the ancient community in a diachronic process. Rendtorff is joined by Isaac Kalimi, who agrees that they are two different methods, each with its own distinct goals and procedures ("Religionsgeschichte Israels oder Theologie des Alten Testaments").

58. Albertz, *Persönliche Frömmigkeit und offizielle Religion.*

and positions clearly and concisely.[59] He begins by noting that in Germany the theological faculties no longer regard the history of Israelite religion as a standard subject. This discipline has been eclipsed by Old Testament theology. Dialectical theology that emerged following World War I portrayed the History of Religion in a negative light, so the interests of theological faculties developed in theology and not in history. Albertz counters this trend by asserting that the History of Religion approach has more value for understanding the Old Testament than does the discipline of Old Testament theology. Indeed, he goes so far as to argue that the History of Religion offers a better understanding of Old Testament theology than other approaches.

Albertz makes the following assertions. First, the History of Religion approach must offer a historical construction devoid of dogmatic principles of division and selection. Second, this approach allows the investigation of later Judaism and early Christianity. Terms like *Hebraism* are to be excised, along with the devaluation of the Torah. The Protestant assessment that the high point of Israelite religion was represented by the message of the prophets may not be substantiated. Further, this method is not a mere intellectual history of ideas, but points instead to what Israelites, both men and women, in their sociohistorical context believed and practiced. This approach places side by side a political history and the societal development of Israel in order to determine the ideologies of those whose interests were at stake in establishing and maintaining certain beliefs and practices. This allows the recognition that there were substantive changes in religion over the centuries. The History of Religion sets up a dialectical model in which the different, pluralistic views of the traditions of various social groups unveiled in the Hebrew Bible are brought into play. This approach allows Christian dialogue with non-Christian religions and does not attempt to formulate the uniqueness and thus the superiority of one religion over another. Finally, this method describes the postexilic period more appropriately and requires interpreters to refrain from describing it as a decline, a view that is a Christian judgment that often has obviated dialogue between Jews and Christians.[60]

---

59. Albertz, *A History of Israelite Religion* 1, 1–21. In his paper given at the Society of Biblical Interpretation International meeting in 1993, Albertz called for the reorientation of biblical studies with the major focus to be placed primarily on the history of Israelite religion instead of on biblical theology. Later, in 1994, in his discussions in the SBL International meeting at Leuven, he expressed regret that he had been misunderstood. He emphasized that he was not calling for a dismissal of Old Testament theology, but rather was contending that the discipline of the History of Religion should have priority over that of biblical theology.

60. Albertz, *A History of Israelite Religion* 1, 11–12.

It is also clear from reading Albertz that he offers several other important positions for discussion. One major area of contention is the making of value judgments. Of course, every historian makes judgments as to what transpired, why it occurred, when it took place, who engaged in the activity, and what its results were. However, Albertz goes a step further and contends that even those scholars who make use of the History of Religion tend to make value judgments as to what is of merit in Israelite religion as opposed to beliefs and practices that are judged to be unacceptable and perhaps even unsavory. For Albertz, no scholars, including those engaging in the discipline of the History of Religion, can be totally objective.[61] However, controls must be established that keep the investigation from being completely subjective. Data must be brought into view and evaluated as objectively as possible to set forth the fundamental tenets and practices of Israelite religion. The historian of religion should not make affirmations of truth and establish what is normative. This scholar should not allow church dogmatics to influence the selection and evaluation of data for the reconstruction of Israelite religion. Albertz is critical of systematic presentations of Old Testament theologies, doubting there is any legitimate way of describing Israelite religion in a way similar to the efforts of Eichrodt. It is extremely difficult, and perhaps impossible, to discover any system for Old Testament theology that corresponds to Israelite religion. This is seen by the continuing failure to find a center for any systematic formulation. While Albertz is not opposed to a historical presentation of biblical theology, he does find fault with thematic and systematic presentations that are influenced by systematic theology and originate in philosophical idealism.

The religion of Israel, as described by Albertz, consists of the following major diachronic (chronological) and synchronic (thematic) sections:

- Israelite religion prior to state formation—small family groups, a liberated larger group, the religion of the prestate alliance, and family piety
- Israelite religion during the monarchy—the formation of a monarchical territorial state, the dispute over the religious legitimation of kingship, the main state cult in the south, the main state cult in the north, the dispute over official syncretism

---

61. Crüsemann ("Religionsgeschichte oder Theologie?") argues that neither biblical theology nor the History of Religion may be completely objective. To claim the contrary, in his view, is pseudo objectivity. In addition, he is rather skeptical of Albertz's hope that an increasing consensus about Israel's religion will emerge, for there is as much variation in this field as there is in Old Testament theology.

in the ninth century, the theological controversies in the social and political crisis of the eighth century, family piety under the late monarchy, the Deuteronomic reform movement, and the political and theological controversies after the death of Josiah

- Israelite religion in the exilic period—sociological developments during the exile, the struggle over a theological interpretation of the political catastrophe, the support for Yahweh religion from family piety, and toward a new beginning

- Israelite religion in the post-exilic period—political and sociological developments in the Persian period, the key experience of the failed restoration, the struggle over the identity of the community, the social and religious split in the community, the convergence of the religious strata and the dichotomy between official and personal piety, the rise of the Samaritan community, and a prospectus on the History of Religion in the Hellenistic period

In this last period, Albertz traces the sociological developments, the scribal ideal of a theocracy (Chronicles), Torah piety, and the late prophetic and apocalyptic theology of resistance. While chronological, this treatment of Israel's religion is also synchronic in noting the contrasts between personal piety and popular religion on one hand, and the changing official religion on the other.[62]

It is important to note that Albertz does not hesitate to pose the question of Israel's religious relevance for the contemporary world. He argues that the History of Religion allows interpreters to address theological controversies in the church that, by analogy, might well propose a solution. This solution is possible by noting that the religious history of Israel and early Christianity may provide important insights into similar problems today. However, this argument by analogy, often used by biblical theologians in speaking of the relevancy of a particular point of view in one of the two testaments, lacks controls and allows for individual judgment to run amuck. Nevertheless, Albertz attempts to respond to the accusation normally leveled against the method of the History of Religion, i.e., that it has no interest in theology and the teachings and issues of the contemporary church, by arguing just the opposite is true. He makes the highly

---

62. The so-called minimalist historians argue that "Israel" of the Old Testament is a fiction that cannot be identified with a sociohistorical community. See Lemche, "Warum die Theologie des Alten Testaments einen Irrweg darstellt"; and Thompson, "Das Alte Testament als theologische Disziplin"). See also Davies, *In Search of Ancient Israel;* Thompson, *Early History of the Israelite People;* and Lemche, *The Canaanites and their Land.*

questionable argument that, on theological grounds, the History of Religion, more so than biblical theology, has significance for the contemporary world and the church. In addition, he brings to his task sociological and anthropological methodologies that were especially, though not exclusively, of concern in North America.[63] For example, one may compare his views about a liberated Israel with those of his American contemporary, Norman Gottwald. He even makes use of the criticism of American Jewish scholars directed toward the contemporary theological enterprise as being inclusive of different expressions of Christianity but exclusive of the Jewish experience and understanding. Yet he also continues down the well-worn path traveled by the historians of religion who have preceded him. For example, he is heavily influenced by Scandinavian scholarship when he considers royal ideology in ancient Israel to have been quite close to ancient Near Eastern sacral, even divine, kingship. This dependence may also be noted in his characterization of royal religion in Jerusalem as heavily syncretistic.

Finally, one should recall the salient points of difference between Old Testament theology and the history of Israelite religion that Albertz conveniently summarizes. He prefers the approach of the History of Religion for the following reasons:

- Because it corresponds better to the historical structure of large parts of the Old Testament;

- Because it takes seriously the insight that religious statements cannot be separated from the historical background from which they derive or against which they are interpreted;

- Because it is not compelled to bring down its varying and sometimes contradictory religious statements to the level of intellectual abstraction;

- Because it describes a dialogical process of struggle for theological clarification, demarcation, and consensus forming that clearly corresponds to the present-day synodical or conciliar ecumenical learning process of the churches and Christian-Jewish dialogue;

- Because it sees its continuity, not in any religious ideas, which have to be appropriated by Christians, but in the people of Israel itself, to which the Christian churches stand in a brotherly and sisterly relationship through Jesus Christ;

---

63. Albertz, *A History of Israelite Religion* 1, 18–19. In addition to his dependence on Berger and Luckmann, *The Social Construction of Reality,* he also makes use of Lanczkowski, *Einführung in die Religionsgeschichte.*

- Because a consistently historical approach dispenses with any claim—even a concealed one—to absoluteness, but deliberately does theology under an eschatological proviso that befits a minority church in a multireligious and partially secularized world community; and

- Because it facilitates dialogue with other religions.[64]

Reply to Albertz: Jahrbuch für biblische Theologie

The appearance of the two-volume work by Albertz has provoked a considerable debate. In 1995, the *Jahrbuch für biblische Theologie*,[65] which includes essays by Old Testament theologians, historians of religion, and contemporary theologians, replied in detail to his work. Most of the respondents agree that it is important to follow, at least in a limited fashion, the direction to which Albertz points. At the same time, these respondents ask significant questions that Albertz does not always clearly answer. Others have been forcefully critical of many of the views of Albertz when he speaks theologically.

This 1995 collection of critical responses to Albertz also contains two of his own essays. The first sets forth his basic positions for preferring the History of Religion to Old Testament theology.[66] The second contains his response in which he argues that Old Testament theology, while it ought to be an exegetical, historical, and systematic enterprise, still belongs to the sphere of the church, whereas the history of Israelite religion offers Old Testament theology a concrete material basis, even while by necessity dispensing with normative judgments.[67] It is not possible, according to many of these critics, to assert that the History of Religion may assess what is true and important for modern faith and practice.

I shall not rehearse the other arguments for and against the position of Albertz in this collection of essays, save by way of a brief summary. Several of the respondents (Lohfink, Spieckermann, and Stemberger) see the cardinal question of hermeneutics to be the problem of the Christian Old Testament over against the Jewish Hebrew Bible. Is biblical theology a Christian, theological discipline which must be placed in the context of seeking the truth for Christian communities in the context of its protean expressions, or is it to be an undertaking that includes both Jews and Chris-

---

64. Albertz, *A History of Israelite Religion* 1, 16–17.

65. Janowski, *Jahrbuch für biblische Theologie* 10 (1995). Several of these essays are mentioned above.

66. Albertz, "Religionsgeschichte Israels statt Theologie des Alten Testaments!"

67. Albertz, "Hat die Theologie des Alten Testaments doch noch eine Chance?"

tians? Pannenberg, for example, points to a large spectrum of impulses and actual themes that the significance of the Hebrew Bible sets forth for the Christian faith. Finally, two essays (Koerrenz and Fuchs) deal with the practical matter of the manner in which the God of Abraham, Isaac, and Jacob and the faith in the Father of Jesus Christ may be operative in the present reality of life. I return to the definition of the concept of biblical theology articulated by James Barr, which provides a convenient description of the salient features of the arguments of Albertz that may be either affirmed or seriously questioned. Barr has dealt in detail with the relationship between biblical theology and the History of Religion.[68] In returning to the prominent points of his definition, we note that, for Barr, there have been several major ways of defining and understanding the concept of biblical theology and that one may pose them as contrasts to the arguments of Albertz:

- Biblical theology is "something new," in the sense that it is searching for something that is not already "known." It is not "something already laid down in a past or ancient tradition." Rather, it "is something that has still to be discovered." Albertz is clear when he describes the religions of Israel's and Judah's past, but he is not at all clear when dealing with contemporary faith and practice. He has no methodological criteria for engaging contemporary faith and practice. Rather, he appears to set forth his own value judgments as to what is or is not normative, and he chooses to say what, if anything, an ancient belief or practice may say to a contemporary issue. This lack of clarity obfuscates any serious effort to engage Biblical theology with contemporary faith and modern issues.

- Biblical theology "possesses an ecumenical potential," even though the "actual theologies that have emerged have been very different." Albertz argues for the cogency of this point. However, he is not clear what one is to do when salient points of faith clash. One has diversity but no constraints whatsoever on pluralism and no criteria for engaging in dialogue.

- Biblical theology must have "features and aspects that are analogous to the working of theology in the proper sense." This point is at odds with what Albertz attempts to accomplish. Contemporary theology in its variety of expressions (e.g., systematic, feminist, narrative, *and* postcolonial) is not at all comparable to what Albertz does in his historical, chronological

---

68. Barr, *The Concept of Biblical Theology*, 100ff.

investigation of the development of Israelite religion. It is true, of course, that most contemporary theologians make use of theologies of the past (e.g., Luther, Calvin, Aquinas, Barth, and those of the Bible), but with the purpose of articulating a contemporary theology focusing primarily on the present that has engaged the past.

- Biblical theology achieves "clarity only when it is understood to mean theology as it existed or was thought or believed within the time, languages and cultures of the Bible itself." This historical orientation of biblical theology is in line with that approach of Albertz, although he concentrates as much on popular piety as he does on the biblical text. Furthermore, he does not privilege Scripture, but rather recognizes that religious ideas and practices were followed largely due to the ideologies of different social groups.

- Biblical theology does not obscure the fact that doctrinal (systematic, dogmatic, or constructive) theology and biblical theology have different purposes. Biblical theology is a descriptive, historical discipline in contrast to dogmatic theology (understood as the articulation of what is to be believed by Christians) that issues from the variety of Christian communities. This distinction is not made in Albertz's approach. In the engagement of Scripture, hermeneutical decisions as to what is or is not normative for the faith are made by the church, not scholars standing outside the Christian community.

- Biblical theology recognizes that biblical writers were influenced by earlier and contemporaneous ancient Near Eastern and Greco-Roman cultures and religions. One should avoid arguing that the "distinctive features" of the biblical texts are expressive of true faith in contrast to the false views of so-called pagan religions. On this point, Albertz agrees with Barr.

- Biblical theology is the basis for contemporary theology. Revelation through biblical writers and their texts compares and contrasts with understandings of God and/or the sacred that may derive from human reason and the experiential understanding of the world. Albertz would agree with this argument up to a point. He does not privilege the Bible, but rather views popular religion to be on an equal footing with Scripture. Thus, he does not offer a distinctive place to the roles and functions of the Bible in shaping hermeneutical discourse and normative faith in the church.

- Biblical theology focuses its gaze, not on parts of the Bible, but on the Bible as a whole. This means that Old Testament theology is the first step in constructing a theology of both testaments. Albertz certainly reconstructs the historical development of Israelite religion, but he does not suggest ways the New Testament is to be handled in the overall enterprise of biblical theology.

Thus, Barr would not consider Albertz's approach to be a theological one. However, while it is clear to all that the two disciplines differ in approaches and objectives, there is a growing recognition among scholars that they share a great deal in their respective treatments of the Hebrew Bible. No biblical theologian may reject the historical approach as at least a major part of what this enterprise entails. Rather, the scholar knowingly participates in both disciplines, while acknowledging that the two methods contain different objectives. This is the point made by James Barr near the end of his treatment of the History of Religion and Old Testament theology in *The Concept of Biblical Theology:* "The relation between Biblical theology and the History of Religion is and should be one of overlap and mutual enrichment. And the ultimate reason for this is that the stuff of which Biblical theology is built is really Biblical religion, or . . . those elements of Biblical religion which are commended, supported and advanced by the main currents of the Bible."[69] Indeed, the History of Religion provides Old Testament theology with insights and understandings that otherwise would be impossible to obtain. However, the two approaches are not to be equated.

Different Objectives of the Two Methods

It is clear that the two methods have different objectives, although they provide each other important insights.[70] The *Religionsgeschtliche* approach seeks to set forth a descriptive account of the development of the religion of Israel, without reading the theological or ideological perspectives of the interpreter into these texts and their contexts of social and material culture. Old Testament theology, by contrast, emerges out of the context of the church and seeks to determine and interpret the major beliefs of ancient Israel that may be related to the theological concerns of the church.

---

69. Barr, *The Concept of Biblical Theology,* 135. Later he notes, "The History of Religion must be accorded full recognition and importance by Biblical theology. The two cannot be separated and works on the latter must recognize not only the material of the former but also the positive theological importance of its researches and results" (p. 138).

70. As noted earlier, Rendtorff ("Was haben wir an der Bibel?") doubts that a debate is useful.

This does not mean that the interpreter standing within the context of the church is necessarily subjective in his or her analysis. Even so, the concern of the latter is to determine what is normative for the believing community and what is useful to the church in expressing its faith.[71] The History of Religion approach does not and, indeed, cannot make normative judgments for the church. The History of Religion approach sets forth the many different beliefs of ancient Israel in a diachronic portrayal that interacts with the different religions and cultures of the ancient Near East and early Greco-Roman world. The value of these beliefs and practices for the church is not addressed, but rather everything is included in the historical description. In addition to avoiding value judgments for what the church is to believe, historians of religion make use of history as the structure for arranging and interpreting material culture and articulate the diversity that exists in the culture and the biblical text. Finally, the History of Religion approach is as concerned with describing popular religion in ancient Israel as it is with the official religions of the nation of Israel and its major social institutions that are set forth in the text of the Old Testament. Indeed, to write a history of Israelite religion, the historian takes into consideration both the material culture and the text of the Old Testament.[72] Old Testament theology may benefit in its understanding of the Bible by making use of material culture and popular religion, but it nevertheless gives primacy to the canonical texts.

These commonalities and differences between the two disciplines have produced a creative tension that has continued during the past two centuries for various reasons.[73] First, there is considerable diversity of beliefs and practices in the Hebrew Bible itself, because it was written and edited over a millennium. This militates against finding a center or unity in the theology of the Hebrew Bible. It is doubtful that scholars will ever agree on a thematic center that unites the diverse biblical texts.

Another source of creative tension is that the final redaction occurred late in the history of Judah, likely in the third century B.C.E. This opens the possibility that later editors reshaped earlier texts to support their

71. One Old Testament theologian who especially emphasized reading the Old Testament for its theological and normative significance for the church is Vriezen, *An Outline of Old Testament Theology.* He distinguishes clearly between Old Testament theology and the history of Israelite religion. See also his volume *The Religion of Ancient Israel.* An Old Testament theologian who "Christianized" the Old Testament was Vischer, *Das Christuszeugnis des Alten Testaments.*

72. See Toorn, *Family Religion in Babylonia, Syria and Israel;* and Albertz, *Persönliche Frömmigkeit und offizielle Religion.*

73. Hayes and Prussner, *Old Testament Theology,* 264–67.

own theologies (and ideologies) and to reflect their different historical and social contexts. Even so, they often did not eliminate earlier beliefs and practices. However, differentiating between the original and the redactional understandings of the text is an extremely formidable task.

Third, many scholars, biblical theologians included, agree that the "Old Testament is a history book," although the term *history* is used in a variety of ways.[74] The description of the Old Testament as a "history book" fits the chronological development of the tradition complexes of the Hebrew Bible over many centuries and reflects the fact that large parts of the Hebrew Bible are narratives or stories (e.g., the Deuteronomistic History and the Chronicler that are concerned with "historical" developments. This is von Rad's understanding, and he appears to me to be correct).

In addition, histories of Israelite religion focus on beliefs and practices of ancient Israel in the context of the ancient Near East and the eastern Mediterranean worlds, while the theology of the Hebrew Bible deals especially with the idea of divine revelation, i.e., God speaking in and through human words.

A fifth cause of creative tension is that the relationship of the Old Testament to the New Testament in the History of Religion approach is a historical, chronological development that moved from ancient Israel through the variety of Jewish communities into the early church and the synagogue.

Sixth, while there is a historical continuity between ancient Israel and early Christianity, there is no privileging of a text, a testament, or a religious affirmation.

Finally, Karl Barth's disdain for religion as a human means to achieve salvation and theology as the Word of God that reached its culmination in Jesus Christ as the "Word made flesh" intensified this tension between the two fields. For Barth, "religion is the concentrated expression of human unbelief."[75] Christianity, according to Barth, is not a religion, but rather a community formed by revelation through the Word. This means that, for dialectical theology, the History of Religion approach to Israelite religion and early Christianity is illegitimate as an approach to theology. The Bible, rather, is the revelation of God to humanity, demanding a "yes" or "no."[76] Given this extreme position, there would be no authentic place for the History of Religion approach in doing Old Testament theology. Few Old Testament scholars, save for Brevard Childs and some of his students,

---

74. Hayden White, *Metahistory.*

75. Barth, *Church Dogmatics* I/2, 303.

76. Hayes and Prussner, *Old Testament Theology,* 266–67.

would accept Barth's understanding as the basis for carrying out biblical theology. Barth's repudiation of the History of Religion for theology attracts few devotees in the present world of biblical theology.

Approaching Old Testament Theology through the History of Religion

In addition to Albertz, other significant scholars have undertaken to use the History of Religion as an approach to construing at least the historical basis for Old Testament theology.[77]

Werner H. Schmidt

One of these is Werner H. Schmidt.[78] For Schmidt, a theology of the Old Testament is unthinkable without taking into consideration the history of Israelite religion, even as the reverse is also true.[79] At the same time, he argues that a history of Israelite religion does not simply describe the origins and development of religion among many, but also sets forth the unique features that place it apart from and above other religions. However, the Old Testament not only enters into disputation with other religions of the time, but also engages in self-criticism. Furthermore, the religion of Israel is not without its own intrinsic value judgments.

It is clear that Schmidt's primary interest is not to present the religion that was practiced historically by different social groups of ancient Israel. Rather, his focus is on select social circles in ancient Israel that present their own theological views that may influence the present understandings and beliefs of the church. For example, Jeffrey H. Tigay and he have argued for the combination of the History of Israelite Religion and Old Testament theology by focusing especially on the central theme of the first commandment, which came to be understood eventually as monotheism.[80] Indeed, Schmidt considers the first commandment to be at the center of Israelite religious faith.

---

77. Hermisson (Alttestamentliche Theologie und Religionsgeschichte Israels) argues that both are needed to carry out the task of Old Testament study, and it is clear that the two are not completely separated. According to Hermission, the history of Israelite religion enables one to recognize that Christian faith is based on historical events that come to expression in the texts of the Old Testament. Cf. Ebeling, "Was heisst 'biblische theologie'?"

78. Schmidt, Vielfalt und Einheit alttestamentlichen Glaubens 1, especially the discussions of "Psalmen und Weisheit," "Theologische Anthropologie und Jeremia," and "Theologie des Alten Testaments."

79. Schmidt, "'Theologie des Alten Testaments' vor und nach Gerhard von Rad." Cf. Westermann, "Das Verhältnis des Jahweglaubens zu den ausserisraelitischen Religion."

80. Albertz, "Jahwe allein!"; and Stolz, Einführung in den biblischen Monotheismus.

Schmidt cannot envision an Old Testament theology that does not enter into relationship with the history of Israelite religion.[81] He follows a chronological development of Israel's theology and religion by tracing them through several periods: nomadic prehistory, early history after the settlement, monarchical period, and the late period. However, he then places thematic sections under each of these particular historical periods. In addition, he has eight excurses that deal with topics of Old Testament theology: redemption, the commandment on the Sabbath, the "Spirit" of God, covenant, election, offerings, the world of God, and death and hope beyond death. He also articulates the relationship between the testaments by accenting the element of hope and future orientation in the topics of the kingdom of God, the Son of God, messiah, Zion, and prophecy. What gives this variety of religious and theological expression its unity is the first commandment.[82] This uniqueness of Israel's God is based, not on holiness, but rather on the zeal expressed in the first commandment.

A. H. J. Gunneweg

In addition to Albertz and Schmidt, A. H. J. Gunneweg, in his *Biblische Theologie des Alten Testaments,* has written another important volume that uses the method of the History of Religion to assist in shaping an Old Testament theology. This is underscored by the subtitle: *Eine Religionsgeschichte Israels in biblisch-theologischer Sicht.* (A History of Israelite Religion from its Biblical and Theological Perspective).[83] For Gunneweg, Old Testament theology combines a descriptive, historical articulation of the religion of Israel with theological reflections on its importance for the theology of the church. Theological reflection is focused on the Christian canon, and for Gunneweg, this means ultimately the privileging of the New Testament.[84]

---

81. Schmidt, *The Faith of the Old Testament,* 4. Tigay *(You Shall Have No Other Gods)* has argued on the basis of Hebrew inscriptions that there is no substantial evidence that Israel, at least in and around Jerusalem, violated the first command by engaging in polytheism. His views, while carefully expressed, have not convinced many Old Testament historians of religion, who see religious pluralism, including polytheism, as an important feature of religious expression even in and near Jerusalem. Indeed, the archaeological finds of numerous female figurines in Jerusalem undercut his position.

82. Schmidt, *The Faith of the Old Testament,* 83.

83. Gunneweg, *Biblische Theologie des Alten Testaments,* 9–36. See also his *Vom Verstehen des Alten Testaments.*

84. Gunneweg, *Biblische Theologie des Alten Testaments,* 161. Pannenberg ("Die Bedeutung des Alten Testaments") agrees with the argument that the Old Testament is also a Christian book. Since the God of the Old Testament is indeed the Father of Jesus Christ who was sent into the world to redeem it from sin, the Old Testament should be read as a book that is a part of the Christian canon. The Old Testament tells of God as creator, as the one

Gunneweg makes an important case for the role of the History of Religion in assisting the writing of an Old Testament theology.[85] He begins by reviewing scholarly literature that discusses the difficult problem of establishing the relationship between the two methods. He then presents his own views. He argues, first of all, that the subject of an Old Testament theology is not the setting forth of the themes of divine revelation. The subject, instead, is both the understanding of God and human self-understanding. He further argues that the historical character and situations of the understandings of God and the Israelites should not be forgotten. These understandings, both of God and of the self, are not absolute, but rather are historically conditioned and therefore relative. A dialogical subject-subject relationship stands between the present interpreter and the past that is interpreted. But there is a temporal and cultural separation between the two. In addition, Old Testament theology is a historical science and is not to be seen as a precursor to the theology of the New Testament.[86] The Old Testament resists the schemes of promise and fulfillment, type and antitype, and law and gospel. The Old Testament also resists the systematic themes of dogmatic theology. While it is a part of Christian theology in that it belongs to the Christian canon, the Old Testament may not be interpreted christologically. In examining the relationship between the Old and New Testaments, however, it is clear that the New Testament is the basis for the reception of the Old Testament by the church. Indeed, the Scripture of the early church was the Hebrew Bible. This recognition allows Christians to meet the possibilities of existence in and understanding of the world that may be connected to those in the entire Bible. This means, then, that the Old Testament is not a book foreign to Christians. The Hebrew Bible enables movement into the realms of both Christianity and Judaism. Finally, the selection of the Old Testament by the early church as an important part of the Christian canon modifies the Christian message, since this earlier testament is presupposed. The major impact of the Old Testament is found in both its theological themes of monotheism, creation, election, and the people of God dwelling among pagans and its collection of psalms as the hymn and prayer book of the

---

who is different from his creation, and as the redeemer of his people in the salvific events of history, a redemption that culminates in the coming into the world of Jesus Christ to announce the advent of the reign of God. The church has the obligation to continue to be the elect people and to fulfill the law. Without the Old Testament, Christian faith is not understandable, and its historical grounding would have to be replaced either by mythology or the deification of humanity.

85. Gunneweg, *Biblische Theologie des Altens Testaments,* 138–43.

86. Thus, he opposes the position of Vischer, *Das Christuszeugnis des Alten Testaments.*

early church.[87] Most importantly, then, the Old Testament is to be preached and taught as a Christian book in the life of the church.[88]

Erhard Gerstenberger

A final key example of the use of the History of Religion in doing Old Testament theology is found in the volume by Erhard Gerstenberger.[89] His central concern is to make clear the diversity of theological views that emerge from the changing sociohistorical contexts through which Israel lived. This sets the stage for the various and often diverse theologies that have arisen in the contemporary world. Gerstenberger then outlines the developing Old Testament theologies that reflect the major sociohistorical periods in Israel.

However, before proceeding with his description of Old Testament theologies, Gerstenberger sets forth his major assumptions.[90] He first considers the issue of the context of the author of the theology. He contends that "any theological 'approach,' including any exegesis of the Old Testament and any 'theology' of the Old Testament based on it, is subject to its own limited, concrete, contextual conditions and therefore cannot be absolutized." In enlarging this contextual setting of the theologian to include the globe, Gerstenberger entertains a postcolonial perspective in recognizing that all interpreters have their particular space and time for existing in the world that are remote from those of the Old Testament. Yet he cautions against capitulating to the view that there is an unbridgeable historical abyss that separates the contemporary interpreters from the past of the Hebrew Bible. Indeed, this text has had and continues to have enormous influence on contemporary cultures and thinkers. Thus, in dialogue with its interpreters, these ancient texts continue to say different things to the successive generations over the millennia. This continuing dialogue is not to be ignored in theological inquiry. Or, in the words of Spieckermann, "The message of God's acts of salvation for Israel and the world is the theme of a Biblical theology," and, "Its foundation for the reality and knowledge of these acts of deliverance resides in the definitive salvation of the world in Jesus Christ."[91]

It is the case, of course, that our own present worldviews and various cultures differ widely from those of the Bible. While there are links to the biblical past in regard to theology, there are also serious differences. We

87. This point is also made by Spieckermann, "Die Verbindlichkeit des Alten Testaments."

88. Spieckermann agrees: "The theology of the Old Testament is a Christian document" ("Die Verbindlichkeit des Alten Testaments," 45–46).

89. Gerstenberger, *Theologies in the Old Testament.*

90. Ibid., 5–18.

91. Spieckermann, "Die Verbindlichkeit des Alten Testaments," 29–30.

cannot help but read and make judgments about biblical and contemporary theologies from our own various contexts. Gerstenberger adopts the perspective of liberation theology when he argues that we in the West live in a privileged society and culture that has profited from colonizing Third World peoples and exploiting marginal populations. Those from the margins read the Bible very differently from those who live in the center. The elite of the West enjoy their privileges that often derive from their oppression of the poor. In addition, a feminist perspective permeates Gerstenberger's thinking when he acknowledges that we are often trapped in a sexist, patriarchal society and tend to understand the Bible from the perspective of white males of privilege. Our Old Testament theologies are decidedly male in using male images and metaphors to describe God, in deprecating women, and in attributing roles of power to men. These are true at times in both the text and the understanding of the reader.

Thus, before writing an Old Testament theology or theologies, one must engage one's own prejudices and contexts and bring them into the open. "The epistemological, social, economic and gender-specific conditions of our time are so different from those of antiquity that we must first relate any statement of the Bible . . . to this reality of ours and discuss it before it can be a stimulus and criterion for our theological decisions."[92]

Gerstenberger also discusses the problem of canonicity. There is not one single canon, but rather three that may constitute the text for Old Testament theologies (the Jewish Tanakh, the Roman Catholic expanded canon, and the Protestant canon that is arranged so as to reflect theological perspectives of Christianity). This brings into serious question, even from the start, any canonical theology as normative (thus criticizing Childs and Rendtorff). Furthermore, the canon, regardless of which one, represents a collection of literature that has no single theology, but rather contains numerous theologies that often conflict. Further, while it is clear that a Jewish community eventually selected and gave its approval to a certain body of texts and that the final form of these texts had their own theological menus, one cannot claim the superiority of the canonical text or collection over against earlier forms of books that were shaped in a different time and at times divergent settings or even noncanonical writings. This means, then, that Gerstenberger is opposed to giving the final form of the canon a position of superiority in shaping theology. He contends that, since we cannot limit ourselves to the canonical texts, we need to be aware as best we can of the faiths of ancient Israel in their contemporary environments, some of which are enhanced by archaeology and other written sources. This means, then, "we may not read the Biblical texts as a

---

92. Gerstenberger, *Theologies in the Old Testament,* 12.

uniform norm of faith." These canonical texts "have no absolute claim to validity."[93] Furthermore, he contends that the witness of other ancient Near Eastern religions points to important elements of faith, meaning we as interpreters are to be open to these neighboring cultures and their religious insights. In the final analysis, we must keep in mind that the Hebrew Bible is a conversation partner that assists us in addressing our own significant issues. My response to Gerstenberger is that, while I acknowledge that the religions and cultures of the ancient Near East often influenced Israel's own understanding of faith and practice, we still stand with a religious tradition that has made certain affirmations that define our identity, beliefs, and practices.

Gerstenberger makes ready use of recent sociological studies in his work, and thus has availed himself of a great deal of social scientific research that has blossomed in the past quarter century.[94] Applying these theoretical methods and Old Testament scholarship to the history and theologies of ancient Israel and early Judah, Gerstenberger delineates five major social constructions that influence Israel's varying views of God and social ethics. These are the family and clan, the village and small town, the tribal alliances, the monarchical state, and the confessional and parochial communities in the exile.

Beginning with the family and clan, Gerstenberger notes that this type of personal piety or familial religion involved the social world of the household[95] that went far back into the mists of the early beginnings of Israel's forebears yet continued to be the setting for the local, popular form of Israelite and early Jewish religion as late as the rise of rabbinic Judaism.[96] While in practice everyone shared the household possessions, the father was the *pater familias* who owned and presided over everything in the familial estate, from animals to material elements to household slaves. Even other members of the family were under his dominion. The household typically survived on a subsistence level through farming and the pasturing of small cattle, sheep, and goats. The household members recognized that the earth, the sun, and the rain gave life and nourishment to flocks, produce, and people. Subsequently, deities responsible for the fertility of fields and vineyards, flocks, and human offspring became honored and even worshipped by the family in order to derive from them the powers of fecundity necessary to survive. By contrast, demonic powers that threatened the household and brought sterility to the family, flocks, and soil

---

93. Ibid., 16.
94. Ibid., 19–24.
95. Perdue et al., *Families in Ancient Israel*.
96. Gerstenberger, *Theologies in the Old Testament*, 25–91.

were to be repelled through magical means as well as by means of the powers of the household gods. Sacrifices were offered to communicate with the family gods, assuage them, and provide for their needs. It is particularly in the religion of the ancestors that the family deity became a companion who dwelt with the household, blessed it with life, and commanded its allegiance (Gen 28:20-21; see the "Mighty One of Jacob," the "Fear of Isaac," and the "Shield of Abraham").[97] These household gods were even depicted in the form of images (*těrāfîm,* תרפים; Gen 31:19, 30-35) and were provided a shrine in a special location in the house. Even when one deity was the god of the clan, this worship occurred in the context of a polytheistic world in which there were many divine beings.

Female images were frequently found in Israel as figurines or seal images. In the second millennium, these were generally depicted nude with sexual powers portrayed by erotic and fecundated forms that were often exaggerated. Later images were depicted with twigs, plants, trees, and animals to demonstrate the fertility of the goddesses and their dominion over the world of creatures. One frequent example of a male figure is Bes, originally an Egyptian guardian of birth and child care who also repelled demons. Amulets of Bes were found throughout ancient Israel in the time of the monarchy and exile, pointing to the god's widespread worship. The household cult in Israel also included Baal and Asherah (see, e. g., Deut 18:10-11), thus eliciting its strong condemnation by the Deuteronomists.

Gerstenberger sets forth the second sociohistorical stage and its theology in chapter 5 of *Theologies in the Old Testament:* deities of the village community.[98] The ethos of the village was based on the principle of family solidarity, while the families largely related by blood and marriage together toiled on common fields and pastured herds. Their religious beliefs and practices were based on these shared tasks. Presumably these villages worshiped storm and fertility gods and goddesses in open-air sanctuaries, with standing stones *(maṣṣēbôt,* מצבות*)* representing the male deities and trees and wooden pillars portraying female deities *('ăšērôt,* אשרות*)*. These deities also blessed the villages with fertility through the sending of rain and the fructification of soil and increasing the fertility of herds and families. These deities, similar to Baal and Anat of Canaanite mythology, were also warriors who protected the villages from their enemies. The theology of the villages was based, then, on the everyday struggles for survival and solidarity in work, defense against enemies, and legal decisions. The deity

---

97. See Alt, "The God of the Fathers"; Bernd-Jörg Diebner, "Die Götter des Vaters"; and Matthias Köckert, *Vätergott und Väterverheissungen.*
98. Gerstenberger, *Theologies in the Old Testament,* 93–110.

of the village was not only its leader, but also the originator and protector of laws and customs that undergirded its social life. Thus, the village god was the deity of fertility, war, and law.

Gerstenberger then addresses the god and goddess in the tribal alliance.[99] He begins by rejecting Gottwald's thesis of the origins of liberated Israel resulting from a peasant revolt of underlings in the Canaanite city-states uniting with slaves who gained their freedom from Egypt and worshiped Yahweh as the deity of liberation.[100] Gerstenberger argues instead for a group of tribes that were independent and on occasion formed tribal alliances for military and legal reasons. It appears that pre-state Israel already had begun to worship Yahweh, possibly at a tribal shrine where the tribes celebrated their theology based on military victories against common enemies. Yahweh religion, more than likely, originated from outside the tribes and possibly was borrowed from desert peoples such as the Kenites or Midianites. This deity would have been a storm and warrior deity, much like Baal (Ps 29), Adad,[101] Chemosh, and Resheph.[102] As a god of war, Yahweh[103] led the combined militias of various tribal groups into battle against a threatening enemy (see Judg 5; Hab 3:5-7). A liberation theology emerged from these portraits of the divine warrior who freed the slaves and defeated tribal enemies.

Kingdom theologies are the next development in ancient Israel and Judah.[104] The monarchic state was a centralized and bureaucratic system ruled by the king who presided over a royal entourage of officials. In Judah, the divine promise of a Davidic descendant was embodied in the bold oracle of Nathan (2 Sam 7; Ps 89). Yahweh is the one who chose David and his descendants to rule over the kingdom and selected Zion as his divine dwelling place in a sacred location adjacent to the palace (Pss 46, 48). Key to the royal ideology is the kingship of God, who chose as his son the human ruler on the day of his enthronement (Ps 2:7) and was understood by some court poets to be divine (Ps 45:7). The religion of the state focused on the kingship of Yahweh, the election of the House of David, and the divine dwelling on Mount Zion in the Temple. The coronation of the human ruler (2 Sam 5:1-5; 1 Kgs 1:32-40; and 2 Kgs 11:4-12) included the presence of Yahweh, the anointment of the new ruler, his riding of the royal mule, and his drinking from the sacred spring of Gihon (see the royal Psalms, 2,

---

99. Ibid., 111–160.
100. Gottwald, *The Tribes of Yahweh.*
101. Keel, *Die Welt der altorientalischen Bildsymbolik.*
102. M. Smith, *The Early History of God.*
103. P. Miller, *The Divine Warrior in Early Israel.*
104. Gerstenberger, *Theologies in the Old Testament,* 161–205.

45, 89, 110, and 132).[105] Ruling on behalf of Yahweh, the king was the one who brought fertility to the land, established and maintained justice, and led the army.

Gerstenberger then examines the faith community of Israel during and following the exile. Now the commandments and the salvific narratives are written down eventually to become the basis for a scribal religion. In addition, monotheism develops in its full form, allowing Israel to worship Yahweh in a foreign land and to negate the existence of other deities (cf. the wisdom texts, including Wis 13–15). With the exiles in Babylon, the Jews began to encounter mythologies that influenced their religion, including those that had to do with creation. Especially important was the Babylonian god Marduk's defeat of Tiamat, the personification of chaos. Following the death of Tiamat, Marduk creates the world, a mythological theme that is reflected in the Bible (tĕhôm, תהום; see Gen 1:2; Pss 18, 77, 104, 114; and Isa 52:7-8). Yahweh, the supreme deity, created both the cosmos and humanity (Job 38:4-11; Ps 8). Images of the defeat of chaos are found in the Yahweh speeches in Job 38:1—42:6. This use of ancient Near Eastern creation imagery in Job, among other sapiential texts, points to the international character of wisdom theology. By the fifth century B.C.E., the Torah was shaped into its final form, followed by the canonization of the prophets approximately at the beginning of the second century.

Thus, from Gerstenberger's theologies, one discovers the major understandings of Yahweh that arose within the context of the changing social settings of ancient Israel and early Judah. The issues that are not addressed are both historical and theological. In regard to the History of Religion, there is no doubt that the changing social systems of early Israel played a substantial role in the development of understandings of God. Thus, from Gerstenberger's theologies, one discovers the major understandings of Yahweh that arose within the context of the changing social settings of ancient Israel and early Judah.

However, there are also critical questions to discuss. Is Gerstenberger's history of Israelite and Judahite society and the developing religions and views of God truly a theology, or do we find more of a social, religious history? To write a theology, is it not necessary to approach the biblical text from the context of the church? What of the New Testament in the Christian canon? How does one determine what is truly theologically appropriate for the church in the present? For example, had Gerstenberger developed a theology of liberation from the social development that clashed at times with state religion, one might find some common thread

---

105. Von Rad, "Royal Ritual in Judah," 167–73.

running through this collection of social traditions that contained varying theological perspectives. And what of postcolonialism and feminism that he mentions in his compelling introduction? Could a postcolonial theology born of Israel's and Judah's own social and historical experience not be isolated and written? And what of the strong possibility that women found in other cultic expressions—say, those associated with Anat or Asherah—a freedom that challenged the male domain of Yahwism? These are interesting and important questions to which Gerstenberger's responses would be most intriguing to read. But he does not raise or answer them. While Gerstenberger has produced a potentially important theology that provides a careful review of Israel's changing theological perspectives within the context of the development of its social and cultural world, he ultimately draws back from his own critical approach outlined in his introduction.

The Theology of Jeremiah and the History of Religion

Jeremiah in the Theology of A. H. J. Gunneweg

Like many Protestant scholars before him, Gunneweg regards Jeremiah not only as the last of the series of great First Temple prophets, but also as the one who represents the high point of this group of exceptional proclaimers of the divine word.[106] Dating the origins of his prophetic call to the thirteenth year of the reign of Josiah (626 B.C.E.), when Judah had achieved independence from the other nations of the ancient Near East, Gunneweg describes the national crisis soon to engulf both the life of the nation and its leading spokesperson. This, of course, was precipitated by the death of Josiah in 608, according to Gunneweg's chronology, and soon led to the colonization of Judah, initially by the Egyptians after Necho II had succeeded in vanquishing the Judahite king's army at Megiddo, and then by the Babylonians under Nebuchadnezzar II in 605 B.C.E. Two major deportations then occurred, the first in 597 B.C.E. and the second in 586 B.C.E.

As do many earlier Jeremiah scholars, Gunneweg uses these events to provide a chronology of the activities of the prophet. From 626 B.C.E. to the beginning of the Josianic reform, Jeremiah was dependent on Hosea by regarding the wilderness period as the time of the pure love that developed between Yahweh and Israel. This was followed, according to both, by the entrance into the land and the Baal apostasy and religious syncretism. Both prophets condemned this religious development. In this period, the

---

106. Gunneweg, *Biblische Theologie des Alten Testaments*, 198–201.

theme of repentance became paramount in Jeremiah's preaching. Only a total and complete return to Yahweh could save Israel from total destruction and lead to a new beginning with him as their Lord. However, in the period following the decline of Assyrian suzerainty and the carrying out of the reform of King Josiah, Jeremiah chose to remain silent. Reform and restoration suddenly ended with the death of Josiah.

At that time, the second period of Jeremiah's prophecy began to unfold (608–597 B.C.E.). In a sharp polemic, Jeremiah attacked the false theology of the temple's guarantee of Judah's future based on this symbol's indication of Yahweh's abiding presence. Because of this opposition to the temple, Jeremiah became the victim of increasing persecution by his own priestly family, including later the population of the city, many of its officials, and the court, especially Jehoiakim. He was threatened with death. When the Babylonians defeated Egypt and Judah came under the hegemony of the enemy to the north, Jeremiah announced that Yahweh's judgment had been effectively carried out. Baruch, the scribe and friend of the prophet, was called upon to write down the sayings of Jeremiah to this point. Jehoiakim's angry response and effort to take the prophet captive required Jeremiah to go underground. However, in 597 B.C.E., the first siege and surrender of Jerusalem to the Babylonians occurred. Jehoiakim, the successor to Josiah and Jehoiachin, was assassinated, and the city surrendered. Nebuchadnezzar placed on the throne another son of David, Zedekiah.

Now Jeremiah began the third period of his prophetic activity, a period that continued until the fall of Jerusalem and the major exile in 586 B.C.E. Jeremiah explained this defeat and subjugation as the act of Yahweh, who used the Babylonians to carry out his divine judgment against his wayward people. This judgment brought to an end the independence of the state and the monarchy. In this decade, Jeremiah preached that the nation and the king are to be a reflection of the righteous order of Yahweh, but concluded they had failed. Jeremiah also opposed the false prophets who easily predicted salvation only to be proven wrong by the actions of Yahweh.

Yet there was the issue of the future survival and salvation of Israel in subjection to the foreign despot, and it was here, following the devastation of the city, that Jeremiah entered into the last phase of his ministry. What would continue to live beyond the state and monarchic forms would be the continued existence of the people and their inhabitation of the land. According to Gunneweg, Jeremiah here prefigured a theology of the cross, thus connecting his experiences and those of his people with Jesus Christ and those for whom he suffered and died. Jeremiah was placed in prison as an enemy who encouraged the leaders of the nation to bow the knee to the invader. With the fall of Jerusalem, he was freed by its conquerors and allowed to remain to rebuild a new people of God. However, he was eventually forced to accompany revolutionaries opposed to Babylonian rule in their flight to Egypt. Even here, the prophet continued to make his words heard, until his eventual death in this foreign land.

What is especially noticeable about Gunneweg's treatment of Jeremiah is the prophet's placement within the history of Israel. His theological value is found in the prophecies of judgment and salvation he announced during this period in which Judah was swept away by powerful Babylonian forces. Gunneweg also points to the New Testament when he explains that Jeremiah's suffering prefigures a theology of the cross that becomes so important in the New Testament. This approach is little more than a history of the "life" of the prophet as it interweaves with the larger history of Judah. The theological contribution of this prophet is seen primarily in his words of judgment and salvation and in his prefiguring the life and message of Jesus.

Rainer Albertz and the Theology of Jeremiah

Albertz describes the religious views of Jeremiah within the context of one major historical development.[107] That development was the final years of the political existence of Judah and its conquest by the Babylonians and their incorporation of the small nation within its empire, a period that he entitles "The political and theological conflicts and disputes following the death of Josiah." Albertz remarks that Jeremiah's early preaching announced divinely guaranteed success for the political and military expansion of Josiah, a view that was shattered by the death of Josiah at Megiddo. This tragic event led to the prophet's reformulation of his understanding of Yahweh and the nature and destiny of Judah.

While the king was strongly identified with the Deuteronomic reform, his death did not derail completely the efforts of the reformers to continue their reformation of Judah's religion and society. While the ʿam hāʾāreṣ placed Josiah's successor on the throne (Jehoiachin), the Egyptian pharaoh infuriated them by removing him in favor of Jehoiakim, a pro-Egyptian ruler. However, Egyptian suzerainty followed by Babylonian rule for all intents and purposes ended the reform of Judahite religion and even led to social disintegration of the bonding of the different groups. The aristocracy's social oppression of the poor returned with a vengeance. The reform had failed to reinvigorate religious faith and social justice in the nation. This social conflict grew more intense, with most of the priesthood in Jerusalem advocating their own self-interest in the cultic theology of

107. Albertz, *History of Israelite Religion* 1, 236–42.

the temple. They advocated a theology of divinely guaranteed protection, based on an arrogance and certainty attacked by Jeremiah, who called its advocates "deceivers." The royal court split into two political factions, one supporting the political position of Jehoiakim and his policies of social oppression and the other opposing him. It was to the latter faction that Jeremiah belonged. Jeremiah announced the coming of divine judgment, especially against the wicked officials and the king they supported. The aristocracy belonged to the first group, called "wicked" by the prophet, while the "people of the land" were a part of the second. Albertz speculates that Jeremiah even proclaimed the death of Josiah as a divine judgment, making him unpopular with both groups. It is now apparent that Jeremiah distanced himself from the reform.

When the Babylonians defeated the Egyptians and subsumed Judah into their expanding empire, Jeremiah counseled willing submission, since Nebuchadnezzar II was the instrument of Yahweh in history. However, political aspirations led to Jehoiakim's revolt, resulting finally in the first major exile in 597 B.C.E. Jehoiachin, placed temporarily on the throne, had not been able to resist the subjugation of the state and the ensuing exile. Zedekiah, placed on the throne by the victorious Nebuchadnezzar II, vacillated between supporters of subjugation and revolutionaries looking to Egypt for an ally. The high priest Seraiah and a band of temple prophets who included Hananiah finally persuaded the ill-fated king to rebel. The aristocracy and the king, blinded by the Babylonian authorities who sacked Jerusalem, were then sent into exile. The opposing faction, to which Jeremiah and Ezekiel belonged, was led by Zephaniah and was pro-Babylonian. Jeremiah strongly resisted revolution against the Babylonians and dashed the hopes of the first exiles in 597 B.C.E., who longed for a return to the homeland. He strongly opposed the theological argumentation of the national reform party, who promised the population of Jerusalem the city's invincibility and that there would soon be a restoration of the nation and a return to self-rule. This was none other than Zion theology long advocated by the nation. This group severely persecuted this prophet, imprisoning him, until his release came with the destruction of the city. Thus, one has two theologies clashing: the national reform movement that proclaimed Yahweh's coming salvation and freedom from the oppressive rule of other peoples, a theology grounded in Zion and even Davidic traditions, and the view that saw the death of Josiah as the inauguration of a new time of divine judgment. The only hope for the future was repentance and acceptance of foreign rule. This clash even continued during the governorship of Gedaliah, who was assassinated by zealots. This group of firebrands forced Jeremiah to accompany them in their escape to Egypt. The darkness of the exilic period had descended.

Evaluation

The fundamental questions that must be addressed in this debate center on the definitions of biblical theology and the History of Religion, their settings, and their objectives. Is biblical theology a historical enterprise in which the variety of views about God held by Israelites and Judahites, elicited from both the Bible and material culture, is set forth in diverse and multiple expressions? Albertz and many other historians of religion reach this conclusion. In addition, a strongly historical approach makes it impossible to speak of a single biblical theology with a common thread that weaves together the religious faith of the biblical communities. Instead, it is necessary to speak of many different theologies existing at different times and in a variety of different settings. This allows for pluralism, but how may it be restrained and kept from ending in relativism or theologies of personal preference? Furthermore, on what basis does the historian make value judgments about the developing theology described? Regardless of the position of Albertz, issues of contemporary importance would be of no real concern to the historian of religion in following a scientific method-ology. Indeed, why would anyone care what any ancient community in a particular time and place thought about God? This type of work, while constructive in the sense of historical reconstruction of the past, is descrip-tive and not constructive in attempting to shape the faith of Israel and contemporary belief into a holistic formulation.

Biblical theology, by contrast, has to do, at least in part, with revela-tion, that is, the effort to find a divine voice that exists within the multiple voices of the text that addresses Israel and Judah, as well as the church. This effort, of course, is based on the commitment of the scholar to the Christian faith. Without this commitment, the Bible becomes simply an antiquarian document and Israelite religion no more than the views and practices of a people from the distant past that have no obvious relevance to contemporary Christian life.[108] We should not, in my opinion, abandon historical analysis in order to reconstruct the faith of Israel. But the goal of this reconstruction is to enable the contemporary church to hear that divine voice and to allow it to speak to today by the engagement of the faith of the past with the beliefs of the present. The Bible contains multi-ple voices, each of which must be critically engaged and assessed in order to differentiate between what is appropriate for modern faith and practice and what is not. To use Gadamer's hermeneutic, there is an encountering of visions from the past and the future that leads to a new Word of God for contemporary existence to be faithful.[109] And the visions of the present

108. See Spieckermann, "Die Verbindlichkeit des Alten Testaments," 26–27.
109. Gadamer, *Truth and Method*.

must come from a variety of present cultures and from both men and women. Western hegemony and paternalism in the constructive enterprise are no longer acceptable.

Finally, biblical theology for Christians cannot be carried on as though the Christ event has not occurred. The New Testament witnesses to this new and decisive act of God in ways that shape our understanding of Christian faith.[110] Christians read the Hebrew Bible through the eyes of both the church and the New Testament, not to distort its message, but rather to understand it as speaking eventually to them in all of their various contexts and identities as men and women, gay and straight, ethnically different, and culturally diverse. In setting forth the theology of the Old Testament, readers are not to "Christianize" its understanding. Yet there are the realities of the faiths of the New Testament and the ongoing church that also may not be ignored. It is through the encounter of the proclamation of the church with biblical theology (both Old and New Testaments) that Christians through the generations extending into the present may hear a Word that is decisive for faith and life. The formulation and working out of this decisive Word is the complicated, often uncertain, but also necessary task of the contemporary church. To appropriate a statement of Gerhard von Rad, "Each generation of Israel (or, the Church) must determine what it means to be Israel (or, the Church)."[111] I would add to his statement "in all of its contexts and identities." It is then, and only then, that dialogue with non-Christian religions, including Judaism, authentically may take place. And, as David Tracy long has recognized, having engaged in authentic and open dialogue, we find ourselves changed.[112]

I have chosen to set forth as illustrative of the theology of Jeremiah the views of Gunneweg and Albertz, two representatives of the *Religionsgeschichtliche Schule* who advocate the position that this approach is the proper one for articulating biblical theology and even eventually the Bible's contribution to systematic theology. However, while Gunneweg at least makes the theological affirmation that the suffering of the nation and its prophet, Jeremiah, prefigures a theology of the cross, there is no other indication of engaging this prophet's theological viewpoint with those of the larger canon and then the teachings of the contemporary church. Albertz is even less forthcoming in making connection with anything that

---

110. Spieckermann ("Die Verbindlichkeit des Alten Testaments") writes, "The New Testament directly witnesses to Christ. Its message cannot be set forth without the knowledge and use of the Holy Scripture of the Jews found in the Septuagint. The New Testament's thought world and language emerged out of this text."

111. Von Rad, *Old Testament Theology,* 2:444.

112. Tracy, *The Analogical Imagination.*

would conceivably be a more comprehensive biblical theology, and he makes absolutely no effort to engage contemporary theology. Two questions, then, must be raised: In what way does either of these treatments articulate either a biblical theology or a theology that encounters the issues and faith of the contemporary church? And how do these summaries do anything more than set forth a small aspect of the history of Israel? To argue broadly, but also vaguely, that the History of Religion is the proper way to set forth the theology or theologies of the Bible and that this in turn assists in shaping the faith of the contemporary church is to make bold claims that require some clarifying indications. Jeremiah would be a good example. However, both of these treatments of Jeremiah offer nothing more or less than a history of the life of the prophet and the major themes he announced. These are no different from what one would discover in any standard Old Testament introduction or history of Israel.

3

From Eurocentric History to Voices from the Margins: Liberation Theology and Ethnic Biblical Interpretation

"We Drink from Our Own Wells."

—*Gustavo Gutiérrez*

Introduction

LIBERATION THEOLOGY HAS MANY, DIVERSE EXPRESSIONS, INCLUDing postcolonial, womanist, Asian American, African American, Hispanic, *mujerista,* feminist, and gay-lesbian, to name some of the more general categories.[1] Within these larger areas, there are significant varieties of formulation. However, much liberation theology and many liberation movements, which may not have an overtly theological component, generally operate out of a social model of conflict (Marxist, neo-Marxist, or radical socialist). Additionally, liberation theology has identifying themes that are common to most of its protean expressions: solidarity with the oppressed, the raising up of the downtrodden, the humanization of social structures that deny full humanity to certain groups, the empowerment of oppressed groups to live lives of integrity, the value placed upon the experience of oppressed peoples, and the rejection of authoritarianism and hierarchy. Since feminist, womanist, and postcolonial theologies will be addressed in a following chapter, this chapter is limited to a brief discus-

---

1. We shall deal with feminist theology in chapter 4. For a basic introduction to Latin American liberation theology with bibliography, see Ferm, *Contemporary American Theologies.* Among the classics of Latin American liberation theology are Gutiérrez, *A Theology of Liberation* and *We Drink from Our Own Wells;* Bonino, *Doing Theology in a Revolutionary Situation;* and Segundo, *Liberation of Theology.* For introductions to Latin American liberation theology, see Boff and Boff, *Introducing Liberation Theology;* R. Brown, *Gustavo Gutiérrez: An Introduction to Liberation Theology;* and McGovern, *Liberation Theology and Its Critics.*

sion of major themes in Latin American liberation, a Hispanic theology of exile, and African American theology.[2]

Liberation Theology in Latin America

Blazing the path for a new and commanding theology, Latin American theologians since the 1970s have articulated a passionate approach to God, society, and marginal social groups, usually identified simply as "the poor." Originating in countries in which the poor often have long been victims of oppressive regimes that have extended policies formulated during the periods of European and American colonialism, Latin American liberation theology has important defining features, which undergird its diversity of expression. The starting point is the realization that for Latin American liberation theologians, context is critical. Subsequently, they have argued for a theology that reflects the situation and culture of Latin America and not the history, issues, and culture that provide the context for European and American theology. Central to liberation theology, of course, is the emphasis placed on the practical application of the Bible's emphasis on liberation and continuing reflection on its practical application. There has also been significant use or adaptation of sociological conflict theory, particularly Marxism or neo-Marxism, in giving this theology a social critical basis.

While the focus of liberation has been on the humanization of the poor by freeing them from the degradation and dehumanization of poverty, there are also the related theological objectives of freedom from sin, selfishness, and oppression. These include both oppressor and oppressed, for the undermining of injustice liberates and redeems not only its victims but also its practitioners. Practice and critical reflection on practice are the twin features of liberation theology, and together form what theologians call praxis. For some liberation theologians, orthopraxis takes precedence over orthodoxy as the primary consideration for theological reflection.[3]

When interpreting the Bible, liberation theologians largely base their objective of freeing the oppressed on the exodus from Egypt and the teachings and actions of Jesus in the Gospels. Liberation for the downtrodden is the actualization of the commandments of God to love and care for the neighbor. Love is actualized in solidarity with the oppressed, in experiencing their lot, and in capturing their vision of both life with God (spirituality)

---

2. For the impact of liberation theology on the churches in North America, see Tabb, *Churches in Struggle*.

3. See Boff and Boff, *Introducing Liberation Theology*, 49–63.

and the divine reign (social justice). In Latin America, the victims of so-cial injustice are most commonly the poor, although liberation theology includes all people and groups who are the victims of various kinds of oppression. To enter into solidarity means to oppose the oppressors, those modern pharaohs whose repression leads to the victimization of the downtrodden. Yet to enter into solidarity also means recognizing all peo-ple, including the poor, are fully human, a fundamental view that is often denied by oppressive social systems.[4] Thus, the task is to proclaim a liber-ating theology in a world that is often inhuman in its treatment of the oppressed. Conscientization is the means by which the oppressed achieve their full human dignity. This usually involves active struggle in various forms. Struggle is directed against oppression in both the spiritual and human (sociopolitical) realms. And for some liberation theologians, rad-ical means may be used in the struggle for liberation, including not only passive resistance but also active revolution against tyrannical regimes.

The experience of the oppressed is seen as a defining, epistemological characteristic for liberation theology. Their piety, compassion, love, cele-bration of life, serenity, and moderation are the defining features of faithful living. Theology, which is not informed by their experience and conse-quent vision of God and the kingdom, is limited in its scope and impov-erished in its character.[5]

For liberation theology, God is one who expresses partiality toward the poor: "God is especially close to those who are oppressed; God hears their cry and resolves to set them free (Exod 3:7-8). God is father of all, but most particularly father and defender of those who are oppressed and treated unjustly. Out of love for them, God takes sides, takes their side against the repressive measures of all the pharaohs."[6] God is the redeemer (*gōʾēl*) of the Old Testament, the one who saves the poor from their af-fliction. This same redeemer freed the slaves in Egypt and called them to become the chosen of God in order to liberate other captives from their prisons. The revelation of God occurs in the historical setting of the liber-ation of the oppressed. The paradigmatic act for divine liberation in the Old Testament is the exodus.

In Christian liberation theology, Jesus Christ is the one who identified with the poor, suffered their misery, preached to them the good news, opposed and was oppressed by repressive rulers, and through word and deed initiated the dawning of the kingdom, that realm of nearness to God in which justice would reign supreme. The ministry of Christ represents

---

4. Bonino, *Doing Theology*, 81.
5. Gutiérrez, *A Theology of Liberation*.
6. Ferm, *Contemporary American Theologies*, 62.

the paradigm and forefront of active liberation. The crucifixion represents both Jesus' rejection by human authorities and the sacrificial acceptance by God. In the resurrection, life triumphs over death, and freedom over oppression. The resurrection anticipates the culmination of the universal reign of God.

In Christian liberation theology, the Holy Spirit continues to dwell with God's people and becomes the means by which persons are able to live in peace and justice, one with the other. The Holy Spirit, as the divine presence that identifies and struggles with the oppressed, works for the transformation of human society in order to eliminate oppression and discrimination.

The kingdom of God is the goal of salvation history. Working out of a theology of realized and future eschatology, the kingdom is viewed as both present in a partial manifestation and not yet in its final and complete realization. The kingdom embraces all of history as well as its culmination. The manifesto of liberation theology is that faith must be put into action in order to free the oppressed and to enter into community with God until the final culmination of the peaceable kingdom becomes complete. And this kingdom of harmony and justice includes both creation and eternity. With the new heaven and the new earth, creation and history are joined with eternity and time together in their totality as one. In the liberation of history, there is the redemption of creation. And in the redemption of creation, there is the culmination of the kingdom of God.

Finally, the people of God are to be both the sign and the instrument of liberation. In response to the grace of God's salvation extended to them, the church members as the community of the redeemed who embody servanthood are to preach actively a liberating Gospel to all, but particularly to the poor. In the communion experienced by poor base communities, the church shares with others both love and justice. Through action and divine encounter (prayer, worship, and Bible reading), the church and its members experience true spirituality. This spirituality is the wellspring of liberation. Rejecting the tyranny of authoritarianism and hierarchy, these base communities of the poor point the way authentically to the culmination of the kingdom of God that is grounded in egalitarian brother- and sisterhood. In its worship and celebration and in its piety and struggles for social justice, the church embodies the liberation and liberating experience offered to and made possible for all.

Liberation that brings about the humanization of the oppressed may occur only by changing the systemic structure of oppressive societies, including economics and politics. Evil is not simply personal, it is systemic in hierarchical human societies in general. Only in the church's transformation of oppressive structures through active and even revolutionary change can the oppressed be liberated and achieve their full humanity, but so may everyone achieve full humanity, regardless of race, color, creed, national and geographical location, gender, and sexual orientation.[7]

Segovia's Theology of the Diaspora

Fernando Segovia's work,[8] that of a Hispanic American scholar, is in general a form of liberation theology, although it also has strong connections to postcolonialism, discussed in chapter 8. Thus, his work fits at least two major categories in the typology of approaches I have developed for this book. Latino/Latina theology is quickly gaining increasing awareness and influence in North American theological circles and in the church, in part due to the explosion of the Latino/Latina population in the United States. Segovia's voice is important due to numerous insights he has into the theological, social, and political matrices in North America. While he has yet to write a complete diaspora biblical theology, he has set forth clearly the theoretical basis for this ethnic approach that could move well beyond the Hispanic-American community to include other groups of displaced peoples in the world.

Segovia undertakes the task of biblical theology in several seminal writings, including especially two volumes: *Decolonizing Biblical Studies* and *Interpreting beyond Borders*. His methods include postcolonialism, diaspora studies, and cultural/intercultural approaches. His description of postcolonialism mirrors most of what I set forth in chapter 8. Thus, I shall pass over his succinct and clear delineation of the major features of the approach to biblical interpretation and concentrate on cultural/intercultural approaches and diaspora studies.

In his collection *Decolonizing Biblical Studies*, Segovia clearly presents the "competing modes of discourse" that characterize contemporary biblical studies from the perspective of how their various methodological representatives view the text. The differences among the major modes of discourse at work in contemporary biblical scholarship are important to understand, since their approaches and objectives differ significantly. His descriptions are lucid and insightful.

Segovia examines historical criticism's view of the Bible under the rubric "The Text as Means." Historical criticism, which has enjoyed a long and unrivaled history, is experiencing a "broad retreat" during the last quarter of the twentieth and now the early twenty-first centuries. Some of these developments have occurred due to changes in global political and eco-

---

7. Boff and Boff, *Introducing Liberation Theology*, 50–51.

8. For relevant works by Segovia and the other scholars discussed in this chapter, see the bibliography.

nomic realities, especially with the end of colonialism and the emergence of postcolonialism. This has allowed the voices of the Third World to speak and be heard for the first time in the history of biblical interpretation.

Historical criticism, in Segovia's view, has lacked theoretical sophistication and a critical self-consciousness. For this approach, the meaning of the biblical text is located not only in the world that it projects or in the reconstruction of the author, but especially in an adroit combination of both. There was generally little appreciation for or way of getting at the artistic and ideological disposition of the text. Historical positivism has been the theoretical base of traditional historical criticism, since the text has been viewed as "univocal and objective." Yet the history reflected in the text, through a variety of methods, including literary (source) and redaction criticisms and comparisons with the cultures in which it was produced, could be scientifically reconstructed through the methods that had dominated historical research since the Enlightenment: empiricism and rationalism. The ideology of the interpreter was not considered, since she or he approached the text "objectively" and interpreted it according to "scientific" canons of understanding. The text itself was an object, as were the worldviews it posited. One could recapture the history of Israel and *the* historical meaning of the text, understanding *the* as pointing to its one and only true sense. Thus, historical criticism came to view the text as the means to obtaining the single meaning of the biblical text that was intrinsic to the text itself or in the reconstruction of scholars.

Segovia then turns to consider more recent literary criticism in a variety of modes (rhetorical, formalistic, new, and so on), which should not be confused with older literary criticism that focused on sources and redaction. To do so, he considers this collage of methods under a different rubric: "The Text as Medium." These literary approaches, highly diverse as they are, are much more self-consciously theoretical and have to be, since they offer a critique of and alternative to historical criticism.

What holds these various methods together is their collective view that meaning emerges from the interaction of text and reader. The focus, therefore, is no longer the world behind the text or the historical reconstruction of the author, audience, and date of composition. Rather, the meaning sought is the reader's own ideology and understanding of reality engaging those of the text. The two views merge, then, to construe meaning. The move from author and audience to implied author and audience has given room to the issues of narratology, characterization, and point of view. The text is not viewed as a piecemeal collection of sources and redactions put together over centuries, but rather in its entirety and even as a unified whole with meaning and importance. There has also been movement from the text as having one meaning to the slow but increasing recognition that it can have several competing ones. Yet the reader remains the universal interpreter about whom nothing is known. The identity of the reader is not a concern. The result is a strong criticism of historicism, a number of more sophisticated theoretical approaches, and the recognition of the reader's role in shaping the meaning of the texts.

Segovia then outlines the salient features of cultural criticism under the rubric "The Text as Means and Medium." Social science criticism has emerged at approximately the same time as the development and use of newer literary criticism. It too is theoretically self-conscious about the multiple approaches it takes. However, unlike the new literary methods, social science criticism is much more adaptable to the methods and objectives of historical criticism. Social scientists see the text as a means, not to some particular understanding of the time in which it was written, but to the broader social and cultural dimensions of its location. What is especially important is the understanding of its economic, social, and cultural codes, that is, the text as an "ideological whole." However, as in historical criticism, the meaning of the text is understood as univocal. The goal is to get at the world of the culture that resided behind the text. However, flaws mar the efforts of biblical scholars to understand the sociological and cultural methods used to exploit the meaning of the text in order to uncover its sociocultural reality. Largely uncritically accepted without even translating the theory from a modern society to an ancient one, these are expounded by the theoretical model an interpreter chooses to use. The reader continues to be a universal, nameless, and sophisticated intellectual. The scholar offering the interpretation remains (as is in the other major approaches just described) the dominant authority for determining meaning and knowledge. Meaning is in the interaction of text and its original social and cultural context, but construed by a nameless, unknown interpreter whose ideology and social location are either unknown or not considered.

For Segovia, the best approach to determine meaning is from the general area of cultural studies, which he discusses under the rubric "The Text as Construction." This approach questions the possibility of a disinterested writer or, for that matter, an unidentified audience. The readers and their audience are flesh-and-blood people with their own stake in the meaning pursued. What becomes central is the social location of the text, the audience, and the reader-interpreter. No longer is the reader's own voice silenced by the "expert" scholar; it is heard in both the questions addressed to the text and the answers received. Increasingly the reading is influenced by postmodernist theory with the goal of constructing both text and meaning. There is not simply a one-to-one correlation between reader and text, but also dialogue between the various readers from different social locations. In addition, the audience is part of the interpretative mix. This has led to a global hermeneutic in the mode of the postcolonial world and postcolonial approaches to biblical criticism.

Segovia's understanding of cultural studies and its relationship to biblical criticism is developed in detail in the second chapter of his book *Decolonizing Biblical Studies*.[9] He takes his cue from literary criticism's understanding of plot in setting forth what he regards as liberation and decolonization that have been operative in biblical studies. While there is indeed a plot that moves from the beginning to the middle to the end within the framework of a posited progress, there is the ironic twist to this hermeneutic in the recognition that in the new plot, there is not an accompanying new consensus, but rather multiple views emerge. Further, progress is not necessarily linear but multidirectional. In addition to understanding the cultural and social location of the text, the same interest has developed in viewing critically that of the interpreter. Ideological interests are sought in order to understand the interpreter's view of a text's meaning. The fundamental principle is that interpretation is not value-free but rather political in its assertions. The approach of the text and interpreter through cultural studies frees the text from the elitism that had in essence imprisoned it and from the unchallengeable assertions made by the intellectual elitist. Interpretation now moves within the domains of the marginal peoples who have existed on the social and cultural boundary of acceptance because of color, gender, and colonial location. There is no single grand narrative that develops from the Bible and enters into the academic halls of Western universities, but rather many narratives of understanding emerge from the varied contexts of the text and its diverse readership. This approach stimulates dialogue among those existing in both the same and different sociocultural contexts.

In his writings, Segovia's own distinctive concept is his articulation of hermeneutics among the "diaspora" (meaning scattering or dispersion), a Greek term in biblical studies that refers to Jews living outside Eretz Israel. These were the Jews forced into exile by the Assyrians, Babylonians, and later on, the Romans. This diasporic experience of Jews has continued throughout history.[10] Segovia uses the word in a more general sense to refer to people who permanently reside in a country other than the one of their birth. Some actually choose to live in another country. More

---

9. Segovia, *Decolonizing Biblical Studies,* 34–52.

10. Segovia acknowledges the influence of William Safran, "Diasporas in Modern Societies." Safran argues that the Jewish exilic experience has become the "ideal type" for all other diasporas, although Segovia takes issue with his model for the definition and identification of *diaspora.*

important for his hermeneutical method, however, is the use of the word to name the many marginalized peoples in the world who have been displaced and forced to live under the control of a dominant and dominating class in another country, a different culture, and indeed, another world. The reasons for being forced to live in another country are numerous but generally may be subsumed under the related categories of economics and politics. The major experience that people of the diaspora share is migration. Since Segovia is a Latino and an American, he primarily discusses the Latino experience in the United States. He contends that the term *diaspora* and the branch of studies devoted to its explication in modern social, political, and theological arenas are appropriate to relate to postcolonialism. In essence, he understands diasporic studies as a sub-discipline of postcolonialism.

While noting the variations in meanings given by scholars to the term *diaspora,* ranging from maximalist to minimalist understandings, Segovia expresses his preference for a definition that emphasizes geographical dispersion from the homeland and its people to another land and people. He contends that pointing to the Jewish exiles and diasporic experience as the ideal type is "highly problematic." By emphasizing "geographical translations of people in general," Segovia indicates that diasporic studies may be a far-ranging field of discourse to describe the experience of many marginalized groups of people.

Segovia explains that when postcolonialism is taken as the frame of reference for diasporic experiences, then there are certain phases to which one may point. The first is the settlement of large numbers of Europeans throughout the colonized world as a result of their native countries' imperialism. Second, there has been a massive deportation of millions of conquered peoples to new and strange lands, where most originally were exploited as slaves or indentured servants, and many even now continue to live in squalor. More recently, there has been the dispersion of non-Western peoples to the West, largely through the process of legal or illegal immigration. The immigrant populations in the first generation have entered the lower class and worked in very poorly paid positions. Discrimination often keeps them in these marginalized positions of economic servitude.

When Segovia considers the diasporic experience and Christianity, the imperial expansion of the West has led to the globalization that has come to dominate most of the world. Yet this usually has occurred with the same kind of assumed superiority of the West over the former colonized nations in economics, military, culture, and technology. One of the results of globalization has been that Christianity is no longer primarily centered in the West but has become a global religion. This has decreased the influence experienced by the Western church. One statistic quoted by Segovia is telling: the percentage of Christians in the continents and sub-continents of Africa, Asia, Oceania, Latin America, and the Caribbean in 1900 was 17.2 percent. Today it is 60.3 percent and increasing. When this trend is coupled with the ethnic transformation of Western countries and their rapidly increasing diversity, the implications for the directions of Christian theology and the church are far ranging. While the majority of non-Western immigrants in Europe are non-Christians, the opposite is true in the United States.

Segovia then examines the effect this global migration has had on the study of Christianity. The diasporic phenomenon has already had a major impact on the beliefs and practices of Christianity throughout the globe, the West included. This undoubtedly has already begun to influence the academic study of Christianity in the world. Postcolonial and diasporic studies are slowly entering religion departments and seminaries and will dramatically alter the teaching and scholarship of academic institutions. At the same time, these subaltern studies will, without question, eventually become important in shaping biblical theology. Already biblical criticism has confronted questions raised by these sociocultural and political forces. The context of the interpreter, the insight into the writer of the text who was composing from a different social setting, and new understandings of texts are already taking shape. For example, Segovia points to the study of Daniel Boyarin (who he calls a member of the modern Jewish diaspora) that is a detailed analysis of Paul.[11] Boyarin argues that the rabbis taught the renunciation of domination over other people because of the Jewish diasporic experience. The rabbis recognized the threat to Judaism represented by controlling the land of Israel. By emphasizing the community in its ethnic, cultural, and religious features, the rabbis renounced the possession of the land that resisted this particularism and opted instead for the diasporic experience that allowed for Jewish identity to be strengthened and maintained. Paul's universalism and strong criticism of Jewish dependence on the Torah planted the seeds of anti-Semitism in Christianity that erupted in violence when religion and the state were entwined. Boyarin is critical of Zionism, because he sees it as a rejection of the rabbis' vision of the renunciation of power in order to have Judaism and the state united in a way that leads to a reaffirmation of what inevitably becomes domination of others. He proposes a mixture of the rabbinic renunciation of power with Pauline ethnicity, universalism, and solidarity to provide a new vision for the world.

11. Boyarin, *A Radical Jew.*

Segovia then moves into his own understanding of biblical studies as a Latino in a diasporic location. From these factors he sets forth a multifaceted hermeneutic. Biblical studies should embrace the major historical, literary, sociocultural, and ideological elements that are long-standing in the field, but with a renewed emphasis on the social location, not only of the writer of the text, but also of the interpreter. Thus, there should be a study of both the text and the reader construed by an ideological mode of discourse. This approach not only recognizes the context and particular self-interest of the reader, but it also portrays the varieties of real readers behind the text, their positionings, and their self-interests. Segovia also proposes an "intercultural criticism" in which texts, readings, and readers are "others" to be "acknowledged," "respected," and "engaged." Finally, this approach is linked to postcolonial studies that focus on the geopolitical features of imperialism and colonialism. Thus, one regards biblical texts as historically positioned within imperial settings (Roman, Greek, etc.), as positioned within the contemporary world of imperialism and neocolonialism, and as positioned within the postmodern world of readers and readings. In each of these settings, one notes the content and self-interest of both text and interpreters.

Segovia is a strong advocate for taking the "flesh-and-blood" reader seriously, not so much as an individual, but as a member of a community with its own sociocultural features and location. In particular, this location is grounded in the human populations of the Third World, who share the experience of diaspora, in contrast to the colonizers of the First World, who control much of the world's treasure and political power. It is for these Hispanic Americans, the social group to which Segovia belongs, that he articulates a hermeneutic that will allow them to read the biblical text as the "other," that is, the marginalized who are "allowed to surface and describe" themselves and in so doing are acknowledged and respected for their "otherness." This hermeneutic does not allow the text to so overwhelm the "others" that their collective voice falls silent, and they are humiliated by their identity. This model also calls for strategies of reading that are based on the critical study of texts, and that allow for the analysis of the readers. All readers have a say in comprehending from their multiple contexts a collection of literature that had its own social locations.

In most of his hermeneutical reflections, Segovia writes out of his own experience as a Hispanic American scholar. He speaks not only as one who is a member of the diasporic Hispanic community, but also as one who lives among people in North America who are bicultural. This means that they live in two worlds, often with unease due to the tensions that exist between them. Hispanic Americans experience alienation in which they exist as "others" or as aliens in both worlds. In the predominately white European culture, Hispanic Americans are to live a predescribed, predetermined, external script that Anglos have written for them. This script involves the name *Hispanic* (or occasionally *Latino*), the placement into a monolithic mass, an acceptance of a rigid set of values, and a racist portrayal of Hispanics as lazy, violent, passionate, unintelligent, vulgar, and happy-go-lucky. Thus, Hispanics are not allowed to fit the mainstream of the dominant culture. The people who make up the dominant culture fail to recognize or respect the diversity of dialects, histories, cultures, and traditions of the Hispanic worlds from which Hispanic Americans come. Yet the worlds of the different Hispanic populations in America largely no longer exist for them. This means that Hispanic Americans are perpetual "others" in both the dominant American culture, in which they are not valued and respected, and the marginal world of Hispanic communities, who regard them as "outsiders." Other groups, particularly the Eurocentric population, have defined them, their roles, their identities, and their codes of behavior. "Otherness" becomes, then, for Segovia the basis for hermeneutics for this alienated community, both in terms of their stereotypical definition by the external majority and in their experience within this social context.

Another expression for this interpretative enterprise, chosen by Segovia, is *intercultural criticism*. The task, as he sees it, is to give a voice to the "other" that is affirming and defining of the self in a variety of ways: self-appropriation of the past history and culture; self-definition by which these marginalized "others" are to issue their own understandings in their own words; and self-direction that allows the "others" to reclaim and determine their own future. This hermeneutic allows the "others" to achieve dignity and self-worth and to resist the discrimination directed against them by the dominant culture and to struggle for participation in a democracy that honors and respects all humans.

Another important dimension of Segovia's hermeneutic is "the text as other." The text is contextualized, meaning it is a body of literature that had its own social context among a people who themselves were often marginalized as "others." The voice of the biblical text seeks to liberate and empower its audiences by addressing them in their experience as "others." The theory of this hermeneutic is reader-response criticism in which meaning derives from the interaction of reader and what is read. Both the text and the reader have their own social locations that shape their identities, worldviews, and meanings. The readers begin, but do not end, with distanciation, meaning that the social conditioning of the text is of a people and a culture significantly different from their own. This demonstrates that the reality posited by the text is socially conditioned, even as the readers operate out of their own very different social settings. Meaning, therefore, is by its very nature socially constructed. Yet it is engaged with purpose. The Hispanic experience of "otherness," now self-defined, becomes the lens through which to interpret the Bible, even as the Bible transforms the lives of the "others."

Intercultural criticism shows, then, that reality is not only constructed, it is to be engaged. The world of the text is to be critically engaged. The world of the dominant culture is to be critically engaged. In the case of stereotypes, social discrimination, and poverty based on race, the text, interpreted through this hermeneutic, helps in the struggle for justice and dignity. In this way, this understanding of the social construction of reality and the engagement in struggle allow Hispanic Americans to live and think with greater ease within the two cultures in which they find themselves. For Segovia, "a hermeneutics of otherness" coupled with one of engagement become the essence of a hermeneutics of diaspora.

African American Theology and Biblical Interpretation

African American liberation theology applied to the interpretation of the Bible contains many of the themes of liberation theology articulated in the preceding section.[12] However, the difference is the social context of this theology that emerges from a people who are largely the descendants of slaves, kidnapped by slave traffickers and ferried to colonies, in particular, those in the southern United States, and forced to work on plantations. The long history of the African American experience includes an ostensible liberation by the Emancipation Proclamation issued in 1863 by Abraham Lincoln, followed by a difficult struggle for civil rights, culminating in the civil rights legislation of 1964. However, while discrimination on the basis of race, color, and creed has been declared illegal in the United States, racism and its attendant poverty and covert discrimination have continued to plague the African American community.

To address these issues theologically, African Americans have produced a rich tradition that originates in the period of slavery and has continued into the present. Due to the impact the Bible has had on African Ameri-

---

12. For an introduction to African American liberation theology, see Ferm, *Contemporary American Theologies*, 41–58. Among the best examples of African American liberation theology are Cone, *Black Theology and Black Power; A Black Theology of Liberation; God of the Oppressed;* Roberts, *Liberation and Reconciliation;* Jones, *Christian Ethics for Black Theology;* and C. West, *Prophesy Deliverance!*

can experiences as slaves and free citizens over the centuries, new studies are beginning to take shape that provide the methodological basis for an African American biblical theology.

Vincent Wimbush

The work of New Testament scholar Vincent Wimbush represents two major areas: asceticism and, important for this volume, African Americans and the Bible. His hermeneutical approach to the Bible is clearly laid out in his essay "Reading Texts as Reading Ourselves."[13] He, more than any other African American biblical scholar, has articulated a clear and cogent theoretical foundation for doing biblical theology from this perspective. Thus, I begin with his important work.

Wimbush operates out of the critical perspective of the relationship between text and reader. The discourse of the text brings to mind a shared worldview. When a text over a lengthy period of time has continued to evoke a common understanding of reality, it becomes known in a culture as a "classic" or as "canonical." Yet classics also should be approached with suspicion, because readers need to develop a distance from these texts that arise at different times and dissimilar social locations than the canon but also the contemporary communities of interpretation and transmission. This recognition of the otherness of the text allows the reader to approach it critically and to come to understand it with greater cultural clarity, both that of the text and the rather different one of the reader. In addition, classics or canonical texts are not to be defined and interpreted by a single group in a culture or by one generation as appropriate for all future generations. Each cultural group, even in reading classics, should be allowed to understand them in ways that are germane to its understandings and interests.

In a postindustrial reality of transnational corporations and the shrinking of the globe, the contemporary world calls into question many traditional values and understandings, so much so, that some social groups seek to isolate and maintain particular concepts as rising above the rapid change afoot throughout the consortium of nations and peoples. Fundamentalists and reactionaries alike try to maintain premodern values, beliefs, and traditions as a wall of security protecting against the fearful intrusion of change. Other more critical voices, while valuing the traditions and affirmations of the past, seek to transform them into new and engaging understandings emerging from a contemporary worldview.

---

13. Cf. his earlier essay, "Biblical Historical Study as Liberation."

African Americans, while marginalized socially and politically, continue to read the Bible in order to support their struggles for freedom and to interpret the world in view of their own experiences and self-understandings. From the early days of their slavery in America, African Americans heard the Bible read and sung in hymns that became important to their own discourse and provided new ways of interpreting their experiences. Through the years of "freedom" in the United States, African Americans have responded to Christianity in different ways, from small forcibly segregated congregations to large urban churches, from quiet acceptance of racism to active struggles for civil rights, and from fundamentalism to articulations of justice in social activism. Through all of these responses, the Bible has played a key role, even when it has been misused to legitimate racism, apartheid, and colonialism. Orality has played a key role in the reaction to and articulation of the biblical texts, due in part to the prohibition against education by white masters and racists in the eighteenth and nineteenth centuries. Thus, literalism did not enter into the African American interpretations and transmissions of the meaning of the text until the more modern transition of some to fundamentalism. This allowed for the freedom to exercise the religious imagination of African American culture in the interaction with the Bible. Until more recent times, the African American community has not embraced the fundamentalism of certain religious groups due to racism. But now, even they are challenged by this expanding movement in America.

For a hermeneutic to embrace African American interpretations of Scripture, it must be aware, first, of the historical experiences of this community and its readings of the Bible. This serves as the basis for then engaging in a critically reflective approach to biblical texts, culminating in a constructive theology of modern import. If this approach affects the wider school of interpretation in church and academy, it will require a shift in traditional positions and understandings. The traditions themselves would be subject to rigorous criticism and alterations in what is affirmed as knowledge or truth. In addition, this hermeneutical shift requires an understanding of the cultures of the Bible and the reader. Particularly important are those texts that strike a chord in the culturally shaped reader.

In the interpretative process, the text criticizes the reader and his or her audience even as the reader criticizes the text and its culture. Thus, the theme of the oneness of God's human creation speaks against the distortion of community caused by racism. This biblical theme has become an integral part of the African American community. In contrast, texts that speak of the legitimacy of slavery and patriarchy are to be roundly critiqued as misrepresenting the biblical teaching of justice and oneness. For Wimbush, approaches to biblical interpretation that ignore the African American experience risk the danger of eliminating the Bible as a major resource for the articulation of a worldview that is grounded in justice. Wimbush concludes that the social location of the Bible and its readers is fundamental to an appropriate, engaging hermeneutic that leads to world construction.

Wimbush has edited an interdisciplinary collection of 68 essays, most by African American authors, that offer varied responses to the question "How might putting African Americans at the center of the study of the Bible affect the study of the Bible?"[14] This driving question is extended into such areas as the political character of the academic guild in North America. Is the study of African Americans and the Bible weighted in the direction of studying African characters or African origins in Scripture? Or is the concern much more expansive in seeking to move the entire exegetical and hermeneutical orientation of biblical studies away from Eurocentric interests, culture, and understanding of power toward the margins, in this particular case, of African American culture and understanding?[15] The collection answers the formative question by concluding that the "crux of interpretation is not words, but worlds."[16] In the process of interpretation, it is critical to understand what people have done to the text and, in turn, what the text has done to people. The context of interpretation is not the ancient past, but rather the social and cultural locations of the African American communities in the present. Significantly, the authors of this collection come from a wide variety of the humanities, so it is interdisciplinary. Of course, Wimbush, a New Testament expert on asceticism, does not espouse dispensing with historical criticism. Rather, he advocates that the lay communities be allowed to appropriate the Bible in shaping their own understanding of the world.

The volume, *African Americans and the Bible*, is divided into three sections. "Pre-Texts" discusses the backgrounds of texts and meanings, and the possible hermeneutical approaches that allow a contemporary understanding of the Bible. "Con-Texts" concerns the weaving together of the worlds of the African American community as seen by many different scholars. This approach examines the history of this community's encounter with the Bible, including the distortions of white racists in stripping away the humanity of African Americans, the healing necessary before

14. Wimbush, *African Americans and the Bible*.
15. Ibid., 1–43.
16. Ibid., 19.

interpretation can occur, and positive encounters that speak of freedom and hope. "Sub-Texts" speak of hermeneutics from a variety of different perspectives and understandings. One of the noteworthy conclusions reached in this volume is that reading the Bible through the lens of African American interpretation, which is based on particular experiences, provides an important entrée into this sacred text. It is important, since this text was composed largely by those who themselves were marginalized.

One of the principal concerns in Wimbush's introduction to this collection is the recognition that the classics of Western civilization, including those that have emerged from the discipline of biblical interpretation, are produced by and intended for a particular elitist culture of a white, Eurocentric intelligentsia. To take the Bible out of this world, so foreign to many ethnic realities, and place it within one of the marginalized groups—in this case, the African American community—is both a defiant intellectual act and a political one. Black people through their experience have moments of discovery that are important to the hermeneutical enterprise. Even more important, this repositioning of the Bible's context allows for a critical examination of the white consciousness of privilege and how that creates problems in the interpretation that issues from it. The foregrounding of the Bible in African American reality asks, not about the specific meaning of a particular text within an ancient culture, but about how meaning is achieved in relationship to and through Scripture. Of course, there is no single African American reality. Diversity characterizes this community, as it does others in the disparate cultures of the globe.

The Goal of Biblical Studies

Modern biblical studies are characterized by a variety of assumptions. These include the view that the goal is to recapture the meaning of a text within its original historical, social, and cultural context. This original meaning is hypothetically recoverable in an objective, exegetical approach. Yet this proposed objective and the resultant meaning occur within and for a historically and socially homogeneous European culture. Thus, the meaning for today is directed toward a culture that assumes superiority, dominance, hierarchy, and political control over other cultures and peoples. In essence, this approach results in the silencing of alternative voices that speak out of their varied and different experiences. The Eurocentric culture has made a fetish of the biblical text that, through elitist hermeneutical application, supports white Western dominance in the world. Those not educated in the sophisticated, highly complex methods of historical criticism can only be silent. The Bible has become mystified and open to understanding only for the priests of exegesis who command the complex methods of analysis.

Historical Criticism in Service to the Present

Furthermore, historical criticism has largely limited the Bible to its historical past, so its voices have very little to say to modern cultures and societies. Secularists in the university, engaged in the so-called social scientific and literary study of the Bible, are hard pressed to explain their interests in this collection of ancient writings, other than to say that they are historians or literary scholars or archaeologists. Thus, they claim interest in the "facts" of the Bible, its cultures, and its societies but divest themselves of any interest in possible relevancy to today or to the questions of meaning that continue to haunt human beings through the generations. This contrasts appreciably with communities of the poor and marginalized, who want the texts to address their own realities and the specific circumstances of their daily lives. If the academy were to respond to this by making, for example, African American communities the heart of interpretation, then the primary emphasis in study would shift to the contemporary period of marginal existence of a people often beset with poverty and the evils of discrimination. Foreground would replace background as the area of primary interpretation, while background would be relegated to a secondary position.

Making African American study of the Bible the major approach of the academy would result in a "more consistent and intense and critical focus on *the phenomenology of social-cultural formation and the creation and uses of sacred texts.*" Thus, the major probing would occur in the critical examination of the interaction of society, culture, and sacred texts. The Bible in this setting is not a transcendent, theoretical entity, but rather an immanent, forming document of values, understandings, and beliefs. This cardinal point recognizes clearly that people form and shape texts that, in turn, continue to form and shape the people and their descendants as a "sacred tradition."

Scripture as Manifesto

This new process of biblical interpretation, in moving away from primary interest in meaning often locked in the past, places its focus on "*the Bible as scripture/manifesto that defines and embraces darkness.*" This is the most important ramification of placing the Bible within the context of the concerns and interests of the African American community. Scripture serves, at least in part, as a manifesto to those who are exiled and marginalized. The world is an unreceptive and cruel place through which to travel. When the Bible is directed to the marginalized and the harsh circumstances of their daily existence, then it reflects their own experiences and ceases being a text that legitimizes the oppressors. The Bible becomes not only a document of hope for the marginalized, but also a collection of texts that capture marginality, liminality, pain, and exile.

The experiences of African Americans as exiles and slaves can shed important light on the worldviews of a nation built on the foundations of oppression, greed, and conquest. For Wimbush, this window into the power dynamics of America and the West becomes a means of opening up a world of darkness that continues to blind and repress marginal peoples. Thus, in interpretation, one places into the foreground the Bible in the experiences and history of African Americans and then moves backward into the times of origins. Religion and culture cannot be separated. They are intrinsically one. The issue is where to begin the examination of this relationship: the historical past or the contemporary life of marginalized peoples.

According to Wimbush, darkness becomes, then, a mode of seeing, orientation, and understanding in a world of collective pain, especially for those who have existed on the underside of history. We must learn to read darkly and, through the darkness that becomes so readily evoked, learn to see the Scripture as a text of pain and a foundation for oppression. It is a reading that is nuanced by and captured in the three formerly described sections of "Pre-Texts," "Con-Texts," and "Sub-Texts." This structure becomes cyclical rather than linear, because it involves a durative process of the making of the self and the world that never ends. This reading ultimately becomes a reading of the self and not primarily of the text, a reading that may be disruptive and frightening but also is poignantly true.

A Changing Relationship with the Bible

Finally, in his primer *The Bible and African Americans: A Brief History,* Wimbush returns to his essay in Cain Hope Felder's collection, *Stony the Road We Trod,* and expands and reworks its major points. This work again initiates the subject of approaching the Bible within the context of the African American experience. Wimbush writes clearly of the Bible's function as a contributor to the "language-world" of African Americans who use its words in church, jazz, poetry and other types of literature, and colloquial speech. These become the media for the cultural contact of the Bible with the African American communities. This emphasis on the biblical language-world was inherited from the Europeans who came to this country to found the new Israel and to escape the tyranny of church domination in their mother nations. It should come as no surprise, then, that the enslaved and marginalized peoples in the newly emerging America should also see the text as a liberating force. The Bible's images, stories, and rhetoric, indeed its entire language, became central to the imagination of the African American slaves and from them to later generations. While African slaves were cut off from their culture and the language of their homelands, deemed inferior by their masters, they learned to communicate with each other through the language-world of the Bible.

Awe and respect of the early generations gave way to "befuddlement and contempt," as African slaves could not simply identify inspiration, revelation, and the sacred with a book. God was everywhere and located in all things. Yet this "befuddlement and contempt" led, not to the rejection of the Book, but eventually to a reverence for its importance. What attracted these early generations the most were the stories of bondage and liberation that spoke to their own experiences as slaves. Whether read or heard for understanding God and the righteous, or read backward to ward off demons, or randomly used to tell fortunes, the Bible came to permeate black culture. These readings no longer associated the Bible simply with the white privileged class, but now came to speak directly to the African American experiences.

A third reading developed in the northern states from the early period of the nineteenth century to the outbreak of the Civil War. Some African Americans in the pre–Civil War North were "allowed" to educate themselves. From this time on into the twentieth century, they began to develop a sharp social criticism of the world of the dominant white Europeans and their descendants. Among these who succeeded in doing so were those who challenged the myth of America as the "promised land." It may have been a land of promise for whites, but for African Americans, it was a place of exile, pain, and humiliation. Their experience was opposite to that of the white Europeans, who found in America a "land flowing with milk and honey." Black rhetoricians waxed eloquently about the oneness of humanity, the negation of difference, and the kingship of God over all peoples who were created in the divine image (Gal 3:28). They approached the social evils in their experiences with the biblical texts that condemned injustice. They condemned the society in which their communities existed for its social transgressions, and began the movement to black independent churches not controlled by whites. And their reading of the Bible ranged from apologetics to radicalism in responding to a white racist America. Their major goal was not only acceptance as human beings, but also integration into the larger society.

A fourth reading, that of fundamentalism, will not be considered here. However, if you are interested in the particular impact of fundamentalism on African American religion and its own distinct formulation, I encourage you to read this section of Wimbush's book.

The fifth and final reading is womanist theology, considered in chapter 5.

Cain Hope Felder

The approaches of liberation theology and African American interpretation are also found in the writings of Cain Hope Felder.[17] His volume *Stony the Road We Trod* has become a classic in African American biblical studies, blazing the trail for many other important studies to follow. Another important volume by Felder focuses attention on race and racism.[18] In this brief study, Felder examines race and racism in six succinct chapters: "Race and Sacralization in the Old Testament," "The Curse of Ham," "Old Testament Geneaologies," "The Narrative about Miriam and Aaron," "The Doctrine of Election," and "Secularization in the New Testament." In his introduction, he articulates clearly his objective in the study: the "profound difference in racial attitudes between those in the biblical world and in the subsequent history of Eurocentric interpretation." There do not appear in texts of antiquity any detailed definitions of race or theories about ethnic differences. While the Bible recognized differences in color, these were not used to support a political ideology that justified slavery or mistreatment of others. Indeed, it is not until the period of the Enlightenment that these categorizations and theories began to develop and to receive "scientific" explanations. These became the basis for white racism that developed so strongly and pervasively in the post-Enlightenment world. Even the Israelites themselves understood themselves as a motley group (a "mixed multitude") of different ethnic peoples with diverse cultures. The term *Semite* offers no real help, for it largely referred to a linguistic element that included Hebrew, Northwest Semitic, and even Akkadian and Ge'ez. Likely these groups were Afro-Asians. Thus, race and racism are relatively modern developments and are not in the world of the Bible.

The Hebrew Bible evidences a process of "sacralization," which Felder defines as taking an ideological concept and inserting it into the tenets of religious faith. This process was undertaken by particular groups to serve their own interests. Different is the process of "secularization," in which a religious concept of seminal value is weakened by sociopolitical and ideological processes. These are present in the Bible and have opened the door to matters of race and racism, but their full-scale development is a modern phenomenon. Race and secularization are illustrated by a number of texts in the Hebrew Bible that have been interpreted by racists.[19] The first is the "curse of Ham" in Gen 9:18-27, which was used first by the rabbis of the early Talmudic period and the church fathers to demean black people.

17. See especially Felder, *Stony the Road We Trod* and *Troubling Biblical Waters;* and Gates, "Ideology and the Interpretation of Scripture."

18. Felder, *Race, Racism, and the Biblical Narratives.*

19. See also Felder, *Troubling Biblical Waters.*

What is actually at stake in this text in the J narrative is the understanding that all of post-flood humanity derives from the three sons of Noah. Following this, the various destinies of particular groups tracing their ancestries back to these sons are set forth. In Felder's view, this is a prime case of secularization in which particular peoples and cultures are set forth as blessed or cursed. Because of Ham's disrespect of observing the nakedness of his father, his son, Canaan, is cursed, while Ham's two brothers (Shem and Japeth) are blessed. This version of the story is politically inspired to justify Israel's conquering and domination of the Canaanites. But the curse as early as Talmudic Judaism began to be interpreted as the explanation for the black-skinned Africans.

Another text that illustrates the process of racism and secularization is the "Table of Nations" (in Gen 10; cf. 1 Chr 1:1—2:55), which consists of two sources, J and P, separated likely by several centuries. These are catalogs of peoples and individuals, not examples of ancient ethnology. They do not have as their intent the establishment of ethnic differences between the peoples of Africa and Asia. The motive that derives from this table is theological. The one in 1 Chronicles obviously places its interest in the descendants of Shem, while the older J narrative's list was the first and then was expanded by P. Throughout it becomes clear that the descendents of Shem lessen in importance in order to make way for the Israelites, the chosen people who received the blessings of salvation history. However, not even Israel is made racially or culturally superior to the other nations, showing that the concern is theological and not racial as argued by racists to uphold the view of superiority of certain ethnic groups and the inferiority of others.

A third biblical text is the narrative told of Miriam and Aaron in Numb 12:1-16. In this story, the brother and sister of Moses criticize him for having taken a Cushite wife. Is it due to her color? This may be the case. The LXX understands the criticism as due to her color, and the affliction of Miriam with leprosy (v. 9) results in her becoming leprous, "as white as snow." While Aaron's position as priest preserves him from a similar fate, it is clear that the two are rebuked due to their prejudice concerning the woman's dark skin.

Randall C. Bailey

Bailey's major contribution to African American studies is his editorial work for a recent *Semeia* issue.[20] In the introduction, he sets forth the major works that have appeared in African American biblical scholarship.

---

20. R. Bailey, *Yet with a Steady Beat*. He briefly introduces this collection of eight essays and three responses on pp. 1–7.

He begins with the 1989 issue of *Semeia,* coedited by Katie G. Cannon and Elisabeth Schüssler Fiorenza and entitled *Interpretation for Liberation.* This collection, primarily of black scholars (save for one) who are women (save for one), began the conversation about the interpretations of the Bible in the African American community. In his collection, *Stony the Road We Trod,* Cain Hope Felder structures the major sections of the volume to include hermeneutics, the role of Africa in the life of ancient Israel, and the discussion of key biblical passages important in the black community. Two areas remained to be addressed: historical criticism in this tradition and its history of interpretation.

This collection was followed by the 1994 issue of the *Journal of the Interdenominational Theological Center,* comprising a group of articles that were written by African American scholars and read in the African American Theology and Biblical Hermeneutics Group of the Society of Biblical Literature. These essays are primarily exegetical. Vincent Wimbush's *African Americans and the Bible* appeared in 2000 and contains sixty-eight essays that cross disciplinary boundaries in order to demonstrate the ways black people in the United States have used the Bible in the various facets of culture. What unifies this collection is not only its subject matter, but also a new cultural criticism that seeks to demonstrate how a variety of ethnic cultures pursue their defining work in all aspects of life. These works filled two major gaps left by Felder's influential work.

Bailey's edited collection, *Yet with a Steady Beat,* presents a variety of African American studies of the Bible, including the Deuteronomistic History, the Psalms, and Paul, and the hermeneutical methods at work to carry forth this tradition of interpretation—in particular, ideological and narrative criticisms. The various issues that appear in this volume are ethnography in the ancient world, the use of laws that affect the poor in Deuteronomy and their relationship to poor communities in America, black folk tradition that intersects with biblical texts, and passages in the Bible, especially those that deal with liberation, that have been important in African American theology. Adding to the value of these studies, most are interdisciplinary in scope and approach. Social location appears as a dominant concern, not only in the essays themselves, but also in the three responses to them. This parallels the attention given in other examples of liberation theology in this volume.

Randall Bailey has published an important essay on the academic interpretation among African Americans in *African Americans and the Bible,* edited by Vincent Wimbush.[21] In this essay, he delineates four major trends

---

21. R. Bailey, "Academic Biblical Interpretation."

that have developed in the African American academic study of religion: pointing to African presence in the text, describing racist and white supremacist interpretations, placing readings within the social location of the African American community, and describing the academic study of the Bible by African Americans as ideological criticism. He notes in this five-year-old study that forty-five African Americans (eleven of whom are women) in the United States have doctorates in Scripture.

Jeremiah and a Theology of the Diaspora

The most important crisis facing the people of Judah was the Babylonian conquest, the forced exile of its leaders from its homeland to a new and strange land, and the requirement of both exiles and those who remained behind to develop a new metanarrative that provided a theological basis for existence. Segovia's theology of diaspora and the book of Jeremiah engage each other in developing a *modus vivendi* for human existence in a strange and foreign land.

The community in Babylon because of the first exile (in 597 B.C.E.) is described in the prose narrative as the "good figs," as contrast to the "bad figs," who represent those who remained in Judah, including especially Zedekiah and his officials (Jer 24). The "good figs" are told they will become the remnant from whom Yahweh will build a future people, but only after the experience of the exile. Historically, this narrative is likely an apology for the exiles in Babylon who returned to their homeland and encountered the stiff resistance of the "people of the land."

The Book of the Covenant (Jer 30–31), probably comprising oracles to the exiles by prophets who were disciples of Jeremiah, also speaks of a people who are the recipients of Yahweh's everlasting love (*ḥesed*). These will return home one day to Zion, where they will praise Yahweh for having delivered them. In this new and inviting world, the people of Israel, those in all areas of diaspora, will return, including even children, pregnant women, the blind, and the lame. Together they will become once more those who are remade into the people of God. This leads to great celebration and a cessation of lamentation.

However, until that restoration, the exiles are admonished to settle down and raise their families in exile (cf. the letter to the exiles in chapter 29). To follow Segovia, this equips a diaspora people with the insight based on experience that God does not abandon them even in a foreign land. They are not encouraged to acculturate into Babylonian culture and society, but their existence as the "other" provides them the deep appreciation and joyous celebration of life that will come to fruition one day in the future.

Jeremiah and African American Biblical Theology

Contemporary biblical theologies that have commanded the most attention in biblical studies have largely ignored marginal peoples. However, a focus on this area provides interesting insights. For example, the Bible contains no evidence of racism directed toward people of color. Indeed, it is not uncommon to discover that Africa and Africans play a significant part in the biblical literature. One case in point is the Ethiopian eunuch who bears the name Ebed-melech ("servant/slave of the king") in Jer 37:11—38:13. Jeremiah had been imprisoned by officials who were pro-Egyptian and supported the rebellion against the Babylonians. Jeremiah had long preached submission to the Babylonians, a message thought by zealots to be traitorous (cf. chapter 27). Persuaded by the pro-Egyptian party seeking Judean independence from Babylonia to appeal for help from the newly installed Egyptian king, Hophra (589–570 B.C.E.), Zedekiah rebelled against the Babylonians in 589 B.C.E. After the Babylonian forces had laid siege to Jerusalem, they were forced to withdraw temporarily in order to meet the Egyptian threat from the south. Rejoicing followed this supposed deliverance. During this respite, Jeremiah sought to leave the city and go to Benjamin to receive his share of his household's property.

However, he was accosted by a sentinel at the Benjaminite Gate, accused of deserting to the enemy, and arrested. Whereupon, his pro-Egyptian enemies, officials who had the king's ear at court, learned of this and had him arrested for sedition and desertion. He was imprisoned, with the king's permission, in a cistern of the king's son, located in the court of the guard.

As Jeremiah sank into the mud, his fate appeared to be sealed. However, Ebed-Melech, an Egyptian eunuch in the king's palace, appealed to the king to spare Jeremiah. This African official was given three men to remove Jeremiah by rope from the cistern, although the prophet was forced to remain in the court of the guard. Once again, visited by the king, Jeremiah counseled surrender to the Babylonians. What is interesting is not only the important act of deliverance that likely saved the prophet's life, but also the realization that this Ethiopian is the one marginal person who has an important narrative role. This case and many others point to the significance of Africa and Africans in Israel and the ancient Near East in history and theological tradition.

Evaluation

Since the 1970s, liberation theology has developed into a major approach to biblical and contemporary religious understanding. Indeed, its further expansion is witnessed in a variety of specific forms, including Latin American, feminist, African American, Hispanic, *mujerista*, womanist, and postcolonial theologies. In this chapter, we have dealt with three expressions that grew out of historical criticism. In the typology we have developed, the movement from history to liberation does not mean the abandonment of history as a theme and as a method, but rather an appropriation of history to point to the historical development of liberation among marginalized communities of people.

The contributions of ethnic formulations of Old Testament theology may be summarized under two major categories. The first is the sensitivity that scholars who come from marginalized peoples bring to the text, allowing them to gain theological insights that escape majority interpreters. Too often, people who articulate the theology of the text stand within the context of majority classes and cultures, which fail to recognize theological points that are significant contributions by the marginalized. The role of Ebed-Melech, an Egyptian eunuch who rescued Jeremiah from death in a cistern, is not only important for understanding the identity of a marginalized foreigner, whose native rulers belonged to the twenty-sixth dynasty that had been preceded by the Cushite twenty-fifth dynasty composed of rulers from Ethiopia. He also was likely an Egyptian official who represented the interests of his Egyptian dynast, yet saved the leading prophetic voice of the pro-Babylonian party. There are many similar examples of the marginalized who participate in the narrative memory of ancient Israel whose own forebears were proclaimed to be slaves liberated from Egyptian tyranny.

The second category is the insight that marginalized interpreters bring to Old Testament theology. This insight is born of the experience of oppression and victimization in a majority culture. Segovia's understanding of the theology of the diaspora, for example, is enriched by the experience of his ethnic ancestors, many of whom, against their will, have found themselves in a land that belittles minority ethnicity (in his case, that of Latinos and Latinas). When Old Testament theology is understood as having the responsibility to address contemporary issues of racism, poverty, and the like, the experience of living in a foreign land awakens the text to new life. The implicit claim for the superiority of Eurocentric theology can no longer be affirmed in a diverse world of many cultures and traditions.

4

From Exclusion to Inclusion:
Feminist Interpretations of History

We all belong to one Spirit. Those who oppress long for this belonging, but ownership does not permit belonging. . . . If we are one with Creativity itself, if we choose not to oppress, then the waters, the land, the cosmos, and our fellow creatures will teach us about belonging. The belonging is to those who choose to be as one with Life itself. And if we give up the notion of owning some piece of creation that is outside the sphere of our own bodies and minds, we may belong.

—*Karen Baker-Fletcher*

"Dancing in the House of Wisdom" or "Waltzing in Widsom Ways" means stepping and twirling—creating an interpretative, communal dance and breaking out of the rhythm of the rigidity of culturally ascribed dance steps. I visualize a diverse group of wo/men dancing in a circular formation inside the pillars of an open-air house—their dance circle open, ready to accept the reader inside. The dance could be edifying to the mind, body and spirit of the reader.

—*Linda Ellison*

Introduction

THE FIRST QUOTE FROM THE WRITINGS OF THE WOMANIST SCHOLAR, Karen Baker-Fletcher, comes from her journal of reflections and the second from Linda Ellison in a paper written for "Gospel Stories of Women," taught by Elisabeth Schüssler Fiorenza.[1] With these quotes, two women depict in entrancing language the deep-seated feeling of one who longs to become a participant in the concord of the cosmos. The choice that we make not to own or oppress generates this aesthesis of the harmony of the elements that allows us to belong to the cosmos that is generated by the life-giving Spirit. Further, the image of the dancing goddess and her maidens invites women into the captivating, shared dance of participation in the task of revealing the intricacies of the Scripture. Among the religious symbolizations of this merging with the cosmos and the text through creativity and the renunciation of oppression is the goddess

1. Baker-Fletcher and Baker-Fletcher, *My Sister, My Brother*, 295–96.

Hokma/Sophia, who as the daughter of God, orders a world of aesthesis through playful dance and inviting words of her maidens who seek to join in the banquet inaugurating her reign as the Queen of Heaven.

These quotations lead us into another realm of biblical theology and hermeneutics, that of feminism. The goddess Wisdom and her maidens in Near Eastern, Israelite, Jewish, and Hellenistic religion, together with the spirituality expressed in the devotion and study of her followers, integrate reality into a harmony of the cosmos through the loving dance of creative joy and the call to take up the path to insight and life. In many ways feminism captures the images of the dance of the Spirit that makes all things one, overcoming difference and polarization. Indeed, the vision of feminism is to awaken once again goddess Wisdom to dance with her followers and shape a world of blissful oneness.

Feminist Theology

Feminist theology began to achieve significant prominence in the 1970s, accelerated by the activism of women struggling for full civil rights and liberation from patriarchy and sexism during the past century.[2] There is, of course, a lengthy history of feminism in every political, social, and religious sphere that may be traced over the centuries. Especially significant resources for feminism and struggle are available from the nineteenth century.[3] In addition, while there is common cause among feminists, there is also significant diversity. Feminism is best characterized, not as a method or an ideology, but much more as a consciousness that emerges from identity constructed by place, experience, and gender. This consciousness, as it were, is particularly true of women, because of their common, shared experiences. However, males may themselves, with significant effort, develop this consciousness, at least through empathy and a developed awareness of the destructiveness of patriarchy. There is great variety in regard to theory, method, analysis, and objectives among feminists.

2. Among the many important works in feminist theology are Carr, *Transforming Grace;* Daly, *Beyond God the Father;* Heyward, *Touching Our Strength;* Ruether, *Sexism and God-Talk;* Russell, *Human Liberation in a Feminist Perspective; Feminist Interpretation of the Bible;* and Thistlethwaite, *Sex, Race and God.* Two fine surveys are Clifford, *Introducing Feminist Theology;* and P. Young, *Feminist Theology/Christian Theology.* For an example of feminist biblical interpretation, see Newsom and Ringe, *The Women's Bible Commentary.* Trible's article "Five Loaves and Two Fishes" provides a succinct summary of feminism and its impact on biblical theology. See also Bass, "Women's Studies and Biblical Studies"; and Sakenfeld, "Feminist Perspectives on Bible and Theology." A comprehensive, well-written overview of feminist biblical studies is V. Phillips, "Feminist Interpretation."

3. See especially Lerner, *The Creation of Feminist Consciousness;* and Selvidge, *Notorious Voices.*

In addition, the theoretical discouse and its applications have not remained static. Increasingly, scholars have argued for a heuristic model that distinguishes between first-generation feminist theology and the second generation, and perhaps even a third. The first generation concentrated mainly on the critique of patriarchy and pointed to the limitations of theology that did not take women's issues and experiences seriously, while the second generation moved beyond critical evaluation to a more systematic presentation. The reshaping of theological language and method has been under way in contemporary feminist hermeneutics and modern study of the Bible for over a generation. New feminist theologies, including biblical studies, have appeared to reshape the discourse of the academy and the church.

Important themes and emphases unite the diverse expressions of feminist theology. Women's liberation is a multifaceted response to systemic oppression and victimization, using a variety of strategies to effectuate social, economic, political, cultural, and religious change that not only will eventuate in the equality of women, but at the same time will lead to the recognition and authentication of their full humanity. Many forms of social existence use gender to support male domination (patriarchy) and female subordination. The ideological undergirding of patriarchy is sexism, both open and covert. Feminism actively seeks to identify the various manifestations of sexism, misogyny, and patriarchy—forces that exploit and subordinate women—and then to subvert them by means of a variety of different strategies. As a manifestation of the sinful distortion of the image of God that involves both male and female, patriarchy is prophetically opposed and theologically subverted.[4]

Since sin permeates all areas of human life (including political expressions and power relationships, society and social institutions, sexuality, economics, class, and family), feminists operate on the understanding that sexism is but one of many related forms of pervasive oppression that also include racism, fascism, exploitative capitalism, and colonialism. Thus, there is often an explicit concern to work with other oppressed groups to subvert all forms of oppression that lead to the denial of full humanity to any person or group. Indeed, there is at times even an expressed desire to liberate the oppressor from his efforts at dehumanization of victims, including women and societal marginals.

In the examination of sexist exploitation of women, feminists have recognized that religion has been used or misused to oppress women and other groups. This has led some feminists to reject religion, including Judaism and Christianity and their sacred texts. However, to dismiss religion and its sacred texts may result in ignoring the powerful motivating

---

4. Trible, "Five Loaves and Two Fishes," 281.

force these play in shaping lives and cultures. In addition, to reject the Bible as hopelessly sexist is to accept the authenticity of the arguments of male interpreters and thus to allow the misogynistic character of much of the Bible to remain unchallenged. Thus, feminism proceeds on two fronts with regard to the Bible. First, it questions the interpretations of male scholars concerning history and the Bible and articulates, where possible, appropriate feminist interpretations and reconstructions of history, and it rejects the authority of an unchallenged Bible to threaten to continue to oppress women. Additionally, religion is recognized as a powerful means by which to achieve liberation. To this end, there is a critical evaluation of religion and sacred texts in order to deny to authentic religion myths, stories, rituals, symbols, and language that are oppressive, yet at the same time to discover or recover as well as create new religious language and celebrations that are liberating.

Feminists, including literary critics, historians, and biblical scholars, have sought to recover women's stories in the Bible and Christian tradition in the effort to recognize the important contributions of women in religious history that had been lost, forgotten, or suppressed by patriarchy and are suggested by the various stories and poems present in Scripture. There are various means of getting at these stories, including a "hermeneutics of suspicion," that attempt to identify evidence of patriarchy's efforts to suppress women's voices. This recovery of women's history represents, not merely an antiquarian interest in the past or the expression of pride in women's accomplishments, but also the desire to uphold and affirm the full humanity of women and to find new models for feminine leadership. The implication is that women, once this status is achieved, would not be forced into male patriarchal models of leadership that are oppressive and at times antipathetic to authentic feminine existence.

Feminist literary critics engage in pursuing the nature of language. They have recognized that, due to the enormous creative power endemic to language, "whoever names the world owns the world." In large measure, men have dominated the naming process. Thus, discourse needs to be carefully scrutinized, and sexist interpretations, translations, and meanings expunged.

The question of translation of the Bible is a key aspect of understanding the power of language. Through language—in this case, that of Scripture—the world is created. The language of the Bible, believed sanctioned by God and the church due to the texts included in the canon, can either liberate or dominate, set free the captives or enslave them, and erect or remove boundaries that separate people into classes, ethnicities, and genders or that create social stigmas associated with poverty and other features of "otherness." Until the appearance of *The Woman's Bible*, translated by Elizabeth Cady Stanton, all the translators of the Bible in the West had been men, including Jerome, Luther, the King James scholars, and the group of men appointed to do an Authorized revision of the King James Version.[5] Among the goals of Stanton's work was to retranslate the texts that referred to women and especially that became the basis for male domination of women. Seven women worked with Stanton in producing this new Bible. After the first volume appeared, the National Woman Suffrage Association in its 1896 convention disavowed any connection with it. While Stanton and her group lacked skills in translation, because most evidently did not know the original languages of the Bible, the impact was still significant. The passages dealing with women were cut out, placed into a blank book, and then interpreted. The commentaries are critical of patriarchy but affirm the major theological tenets the Bible contains. Women also were created to experience freedom and to seek after happiness. Passages that are humiliating and dismissive of women cannot be understood as written in accordance with divine will.[6] This translation became the first women's Bible, the first women's commentary, and the first feminist theology of Scripture. Stanton's work as a suffragist and feminist has considerably influenced the feminist movement in the Western world.

Recognizing that traditional God language is largely patriarchal (God is father, king, lord, warrior, and suzerain), feminists emphasize that God is beyond gender (male or female), even though there are metaphorical ways of talking about God in sexual terms: God as male, but also God as female. Inclusive language is broader in scope, however, than the matter of God-talk. Religious language describes human beings as well as God, and even language about God says a great deal about human identity. Thus, to limit metaphors for God to male terms (father, king, ruler, warrior, and lord) creates and legitimates a social reality in which males rule over women, who are placed in a subordinate role and even dehumanized.[7]

---

5. For a history of the English translations and versions of the Bible, see Metzger, *The Bible in Translation*. One of the developments in the history of the translation and versions of the Bible in English is the effort made by the NRSV to translate Hebrew and Greek words for humanity as *human beings* or other non-gender-specific terms, if it is clear the text is referring not to gender but to humans. However, more problematic is the translation of language for God, particularly the gender pronouns. The proclivity of the NRSV was to eliminate masculine references to God, as directed by the Division of Christian Education of the National Council of Churches (which holds the copyright of this version), if possible. Yet, sorting out what is culturally required by the historical context and what is liturgically and morally defensible for a version so readily used in the mainline Protestant churches has continued to be a very difficult and perplexing matter.

6. For a brief summary of the work of Stanton and the nature of *The Woman's Bible* see Clifford, *Introducing Feminist Theology*, 46–49. For a more detailed study, see Griffith, *In Her Own Right*.

7. "Patriarchal language for God promotes an entire way of thinking, social constructions of race, class, and gender, for instance, that benefit males, especially white, affluent males" McFague, "Mother God," 138–43.

Traditional language of the Bible and culture may be demeaning to or affirming of women. This recognition assists in the effort to shape a contemporary discourse in society and religion that recognizes the full humanity of all. Other metaphors for God, some new and others suppressed or lying fallow within the tradition, have been proposed, including, for example, God as mother, friend, and lover.[8]

Of course, feminists have raised and addressed many other questions and concerns that affect contemporary and even biblical theology. For example, feminists raise the question as to whether there is a distinctively female experience, consciousness, or embodiment that separates women from men and often conclude with an answer in the affirmative. This has major epistemological implications for various disciplines and their practice, including theology: feminists may use women's experience as a source for doing theology or even as a norm that evaluates theological expressions, including those in the Bible.[9] For feminists, theology that does not take into account or reflect women's experience is inauthentic. And this point may be taken a step further by the argument that women's experience should contribute to the norms for evaluating theology.

Related to the matter of women's experience is the question of the relationship between the sexes. Are they enemies or partners or individuals with their own experiences and contributions? How may they relate authentically to others, male and female, in ways that affirm the full humanity of all, including in particular marginals who are not, as often portrayed, simply poor men, but also impoverished women who have their own, even greater struggles for survival and dignity?

Feminist Interpretations of History

As one would expect, feminism as a social, historical, and theological lens through which to present biblical theology is complex. Indeed, the variety of feminist, womanist, and *mujerista* studies are varied and may be found in every chapter in this introduction that outlines different approaches to biblical theology. But for the sake of a general discussion, which this introduction must necessarily be, let me greatly oversimplify, without too much reductionist misrepresentation, by dividing feminist biblical interpretation into two main, though often related, approaches: historical and literary. Schüssler Fiorenza is critical of this bipolarity, since it represents to her the patriarchal dualism that she seeks to deconstruct.[10] However, it seems clear to me that this duality of those who affirm history as the con-

---

8. Sallie McFague, *Models of God.*
9. See P. Young, *Feminist Theology/Christian Theology,* 49–69.
10. See her rejection of this dichotomy in *Sharing Her Word,* e.g., 9–12.

text for understanding the origins and development of tradition, as she does, and those who reject history as a concept and an approach that has no bearing on the meaning of texts, something that one sees in the writings of many postmodern feminist biblical scholars, has merit, heuristic as well as methodological. Feminist biblical scholarship that is strongly grounded in history and the goal of historical reconstruction, as has been the case with biblical interpretation in general, has blended well with social-anthropological theories. Working with a hermeneutics of suspicion, feminist historians have long been aware of the male silencing of the voices of women and the elimination or at least diminishment of their contributions to Israelite and Jewish history and religion. This has led to largely distorted historical descriptions of a male-dominated religion and society, which in turn have provided the basis for a biblical theology that is ideological, sexist, oppressive, and severely damaging to modern faith and values in the church.

Feminist historians take two separate but related directions in interpreting Israelite religion, society, and biblical texts. The first direction involves recognizing the significance of women in Israelite and early Jewish history and the texts upon which this rests and to attempt to recover their voices and roles in the reconstruction of biblical history by examining narratives, stories, and poems as important source material. At the same time, because so much of biblical knowledge has been produced by males, arguably to promote their self-interests in society and church, feminists are "suspicious" of past studies. These either may be cleansed of sexism or replaced by feminist interpretations that are geared to discovering the place of women in the sociopolitical and religious world of ancient Israel, early Judaism, and primitive Christianity.

The second direction is to include the importance of noncanonical texts and data from material culture that also points to the status and roles of women. This second perspective results from the fact that much of the biblical literature is patriarchal and paternalistic and that the contributions of women, if not totally eliminated, were reduced in significance and at times even presented in demeaning ways. It is impossible to shape a biblical theology that engages contemporary faith without recognizing historical and biblical sexism and without attempting to reconstitute the roles and voices of women.

A second approach taken by feminist interpreters of Scripture concentrates on the literary construction and meaning of texts. This approach often dispenses to a large degree with history, considering it to be a largely useless enterprise in liberating women to achieve their rightful place in the world. The male codes of reading the Bible, particularly those that are linked to historical criticism and Eurocentric theology that privilege the interpretations of white Western men to the exclusion or even shameful debasing of feminist, womanist, egalitarian, postcolonial, and postmodernist ways of understanding and interpreting Scripture, are inherently based on the patriarchal history of the (largely male) persons who wrote and redacted the Bible. This twin bias cannot be escaped simply by feminists looking for tiny pieces of history that point to more significant female roles. Literary criticism of various types, postcolonialism, and postmodernism, as we shall see in later chapters, offer women vital and fruitful means of articulating the theology of the biblical text and engaging modern theology for the contemporary communities of faith.

In this chapter, I shall examine several feminist historians who build on the basis of historical criticism and social-anthropological theories a feminist historiography, one that liberates men and women from the desperate imprisonment of a largely sexist historiography that has frequently produced distorted portrayals of biblical theology engaging the contemporary meanings of faith. At the same time, feminist work in contemporary hermeneutics will also be outlined. The two feminist biblical historians I have chosen to discuss briefly are Elisabeth Schüssler Fiorenza and Carol Meyers.

Elisabeth Schüssler Fiorenza

Introduction: Feminist History

Feminist studies of the Bible, which have as their objective historical reconstruction, have focused on two related areas: (1) the significant sociohistorical role women play in the history of ancient Israel and the early church and (2) the articulation of a critical feminist hermeneutic as both a research tool into the past and an interpretative method for present theological discourse.[11] Both of these areas are addressed in the writings of Schüssler Fiorenza[12] (New Testament), as well as Carol Meyers (Hebrew Bible), discussed in the next section.

The role of women in Israelite society and cult, along with feminine sexuality and the turn of women to goddess worship and intermarriage with non-Israelites, have been and continue to be areas of particular interest in

---

11. This differentiation is set forth frequently in the writings of Schüssler Fiorenza. See, e.g., *Bread Not Stone*, afterword, 152. Yet this hermeneutic is used also as a research tool in exposing sexism in the writings and social construction of the early church and in reconstructing early historical narrative and the roles women and the feminine played in the origin and expansion of early Christianity.

12. For a listing of her most substantial writings, see the bibliography.

feminist biblical interpretation.[13] The reference to Paul's relationship with prominent women points to their active role in the expansion of early Christianity. The feminist historical critic argues that the modern historian works with the principle of selectivity based on the key role played by self-interest. Thus, while male scholars have developed rigorously reconstructed histories and interpretations, they have operated out of their own patriarchy. Feminist interpreters are to be as rigorous as their male counterparts and at the same time work from the basis of women's self-interest in liberation from male domination. Thus, their work is also selective in what they construe as fundamental to the history of ancient Israel, early Judaism, and the primitive church.

In addition to Paul and women, a special area of interest to feminist New Testament interpreters has been Jesus' circle of women. While earlier scholars tended to place Paul in the camp of those who opposed important roles for women, because of the culture's presumed sexism both in Judaism and in the Greco-Roman world, Jesus was interpreted to be the liberator of women. However, this simplistic dichotomy has been brought under critical scrutiny because of an inherent anti-Semitism in the interpretation. A more lucid and less slanted view is emerging in scholarship involving early Christianity concerning the complexity of views of women in the early environment in which Jesus and Paul lived.[14] For example, Amy-Jill Levine has argued that we need a clearer understanding of Jewish purity laws in the first century C.E. before declaring Jesus to be one who repudiated these in acts of courageous liberation of women and men suffering under Roman imperialism.[15] In addition, it is clear on the basis of extra-biblical cultural data that women played significant leadership roles in Jewish synagogues and were at times important patrons.[16] Thus, to

---

13. See, e.g., the work of Carol Meyers. One should also consult Athalyah Brenner's numerous writings and edited volumes. Brenner combines in her work the roles of feminist literary critic and feminist historian. One of her major points that is fundamental to historical interpretation is her emphasis on a hermeneutics of suspicion in identifying the historical and social roles of ancient Israelite women and their representation in texts written by men. Brenner, *The Israelite Woman.* Brenner's editing of a multivolume commentary (*The Feminist Companion to the Hebrew Bible*) is a rich resource of feminist interpretations of biblical texts. See also the essays in Day, *Gender and Difference in Ancient Israel,* which briefly construe the roles of women in Israelite society.

14. See Plaskow, "Anti-Judaism in Feminist Christian Interpretation." See also Plaskow, *Standing Again at Sinai;* and Kellenbach, *Anti-Judaism in Feminist Religious Writings.*

15. Levine, "Second Temple Judaism, Jesus, and Women." See also Levine, "*Women Like This.*" There is no evidence that these laws were understood by women to oppress them.

16. Brooten, *Women Leaders in the Ancient Synagogue.* See also see her theoretical essay, "Early Christian Women and Their Cultural Context," and her volume on love and sexuality between women in the early church, *Love between Women.*

contrast Jesus as the liberator of women with a supposedly misogynistic Judaism presents an interpretation that is rife with anti-Semitism.

One of the epoch-making books in the history of New Testament studies and their engagement with contemporary theology is Elisabeth Schüssler Fiorenza's *In Memory of Her*. Striking like a thunderbolt the presumably unassailable tower of male interpretations that had dominated society, academy, and church for two millennia, Schüssler Fiorenza's book proposed a dramatically new reading of early Christian history and theology. Not since Karl Barth's *Der Römerbrief* appeared in 1919 to assail and ultimately severely restrict the dominance of the approach of the History of Religion in biblical interpretation and to shape a theological revolution that culminated in neo-orthodoxy has a book had the impact of Schüssler Fiorenza's reconstruction of early Christianity. Indeed, in both biblical and theological studies, her work has revised methodological and hermeneutical approaches by raising and answering questions that had been either ignored or given little weight: the self-interest of writer and interpreter, the hermeneutics of suspicion, and the marginalization of women (and other groups in her later writings) that silenced their voice and ignored, if not almost eliminated, their roles in the origins and expansion of early Christianity. While others wrote of these and similar emphases, it was *In Memory of Her* that brought them together in a compelling reading of the New Testament and the early church. While she is not the first feminist biblical scholar who takes a historical approach to her work, she is certainly the most profound and influential in her combination of rigorous historical study and theological hermeneutics.

In Memory of Her

In Memory of Her, which paved the way for a critical feminist theology of early Christianity, was published originally in 1983 and then revised and reissued in 1995. In the first part of this classic, Schüssler Fiorenza lays out clearly in three succinct chapters a feminist critical hermeneutics, a feminist critical method, and a feminist model of historical reconstruction. These methodological chapters are followed by two additional ones that enter into the realm of contemporary hermeneutics: "Women's History as the History of the Discipleship of Equals" and "Tracing the Struggles: Patriarchy and Ministry."

The book receives its title from Mark 14:9, which tells of an unnamed woman who anoints Jesus. In spite of the promise that "what she has done will be told in memory of her," whenever the Gospel is preached throughout the entirety of the cosmos, her name has been forgotten, and her story has not been told. The author of the Fourth Gospel chose to identify her with Mary of Bethany, the sister of Lazarus and the friend of Jesus. Luke, who does not tell us her name, makes her no longer a disciple but rather a sinner whom Jesus forgives. Even in the Eucharist, those who are mentioned are not this unnamed woman or even the later traditions about her, but rather the story of Peter who denied Jesus and Judas who betrayed him. They are remembered, while this faithful disciple is forgotten. Indeed, in the Passion narrative in Mark, the loyal disciples of Jesus are the women. Yet even they are rarely mentioned. Instead, a betrayer and a coward are remembered.

Schüssler Fiorenza sets forth in the introduction two purposes for the reconstruction of early Christian history as women's history: the effort to remember and reclaim their story and also to reclaim this history as the history for both women and men in every time and location. She thus identifies herself not only as a feminist historian, but also as a feminist theologian. She recognizes the New Testament as both a historical collection of writings and as Scripture for the contemporary world. She stresses in the very beginning that she combines a historical and theological critical approach with biblical-historical hermeneutics. This is the fundamental key to understanding her work.

Methodology

She articulates then her basic methodological approach. First, she is a historian and, as such, engages in the historical-critical interpretation of the collection of books found in the New Testament canon. This she combines with the social-historical approaches and the results that began to contribute substantially to biblical studies in the 1970s.

In approaching these texts through a critical feminist theory, she does so with the predisposition to consider them products of an androcentric, patriarchal culture in history. Thus, she works with a hermeneutics of suspicion in analyzing texts that may have eliminated women, silenced their voices, and created a culture of male elitism and sexism in the early church. Further, the prevailing interpretations of the text in the church and the academy have been written mainly by male scholars themselves caught in the web of patriarchy and sexism. This orientation has slanted a great deal of biblical scholarship and contributed to the attempt to silence women, not only in the text, but also in contemporary interpretation.

The sociology of knowledge teaches us that "objectivity" is an impossible goal even in scientific research. All interpreters are caught up in their own biases, partisan politics, and self-interests in the promotion of their theories, their work, and their place in the world. These ideological orientations have colored much of the research into the meaning of the New Testament and the history of the early church. All historians work within a self-constructed frame of reference that is judged by others as to its efficiency and integrity. Historical work therefore is referential, emerging colored and shaped by the features of these frames of orientation. Further, historical work is and must be selective in regard to the data selected to make and then support interpretation. However, the collusive elimination of women has appreciably distorted the early history of the foundation and expansion of early Christianity.

Feminists reject the patriarchal authority of revelation avowed by church officials who see their critical work as undermining the faith. In the post–Vatican II period, Scripture indeed is considered to be inspired, authoritative, and revelatory, but not all texts in the canon are Scripture. If the Bible is to address women in their lives and circumstances today, this discriminating judgment becomes a key cornerstone of interpretation.

This quest for and discovery of women in the past, including those who were active in the origins and expansion of early Christianity, resides in the collective memory of the early and succeeding generations of the church that allows contemporary women to unite in sisterhood with their ancestors in the faith. Thus, this is an "engaged" historical and hermeneutic endeavor, not a dispassionate exercise in intellectual pursuit of interesting table talk. We are now in a paradigm shift, claims Schüssler Fiorenza, from an androcentric model to a feminist one. This has significant implications for the transformation of society and the creation of a new world in which to live. The new world breaks in, not with a whisper, but with a shout that creates conflict and struggle until it achieves the fullness of discourse that provides both meaning and direction. The new world comes through the liberation of marginals from patriarchy that dominates, controls, manipulates, and dehumanizes its victims.

Model of Reconstruction

In her initial chapter, Schüssler Fiorenza surveys the history of theological feminism from earlier times to her own time by placing it within a variety of schools and traditions, beginning with the suffragist movement in the late nineteenth and early twentieth centuries. She concentrates initially on Elisabeth Cady Stanton and then moves into neo-orthodoxy and its scholars, who include Letty Russell, into the sociology of knowledge and the work of Mary Daly, and finally into liberation theology. While summarizing in her critical review the strengths and weaknesses of these earlier approaches, she feels her method of analysis and hermeneutics is most akin to that of liberation theology. Here she makes her case for the importance of the symbiosis of historical reconstruction and theological envisioning. The goal is not only the liberation of women from the control of men, but also the elimination of patriarchy from the Christian community and faith. Feminine identity is not biological, but rather experiential in that women bond together by means of the common experiences of struggle against patriarchal culture and history. This goal is made possible, historically speaking, through the activation of memory. Women's experiences of oppression and liberation become the feminist canon and theologically authoritative basis for life. Thus, she sets forth her approach as a Christian feminist theology of liberation.

For Schüssler Fiorenza, the locus of revelation is not Scripture, but rather the ministry of Jesus and the *ekklēsia* of the women who are called to become his disciples. The goal of feminist critical method is to "break the silence" developed by androcentrism that keeps women in the shadows and to bring them forth into the light in order to reconstruct their role and language in the history of the origins and expansion of early Christianity. Thus, feminist critical method seeks data and clues that enable this historical task to take place. This requires not only historical efforts to discover these materials about and by women, but also the dismantling of the framework of systemic androcentricism that pervades Western culture and the chauvinistic historical-critical method pursued by men. Thus, historical-critical scholarship can point to the problem of the absence and marginalization of women, but it cannot deconstruct its own hermeneutical framework of interpretation. This androcentrism is evident in translations (e.g., the use of the term *men* for "people," *man* for "person," and male imagery for God) and interpretation. Examples include the understanding of the name Junia as a shortened form of the male name Junianus, instead of regarding it as a frequently occurring female name, and the regarding of Phoebe in Rom 16:1-3 as a servant or helper, instead of as one who held the office of deacon, an influential role in the early Christian community (cf. 1 Cor 3:5-9). Androcentrism is also apparent in the election of sources by refusing to give proper weight to those that deal with women. This is seen even in the Gospel of Luke, for example, who indicates that Christianity's mission was almost entirely a male affair.

One may also see a significant degree of patriarchy in the process of canonization and the function of canon theologically in the early church. Canonization, in Schüssler Fiorenza's view, occurred during the time of intense struggle over the role of women in the church and, in particular, their leadership. With the patriarchal supremacy that emerged from these conflicts, canonization was a decidedly antifeminine process that included the depiction of women's views as heresy. It was the "orthodox" church and its male leadership that gained the upper hand in arguing that it preserved the true line of continuity with Jesus and his disciples. This culminated in the doctrine of apostolic succession. The various splinter groups of Christians sought to establish their relationship and identity with this true line of succession. These included not only the male-dominated "orthodox" Christians, but also Montanists, gnostics of different kinds, and women who pointed both to Mary Magdalene, Salome, and Martha as belonging to the line succession and to prophetesses who continued to speak divine messages. Those upholding these women stressed the women prophets in apostolic times (see those mentioned in Rom 16), emphasized the egalitarian body of Christ in Gal 3:28, and even preserved texts in which women were key participants (see, for example, the Acts of Paul and Thecla). Yet the androcentric party pointed to the lack of the women among the disciples Jesus commissioned to preach and to their absence at the Last Supper. Deutero-Pauline household codes were composed that were designed to place women in roles of subjection. This antifeminine, androcentric view continued into the church fathers (cf. especially Tertullian), whose polemics against women demonstrate that this contestation of women's role continued well into the third century. Women were made to be responsible for the entrance of sin in the world through the Fall, for the temptation of the angels who fell from heaven, and ultimately for much of church heresy. Thus, the canon became the document of the androcentric, antifeminine group, who won this battle of the book in the history of the early church.

Since this is obvious, the response of the feminist historian must be one of suspicion in examining the "evidence" of Scripture that is antifeminine. In addition, it is through the consideration of sources that are noncanonical that this male bias especially may be exposed. What occurred in Christianity was no less true in Judaism. These androcentric texts of much of the canon do not reflect history, but rather reveal the sexism of the canonizers. Schüssler Fiorenza argues that historians must use their imagination, intrinsic to historiography, in retelling the story of Christian origins and the expansion of the church.

Schüssler Fiorenza then articulates her model of historical reconstruction that facilitates the rewriting of early Christianity. Historians of every persuasion no longer operate with the naïve assumption that they may set forth what really happened, although this view is pervasive in popular circles. Nevertheless, historians for most of the modern period since the Enlightenment have espoused the simplistic view of the formation of the church from the ministry of Jesus to the apostles, to the establishment of communities, to the victory of the Great Church in the time of Constantine. This reconstruction was guided by the philosophy of positivism in which data existed as "real" entities, the interpreter could lay aside personal values and beliefs, and the construal of data into what actually happened according to the principle of cause and effect. However, in the period since World War II, other philosophies of history were constructed that supplemented those of Romanticism, idealism, and positivism, with the result that even positivism no longer prevails as the singular, unquestioned philosophical frame for writing contemporary history.

Historians have long recognized that good history writing requires a "unifying vision," born of the imagination, that guides the inspiration, goal, and interpretation of the data in a compelling way that makes sense within a particular philosophical framework, whether positivism, Marxism, neo-Marxism, feminism, postcolonialism, and so forth. Historians argue over the various "visions" and the construal and interpretation of the data in a particular relationship that leads to the reconstruction of the past. For feminist historical reconstruction, new questions must be asked and answered within the conceptual framework of an interpretative model that reconstrues the evidence in new and convincing ways. However, this does not mean that its reconstruction is the answering of the overarching question of "what really happened?"; rather, possibilities are articulated to explain and interpret the past within one dominant scenario.

The feminist model gives a significant place to the social categories of the disinherited and the marginals to whom the gospel was preached and who formed the core of the early communities. Those who were not among the privileged included not only the poor and illiterate, but also intellectuals, foreigners, and former slaves who had their own intellectual and experiential resources but lacked the sociopolitical power and status to set them forth in public view and written texts. Various social models have been proposed by New Testament historians who portray the early Jesus movement as "aggressive," "revolutionary," "charismatic," or "millenarian." These models have pointed to the antifamilial or afamilial character of the early Christian movement. At times an ethic of *agape* is isolated from texts that smooth over inequalities of members. While different in details, these reconstructions explain the process of the gradual patriarchalization of the church, the movement from charism to church office, transition from a radical love ethic to an ethos of privilege, and from egalitarianism to hierarchy. Yet a feminist model of historical reconstruction is to analyze this developing patriarchalization of the Christian community and to reflect upon it theologically.

In dealing with the problems of writing women's history, the feminist historian understands that the ideas of men about women, reflected in the data and its interpretation, do not necessarily reflect women's historical reality, since so much of the materials and their interpretation issue from the androcentricity of antiquity. Feminist historians require a theoretical framework for the interpretation of women's historical experience.

This theoretical framework Schüssler Fiorenza finds in the commonality of women's historical experiences and their struggles to achieve full humanity within the private sphere of the family and the public domain. In this model, religion emerged as a "middle zone" between the private and public spheres. Hellenistic mystery cults were often subversive of the order of patriarchy in the household and the larger society. Yet these associations provided the contexts for women's symbolic deconstruction of patriarchy and independence. This attracted women to early Christianity and Judaism. Thus, the afamilial orientation of these religions allow androcentric texts and their symbolizations to be understood. The hostility toward these groups of women emanated from "middle-class" patriarchal households attempting to subject women to menial status. But for a time, the women who participated in early Christianity and the emancipation of marginal groups points to its anti-state, antipatriarchal demeanor in the larger hierarchic, male-centered Greco-Roman world.

The Feminist Reconstruction of Early Christianity

Schüssler Fiorenza points to three important issues that confront the historian in attempting to reconstruct the history of early Christianity:

1. Are there two distinct and different forms of early Christianity, or are these differences simply the creations of the extant literature?

2. How is historical criticism used to move from the gospel literature to the historical Jesus and the early beginnings of the movement?

3. Especially important for her work, how can the story of Jewish women be reconstructed when the sparsity of texts and the patriarchy of surviving literature make it a very difficult process?

In the second section of *In Memory of Her,* she traces topics identified by these titles: "Jesus Movement as Renewal Movement with Judaism," "The Early Christian Missionary Movement: Equality in the Power of the Spirit," and "Neither Male nor Female: Galatians 3:28—Alternative Vision and Pauline Modification."

For Schüssler Fiorenza, the Jesus movement was one of numerous renewal movements in Judaism in the first century C.E.: apocalyptic, prophetic, and cultic. The role of women in these groups is difficult to articulate, since there is no direct information in the sources. It is likely the Sadducees and Pharisees interpreted women in terms of the written Torah, including matters like marriage and purity rules. We are unclear as to whether the Pharisees allowed women to enter their ranks. In Qumran, while burials and infrequently the literature have revealed the presence of women and children in the community *(Manual of Discipline* and the *Rule)*, the woman's role is not known. Certainly, the construction of the community was based on the model of a male military camp. In the view of Josephus *(Antiquities* XVIII.21), the Essenes did not bring wives and slaves into the community because they believed women would bring dissension and slaves injustice. Wisdom and apocalyptic were also negative in their views of women (see especially Ben Sira). Yet not all ancient Jewish literature was sexist. The book of Judith, which Schüssler Fiorenza dates to the first century B.C.E., is a heroic biography that indicates women had the rights to inherit property, manage their husband's estate through a woman steward, reject remarriage, and decide to dedicate their life to a strict religious observance. Judith was well educated, articulate, and beautiful (a beauty that could not have been veiled) yet could use her feminine gifts in the treacherous murder of an evil man who was captivated by her charm and made the fatal mistake of disregarding her strength of resolve and wisdom. Her victory is viewed as the victory of her people and demonstrated the justice of God, who was compassionate toward the oppressed. She lived to age 105 and distributed her wealth to her husband's and her own families. This romance points to a different view of women in the time of renewal movements.

The Jesus movement understood, as did other groups, that Israel is the elect of God and that the kingdom of God was already present. Disregarding essentially the Torah and the temple, this movement understood humanity in terms of the wholeness of creation. Everyone is invited to participate in this new Israel—men, women, and sinners. Thus, the miracles of Jesus reflect this wholeness in the healing of men and women, and his table fellowship is equally inclusive. Those who were allowed to participate in this *basileia* included not only men and women, but also the infirm, sinners, prostitutes, tax collectors, the persecuted, the poor, even those who were outcasts from their own communities. Among the followers of Jesus were women: Mary of Magdala, from whom seven demons were excised, the woman who washed Jesus' feet, Mary his mother, and Mary and Martha, the sisters of Lazarus. The Syro-Phoenician woman healed by Jesus is told to go and proclaim what has happened to her, and the deformed woman who praised God testifies to Jesus' healing that came by means of the power of God. The woman who anoints Jesus in Mark engages in a prophetic act that proclaims through her action Jesus is the Messiah. Thus, whenever the gospel is preached, the act of this woman prophet is to be remembered.

Perhaps the most provocative and yet controversial thesis of Schüssler Fiorenza is her representation of the "Sophia-God" of Jesus and the discipleship of women who followed him.[17] The parable of the shepherd looking for the lost sheep and the woman searching for her lost silver coin is likely taken by Luke from Q to emphasize the joy that results from finding the lost. One of the images, then, is of God as a woman searching for one of her lost coins, a metaphor that is a striking, atypical image of God in the first century C.E. According to Schüssler Fiorenza, the Jesus traditions present a gracious God in the image of divine Sophia, as indicated in a Q saying in Luke 7:35 where Sophia's children include sinners, tax collectors, and prostitutes. For Q, Jesus and John are the most eminent of these children, but Matthew later identifies Sophia with Jesus. Jesus-Sophia is justified by her deeds. In Jewish wisdom, the cult of the goddess is integrated into the theology of monotheism and the gracious goodness of Israel's God. Sophia is teacher, beloved, sister, wife, mother, and queen, and she is the instrument of divine creation who makes all things new. While known by many names in the extant literature, Isis, the closest Hellenistic representation of Wisdom, is a very important one. Divine Sophia becomes the offspring and even consort of Israel's God. At other times God assumes the language and form of the goddess. Thus, Sophia is at first identified with God and then, later, with Jesus, since he originally understood himself as the prophet and child of Wisdom. The language of Jesus appropriates on occasion that of Wisdom (cf. Matt 11:28-30). Her envoys, originally understood as John and Jesus, are persecuted and killed (Luke 13:34, Q).

The disciples of Jesus were to continue the preaching, teaching, and works of Jesus, who initiated a movement of equals. Eventually they not only imitate his/her works, but also come to understand the community he/she envisioned as Jesus-Sophia. Eventually this community came to include not only Jews of all social and gender strata, but also Gentiles. The Jesus movement had as its driving force the liberation from patriarchal structures and the establishment of a community of equals. Economic exploitation and patriarchy are to be understood together, especially when it is recognized that in the first century widows and orphans were those who had the greatest need. The preaching of Jesus sought to disassemble

---

17. See the development of this view in *Jesus: Miriam's Child, Sophia's Prophet.* Not all feminists agree with Schüssler Fiorenza's reuse of the Sophia imagery in the construction of the ministry of Jesus and her later identification of Jesus with Sophia. Schottroff, in "Wanderprophetinnen," argues against this by noting that "Wisdom" in Israelite and Jewish religion belongs to patriarchal wisdom circles of male sages who are teaching elitist men. Levine, a Jewish feminist New Testament scholar, also questions whether Q is actually so positive toward women. Levine, "Who's Catering the Q Affair?"

the structures of poverty and patriarchy by establishing a community in which human relationships were understood in new ways. This was a community of equals undivided by social status, gender, and ethnicity.

The second period in the development of early Christianity reconstructed by Schüssler Fiorenza is the missionary movement. Sources that deal with this movement are lacking for the critical period between 30 and 50 C.E. The letters of Paul were written in the 50s until the middle of the 60s, while Acts is a literary source best positioned as coming at the end of the first century C.E. Acts does not appear to be aware of the Pauline correspondence and contains many problems that were addressed by Paul's letters. In addition, the two major figures of Acts are Peter and Paul. In it no women were among the original apostles, nor were they among the Hellenists in Jerusalem or singled out as important in the church at Antioch. However, women are mentioned as being significant players in the expansion of the early church. These include Tabitha, Jappa, and Lydia, who are mentioned as important persons in Antioch, Thessalonica, and Beroea. Damas in Athens, Prisca in Corinth, Drusilla, the wife of governor Festus, and Bernice, the wife of Agrippa, held significant social rank and public stature. Acts especially refers to women who are well known in their social environs and are wealthy.

In Rome women of elevated social status were among the Godfearers and proselytes of Judaism. As was true in Judaism, the Christian evangelists required the hospitality of the "house churches" held in the homes of the elite who had become early converts. Barnabas appears to have been prosperous, and Paul was a Roman citizen from a Hellenistic family of privilege. The Pauline correspondence mentions women among the coworkers of the apostle: Prisca, Apphia (a sister), Phoebe (sister, *diakonos*, *prostasis*), and Junia (apostle). These women were his fellow laborers to whom the Christians were to be subject and who engaged in admonishment. In Rom 16:6, 12, he commends Mary, Tryphaena, Tryphosas, and Persis for their hard "labor" in the world. Schüssler Fiorenza concludes that Paul regarded women as equals in his work. In Phil 4:2-3, Euodia and Syntyche "competed" as in a race alongside Paul. Phoebe is a minister of the entire church of Cenchreae, not simply a pastor to women. There were also missionary couples, including Prisca and Aquila and Andronicus and Junia, who are linked together in the missionary movement, but the women are not called "wives," but rather colaborers. The Acts of Paul and Thecla presents a woman missionary who "teaches the word of God," a person to whom even as late as the third century, women in Carthage appealed for their authority to teach. Her relationship with Paul is one of spiritual love.

Schüssler Fiorenza's analysis of the missionary movement takes into consideration the house church. House churches were not only the domiciles where missionaries were received and given hospitality, but also the location of proclamation and worship. Whether the entire family, consisting of members, servants, slaves, and unmarried women relatives, converted to Christianity when the owner of the house did is not clear. But the social strata represented in the house churches point to the variety of groups who were members of the early Christian communities. Of course, the meeting place of the household was the common location for the celebration of other Eastern religions. These house churches were egalitarian, admitting into membership people from every social stratum and making no differentiation between male and female. However, the missionary movement did not find its prototype in the Greco-Roman patriarchal household or in the patriachalism that was less harsh in its male domination.

Once again Schüssler Fiorenza's understanding of the Sophia myth enters into her analysis of the theological depiction of the Christianity of the missionary movement. An important facet of this theology was the power of the Spirit present among the believers. In 1 Cor 1:24, Christ is preached to both Jews and Greeks as "the power of God" and the "Sophia of God." Thus, there is the identification of the Spirit with Sophia that leads to divine presence, life, and liberation. Believers "in Christ" are possessed by God's Spirit and the Spirit of Wisdom. Faith becomes the basis for salvation. The Christian community becomes the "new creation" (2 Cor 5:17). The resurrected Christ is identified with both the Spirit of God and the Sophia of God. The Lord of the Jesus movement is no longer a prophet of divine Sophia, but has now divine Sophia herself. This theology is expressed in the pre-Pauline hymns of Phil 2:6-11, 1 Tim 3:16, Col 1:15-20, Eph 2:14-16, Heb 1:3, 1 Pet 3:18, 22, and John 1:1-14. These proclaim in language taken from Hellenistic Jewish wisdom theology and contemporary mystery religions the universal scope of salvation in Christ. Thus, mythological language from Hellenistic Jewish wisdom and from the myth of Osiris-Isis is used to shape the discourse of the missionary movement's Christology. Similarities may be found in gnostic texts.

Yet, for Paul, this theological discourse is not allowed to exist in an ahistorical mythical framework, but instead is grounded historically in the earthly Jesus and continued through his community especially by means of placement in the context of moral paraenesis. This Christ-Sophia has come to the dwelling place of humanity to fashion a new people to be the "sons and daughters of God," an egalitarian community that allows no dichotomies (Gal 3:28). In Paul's theological understanding issuing from the baptismal formula of Gal 3:28, the tension between the early Christian community and the larger society is neutralized. Nevertheless, women are admonished to make some accommodations to the society in which the community exists. And in the marriage of believers to nonbelievers, the believers are not to separate from their pagan spouses. Wives' behavior is subjugated to husbands, and women are to refrain from speaking in the assembly. Thus, his theological understanding of equality between the sexes in the faith is compromised in society and worship. These limitations become the basis in the post-Pauline tradition for the elimination of women from leadership of the entire community, and for limiting their ministry only to other women.

In the third section, Schüssler Fiorenza traces the emergence of patriarchy in the church. Most of the New Testament literature, save for the epistles of Paul, was composed in the last third of the first century. The Christian community of this period appeared to be experiencing difficulties with the Greco-Roman society in which they lived. This led the church into an adoption of the patriarchal social features that characterized life in the different locations of the empire. However, while the post-Pauline and pseudo-Petrine writers attempt to restrict women's roles in the community in order to make it acceptable to the understanding and rules of decorum in the later society, it is important to note that the evangelists Mark and John, as known in the tradition, create for women an apostolic and ministerial leadership. These narrators perpetuate the roles of women from the early Jesus movement, leading to a clash of visions that would end only with the victory of patriarchy in the coming centuries.

The epilogue to Schüssler Fiorenza's book, titled "Toward a Feminist Biblical Spirituality: The *ekklēsia* of Women," lays out in comprehensive form her hermeneutical construction. Schüssler Fiorenza works out the implications of her historical reconstruction of early Christianity by addressing its "spiritual implications." These are developed in more detail in subsequent books, which will be examined in the following section, but her initial reflections are important to mention at this point. She speaks as a feminist whose experiences as a woman have led to her bonding with her sisters who have had and continue to have a similar set of experiences. This sisterhood provides both empowerment and the stimulus for seeking to establish a discipleship of equals. This feminist community will no longer be content to exist on the margins of the church but rather, in solidarity with all people everywhere who are oppressed and impoverished, will enter into the mainstream of the church and bring about a transformation of both its vision and its way of living and believing.

The term *ekklēsia* is a political one from the world of the early church and refers to an assembly of free citizens to make their own decisions in political and spiritual dealings. This term thus refers to the goal of empowered women to participate as full-fledged members of the church and to engage in its decision-making processes. Thus, women, existing and acting in solidarity, are to live out and realize a new vision of a truly egalitarian church by which the world is transformed. The sources from earliest Christianity provide support for this experience, as do the women in the faith who have gone before. This earliest form of Christianity consisted of relationships, not doctrines, mystical migrations, and cultic rituals.

The objection that the *ekklēsia* of women is not inclusive fails to realize that the Catholic Church has always had communities of women. Indeed, the Protestant Reformation's elimination of these communities has contributed to even greater patriarchy. The Roman Catholic Church has sought to control women's communities by male hierarchy, liturgy, law, and spirituality. Yet there have always been communities of women who have continued to exist free of clerical control. Their history and spirituality are recognized as the heritage for a feminist liberationist hermeneutic. Schüssler Fiorenza responds to the commonly voiced objection that this community does not embrace men. Yet the centuries of male hierarchy have exacted their toll on women, and it is not possible now to build the community of egalitarianism that still waits for realization in the future. The images of tradition that women embrace include the exodus, which signifies women leaving all behind that has imprisoned them, including a loving community with men. Women are to live in their own communities, abandon the structure of the patriarchal family, and engage in the quest for liberation. The spirituality of this community comes from the presence and indwelling of Sophia-Spirit, the solidarity of women based on experience and relationship, and the active engagement of liberation. As long as women are defined as sexual beings by the church, they cannot say, "This is my body." Women's bodies have been raped, battered, sterilized, and made the subject of males seeking to control their reproductive systems through male legislation. This community is the center, then, where the memories of women in the past and the enactment of liberation and equality in the present and future must occur. Only in this community are women able to celebrate their foresisters' deeds and lives in "memory of her." "In breaking the bread and sharing the cup we proclaim not only the passion and resurrection of Christ but also celebrate that of women in Biblical religion."[18]

18. Schlüssler-Fiorenza, *In Memory of Her*, 351.

Christology: Miriam's Child and Sophia's Prophet

Schüssler Fiorenza presents her understanding of Christology[19] by focusing especially on the theoretical frameworks for the discourses as Jesus Christ. Her concern is the possible "contamination" of the interpretation of these discourses by their social locations in the academy and the contemporary church. It has become a truism that the Bible, history, and theology have assisted in shaping the major metanarratives of Western society that are hierarchic and controlling in the worldviews they encapsulate. So, Schüssler Fiorenza asks, within this larger setting, what would a feminist Christology look like? A feminist Christology must develop and exist in the face of contrary religious and academic opposition and by disputing the sense of helplessness pervading the media reports of world events over which there appears to be no control. This Christology seeks to empower the marginals, victims, and oppressed, whose dreams are often shattered by contrary forces of oppression. Two worlds stand before us: one of a radicalized democracy in which all participate to improve their lives and one of a dictatorship of controlling and privileged nation-states, whose policies advance the well-being of only a small percentage of the global population. "Ludic" or even nihilistic theories of postmodernists engage in games that offer no salvation from destructive forces. A critical feminist liberationist hermeneutic attempts to engage in the establishment and proliferation of radical democracy and economic justice for all. Religion's role in these matters will depend on whether some will adopt a feminist liberationist mode or be driven by patriarchy and/or fundamentalism. Schüssler Fiorenza seeks a hermeneutic that blends a common rejection of oppression, racism, exploitation, heterodoxy, and colonialism.

Christological doctrines and formulations were formed at the time the so-called orthodoxy gained prominence, beginning in the Constantinian church of the Roman Empire. The "kyriarchal[20] order of the household" was the paradigm for the universe, the state, and then the church as understood in the fourth and fifth centuries, when the Nicene and Chalcedonian creeds were promulgated as the summary of the Christian faith. The Chalcedonian creed in particular was political in that it was shaped by the imperial

19. The book bearing this title speaks of Jesus as both the child of Miriam and the messenger of Woman Wisdom, who continues to lead the church toward the realization of egalitarian vision.

20. See, e.g., *Bread Not Stone,* afterword, p. 211, n. 6. There she defines kyriarchy as "a social and discursive system that interstructures gender, race, class, and colonialist oppressions and has as its focal point women at the bottom of the sociopolitical and religious pyramid." She considers her use of the word *patriarchy* in this sense to require more explicit definition. She views patriarchy, or the power and control of men, to be one of the structures of kyriarchy, a much more encompassing term.

politics of domination and exploitation. It introduced a series of dualisms between fatherhood/masculinity, divinity, and eternity and motherhood/ femininity, the earthly, and humanity. Placed in opposition are genders, church and world, religion and nature, and heaven and earth. Yet the Chalcedonian creed included also a reference to St. Euphemia's Oratory, which gave ideological space to the feminine. Upon this feminine element, feminist critical hermeneutics may build. And the setting for this formulation is the *ekklēsia* of women. This gives space and nurtures a discourse for women that is in opposition to the kyriarchy of the early and modern church.

Schüssler Fiorenza refines in her second chapter the key issues in feminist Christology. First, the myth of "true womanhood" that defines women's roles in regard to their elitist husbands essentially makes them the appendages of classism and racism. The goal of this definition is kyriarchal, born of classism and not anthropology, while it is opposed by a Christology that rejects hierarchy and patriarchy. Further, elite clerical males who argue Christ was not a woman also espouse a kyriarchic theology that is contradicted by a Christology of the suffering Christ who, like women, including female slaves whose children were sold into slavery, undergoes the same type of oppression and dehumanization nourished by overt racism. The incarnation does not extol the maleness of Christ, but rather points to the belief that he was born of God and a woman, Mary. Thus, kyriarchal Christology is not normative for Christian faith, experience, and practice. A feminist liberationist Christology proclaims a God, not in systematic formulations, but rather in terms of justice that subverts kyriarchal domination. This Christology requires theologians to assume responsibility for their hermeneutical frameworks and for the interpretations they develop. Theologians are to engage in a battle against kyriarchic power structures that dominate and oppress marginals. The various christological images in Scripture and theology are exercised to achieve this emancipation of captives.

While Christology is important for Schüssler Fiorenza's feminist theology, she argues that soteriological concerns take precedence over this theological feature. This is because women in a variety of religions are to join together in the struggle for liberation. She also places the social-cultural dimension over the individual-anthropological one. The feminist struggle is a global one with the goal of transforming and dismantling the kyriarchy that permeates all religions, cultures, and nation-states.

The theology of the cross has the endemic problems of presenting Jesus' death as self-sacrifice, radical obedience, and atonement. This theology provides a religious value for suffering and death that, unless proclaimed within the context of the empty tomb, can become debilitating to any striving for liberation. The God of the empty tomb is the one who takes up dwelling among the living, not the dead. In the celebration of the *ekklēsia,* women experience and testify not only to the suffering of Christ but also to the risen Lord who dwells in their midst and enables them to experience new life.

Schüssler Fiorenza comments on what has been one of the most puzzling features of the New Testament. While Jewish and Gnostic literatures said a great deal about divine wisdom, set forth in feminine imagery, the early canonical writings have preserved only a few traces. These features of Woman Wisdom were either reconstrued through the male image of the Logos or reattributed to Mary the mother of Jesus. However, this rediscovery of Sophia-God and Sophia-Christ is based on the recognition that language is constructed through sociocultural means and is not reflective of reality. The attempt to attribute gender to an entity due to the use of a masculine or feminine noun is wrongheaded and must be abandoned. While the feminist liberationist scholars do not simply reconstruct and reuse the language of wisdom theology in early Christianity and Judaism, they nevertheless are compelled to struggle with masculine conventional language for God and the male authority derived from this language. The goal is the deconstruction of the sex/gender system used to formulate the patriarchal theology of God and Christ.

Finally, Mary the mother of Jesus has been mythologized to such an extent that the church has essentially stripped her of all her humanity. Yet Roman Catholic theology has been able to provide a rich resource for viewing God as present in a woman and in using feminine discourse to speak of incarnation and liberation. The rescuing of her humanity is necessary for a feminist liberationist theology. It is necessary because it presents a young Jewish woman, who is pregnant out of wedlock, turns for help to another woman who praises her and the child she is bearing, and sings the magnificat to the God who has elected her. This humanity of Mary speaks a discourse of liberation from the domination of kyriatric laws that proclaim a child born out of wedlock to be a bastard and the woman who bears him/her to be a sinner, having defiled herself with illicit intercourse. She struggles for dignity and self-worth and becomes the Mary to whom women victims look for their identity and comfort.

A Critical Feminist Liberationist Hermeneutic

Schüssler Fiorenza has continued to produce a steady stream of provocative texts outlining her hermeneutical approach with the addition of new insights and applications to historical issues. Here I shall only briefly touch on the key themes she articulates in her writings. She constructs a model of interpretation that engages Scripture both historically and theologically in present discourse. The model, as she sees it, overcomes the hermeneutical gaps and separations between past and present, sense and meaning, critique and consent, explanation and understanding, reading behind and in front of the text, and distanciation and empathy.

In her statements on hermeneutics, Schüssler Fiorenza articulates the distinctive features of her thinking and theological reflection. She constructs a model of four parts that delineates the significant strategies of critical feminist liberationist hermeneutics:

1. The first strategy is to begin exegetical and theological work with a hermeneutics of suspicion toward male, traditional interpretations of the Bible and theologies that have resulted in either debilitating interpretations of the feminine in the biblical world or in silencing and making invisible women in these social worlds.

2. Another interpretative strategy emphasizes "memory" (the major tool of reconstruction) that enables the careful scholar to search for, discover, and analyze biblical and nonbiblical sources for constructing a historical narrative that stands in opposition to the sexist narrative of men in the church's history and in the history of interpretation.

3. The process of evaluation includes affirming the authentic dimensions in the text and understanding and then proclaiming these through word and deed—i.e., through preaching and writing that allows feminist narratives entrance into the sacred domain of the church and the halls of the academy.

4. The activity of imagination builds on the historian's long-held recognition that reconstruction and interpretation are not limited to "facts" that interpret themselves through the canons of reason and empiricism, long a traditional argument of what has been the dominant approach to historiography, i.e., positivism. In addition, imagination is invoked in other forms of experience, including the creation of and participation in liturgy and ritual, spirituality, prayer, art, and writing and singing hymns.

These four strategies especially gain their power from within the community of wo/men[21] who derive insight and strength from each other's

---

21. She began to use the term *wo/man, wo/men* in her 1994 book *Jesus: Miriam's Child, Sophia's Prophet*. She uses the term to underscore the instability and ambiguity as well as the linguistic inclusivity of the words *woman* and *women*. Wo/man, she explains, is defined not simply by gender but also by race, class, and colonial structures of oppression. The term is inclusive and means in most places "people" (*Rhetoric and Ethic*, 9).

experiences and understandings and seek to transform the interpretative and social worlds accessible through exegesis and constructive theology. These experiences and understandings eliminate the "malestream"[22] traditions that have led to the demeaning and marginalization of women. This critical feminist liberationist hermeneutic engages and seeks to countermand the dominance of the positivist, male-oriented, scientific paradigms of academy and church.

Schüssler Fiorenza also speaks of a paradigm in theology that is given life by the variety of liberationists. This paradigm shift at work in her critical theology of liberation is a movement away from the modern "malestream" of tradition and engagement. The four elements of this shift she calls changes in interpretative goals, in epistemology, in consciousness, and in the central theological questions.[23] Change, as she uses the term, is not passive, but active. She means that her critical theology of liberation is an effort to transform sociopolitical and hermeneutical realities at work in the globe that oppress rather than liberate. Who are the interlocutors of her hermeneutic? They are the marginals who have been forced to exist on the social and cultural peripheries of collective life and whose voices are silenced by the dominant paradigm of control. The proper scholarly decorum is not neutral objectivity, but rather active, militant resistance to oppressive structures and direct engagement in the efforts at transformation leading to liberation. This world of oppression can be transformed with active involvement in the process of creating change. It is not closed or impervious to countermeasures designed to subvert its power structure.

In *Rhetoric and Ethic*, she sets forth her understanding of language as a form of power. She seeks to engage biblical scholars in the transformative work of justice by seeing clearly and accepting their responsibility to use the power of their language in interpretation for the cause of struggles for emancipation of marginals from oppressive power structures.[24] This does not mean that this awareness and appropriate use of the power of language

22. This is a term she coins to describe the dominant male theological tradition that has developed throughout Christian history and male exegetical interpretations of Scripture.

23. These questions, clearly described in *Bread Not Stone*, afterword, 169–72, are the constructive theological basis for her work.

24. She argues, "A critical rhetorical-emancipatory process of interpretation challenges practitioners of Biblical studies and readers of the Bible to become more theo-ethically sophisticated readers by problematizing both the modernist ethos of Biblical studies and their own sociopolitical locations and functions in global structures of domination. At the same time, it enables them to struggle for a more just and radical democratic cosmopolitan articulation of religion in the global polis" (*Rhetoric and Ethic*, 54).

Mary Ann Tolbert is one of the editors, with Fernando Segovia, of *Reading from This Place* 1, which contains numerous, provocative essays dealing with the politics of social location and the interpretation of the Bible in the academic guild. Her concluding essay's title

is limited to the canonical writings of Christianity or that only the intellectual or expert may participate. Traditions and peoples of other religious traditions may also become involved in shaping a new world paradigm that eliminates elitist power structures and sets up structures of justice and humanity for all. Finally, this hermeneutical effort occurs within the sociopolitical structures operative in the world and seeks to change them through active confrontation. This effort becomes all the more imperative when it is recognized that what is at stake is humanity and humanization— indeed, survival itself. The social context for this activity begins within the community of wo/men, who gather strength, and then launch their resistance to and overthrow of kyriarchy. In *But She Said,* she characterizes this wo/men's *ekklēsia* as a radical democratic movement that has its origins in the efforts of the suffragists and the prophetic leadership of Elizabeth Cady Stanton.

One other dimension of her hermeneutics should be recognized, for it is critical in gaining insight into her interpretation of the Bible and theology. This is, to state it simply, the matter of context. All ways of interpreting the Bible, history, and contemporary society and politics occur within the location of a particular context. The three elements that come together for an interpretative moment but then shift into other arrangements, are the texts, the readers, and the contexts, not only of the text, but also of the different interpreters. As the arrangements continue to shift, so does meaning. This explicitly requires the hermeneutical process of reflection in which interpretation takes cognizance of the differences of the contexts of texts and readers and seeks to engage in sociorhetorical, epistemological,

---

directly states this relation: "The Politics and Poetics of Location." This volume was generated at a national conference at Vanderbilt University that took into view diversity, the impact of social location on interpretation, and the paradigm of power generated in and sustained by the academic study of religion but also present in many forms of Christianity. Her essay, which brings together the salient points of the discussions held at Vanderbilt, emphasizes that individuals and groups cannot so transcend their social locations that these are irrelevant to understanding both the people who composed, edited, and transmitted the Bible and later interpreters. She understands postmodernism not as a rejection of history or even of Enlightenment epistemology, but rather as a critical response to its excesses. The arguments of the Enlightenment about the natural condition of human beings and the "objectivity" of interpretation are rejected, but not the realization that social location plays a dominant role in thinking, writing, and interpreting. Postmodernism must seek to be based on Derrida's nihilism regarding uniformity or even indigenous rights, if it expects to engage in transformation of the social reality. Otherwise, it enters into a quiet passivity that has nothing substantial to offer. Tolbert prefers the politics of location that involves not only space, but also gender, race, and economics, to name some of the most important. This should enable the development of numerous alliances of social and ethnic groups to come into actuality and resist marginalization as unacceptable.

and ideological analysis. The hermeneut must be properly attuned to the power structure at work inside and outside the written documents and recognize that texts and interpretations invariably are shaped ideologically by self-interests. No text and no interpreter are interest-free. Meanings must be constructed and reconstructed in a continuing quest for liberation for all peoples of the world.

Schüssler Fiorenza explains that while there are different hermeneutical models at work in the church, hers is one that operates within the theological world of post–Vatican II, in which the Roman Catholic Church allowed not only the use of critical method, but also the recognition that not all Scripture is revelation, save for texts pertaining to salvation. Yet neither the Roman Catholic Church nor the Protestants have clearly articulated what "wo/men's" salvation actually is. Indeed, this revelation cannot be made once and for all. But it must be captured within the sociorhetorical structures at work for emancipation.

Her most important work, perhaps, for discussing her hermeneutical principles is *But She Said,* published in 1992. Here and elsewhere she contextualizes her hermeneutic within the history of theological approaches, especially taking note of the period since the Enlightenment, and demonstrates how her hermeneutic resonates with other liberation theologies that address the issues of marginals and—especially distinctive for her— the "radical democracy" of the past century in America that has witnessed feminist struggles for ending discrimination, obtaining justice, and unleashing the power of liberation.

Schüssler Fiorenza points to the fact that feminist scholars have long recognized the silencing of wo/men that has occurred in world history and the church. This silencing she interprets as due to kyriarchy, i.e., the domination of elite, propertied men over women and other men. She emphasizes that the purpose of feminist studies in all theological disciplines is to empower women to break the bondage of patriarchy and kyriarchy and to achieve the recognition of their God-given dignity. This means that women have the right, the authority, and the responsibility to speak, an action that includes shaping theological work, biblical studies, biblical hermeneutics, and ethical discourse.

Bread Not Stone

In *Bread Not Stone,* Schüssler Fiorenza notes (as does Gerald West in his postcolonial studies mentioned in chapter 8) an interesting but troubling paradox. On one hand, the Bible is an androcentric, patriarchal, oppressive book that has created misogynist attitudes and actions toward women for the centuries it has existed and been transmitted. Indeed, this very fact of biblical sexism has led some feminists away from biblical studies to other endeavors, whether they pursue a quest to discover cults of goddesses that were not dominated by patriarchy or move to entirely different fields of study. Some of their remarks about women engaged in biblical studies are pointedly critical. Yet, to return to the paradox, the Bible also has been viewed by wo/men, including some feminists, as a source of inspiration and an authoritative resource for unmasking and eliminating sexism at least in some of the biblical content. The biblical emphasis on the struggle for justice has been appropriated by feminist biblical scholars in order to provide a recognized authoritative basis for the quest for justice among all marginals, wo/men in general but also oppressed classes and nations that have suffered and continue to suffer under the heavy yoke of imperialism and colonialism now transformed into an insidious neocolonialism. Thus, the Bible is a two-edged sword that provides inspiration and theological engagement for the undoing of patriarchy yet also is involved improperly in the continued victimization of women and all marginals. The readings of conservative women who buy into patriarchal values espoused in the Bible are not critical feminist readings.

The beginning point in the resolution of this paradox is not with the Bible and its interpretation, but rather with every type of oppressive system that operates to control and demean marginals. Consequently, all experiences of oppressed women (and other marginals, for that matter) begins with the systemic experience of wo/men's dehumanization.

In developing her implications, Schüssler Fiorenza takes issue with structuralists and postmodernists who deny the possibility of historical meaning that may be obtained through critical methods. Indeed, she has been at times viewed (incorrectly, in my judgment) as a scholar who engages in opposing theory with politics so that her own views are significantly misrepresented as political and historical in contradistinction to theoretical. She is subjected to intense criticism for simply painting feminism like a thin veneer over the surfaces of historical criticism. In her view as a historian, she argues that critical method, combined with a critical feminist liberation hermeneutic, allows for the reconstruction of sociohistorical communities and roles in the past, including especially for her, the place and activities of wo/men. Especially important for feminist historians is the search to obtain suppressed data that may be presented in reconstructive work. This type of suppressed data about women may often be fragmentary, but it is still significant in retelling the history of early Christianity.[25]

---

25. For the debate between "The Collective" and the interpretative work of Schüssler Fiorenza, see the former's *The Postmodern Bible*, ed. George Aichele, et al., which will be briefly examined in chapter 7, and Schüssler Fiorenza, *Sharing Her Word*, 15–21.

This data allows for a critical feminist historiographical reconstruction to take shape that both affects and is affected by a critical feminist liberationist hermeneutics.

She describes her hermeneutic as critical feminist liberation hermeneutics because she integrates feminism and liberation hermeneutics and opposes "malestream" languaging by using feminine critical discourse. This interplay of features leads to what she calls "the genre of hermeneutical genre reflection."[26] This reflective enterprise for the historian allows for the imaginative reconstruction of the past in a critically informed way.[27]

As one would expect of a historian with strong theological convictions, Fiorenza has a predilection for tradition. However, she seeks to place her work, not within the male theological tradition of Bultmann, Barth, Schleiermacher, Aquinas, and Augustine, but rather within that of women, named and unnamed, including such pivotal figures as Elizabeth Cady Stanton.[28]

How then does her historical and hermeneutical model relate to the writing of biblical theology? For Schüssler Fiorenza, biblical theology is a "public deliberative discourse of the *ekklēsia.*"[29] The discourse of biblical theology must be constructed by the *ekklēsia,* a pluriform community of all people, who are not differentiated on the basis of class, wealth, education, gender, and geography. Each member of this community must be free to speak in shaping the theological understanding of Scripture. She writes:

> Biblical theology that understands itself as a politics of *ekklēsia* attempts to trace and revalorize the early Christian egalitarian traditions. At the same time it seeks to displace the politics and rhetorics of subordination and otherness that are inscribed in the "Pauline" correspondence with a politics and rhetorics of equality and respon-

---

The chapter on feminism in *The Postmodern Bible* is poorly researched and inadequately argued. The Collective's argument misunderstands Schüssler Fiorenza's work by suggesting that somehow she is not a theorist or that she polarizes by assuming a political stance.

26. See *Bread Not Stone*, 1995, afterword, 156–57.

27. See Collingwood, *History as Imagination.*

28. Schüssler Fiorenza notes two fundamental points made by Stanton in *The Women's Bible:* (1) it is not a neutral book but becomes a political weapon for women in their quest for emancipation; and (2) the texts were shaped by men who never saw or talked with God. Her scholarship was based on the knowledge of Hebrew and Greek and the higher criticism of the day. She has recognized that the Bible has been used by men to keep women in subjection to restrict their emancipation from male domination. Social reform has to be all-inclusive, meaning it must confront inequality in society and in the Bible. She also argues forcefully that the proper translation of the Bible was misconstrued by men. But her fundamental point is the Bible had been politicized by men for the subjection of women to male dominance and control.

29. *Rhetoric and Ethic*, 191.

sibility. It conceives of early Christian writings as taking sides in the emancipatory struggles of antiquity and conceptualizes early Christian community as a radical democratic assembly *(ekklēsia)* of differing theological voices and socio-rhetorical practices.[30]

This radical, democratic politics of equality sets forth a theology of the divine *politeuma,* or city of citizens, that becomes its theological basis and structure. Therefore, the Bible and other resources may be used in the proclamation of a gospel of inclusiveness in which all people share the well-being of reality within the contours of justice. This is indeed the "Kingdom of Heaven"—not an otherworldly unattainable vision of some lofty future, but rather the dwelling place of God and the children of God that becomes the *polis* or city from which the authority of the word goes forth to eliminate oppressive power structures. In this place, the kyrarchic power structures of elitist males vying for domination of the kingdom are confronted, fought, and defeated. This structural base disallows scholars to set forth Christianity as a sectarian movement engaged in conflict that seeks to wrest power from others and to exclude their participation. This base also deconstructs the hetero-orthodox controversies that lead to polarization, victimization, and marginality. This base does not privilege elitist spokesmen, such as Paul, to define authoritatively, once and for all what is true or false theologically, but rather turns to the victims whose voices may be rediscovered, if only in fragmented form, in the canon and other Christian writings.

This type of biblical theology recognizes the necessity of reflection on social-political as well as communal practices and relationships and the importance of moving beyond historical reconstruction to a critical rhetorical engagement of the present in and through the theology of justice and equality that may be discovered particularly in Sophia-Wisdom and embodied in the community of the *ekklēsia.* Once the power of the language of the elite is deconstructed, it is then replaced with the construction of a radically democratic, egalitarian community. Truth is not a hidden mystery revealed only to a select view, as in apocalyptic vision, but is an authoritative norm comprehended by the integration of the voices of the *ekklēsia.* This norm comes through an historical process of radical struggle and debate among equals.[31]

---

30. *Rhetoric and Ethic,* 188.
31. She states that there is a need to "reformulate Biblical theology as a critical rhetoric and politics of meaning that is positioned in the public square of the *ekklēsia.*" *Rhetoric and Ethic,* 193. This means then that biblical studies in capturing this enduring vision can "critically address public political discourses and individual questions seeking for a world of justice and well-being."

As noted above, in *Rhetoric and Ethic*, Schüssler Fiorenza addresses the politics of biblical studies. This politicizing of the field is due in part to the controlling power of language and the linguistic dominion in which patriarchy has taken refuge. To respond to this patriarchy and contribute even more to the hermeneutical debate concerning meaning both past and present, Schüssler Fiorenza develops a "critical rhetorical model of analysis." The first level of this paradigm of communication involves the movement from the rhetor to speech to audience. When this model is no longer operating on the level of speech, but rather on the content of the rhetor's communication that is transformed into a text, then the movement of understanding is from author to text to recipients who seek to understand the meaning in its and their contexts. Understanding the original text in its issuance in the past is one dimension of the process. Interpreting it for the present means placing more responsibility on the recipients to translate its meaning to a new context or contexts. In this mode of interpretation, the modern recipients have the responsibility of constructing new meaning. Schüssler Fiorenza adds that the interpretations of past communities of faith are not to be ignored, but they have contributed to the meanings that the texts have for the present.

In my judgment, this argument is easier for Jews and Roman Catholics than it is for Protestants. *Sola Scriptura* and the rejection of tradition that had gone before the Reformation in order to get to the original texts and their meanings have meant that many Protestant biblical scholars, including especially those who write biblical theologies, have given scant attention to the tradition of interpretation. This has impoverished the work of hermeneutics in Protestant circles. It also has emboldened elitist white males in dominating the construction of theological paradigms. While Schüssler Fiorenza does not model significantly in her own writings the role and place of tradition, at least she endorses the importance of tradition in seeking solidarity with women of the past. In addition, she admonishes biblical theologians, who are concerned with hermeneutical meaning for the present, to engage seriously in coming to knowledge of the history of interpretation.

Most important is the clear articulation of the nature and purpose of biblical theology that Schüssler Fiorenza makes in this volume. She argues that biblical theology is "public deliberative discourse of the *ekklēsia*."[32] By seeing the endeavor in this way, she allows scholars to "re-envision" this discourse by shaping it into a critical reflection on the social, political, and communal aspects of the church, the discipline of current biblical studies, and the important global features of the larger world. Thus, historical and

32. Schlüssler Fiorenza, *Rhetoric and Ethic*, 191.

social critical methods, literary shaping of texts and discourse, and hermeneutical articulation are integrated to form one holistic approach to reflective analysis. Another important result of this type of deliberative discourse within the context of the *ekklēsia* is that it deconstructs the misuse
of language to establish and enforce unjust social and political systems.
The truth of biblical theology depends, then, on its reflective discourse
that engages liberating visions in the Bible that are to be actualized in
communal life. This truth is not something mysterious, incapable of being
directly known, save to a few. Rather, recontextualizing biblical theology
by placing it within the interpretative paradigm of radical democracy and
actualizing it through the deliberative discourse of the *ekklēsia* allows the
text and its reader to engage in the struggle for justice and equality. This
political process replaces patriarchy with egalitarianism and expands the
borders of the *ekklēsia* to include all peoples.

Schüssler Fiorenza develops the unifying thesis that biblical studies,
including biblical theology, should turn once more to the divine *poli-*
teuma (the metaphor of the city in which there is equality and righteousness that bond its citizens together), where Wisdom-Sophia may once
again set forth her all embracing justice and offer well-being to all peoples. In quoting Karen Baker-Fletcher and Linda Ellison, whose words I
used to introduce this chapter, they shift into a poetic mode of discourse
to contend that biblical theology should indeed articulate and participate in "the creative dance between the Spirit and the elements." This
"emancipatory-rhetorical paradigm of interpretation" becomes the discourse that unleashes Wisdom-Sophia's power for life.

Discovering Eve: Carol Meyers's Feminist Social History of Ancient Israel

For over a century, especially since the appearance of Stanton's two-volume
publication, *The Woman's Bible* (1895–1898), feminist interpretations of
the Bible have dramatically affected both the academy and two communities of faith, Judaism and Christianity.[33] The task before all interpreters of
the Bible is succinctly stated by Alice Bach in her recent reader of some of

33. Feminist historians of Israel and early Judaism have made significant contributions
during the past generation. In addition to the two who are discussed in detail in this chapter,
Elisabeth Schüssler Fiorenza and Carol Meyers, see also those who participated in Newsom
and Ringe, *The Women's Bible Commentary.* In addition, see Frymer-Kensky, *In the Wake of
the Goddess;* Bird, "Women's Religion in Ancient Israel"; "The Place of Women in the
Israelite Cultus"; and Ackermann, "'And the Women Knead Dough.'" Important is the comprehensive collection of seminal essays by feminist biblical scholars, including literary scholars and historians, and the bibliography in Bach, *Women in the Hebrew Bible.*

the seminal writings of leading feminist biblical scholars: "Thus, a central challenge is to explore ways in which we can reach the stories of women in a world shaped by male interests." She goes on to state, "We shall have to read with bifocal lenses: aware of our modern attitudes while simultaneously understanding the religious and cultural traditions and practices that shaped ancient texts."[34]

Ethnoarchaeology and the Sociohistorical Reconstruction of Ancient Israel

One of today's leading historians and field archaeologists is Carol Meyers, whose works are characterized by precise methodological application, data collection and assessment, and interpretation in field archaeology, Hebrew Bible studies, and feminist historiography.[35] She uses the theoretical approach of "ethnoarchaeology"[36] in her interpretations of ancient Israelite history and society. Using ethnological information, archaeological material culture, and analogical comparisons that are necessarily cross-cultural due to limited material evidence and the ideological bent (i.e., patriarchy) of much of the Bible, she seeks to set forth the social life of Iron I Israelites in the Western Hill Country, whom she calls "pioneers." She has been particularly interested in the roles of women in ancient Israel, so her insights are important for the work of feminist biblical study. While she is not a theologian, her historical analyses are not unlike those of Schüssler Fiorenza. A needed step is to write a feminist biblical theology that makes use of Meyers's sociohistorical scholarship.

Methodology

Drawing on anthropological studies in general and ethnoarchaeology in particular, Meyers notes clearly several major principles that characterize the relationships between men and women in pre-modern societies.

- No universal set of characteristics governs male and female relationships. These vary from group to group.

34. Bach, "Introduction," xiii.
35. See Meyers, *Discovering Eve;* Meyers, Kraemer, and Ringe, *Gender and the Biblical Tradition;* Meyers, "The Family in Early Israel"; Carter and Meyers, eds., *Community, Identity, and Ideology;* Meyers, "Women and the Domestic Economy of Early Israel"; and Meyers, *Women in Scripture.*
36. Ethnoarchaeology is a method that uses ethnographic information to interpret material culture. Meyers, "The Family in Early Israel," 7. See especially Carter, "Ethnoarchaeology." Among the studies used by Meyers, see Rosaldo and Lamphere, *Women, Culture and Society;* Friedl, *Women and Men;* Gould and Watson, "A Dialogue on the Meaning and Use of Analogy"; and Netting, *Smallholders, Householders.*

- All societies engage in the distribution of labor, and some of this involves gender roles.

- Contributions of the two genders also vary from group to group. In some, women are primarily engaged in biological nurturing and rearing of children, while in others, women are not only engaged in reproduction and the raising of children, but also in the physical work of subsistence farming. Anthropologists have observed that the more involved women are in subsistence labor, the higher their status is in the social group. Also, women engaged in more than 40 percent of the subsistence activities begin to suffer a loss of status. The balance of 60 percent (male) to 40 percent (female) appears to be a stable number.

For the study of Iron I Israel, material culture, when combined with social science methodologies, provides information that aids in the reconstruction of social patterns of organization in pre-state, tribal society.

On the basis of the archaeological record and the method of ethnoarchaeology, Meyers argues that three essential requirements were placed on males in Iron I Israel. The first was participation in military activities in both defensive and offensive undertakings. The pre-state Israelite males, unlike the feudal Canaanite lords (who, as the military caste for command and authority, represented only a small part of the population), were not professional warriors but rather served as citizen warriors of clan villages whose subsistence economies depended on cultivation of the soil and the raising of small numbers of sheep and goats. Warfare, farming, and herding were collective efforts of clan households, although each household was owned by its family, and its dominant male (normally the senior father) was the major authority. The second important requirement was the reclamation of land into arable farmland by the construction of cisterns, clearing of forests and stones, and the building of terraces to preserve the soil on the hills of the hill country in which they settled. This required common, collective work organized by the clan's households. Finally, men had the general responsibility of making the transition to an increasing frontier in the building of what amounted to a pioneer society that would allow economic independence from the surrounding Canaanite city-states. This work included efforts to produce grain in a rocky terrain that had only a thin layer of topsoil and thus generally was unsuitable for farming. The intensity of these efforts to subsist required that women have a high degree of participation in "manual" work, resulting in a concomitant enhancement of status.

What is important for biblical scholars is that there is some corroboration of this in the ancient, formative texts. Meyers takes as her example

Lev 27, a key chapter placed after the Holiness Code (Lev 17–25). This chapter has to do with redemption and the value placed on those who were redeemed from slavery or servitude to other families. In these comparisons based on age and sex, the female ratio varies between 33 and 40 percent. This would suggest a relatively high degree of status for women, as reflected in the stories of women including Miriam, Deborah, and the wise women of Tekoa and Abel Beth Ma'acah. In addition, Meyers indicates the high correlation between the number and variety of goddesses with the status of women. The greater women's status, the larger the number of goddesses. However, there is an exception to this in ancient Israel.

The status of women who worked in physical labor would explain a text like Gen 2–3, which emphasizes the equality of men and women, since the emphasis on the worship of one deity, Yahweh, would not allow for the introduction of numerous goddesses. Thus, this polytheism and binary pairing of the gods and goddesses was replaced by an emphasis on the equality of men and women in early Israel. While this would change in Iron II Israel with establishment of the monarchy and the state, this early emphasis on equality, including status, became a part of Israel's historical memory that enabled later generations to draw upon these early traditions for identity and hope.

Meyers examines the social roles and functions in the largely patriarchal environment of ancient Israel and argues in essence that, while women possessed limited authority in the larger social domain of evolving Israel, they still had considerable power in the domestic side of the household. Her work begins with the ancestors of Israel and continues on through later generations. Her view of the "family household" *(mišpāḥâ)* is that it is largely a kinship group with both residential and economic functions: "The family household thus included a set of related people as well as the residential buildings, outbuildings, tools, equipment, fields, livestock, and orchards; it sometimes also included household members who were not kin, such as 'sojourners,' war captives, and servants."[37] This means that the "family household was not limited to a kinship group, but also to a living group and the materials necessary for existence.[38] Women in the typical household were in charge of agricultural production (food process-

---

37. Meyers, "The Family in Early Israel," 13–14. She notes that family households were not always known as the *bêt 'āb* ("father's house"), but on occasion as *bêt 'ēm* ("mother's house"). Indeed, the former is a social term used on occasion to refer to the community of Israel. The latter term is found in the story of Rebekah (Gen 24:28), Ruth (1:8), and the Song of Songs (3:4, 8:2). Proverbs also refers to family households and women (9:1, 14:1, 24:3, 31:10–31).

38. Meyers, "'To Her Mother's House.'"

ing and preparation) and functions including child bearing, rearing, and teaching; manufacturing of clothing, weaving, and making of ceramic vessels; and organizing and overseeing the labors and responsibilities of the household members that included children, relatives living in the household, servants, hired laborers, and sojourners. This indicated that the household was more a partnership between husband and wife than a hierarchy. Even so, while female power was substantial, it was outweighed by the authority of the dominant male.

Although Meyers does not claim to do biblical theology, it is clear that many of her insights are significant to its construction. Her work is foundational for a History of Religion approach to biblical theology. For example, in her essay "Procreation, Production, and Protection: Male-Female Balance in Early Israel," she emphasizes the communal nature of ancient Israel and points out that the theological depiction of the Yahwist in Gen 2–3 points to the solidarity and equality between men and women. Yet, she asks, is this simply an idealistic articulation of what should or could be, or does it reflect to some extent an ancient social understanding in earliest Israel, before the onset of the monarchy and the rise of the Israelite state? Her answer is that this is more of an ideological depiction than it is a description of social reality. Yet if the balance between gender roles and status can be understood and depicted, then this idealistic representation may be better understood. In the following centuries of statehood, with the rise of the Israelite monarchy, farming villages increasingly came within the orbit of urban and ultimately state sociopolitical structures. The local ways of self-governing gave way to a more centralized system, at least for major decisions. However, the values of the farming communities, issuing in particular from the solidarity of kinship groups, continued to influence legislation, religion, customs, and morality.

A Critical Feminist Liberationist Interpretation of the Book of Jeremiah

Applying a critical feminist liberation methodology to the book of Jeremiah, the first observation is the almost complete lack of references to real women. Indeed, the major players are men: Jeremiah and other prophets, Baruch and the scribes, the kings, and the priests. The voices of historical, named women are silent. However, there are the normal social categories into which the prophet places women (the majority being those of the household or of deviant behavior regarding household moral expectations) and numerous metaphorical and poetic references that are often degrading, with one major exception examined in detail by Phyllis Trible whose work on metaphor and feminist criticism is literary, not historical).

Material culture offers a particularly intriguing counterbalance to this silence in the fact that many fertility figurines from the two centuries prior to the Babylonian sacking of Jerusalem have been found in the city's family houses. This would suggest the flourishing of goddess worship even in the shadow of the great Yahweh temple, and, if Meyers is correct, this would imply an important status for those women in Jerusalem who did not simply yield to the domination by the leading males of the households, priests, and royal officials. This prominence of worship of the goddess (likely the earth mother goddess, Asherah, although Anat also is a possibility) is supported, although in a negative way, by the Deuteronomistic History and the Deuteronomic reform. The DH assault on goddess worship, the low status given to women, and the concern with their sexual purity is a part of Josiah's religious reform that attempted to eliminate the high places throughout Judah and Israel when much of the former Israelite and Judahite regions were brought under imperial control. His assault on the high places and goddess worship also support the strong possibility of the relatively high status at least some women enjoyed during the period of the prophet Jeremiah prior to the defeat at Megiddo by Necho II in 609 B.C.E. The reform not only was political and economical in purpose, but also social in seeking to subject women to a *pater familias* who dominated the household and to an increased patriarchal control in all levels of social, religious, and political life. This collusion of males in the concentrated effort to dominate women by means of the Josianic reform included scribes of significant political power (cf., for instance, the family of Shaphan), the house of David, and especially Josiah, who had ambitions to control again the North where a rival Yahwistic religion and Phoenician fertility cultus legitimated northern rulers, the high priestly Zadokite family of Hilkiah and its desire to have command of the temple cult in opposition to Levitical claims and to priestly roles of women, and centrist prophets of the monarchy and cult prophets who strongly supported the temple service and thus likely also would have also been involved in the subjection of women.

However, Jeremiah is strongly critical of kingship, priesthood, the temple service, and cultic prophecy, but not in order to enhance the status of women. Rather, he was more concerned with reinstituting the Mosaic covenant and tribal authority. The David-Zion tradition was a longstanding theological formation in ancient Israel, since the time of the empire. Its early understanding gave women a considerable amount of self-determination, even to the point of the unrestricted worship of their own native deities. Particularly prominent was the earth mother goddess and her cult that included women priestesses. However, this changed, especially during the time of Josiah. Conservative reactions against this fertility cultus were not simply theological, but also social. Among the social concerns of the reactionaries was the domination of women by eliminating the earth mother cult and its subsequent downgrading of women's status as the providers of fertility for the continuation of the nation.

What I am suggesting is that the prophet's silence about historical women, the degrading images of Israel and Jerusalem as whores and women in heat, and the prohibition of fertility religion indicate he was more than a passive bystander of this assault on the social status of women occurring during the time of Josiah's reforms. Rather, he too participated in this demeaning of the status and value of the feminine gender, forging his own abhorrent views and images. For example, he was anti-king and opposed the temple cultus and its economic and political power derived from the legitimation of the ruling dynasty. But it is also clear that this oppositional stance did not lead to the granting of women a higher status; in actuality, it led to its opposite. The worship of other gods, including fertility goddesses, especially Asherah, that occurred in numerous local high places and, during the reign of Manasseh, even in the temple of Jerusalem was to be forcibly eliminated.

The difficulties of attempting to determine the historical Jeremiah's views of the Deuteronomic reform are well known. We are not completely sure when the prophet began to prophesy, although the prose tradition dates this in the thirteenth year of Josiah (627 B.C.E.; Jer 1:2, 25:3). However, Jeremiah has only one reference to Josiah (Jer 22:15), and that is in the context of a judgment speech uttered against King Jehoiakim (609–598 B.C.E.). Subsequently, it does not appear that the prophet was active or at least known during this transitional time. Furthermore, we should note that the tradition has Jeremiah identified as a Levite from the town of Anathoth, where one of the two major priests of David, Abiathar, was exiled by Solomon. It would seem doubtful that Jeremiah was especially interested in currying the favor of the Zadokites. Indeed, one of his arch-enemies was Pashhur, a priestly official in charge of the temple police and a Zadokite (20:1-6). Jeremiah's language in the poetic speeches of Source A does suggest a relationship to the book of Deuteronomy (3:1-5 = 24:1-4), a relationship that deepens linguistically and theologically with the prose speeches and narratives (Sources B and C) that, in my judgment, are written by Deuteronomic scribes. In addition, Jeremiah is presented as strongly opposed to the Jerusalem temple, its corrupt priesthood, the city of Jerusalem and thus Zion theology, the house of David, and the centrist prophets (7:1-15; 20:6; 22:6—23:8; 26:1-24; 28:1-17). In this opposition and Jeremiah's resistance, women are not mentioned. The goal of returning Judah to a tribal society, dependent on Yahweh, possessed no indication of the increase in the status and human worth of women.

Where does this leave us ultimately in our feminist analysis of Jeremiah and Baruch? Five things are certain. First, Jeremiah had little interest in speaking about historical women. The only specific human females he mentions are his mother and the queen mother of Jehoiachin. Second, his references to flesh-and-blood women comprise social categories that sometimes move into metaphorical language: a woman (48:19), a mother (7:30-31, 15:8, 16:3, 20:14, 17-18), a daughter (11:22, 13:14, 16:3, 19:9, 46:24, 48:46), the poor among whom were women (5:28, 7:6), a bride (7:34, 16:19, 25:10, 33:11), a wife (5:11, 8:10), a widow (7:6, 15:8, 18:21), a mother made childless (18:21), a sister (22:18), a faithless daughter (49:4), widows (49:11), prostitutes, including those active in fertility cults (13:18), women mourners (9:16, 49:3), dancing women in celebrations and festivities (31:13), and a queen mother (22:26). Third, he is especially critical of fertility religion. His criticism is based on the theological reasoning of religious apostasy, although this likely masked his own misogynism because women were active participants, including serving as priestesses, in the mother goddess cultus.

Fourth, his feminine metaphors for a faithful or faithless woman are stereotypical and often degrading. Thus, he portrays Israel/Jerusalem as a virgin (18:13, 31:3-4, 31:21, 46:11), a virgin loved by her beloved (31:3) who joins in a dance of celebration at (her) wedding (31:4), a daughter (6:1, 23; 46:19; 50:42; 51:22), a disobedient daughter who acquired lovers (22:20-21, 32:22), a woman/women (8:19; 48:2; 50:12, 37; 51:30), a lover (12:7), a young bride (2:2, 32), a woman in labor (4:31, 13:21, 22:23, 48:41, 49:24, 50:43), a wayward wife (3:20) who has children (2:9, 3:1, 5:7, 17), a mother (46:27, 50:12), a woman who has lost her children (Rachel, 31:15), whores and fertility priestesses (3:1-5, 6-9, 13; 4:30), a woman in heat pursuing her lovers (2:23-25), a sexually addicted woman who teaches even prostitutes how to ply their craft (2:33), a woman whose sexual addiction is responsible in part for the oppression and death of the poor (2:34), a raped woman (13:22), a woman shamed by lifting up her skirts (13:27), a battered virgin (13:17), an abused woman (50:15), a promiscuous woman abused and abandoned by her lovers (30:12-15), an adulteress/prostitute (13:27), a ritually impure woman (probably menstruating, 13:27), and a promiscuous woman made pregnant by her "lovers" and abandoned (22:22-23). He never once speaks out against the treatment, at times savage, of women, instead choosing frequent humiliating images.

Finally, the female "surrounding [i.e., protecting] a man" (31:22) could be a more liberating image, if Trible is correct in her analysis (see below), in speaking of a future when the current world of power and death will be reversed. Yet this small glimpse of hope for women, if it is indeed correctly interpreted by Trible, does little to counteract the outrageous debasement of women and their humiliation by this "prophet of Yahweh."

The social and metaphorical images of women in the discourse of Jeremiah would have reflected the social picture of their roles during his lifetime. As for the prophet, in examining his references to women in social categories and metaphorical depictions, we find that he normally ignores real women, understands them in largely degrading stereotypes of his period, and depicts them as whores as well as battered and raped victims. His poetic images of the assaulted woman, the most common and frequent metaphor for a city (Jerusalem and other capital cities), are ugly and violent. His strong criticism of fertility religion (11, 17, 17:2-3) and his frequent negative images of women who are sexually unrestrained point to the same concern that one has in Deuteronomic/Deuteronomistic literature: the control of women in the household by the male heads of family that included humiliation and abuse of "wayward" wives and noncompliant daughters and the elimination of the earth mother cult and her priestesses. The legal-priestly, household effort of dominant males to control feminine behavior and to restrict its freedom to choose and to act is restrictive and harsh in Jeremiah's own speeches. Jeremiah likely would have been supportive of the efforts of the Deuteronomic reform (cf. especially 11:1-17) in shutting down the high places where sexual rites were performed, in eliminating the cultus of the earth mother goddess, in rejecting women as priests, in strongly criticizing the royalty (including both rulers and queen mothers) for injustice, and in controlling the women who in his eyes were "wayward." The one possibly positive depiction of women that we shall examine later is discussed in detail by Trible. She asserts 31:22 depicts a woman in the time of restoration as performing the unexpected. She "surrounds a man." However, if Trible is correct in this imaginative construal, it is the single exception to the debasement of women in Jeremiah.

Overall, many women in Jeremiah's time appear to have been involved in the earth mother goddess cult and were not the compliant household servants desired by males seeking domination during this socially turbulent period. Power was not only political in regard to efforts to reestablish the David-Solomonic empire, but also social and sexual in terms of controlling marginal and wayward groups and placing them under the hierarchy of the Josianic kingship. Power took on a religious caste in regard to competing cults, with the Zadokites and Levites vying for control of the temple and the longstanding existence of high places where non-Yahwistic fertility religion was practiced. Finally, gender and sexual power in the household was a major concern, as reactionaries sought to lower the status of women and to create a strongly patriarchal family. Jeremiah did not preach liberation for women. Indeed, it is likely he too was concerned with their increased status and voiced a message of social control. In addition, while he opposed the monarchy and the temple in his period, he was strongly supportive of the elimination of the high places. The worship of the earth mother goddess and the higher status of women that allowed them significant freedom in religion and moral behavior were two areas he sought to eliminate.

Evaluation

The strengths of the models of Schüssler Fiorenza and Meyers and their social histories are many. They both make use of historical criticism, but do so to recapture the social status of women in ancient Israel and the early church. Thus, they have not found it necessary to abandon the work of history writing in their methodology, but at the same time they produce a feminist critical history that enhances the understanding of women in these two different spheres. Each demonstrates that a strong emphasis on material culture allows the writing of women's history and resists the often patriarchal character of the biblical texts. Each recognizes, in addition, that the historian must operate with two fundamental principles in addition to rational analysis and the careful sifting of data: a hermeneutics of suspicion that seeks to detect ideologies inherent in texts and their interpreters; and a use of historical imagination that attempts to set forth what an ancient society's views of women would have been. All historiography, while seeking to avoid extremist arguments and the fabulous inherent in uncontrolled approaches, still requires the imagination to reconstruct the history of a period, an institution, or in this case, a gender. Finally, both scholars recognize the fragmentary nature of the data, both written and material. Even so, their reconstructions of a possible social history are compelling. Both offer biblical theology important insights for carrying out its work: a hermeneutics of suspicion, the importance of material culture in recapturing the theology and ethics of the marginalized, the role of social theory and its application to delineate systems of faith and ethic, and the embrace of important elements of a feminist biblical theology.

5

From History to Rhetoric:
Feminist, *Mujerista,* and
Womanist Theologies

The canon and civil law; Church and state; priests and
legislators; all political parties and religious denominations
have alike taught that woman was made after man, of man
and for man, an inferior being, subject to man. Creeds,
codes, Scriptures and statutes, are all based on this idea.

—*Elizabeth Cady Stanton*

Introduction

THIS QUOTATION FROM THE FRAMER OF *THE WOMAN'S BIBLE,*
Elizabeth Cady Stanton, reflects not only the past, but also for many
women, who continue to be controlled and marginalized by patriarchy,
the present. One of the significant ways of counteracting this systemic
sexism rampant in Western cultures and societies and to engage in the
struggle for liberation is to question not only the authenticity of male-
generated biblical texts that have been used and abused to dominate
women, but also the correctness of their male interpreters who continue
to allow to lie dormant the voices and deeds of women in Scripture, all the
while twisting many texts to reflect a patriarchal reading. One way of proceeding is in the area of literary criticism, which opens a variety of models
for understanding texts in place of historical criticism generally pursued
by male scholars.[1]

Since the 1960s, the methodologies and insights of literary criticism
and the phenomenology of language have been applied increasingly to
biblical interpretation and Old Testament theology and have produced

---

1. The first part of this chapter, which introduces feminist criticism that uses literary
criticism as its primary method of interpretation, the analysis of metaphor, and the contributions of McFague and Trible are taken from Perdue, *The Collapse of History.*

significant results. Among these have been important literary works in the areas of metaphor and rhetorical criticism, the subjects of this chapter. Developments in the study of rhetoric have been combined, on occasion, with feminist hermeneutics to shape new ways of doing Old Testament theology. This is not to suggest that feminist theology is necessarily linked to newer literary criticisms. As noted above, some feminist scholars work out of a diachronic, social-scientific model for liberation theology in similar fashion to Norman Gottwald, while others work in any number of methods and approaches discussed in this overview. For example, two feminist biblical scholars who use historical-critical method within the larger matrix of liberation theology are Carol Meyers and Elisabeth Schüssler Fiorenza, the two feminist historians discussed in chapter 4.[2] However, the contemporary church's concern for inclusive language, especially ways of speaking about and imaging God, is reflected in feminist efforts to pay close attention to the language of the biblical text. Thus, the rhetorical character of texts is examined to find feminine metaphors for God, recover women's stories, undermine patriarchy, and expose sexism.

Mujerista theology is my final consideration in this general discussion of critical feminist interpretation, although there are others, including especially Asian theology, that also should be examined. Part of my justification for not examining Asian American feminism is the fact that our faculty currently has only a Korean historian and theologian who is male, but no Asian feminist. Thus, I am unable to engage this area with considerable insight coming from a colleague, as I have been in terms of other ethnic groups, both male and female.

Feminist Literary Critics and Biblical Interpretation

Some feminist biblical scholars have engaged in biblical interpretation by means of a variety of literary approaches: New Criticism, narrative criticism, rhetorical criticism, and reader-response, to name the most frequently used. Four feminist biblical interpreters, Mieke Bal, Toni Craven, Athalya Brenner, and Phyllis Trible, have been among the leading scholars to develop a feminist literary approach to Scripture. By so doing, they have offered significant insights into Scripture that are helpful in thinking about biblical theology and its engagement with the contemporary communities of believers. While each of these scholars blazes her own path in her methodological and hermeneutical work with significant variations

---

2. Schüssler Fiorenza, *In Memory of Her;* and Meyers, *Discovering Eve.* See also their works listed in the bibliography.

easily recognizable, the important approach that unites their work is feminist literary criticism.

Approach

One of the cornerstones of this hermeneutic is the opposition to the claim of objectivity in doing biblical interpretation. Feminists argue that both the scriptural text and the interpretation are generated by the self-interests of the writers, i.e., the composer(s) of the biblical text and the one who interprets it. Further, each one stresses the importance of the location of text, interpreter, and interpretation. This means, then, that location contains social, political, temporal, and spatial features that combine in producing meaning. A third factor that most distinctively characterizes their work is the approach of texts through a variety of literary methods. They possess remarkable literary skills that enable them to discover the rhetorical as well as historical and social features of texts. They demonstrate how the artistry of a text possesses significance in the holistic construal of meaning. The task of this chapter is to present examples of feminist interpretations of Scripture that affect Old Testament theology in general and the book of Jeremiah in particular. We shall begin with delineating major features of metaphor and then look at metaphorical theology as shaped by a contemporary theologian, Sallie McFague.

Metaphor and Religious Language

Religious language about God is metaphorical in content, function, and meaning.[3] It is by means of its root metaphors that a culture conveys its understandings of God, and thus its most cherished beliefs.[4] However, the effort to understand how metaphor works as an important element of language is often a slippery and elusive task. Nevertheless, the following features are important in the understanding of metaphor.

---

3. Among the many important studies on metaphor, see Barbour, *Myths, Models and Paradigms;* Black, *Models and Metaphors;* Ferré, "Metaphors, Models, and Religion"; Lakoff and Johnson, *Metaphors We Live By;* Richards, *The Philosophy of Rhetoric;* Ricoeur, "The Metaphorical Process"; *Interpretation Theory; The Rule of Metaphor;* Sacks, *On Metaphor;* and Wheelwright, *Metaphor and Reality.* For a detailed application of metaphorical theory to the theology of the book of Job, see my *Wisdom in Revolt.*

4. David Tracy emphasizes, "All major religions are grounded in certain root metaphors.... In a particular religion root metaphors form a cluster or network in which sustained metaphors both organize subsidiary metaphors and diffuse new ones. These networks describe the enigma and promise of the human situation and predescribe certain remedies for that situation." Tracy, "Metaphor and Religion," 80.

One should begin by recognizing that metaphor is more than an example of rhetorical flourish by which a factual, literal meaning is given poetic enhancement. Rather, a metaphor says that one thing is something else. In describing its grammatical and linguistic character, metaphor in essence interfaces two distinctly different objects (tenor and vehicle) within a sentence.[5] The tenor is the principal subject that is conveyed by a vehicle, or secondary subject.[6] Quite often a vehicle that is better known than the tenor describes the latter, since it may be somewhat enigmatic. The vehicle serves as a lens through which to observe and then attempt to describe and define the tenor. A new insight or a point of similarity between the two is seen as being true. In the relationship between tenor and vehicle, meaning for the sentence is constructed. Yet it is not just the tenor that receives meaning and insight; the vehicle also may gain new understanding in this dynamic relationship.

Intrinsic to metaphors is the tension between the "is" and "is not."[7] A subject (tenor) is something else, yet at the same time, it is *not* literally this other thing. There is sameness, yet there is also difference. The proper response to a metaphor requires both "yes" and "no," thereby avoiding absolutism. Literalism accepts the "is" as real but does not allow for the "is not." When this tension between the two collapses, then the metaphor dies or is transformed into something else that is absurd, sterile, or dogmatic.

In a more expanded, philosophical sense, metaphor is "as ultimate as speech itself, and speech as ultimate as thought," being "the instinctive and necessary act of the mind exploring reality and ordering experience."[8] Since language both describes and shapes reality, metaphor moves beyond factual description to participate in the very process of world building.[9] It functions as a semantic building block in the linguistic construction of reality.

The Metaphorical Process

Living metaphors, like humans, are not static and isolated. Rather, they exist in relationship with other words to inhabit meaning worlds of sentence, story, and life. They are not passive and static, but active and changing. Like living creatures, they are in process, dynamic, and open, so they

5. Richards, *The Philosophy of Rhetoric*, 96.
6. Booth, *A Rhetoric of Irony*, 22.
7. McFague, *Metaphorical Theology*, 18.
8. Murry, *Countries of the Mind*, 1–2.
9. Nelson Goodman, in speaking of metaphor, argues, "Far from being a mere matter of ornament, it participates fully in the progress of knowledge: in replacing some stale 'natural' kinds with novel and illuminating categories, in contriving facts, in revising theory, and in bringing us new worlds." Goodman, "Metaphor as Moonlighting," 175.

take on an existence of their own. In addition to their grammatical and philosophical character, metaphors work by taking an implied audience through a process that involves both the deconstruction of previous meaning and possibly even former worldviews to the construction of new and compelling visions. There are several stages in this process.

The first stage is destabilization. In some measure, the metaphorical process begins with the absurd. This means that a vehicle portrays its tenor in a way that is blatantly false, if taken literally.[10] Goodman remarks, "The oddity is that metaphorical truth is compatible with literal falsity; a sentence false when taken literally may be true when taken metaphorically, as in the case of 'The joint is jumping' or 'The lake is a sapphire.'"[11] Ricoeur argues that absurdity is a "strategy of discourse" that destroys the literal meaning of a statement and transforms it into a meaningful contradiction that provides for the possibility of new semantic insight.[12] The first shock, disorientation, is experienced by those who respond to the metaphor, for the ground of meaning is in process of being shifted from one level to another.

The metaphorical process continues with the second stage, mimesis. Through new and even contradictory associations brought to the tenor by its vehicle, the insight is gained that something in this relationship is true. This is the second shock, which Wheelwright calls the "shock of recognition."[13] In one respect, if not more, the tenor and its vehicle have fused, becoming one, but only for those creative moments of reflection leading to insight.

Through reflection and insight, the audience may then come to the third stage in the metaphorical process, that of transformation and restabilization. If the new metaphor is a compelling one, the audience may then be transformed. They experience a conversion in which their understanding of the subject is altered. A powerful metaphor may even recreate the meaning system of the audience, redescribing reality by shaping a new cosmology that provides instruction in the way to live within the new world.[14] And if the metaphor becomes one of the culture symbols shared by the audience, it provides a renewed vitality of understanding. Now disorientation is replaced by a nomos of meaning set within the parameters of a worldview that provides coherence and direction for the culture-producing society. And through the society's rituals of passage, new members may enter into this social world and participate in its beliefs, values, and customs.

10. Ferré, "Metaphors, Models, and Religion," 330; Ricoeur, "The Metaphorical Process," 78–79; and *The Rule of Metaphor,* 199.

11. "Metaphor as Moonlighting," 175.

12. "The Metaphorical Process," 77–78.

13. Wheelwright, *Metaphor and Reality,* 45–46.

14. Ferré, "Metaphors, Models, and Religion," 331; Ricoeur, "The Metaphorical Process," 75.

A new world has been created, all by means of the linguistic construction of reality.

Even with the origination of new metaphors that aid in the linguistic construction of reality, tensions are not necessarily removed or proscribed. Tensions occur in two areas: in the inherent contradictions between the tenor and its vehicle, and in the difficulties that inevitably emerge within a meaning system that is new or has been significantly altered.[15] While it may seem ironic, these very tensions provide life-giving and life-sustaining energy to metaphors and the worlds they build.[16] When tensions are removed, especially by those who wish to misshape metaphor into literal meanings and factual definitions, metaphors either die or become distorted, inflexible, and unyielding. Thus, tenor merges with vehicle, not for moments of imagination and creative reflection, but as a permanent and concrete distortion. This all too frequent occurrence of linguistic dogmatism is destructive to the reality systems of which root metaphors are an important part.

Related to the tensive character of metaphors is the recognition that ambiguity plays an important part in the character of metaphor. Metaphors cannot possess "steno-meanings" that are accepted by all members of a culture. Inevitably, metaphors include a range of possible comprehension grounded, at least in part, in individual experience and understanding.[17] Metaphors may not be given one clear, abiding definition. If this occurs, then the definition transforms them into something vastly different from what they were.

Metaphors, even those that become symbols that carry a culture's systems of meaning and values, are rarely immortal. Within any society, a metaphor may become so commonplace that its power to bear a culture's worldview is lost. No longer capable of transformation, these stock metaphors die, and new ones are required to reconstruct or redirect meaning systems.[18]

Feminism and Literary Criticism: From Theory to Application

This chapter describes several similar approaches to metaphorical/rhetorical theology: the work of contemporary theologian Sallie McFague and the writings of Phyllis Trible, a professor of Hebrew Bible. Both make important use of metaphors in approaching their understandings of theology and the Bible. Of course, other feminists have written important books in this

---

15. This is what Harries refers to as both collusion and collision. "Metaphor and Transcendence," 71–72.

16. Wheelwright, *Metaphor and Reality*, 45–69.

17. Ibid., 33.

18. McFague, *Metaphorical Theology*, 41.

field, including two of my biblical colleagues, Toni Craven and Athalya Brenner.[19] The feminist literary scholar Mieke Bal offers a fertile series of interpretations of Bible narratives that are among the most provocative written by literary scholars interpreting the Hebrew Bible. I shall set forth the details of her work in the chapter on postmodernism.

In addition to McFague, Trible, and later Bal, we shall examine the writings of Renita Weems, a womanist biblical scholar, and Ada María Isasi-Díaz, a *mujerista* theologian whose books have important implications. Of course, we also could have examined the works of these feminist scholars in the chapters on liberation theology, since these features are also an important dimension of their interpretive efforts. Even so, the distinctive features of their work not only include a concern with literary criticism and the nature of language, but also elicit a focus on the nature and function of God-talk within feminist/womanist/*mujerista* perspectives.

Feminist Metaphorical Theology: Sallie McFague

Metaphorical theory has been used by some theologians and biblical scholars who argue that religious language in general and linguistic representations of God in particular involve the important use of metaphors.[20] God becomes the tenor whose vehicles are to provide insight into divine nature and character without the shaping of a linguistic idol construed by literal similitude. And because male and female are made in the image of God, these metaphors for God also say a great deal about human beings and the social systems that they construct. This reflects the dictum that not only are tenors meaning-receiving, they are also meaning-giving. Thus, the use of human terms to describe God also says something significant about human beings.[21]

Religious confessions of faith are judged by some theologians to be metaphorical models that convey meanings and values within a religious tradition.[22] Theologically speaking, these models should provide guidance for the life of faith and action without removing all degrees of tension and ambiguity that are a part of metaphorical language. It is when divine

---

19. Meyers et al., *Women in Scripture;* Craven, *Artistry and Faith in the Book of Judith;* Brenner, *Are We Amused?;* Brenner and van Henten, *Bible Translation;* Brenner and Fontaine, *A Feminist Companion to Reading the Bible;* Brenner and van Dijk-Hemmes, *Reflections on Theology and Gender; On Gendering Texts.*

20. Barbour, *Myths, Models, and Paradigms.*

21. "This is a very important point for religious models because the human images that are chosen as metaphors for God gain in stature and take on divine qualities by being placed in an interactive relationship with the divine." McFague, *Metaphorical Theology,* 38.

22. Ibid., 103; and Tracy, "Metaphor and Religion," 89.

metaphors are taken literally that the creative tension between tenor and vehicle collapses, the two become one, and an idol is created.

Even though Sallie McFague is a contemporary theologian and not a biblical scholar, her work still provides a very important example of metaphorical theology that is suggestive for understanding the nature of language in Scripture and how one might go about the task of writing Old Testament theology. In her work, she makes the significant move from the literary analysis of metaphor to the nature of theological language within the framework of feminist hermeneutics that recognizes the power and abuses of language in shaping reality.[23]

Drawing on many of the features of metaphor presented in the preceding discussion, McFague asserts, "We will not relinquish our idolatry in religious language unless we are freed from the myth that in order for images to be true they must be literal. Nor will we find religious language relevant unless we are freed from the myth that in order for images to be meaningful they must be traditional."[24]

McFague's work covers three related areas that I shall briefly describe: the metaphorical character of the parables of Jesus and other forms of Christian literature influenced by the parables, a metaphorical model for doing contemporary theology, and the presentation of alternative metaphors for God and the world that challenge those that today, to a large extent, have become traditional and conventional. Some of these older metaphors are not dead, for they still wield a deadly power.[25]

Parables as Extended Metaphors

In *Speaking in Parables*, McFague presents Jesus as the parable of God and the parables spoken by Jesus as a model for theological reflection. Parables, which by nature and function are metaphorical, are the form that unites language, belief, and life.[26] Following her description of metaphor, McFague explains the triangular character of parables, a literary form that she considers to be extended metaphors.[27] This character, actually a her-

---

23. In *Metaphorical Theology*, she describes her approach as presenting "a post-Enlightenment, Protestant, feminist perspective which I would characterize as skeptical, relativistic, prophetic, and iconoclastic" (p. x).

24. Ibid., 32.

25. For relevant works by McFague and other scholars discussed in the chapter, see the bibliography.

26. *Speaking in Parables*, 3.

27. She argues that referring to a parable as a metaphor indicates that "the world of the parable itself includes both the ordinary and the transcendent in a complex interaction in which each illumines the other." *Speaking in Parables*, 46.

meneutical model, involves the narrator (Jesus), the esthetic object (the narrative parable), and the effect (on the implied audience). For McFague, no text that has meaning can exist outside of this triangle, even though there is never one single and final interpretation. Through parable, one may come to encounter the vision of the teller (in this case, Jesus), may hear the "voice" articulate, and may see in parabolic vision a self-attestation, although hidden and indirect. McFague calls this the "inverbalization of Jesus as the word." This vision of the world created by metaphor contrasts with the conventional, traditional world of the hearers.

The hearers are interpreted by parables in the responses they make. Whether aligning themselves with the old logic of conventional vision or with the new logic of grace shattering into human history, listeners are challenged to respond to these ultimate questions: What do you say? What will you do? For McFague, the parable itself is characterized by realism and strangeness, and in this dynamic interaction, shock and disorientation turn the world upside down. Yet, through new vision that is both the culmination and the stimulus for the process of coming to belief, the world is recreated, and faith is born anew. Metaphors work, even as their narrative extensions succeed, because they encapsulate human life. Humans are living metaphor, for they too move through process to culmination.[28]

Thus, parables contain the major features of metaphors. They are characterized by the tension between a conventional and traditional understanding of reality and one that is radically different, iconoclastic, and challenging. Following disorientation, the audience sees the new interpretation as plausible, conventional understanding self-destructs, and a new world is born. Reality has thus been redescribed and then reshaped by the linguistic power of the metaphor. Yet what has been assaulted and turned upside down are not only understandings of God, but also the entire socioeconomic reality in which people have dwelt securely.[29] This change is frightening, and the response to new metaphor is fear and even revulsion.

Metaphorical Theology

In *Metaphorical Theology*, McFague takes up the issue of moving from the imagistic language of metaphor to systematic thought for expressing contemporary Christian faith in an engaging and relevant fashion.[30] In doing

28. See Hauerwas, "The Self as Story."
29. McFague, *Metaphorical Theology*, 47.
30. She argues, "Theology begins with a root-metaphor and ends in an ordering, comprehensive system, but even the system, while different from the metaphors that found it, is or should be on a continuum with them." Ibid., 127.

so, she hopes to avoid the idolatry that wrongly tends to accompany some theological language by making metaphors into literal dogma.

This process of movement from metaphor to the conceptual formulation of theology occurs within what she describes as a model. In looking at models in general, she notes four common things that they do. First, they provide a grid through which to look for similarity between the model and what is modeled. They seek out relationships and networks to explain what is less known by what is better known. Second, models make intelligible what is unintelligible or render in clear expression what is often unknown or obtuse. Models also provide a lens for looking at reality by moving beyond them to ever-expanding areas that call for explanation. Finally, models work by depending on paradigms—common sets of assumptions that direct interpretation.[31]

After appropriating these general features of models, McFague then moves into her own specific interests and argues that a metaphorical model, simply defined, is "a metaphor with staying power." That is, the metaphor shapes a comprehensive, ordering structure of meaning, a grid that helps in the organization of thoughts about a topic.[32] Thus, a relational term for God (e.g., father or mother) provides a significant organizing model for understanding the nature of God, religion in general, and even reality itself.[33] And these models provide a guide to life. Conceptual language operates in these models to clarify the ambiguous nature of imagistic language. Yet one should recognize that conceptual language depends on images from which they draw their substance and strength. Thus, models for McFague are both imagistic and conceptual.

Theologically conceived, faith for McFague is not belief in correctly stated doctrines, but rather is a process "more like a story than a doctrine," a position that aligns her with narrative theologians discussed in *The Collapse of History.* Metaphorical theology, she contends, is intermediate theology that examines the ways that the qualities of language, belief, and life come together in parables, and parable-like narratives of story and autobiography that are influenced by the parabolic tradition. However, she argues that any theology "influenced by the parables would be open-ended, tensive, secular, indirect, iconoclastic, and revolutionary."[34]

According to McFague, metaphorical theology stands between primary theology, which is the task of poets who create metaphors, and systematic

31. Ibid., 83–103.

32. She defines a metaphorical model as "a metaphor that has gained sufficient stability and scope so as to present a pattern for relatively comprehensive and coherent explanation." *Models of God,* 34.

33. *Metaphorical Theology,* 23.

34. Ibid., 48.

construction, which is the work of the constructive theologian. Meta-phorical theology sets forth both the imagistic, poetic character of theo-logical language that then proceeds to conceptual formulation that stresses the clear articulation of beliefs in a coherent fashion. To engage in system-atic theology, the theologian first should give attention to the parable or other types of narrative and the metaphors that are central to these nar-rative configurations. Only after this intermediary theology is presented should the theologian set forth a systematic formulation that seeks to bring together a variety of models based on different metaphors into a coherent whole by centering on their relationship to one particular model or theme. Yet, for McFague, theology cannot be completely disembodied, that is, removed from its contextual setting and formulation in life. In its lifelike quality, narrative, of which parable is but one expression, provides the rev-elatory form by which faith comes to exist.[35]

Metaphorical theology, explains McFague, does work with classic texts, beginning with Scripture, and exemplary theologies that are based on the classics to discover important metaphors, including both ignored and con-ventional ones. However, metaphorical theology, as she conceives it, does not concentrate primarily on discovering and then translating ancient met-aphors into modern understanding. Rather, metaphorical theology in seek-ing appropriate God-language does not rely exclusively on the classics, including Scripture, but rather examines many other sources, including the sciences, literature, philosophy, and art. In addition, metaphorical the-ology is not only concerned with the articulation of conceptual frameworks and clarity of expression, but also with the richness of images. McFague also submits that metaphorical theology seeks to "find out" through exper-imentation if something is valid or true. Thus, while classical texts are exam-ined along with a variety of other sources, metaphorical theology is more open than other theologies to experimentation, pluralism, and the power of images.[36]

Metaphorical theologians may not necessarily be engaged in the creation of new metaphors—this is the task of poets—but they must deform old

35. McFague argues that the truth of theological models should be evaluated by several criteria. These include consistency (the components need to fit together while avoiding the idolatry of literalism), comprehensiveness (all of reality is described), the ability to cope with anomalies, the avoidance of absolutism, the capacity to illuminate or make sense of reality and experience, the capacity to organize, the capacity to point out analogies and pat-terns, and the capacity of being relative to contemporary situations and faith. Simply put, valid models "make sense out of human experience." *Metaphorical Theology*, 138–41.

36. "Metaphorical theology is a kind of heuristic construction that in focusing on the imaginative construal of the God-world relationship, attempts to remythologize Christian faith through metaphors and models appropriate for an ecological, nuclear age." *Models of God*, 40; see her discussion on pp. 36–40.

and lifeless constructions that imprison and even deaden God-language. According to McFague, metaphorical theology does not concern itself primarily with content, but rather with the process of coming to belief in a Christian universe while at times despairing over the sinfulness of the present world.

New Metaphors

In *Models of God,* McFague approaches the third area of her work: a presentation of new metaphors that will provoke and transform theological understanding in the postmodern period. By postmodern she means the contemporary period that has emerged after the end of an age dominated by the Enlightenment and its way of thinking. In her view, the postmodern period is a time in which there is a "greater appreciation of nature," a "chastened admiration for technology," an increased "recognition of the importance of language," a greater awareness of the importance of non-Christian religions, the "rise of the dispossessed" who have traditionally been those without status and power in the West, an "apocalyptic sensibility" characterized by the awareness of the dangers of nuclear holocaust and ecological disaster, and an appreciation for the "radical interdependence of life at all levels."[37] For McFague, these are the features that contemporary theology needs to address in a relevant and engaging way.

The problem for contemporary theology, she asserts, is that the traditional models have been grounded in patriarchal metaphors for God and the world. The dominant metaphor for God is the transcendent (absent) king who rules over his kingdom (the earth). Not only is this metaphorical model traditional and conventional, outdated and uninteresting, it has also become dangerous. It is dangerous because it promotes patriarchy, hierarchical relationships, and dualistic thinking (body/spirit, human/ nonhuman, and male/female), and because it wrongly indicates that sovereign power, located in the hands of God or God's chosen, is the force that will promote justice and care for all (human and nonhuman) with the result that the world is kept from entering into the regions of chaos. This acknowledgment of the sovereignty of God leads to passivity and the lack of human responsibility for engaging in efforts designed to enhance well-being for all life.[38]

---

37. Ibid., x.

38. "Language that supports hierarchical, dualistic, external, unchanging, atomistic, anthropocentric, and deterministic ways of understanding . . . is not appropriate for our time." Ibid., 13.

Recognizing the power of language to redescribe and construct reality, McFague turns again to metaphorical theology and asks the evaluative question, Which religious metaphors are appropriate for our time? Theological language, based on new or rediscovered metaphors, needs to take a shape that will subvert patriarchy and hierarchy along with their inherent flaws and dangers and then create a vision that will lead to the assumption of responsibility to nurture and fulfill life in its various forms, all the while being open to newness and change.[39] The intent is not to demythologize religious language of its imagistic, poetic character by abstract conceptualization, but rather to remythologize theological language in order that it may redescribe reality in a provocative and true manner and evoke transformation that is based on new understanding. Metaphorical models, however, dispense with neither conceptualization nor imagistic language. Rather, the two exist in a symbiotic relation, one drawing strength and the other receiving clarity from the other.

McFague considers a variety of sources for new language. She argues that Scripture may be a classic text that endures by redescribing reality and allowing flexibility in interpretation. In searching for new metaphors, McFague looks to human liberation, not patriarchy, as the proper reformulation of the Christian paradigm. The paradigm of Christian faith assaults conventional understandings of power, includes rather than excludes, and is opposed to hierarchy and triumphalism.[40] This paradigm is found in the parables and life of Jesus in the Gospels and reemerges in a powerful way in liberation theology.

In her efforts to remythologize the Gospel for our time, she proposes new or rediscovered metaphors: the world as the body of God, and God as mother, lover, and friend. These metaphors clash directly with the traditional Western model of God as a distant king, a male despot, who rules over his earthly kingdom from afar. This monarchical model promotes hierarchical and dualistic thinking that leads to oppression. The danger of this model is that it threatens life by positing God's distance from the world, God's relationship to humans but not the nonhuman world, and God's control of the world through domination and/or benevolence.[41]

The world as God's body, argues McFague, promotes the ideas of divine immanence, God's care for the physical (not just the spiritual) aspects of existence, human responsibility in that God's body is in human hands, divine suffering as the world suffers, and sin as both the refusal to be a part

39. Ibid., 32.,
40. Ibid., 46.
41. Ibid., 65.

of the world and participation in actions against the well-being of all life that is interdependent. Furthermore, the evolutionary and historical development of the world is a process that is intrinsic to divine activity, rather than something directed by God, but separate from its time, space, movements, and people.

McFague's three relational metaphorical models for God—as mother, lover, and friend—all keep the single model of the world as God's body from deteriorating into pantheism. The metaphor of God as mother presents God as a creator who is intimately concerned with and actively seeks the well-being of life in all of its manifestations. God as lover presents God as a savior whose passion (love for the beloved and suffering) is directed toward reconciliation among all forms of life. God as friend presents God as the sustainer who works with humans to bring about healing to all the components of reality.[42]

This does not mean, for example, that God is defined as mother (or lover or friend) or that McFague is attempting to set up a new hierarchy, only this time a maternal or feminine one. But it does mean that the image of mother is a relational term, like lover and friend, that allows us to consider anew something about which we do not know how to talk.[43] Not coincidentally, these metaphors, she suggests, may replace the traditional Trinitarian metaphors of Father, Son, and Holy Spirit or the more impersonal Creator, Savior, and Sustainer. Throughout her writings, McFague emphasizes that metaphors are always indirect and tentative, although they do make assertions as well as judgments. They suggest certain things about God may be true or provide some insight, but one should always acknowledge that any language about God is inadequate.

McFague's work illustrates how Old Testament theologians may approach the Bible, especially narratives or stories, in order to discover and understand significant theological metaphors and how they operate. Her work is especially useful for understanding Old Testament narratives that provide the form in which life, faith, and values find their unity. Her work also suggests that even the Old Testament theologian, once having assessed

---

42. Ibid., 91–92.

43. Ibid., 33. The dangers in using relational language are sentimentality, individualism, and stereotyping that points to "traditional" male and female characteristics (e.g., women are by nature self-sacrificing and caring, while men are aggressive and assertive). In place of sentimentality, McFague stresses the importance and power of three types of love captured by the three metaphors: the love of parents, lovers, and friends. And in place of individualism, McFague emphasizes that the divine lover's love is for the entirety of the cosmos, not simply for one person or group or species, i.e., humanity. And in place of stereotyping, McFague emphasizes that so-called male and female characteristics are learned through socialization, rather than being intrinsic to gender differentiation.

the metaphorical character of the narrative, may move to a systematic presentation of Israelite faith. However, this move should not cast aside the original, imagistic character of religious language.

Recapturing the Language of Zion: Rhetorical Criticism and Feminist Hermeneutics

Whether they use literary or historical methods, or a combination of both, in their interpretative work, feminist, Caucasian biblical scholars point to the patriarchal character of both the Old Testament and much of the exegesis and biblical theology that represents a white male perspective. Subsequently, they engage in a robust criticism of patriarchy in the text, the scholarly tradition, and the larger cultural ethos of each.[44] The primary goal is to eliminate sexism in interpretative endeavors. There are several ways feminist scholars deal with patriarchy in the biblical text. One of the approaches is the utilization of a "hermeneutics of suspicion," which critically exposes sexist ideologies at work in the text. Other concerns are to discover the suppression of women's history by recovering forgotten stories of women, both in the biblical text and in the vicissitudes of the history of ancient Israel.

Some feminist scholars, as we have noted, have worked mainly as historians to recover women's history in ancient Israelite social life.[45] Thus, the approach to Old Testament theology takes on a decided historical character that uses a wide variety of sources (archaeological, biblical, and other literary data). Other feminists have followed new and developing literary methods to subvert patriarchy in the Bible, give feminist readings to biblical texts, and rediscover or bring to the fore examples of women's stories.[46] Others bring together historical criticism, social scientific analysis, and literary criticism in interpreting the Bible and ancient Israelite history from a feminist perspective.[47]

44. For a discussion of feminist biblical interpretation, see Tolbert, *The Bible and Feminist Hermeneutics;* A. Collins, *Feminist Perspectives on Biblical Scholarship;* Russell, *Feminist Interpretation of the Bible;* Exum and Bos, *Reasoning with the Foxes;* Trible, "Five Loaves and Two Fishes"; and "Treasures Old and New."

45. See Brenner, *The Israelite Woman;* Bird, "The Place of Women in the Israelite Cultus"; "Images of Women in the Old Testament"; Hackett, "Women's Studies and the Hebrew Bible"; Meyers, *Discovering Eve;* and Day, *Gender and Difference in Ancient Israel.*

46. See, e.g., Fuchs, "The Literary Characterization of Mothers"; "Who Is Hiding the Truth?"; Exum, "'Mother in Israel'"; Toni Craven, "Women Who Lied for the Faith"; and Bal, *Anti-Covenant.*

47. Camp, *Wisdom and the Feminine in the Book of Proverbs;* Laffey, *An Introduction to the Old Testament;* and Bird, "The Harlot as Heroine."

Metaphor, Rhetoric, and the Work of Phyllis Trible

While arguing in her article "Five Loaves and Two Fishes" that it is too early to write a feminist biblical theology, Phyllis Trible has recently articulated a set of "overtures" that indicates what this theology might look like.[48] Her initial thoughts include the following three primary assumptions:

1. This type of theology "might locate itself in reference to the classical discipline."[49] In reference to the ongoing debate, she argues that feminist biblical theology would not be content with description, but would be consciously constructive and hermeneutical. Using the metaphor of "pilgrim," she suggests the Bible wanders through time and cannot be locked in the past.

2. A feminist approach to biblical theology operates with the recognition that the Bible is not the property of any particular group, but rather is owned by Jews and Christians, believing communities and scholarly academies, and the world. This approach "is neither essentially nor necessarily Christian."

3. There should be not a single method, but many, and not one approach, but several to unlock the meaning of texts, both obvious and hidden.

Trible suggests that feminist biblical theology should begin with exegesis of texts, both familiar and neglected, always "mindful of androcentricity in Scripture and traditional Biblical theology."[50] Passages that depict God in feminine images should be addressed, as well as neglected texts about women. The meaning of *reh em*, "womb" in the singular and "compassion" in the plural, is a metaphor for talking about God that should be exploited by theological discourse.

Trible then suggests that a feminist biblical theology would move into the area of "contours and content."[51] In contrast to other models, this approach would "focus upon the phenomenon of gender and sex in the articulation of faith."[52] Specifically stated, a feminist biblical theology would begin with Gen 1–3 to interpret the "image of God, male and female" within the mythical context of creation as over against history. Trible argues that the next step would be the investigation of the female in the Bible, but also related literature from the ancient Near East. Even Israelite "folk reli-

---

48. "Five Loaves and Two Fishes," 289–95.
49. Ibid., 289.
50. Ibid.
51. Ibid., 292.
52. Ibid.

gion" would be studied, since women were often denied full participation in the Israelite cultus and thus with some men may have "forged an alternative Yahwism."[53]

Feminist biblical theology, according to Trible, would be especially construed to undermine idolatry, particularly in noting that no one image or metaphor is used to speak of God, and that no single articulation of the faith is normative. Also in the area of language, feminist biblical theology would probe into meanings of words and terms to explore a variety of meanings that are not traditional interpretations. The goal would be to "wrestle" with patriarchal language.

Finally, for Trible, feminist biblical theology "would also wrestle with models and meanings for authority." Authority would center on the reader, allowing for the interpreter to choose what is prescriptive in the text. In dialectic engagement with the text, the Bible might be seen as "authoritative, though not necessarily prescriptive."[54]

Recognizing these proposals as tentative, Trible emphasizes that the thrust of a feminist biblical theology would not only "explore the entire picture of gender and sex in all its diversity," but it would also "wrestle from the text a theology that subverts patriarchy."[55]

Rhetorical Criticism

The origins of rhetorical criticism are usually traced to James Muilenburg, although he himself acknowledged important predecessors, including especially Hermann Gunkel, Robert Lowth, and J. G. Herder.[56] The major task of rhetorical criticism is to define the limits of a literary unit (prose or poetry), uncover the component parts and structural patterns at work in its shape, and point out the literary techniques used in ordering its artistic composition. The focus is the literary work itself, and not the mind of the audience or the understanding of the original listeners. The argument is made that the artistry of the text renders its meaning. The artistic composition and the meaning of the text are inseparable.

The literary techniques that enable a unit to cohere and engage the imagination include anaphora (the repetition of an initial word or words

---

53. Ibid., 293. It is clear that Trible does not advocate writing a biblical theology that uses only the biblical text or that is limited simply to literature. The history of Israelite religion and social organization would contribute to her biblical theology. However, her own specialty has been in literary studies, particularly rhetorical criticism.

54. Ibid., 294.

55. Ibid., 295.

56. For an introduction to rhetorical criticism, see Muilenburg, "Form Criticism and Beyond"; Gottwald, "Poetry, Hebrew"; Jackson and Kessler, eds., *Rhetorical Criticism;* and Craven, *Artistry and Faith*, 11–46. The classic statement is Trible's *Rhetorical Criticism.*

of several clauses, lines, or strophes), refrains (repeated words or phrases at the end of strophes or other subunits), interweaving words or phrases *(mots crochets)* that blend together the entire unit or major subunit, inclusions (the repetition of the opening word or words at the close of the unit, thus marking its boundaries), parallelism of members (strophes or lines within a poem that parallel in some fashion, although there is also a "seconding sequence" in the second part that extends, differs from, or in some fashion changes the idea in the first part).[57] Among the most prominent types are synonymous and antithetical parallelisms. Other features of artistic composition include onomatopoeia (words imitating a sound), alliteration (the correspondence of sounds at the beginning of words), assonance (the correspondence of the sounds of accented vowels), and a variety of different structures for lines, paragraphs (narrative), and strophes (subunits of a poem that express normally one central idea), including chiasms (literally, an X formed by a pattern of lines, e.g., a, b, c, b1, c1) and acrostics (particularly alphabetic ones).

The Rhetoric of the Weeping Rachel in Jeremiah

Trible's elegant piece on the "weeping Rachel" in Jeremiah is found in her enormously influential *God and the Rhetoric of Sexuality.* Drawing on rhetorical criticism and studies of metaphor by scholars including Wheelwright and Ricoeur, Trible contends that the very nature of the Bible is hermeneutical, since, as noted earlier, she calls it "a pilgrim wandering through history to merge past and present." Her book is shaped by "feminist hermeneutics," not meaning an interpretation that only focuses on or is limited to women, but rather the recovery of neglected themes and counter literature, which often lie dormant within the text. Yet it is not enough to awaken sleeping texts to new life, for "feminism" is a "critique of culture in light of misogyny." This critique affects all issues of significant hermeneutical import that pertain to human existence in all of its vicissitudes: race, class, sexuality, ecology, and psychology.

To approach God-language in the Bible, Trible points to four "clues" in the text: hermeneutical, dialectical, methodological, and topical. The hermeneutical clue is found by exploring the tension between God the lover and God the punisher. The variety of meanings and the different "hearings" indicate that biblical theology and hermeneutics should eschew systematizing. The dialectical clue is found in the dynamic between the text and the world, as Scripture is engaged by issues of modern import: liberation theology, ecology, human sexuality, the black experience, and feminism.

---

57. See especially Kugel, *The Idea of Biblical Poetry.*

The methodological clue for Trible is rhetorical criticism that focuses on the totality of a text, stressing and discovering its organic unity. Through its literary crafting, the text comes to life and construes meaning. The rhetoric of the text also awakens the imagination, allowing the interpreter to enter its space and time. Finally, the topical clue is found in Gen 1:26-30. In the compelling language of metaphor, male and female are "the image of God." This means, argues Trible, that male and female are a definition for humanity, just as they are together a metaphor for God. According to Trible, Gen 1:26-30 provides the clue for understanding God in the Old Testament as one who is presented in both male and female images: father, king, husband, and warrior, but also as pregnant woman (Isa 42:14), mother (Isa 66:13), midwife (Ps 22:9), and mistress (Ps 123:2).

In the remainder of the book, Trible works out two objectives. First, she examines feminine metaphors for God. For example, she points to "womb" imagery in the Old Testament, noting that *rehem* in the singular means womb or uterus, but in the plural expands to the abstraction of compassion, mercy, and love. Theologically conceived, God is the one who creates humanity in the womb, prepares the fetus for birth, participates in the birthing, receives the infant from the womb of the mother, and nurtures the newborn from birth through old age to the moment of death. Divine compassion is that of a mother who conceives and carries a child in her womb and is bonded to that life even after birth.

Trible's other objective is to examine narratives that portray the relationships between male and female, including the eroticism of the love lyrics of the Song of Songs and narratives portraying women. For example, she concludes that the story of Ruth is a "human comedy" that provides "a theological interpretation of feminism: women working out their own salvation with fear and trembling, for it is God who works in them." The feminine image is a powerful and central one in biblical faith, says Trible, for it directs the reader to examine the goodness of creation, to explore the eroticism of Canticles, and to witness the struggle for life in the book of Ruth.[58]

Trible's understanding of the metaphor of *rehem* provides vital insight into the nature of God in Jeremiah. Divine compassion, normally extended to Jerusalem, is denied at the time of the invasion of the "Foe from the North" (Jer 16:5), while the survivors of the Babylonian conquest are promised Yahweh's mercy and support (42:12; see 12:15, 30:18, 31:20, and 33:26).

However, the best example of the theology of *rehem* in Jeremiah is found in the poem of the weeping Rachel in 31:15-22. Trible refers to this poem as a drama of voices that "organize structure, fill content, and mold vision to

---

58. See also see her *Texts of Terror* and "Five Loaves and Two Fishes," 279–85.

create a new thing in the land (cf. v. 22b), and this new thing is the poem itself."[59] Using rhetorical criticism with accomplished skill, Trible sees the poem as having five strophes that form a chiasmus, with Ephraim's voice being at the center:

> Words of a *woman:* Rachel cries (v. 15)
> Words to a *woman:* Yahweh consoles (vv. 16-17)
> Words of a man: Ephraim confesses (vv. 18-19)
> Words of a *woman:* Yahweh contemplates (v. 20)
> Words to a *woman:* Jeremiah commands (vv. 21-22).[60]

Woman and female images surround and protect the man, in this case Ephraim, the Northern Kingdom.

According to Trible, the first strophe (v. 15) depicts a weeping mother, the ancestor Rachel, who long ago gave birth to Joseph and then to Benjamin (Gen 30:22-24; 35:16-20).[61] Now, Rachel is heard weeping in her tomb over the death of her children, that is, her descendants who have perished in the Assyrian (and perhaps also the Babylonian) holocaust and whose existence as a people is placed under great threat.

With the voice of Yahweh in vv. 16-17 (strophe II), Rachel is urged to cease her lamentation, for soon her lost children will return from exile. She, Rachel, dominates the focus of this strophe, as it is her future, embodied in the returning exiles, that is assured by the divine voice.[62]

However, with the shift to the third strophe (vv. 18-19), attention is drawn to another voice, this time emanating from a male: Ephraim confessing his sins, turning back (repenting) to Yahweh, and pleading for restoration.

The final two strophes complete the pattern of concentric circles, thereby enfolding Ephraim within the protection of a poem replete with feminine images. Yahweh's voice emerges again in the fourth strophe (v. 20) and claims Ephraim as the child of special delight. Yahweh shares the mother's compassion *(rehem)* for the child, God's "womb trembles" for him.[63] For Trible, it is the voice of the divine mother now who loves her child, Ephraim. "As a result, the poem has moved from the desolate lamentation of Rachel to the redemptive compassion of God."[64]

---

59. *God and the Rhetoric of Sexuality,* 40.
60. Ibid., 50.
61. Ibid., 40.
62. Ibid., 41.
63. Ibid., 45.
64. Ibid.

With the fifth strophe (vv. 21-22), the enfolding of Ephraim is complete. Now it is the voice of Jeremiah that speaks words of redemption. The mood has changed from despair in the opening lines of Rachel's lamentation to hope in the prophetic call to return at the poem's conclusion. One other change occurs: the attention is now on virgin Israel, the daughter, not Ephraim, the son. This adds to the intention of the poem, suggests Trible, in surrounding the male with the female.[65] The last line is the climax of the poem. A much debated line, Trible translates it, "For Yahweh has created a new thing in the land: female surrounds man." The new creation that Yahweh has brought into being is a new reality in which the virile male is surrounded and protected by the feminine: the weeping mother, Rachel; the divine mother, Yahweh; and the daughter, Israel, who surpasses the son. Indeed, for Trible, the poem itself is the new reality.[66]

Not to be forgotten, argues Trible, is the importance of *reḥem* ("womb," "compassion") in the fourth strophe. This uterine metaphor, in Trible's interpretation, encompasses Ephraim, the chosen son, with the divine compassion of the Mother God. It is not only the female imagery of the poem but also the uterus that "nourishes, sustains, and redeems the male child Ephraim."[67]

The metaphor of God as mother, especially noted in the connection of God with *reḥem,* is the theological portrait at the heart of this striking poem. Ephraim is sustained, not by military power and political treaty, but by the divine compassion of God. Indeed, it is Rachel, not Jacob, who surrounds poetically her grandchild and embraces him with her grief. It is the virgin daughter, Israel, who surpasses the son. The movement of this metaphorical poem is also parabolic: the images shatter conventional, male-dominated theology centering on the Divine Warrior and undermine the hubris of rulers and generals that leads them to depend on war and negotiations to bring well-being. Now it is judgment time. It is left to the audience to reorient their theology and meaning system or to turn away in disgust. But acceptance of the reality redescribed by the metaphorical poem requires transforming Judah's entire theology and the social system that it undergirds. The peaceable kingdom would replace active militarism, the strength of women would be affirmed and celebrated, the suppression and subordination of women would end, the patriarchal God would be replaced by a God who is and is not male and female, the children of exile (northern Israelites especially) would return and be nourished

---

65. Ibid., 46.
66. Ibid., 50.
67. Ibid.

by being surrounded by the uterine God, and most importantly, the reign of God would begin.

Womanist Biblical Interpretation

African-American women read the Bible differently than their white, privileged European and American sisters.[68] They and other ethnic women of marginalized peoples also sometimes make use of rhetoric in the shaping of their theological discourse. But just as important is the contribution of social context, especially that of the interpreter, in articulating the literary expression of biblical and contemporary theology. The sociocultural location of African-American women is specifically shaped by a strong history of struggle against slavery, racism, and patriarchy outside of but also within African-American society. As is true in its oppression and exclusion of women and its support of patriarchy, the church historically has been a racist institution. Even the Black Church has tended to support the demeaning of African-American women. The first major challenge of womanist scholars has been to break the bondage into which they have been and continue to be placed by racist and misogynist whites who misuse the Bible to justify both racism and the dehumanization of women. Womanist theology on a political level is the continuing drive for civil rights and the recognition of the humanity and dignity of people of color. At the same time, the Bible also has served as a resource for liberation from racism and patriarchy and for womanist spirituality that develops out of communities of the oppressed who struggle to achieve dignity and humanity for African-American women.

Stories of oppressed women in the Bible provide an identification with African-American women's experience. Thus, the story of Hagar, the Egyptian (thus, African) concubine of Abraham, is especially important, for it reflects the experiences of African-American women who were slaves and even after emancipation continued to be marginalized in the dominant white society, not only by white men but also by white women. Hagar was from a "foreign" country (Egypt) often maligned in the Hebrew Bible and presented as an antagonist of Israel, while, at the same time she was a "concubine" owned by Abraham in every sense of the meaning. Her body was his to claim sexually, while any offspring were his to control, not hers.

---

68. Weems, *Battered Love.* See also Weems, *Just a Sister Away;* "Reading Her Way through the Struggle"; and "Song of Songs." Other prominent womanist theologians include Karen Baker-Fletcher, Katie Cannon, Cheryl Sanders, Jacquelyn Grant, and Emilie Townes (see bibliography).

Economically, she provided for the household of her master and could exist only on the whimsical basis of what he chose to allot her. Because of her ability to bear children, she was hated by Abraham's wife, Sarah, who believed she herself was barren. When the jealous Sarah mistreats her, Hagar takes her child, and together they flee into the wilderness. Due to divine intervention, the child and she survive, and the promise is made that he will be the ancestor of a great nation. African-American women during and after slavery were exposed to similar cruelty and prayed for divine deliverance.[69] They, too, yearn with hopeful anticipation for salvation. This is only one of a myriad of biblical stories with which African-American women have identified.

Womanist Biblical Interpretation: Renita Weems

The scholarship of Renita Weems has been distinguished by womanist theology for her studies in narrative and literary criticism.[70] She takes up metaphorical literary analysis and theology placed within a critical womanist grid in her study of the prophets—Hosea in particular, but also Jeremiah and Ezekiel. She penetrates the thin veneer of moral rectitude of exegetical attempts to support these abusers of women by exposing scholarship's intrinsic sexism. Particularly important are the sexist metaphors of these prophets who are a segment of the male power elite engaged in the abuse and manipulation of women. She notes the prophetic lurid and even morbid fascination with women's bodies and the violence and dishonor done to shame them in the metaphorical language these "divine" spokesmen chose to speak.

Most important in her hermeneutical appropriation of the biblical text for women in general, African-American women, and other marginalized groups is her recognition that interpretation occurs within a social framework of power and that there is no "innocent" reading of the biblical text that has so influenced our global cultures. She dispenses with male-inspired responses that the imagery of violence done to women is simply a "metaphor," meaning that it is a literary expression not to be taken seriously. This view of metaphor is one I have already discarded. Her approach combines gender criticism; newer literary studies, especially New Criticism; critical work on the erotic in theories of literature and other settings; reader-response criticism; and ideological-sociological analysis, especially in observing the inner workings of Israelite society as well as contemporary

69. See Williams, *Sisters in the Wilderness.*
70. Weems, *Battered Love.*

cultures of male dominance. Her book *Battered Love* proceeds in a steady and often provocative unveiling of the interpretive dimensions of her major topic, violence done to women. Chapter 1 describes the nature of metaphor. Perhaps the most important chapter is the second, which describes the sociohistorical context of the metaphors of sexual violence within the interaction of dread and desire and the power structures of Israelite society and especially patriarchal marriage. The next chapter raises the theological questions of the portraits of God that these metaphors depict. Finally, in chapter 4, Weems raises the hermeneutical question of how to engage these texts that write of the brutal actions taken against women, particularly those who are marginalized. Yet she writes not only of the destructive dimensions of sexual aggression, but also of the ways to recover intimacy, love, and romance between males and females. Thus, behind and in front of her work is the nobler vision of gender relationships based on the mutuality of shared love and commitment.

Weems begins with an intriguing question: "Why does the naked, abused female body grip the male imagination?" The prophets appeal to the imagination often by using feminine metaphors to describe the social and religious infidelity of Israel and Jerusalem as promiscuous women deserving of the violence done them. Three prophets have a particular fascination with this metaphor: Hosea, Jeremiah, and Ezekiel. Hosea uses the metaphor to set forth the relationship between the story of his marriage to Gomer, depicted as sexually immoral, and a faithless Israel. She becomes the battered wife who sells her body to survive. Jeremiah uses this metaphor in describing Jerusalem as a wanton whore, while Ezekiel contrasts a daughter and wife who were once beautiful and faithful, but now have become unchaste, libidinous women. These prophets employed these images to shape their speeches of judgment and destruction with the disgust and shame of debauched and abused women. Yet this fascination with the gross mistreatment of women is part of the discourse of their treatment in the Hebrew Bible. They are objects of sexual predatory behavior, victims of rape, forced to exhibit their nakedness, and mutilated, all at the instigation of men. There is a close relationship between patriarchy and violence carried out against women.

It is not enough to forgive this shocking language by arguing that the audiences of the biblical writers and prophets were men. Rather, these "men of God" stimulated through lurid, metaphorical descriptions the sexual fantasies of their male audiences and their sentimental view of two social institutions in which they held power: marriage and family. The household was not only dominated by senior males, but also was the means by which inheritance was orchestrated. Sex in Israelite society was supposed to occur only within the bonds of marriage. Severe penalties, including even death, could be administered for violations of these codes. These prophetic metaphors of loose women contribute to the cultic view of women as polluted and requiring a ritual of cleansing following menstruation, sexually deviant, and dangerous to a male-dominated society. Yet the prophets used this language that originated in the social, political, and religious spheres of Israelite life. These metaphors may have been the prophetic attempt to unveil the obscenity of faithlessness to God and seek, regardless of how demeaning they may be, to highlight the metaphors that describe the intimacy of God and Israel. And yet, according to Weems, these metaphors of wanton women, applied to Israel, did shock Israelites into seeing their relationship to God as degrading. While they did not push the boundaries of male domination, they did force men to see themselves in new and vile ways when worshiping other gods and failing to carry out the commandments of justice in their social dealings. These sexual metaphors of genitalia, breasts, semen emissions, menstruation, and the like were both fascinating and degrading.

Prophets are poets, not demagogues. They draw on the imagery prevalent in their social worlds to transmit their messages of doom and redemption. The social reality in which they lived was one of male privilege, female subjugation, and patriarchal power over women who were members of their household. Metaphors of God were necessary for Israel, since the enigmatic deity cannot be known or depicted by visual images. At this point, Weems makes significant use of the metaphorical theology of her former colleague Sallie McFague, discussed earlier. In the Hebrew Bible, God is normally portrayed by masculine metaphors, while Israel is the wife. The power relationship transfixed on theological gender reflected that of Israelite social understanding of "man" and wife. Even so, marriage is a covenant, and God is presented, not as a heartless, cruel sadist toward his people portrayed in the gender and societal role of the wife, but as a husband who welcomes back his faithless wife. Another metaphorically described relationship is that of God as parent and Israel as disobedient son. In any event, a repentant wife or son (Israel) is welcomed home by a loving and forgiving husband or father (God). The men who heard these metaphorical representations would react in horror and disgust. The prophets used them to portray to their male audiences God's view of their degeneracy and injustice. God is portrayed as both a faithful and an outraged, jealous husband to the promiscuous wife, Israel.

In Hosea, the prophet in chapter 2 legally accuses his wife of adultery, shaming her before their two children and bringing into question their paternity. For her infidelity, she would be shamed by the stripping of her clothing to reveal her nakedness. His charge includes her "falsely" crediting her paramours with providing her support. This shaming of her husband by means of her sexual infidelity and denial that he provided her the substance necessary for life was a double blow to his masculinity and his responsibility in these two roles. Yet, in spite of legal precedent denying the possibility of this, the prophet is willing to take his repentant wife back into his marriage relationship, thus pointing metaphorically to God's desire to forgive his faithless people, if only they would repent. Her return will not only restore the marriage and covenant bond between God and Israel, but the life of the entire cosmos. Moving beyond Hosea, Weems also describes similar imagery in Jeremiah and Ezekiel.

One of the more important insights Weems offers is that in the ancient Near East, cities were usually displayed in feminine guise and often as goddesses who were the wives of male gods. Like women, cities nurture those within them and are vulnerable to violent attack. In Israel, Jerusalem was presented as the wife of Yahweh, but also as a virgin and whore. These graphic images plumbed the depths of human emotions of fear, revulsion, and joy.

Her hermeneutical approach to these texts is largely that of reader-response, i.e., the shaping of the text by the reader who interprets from the matrix of social location. In Weems's case, the social matrix is that of women in general and African American women in particular. Thus, interpretation comes from the marginalized, social placement based on gender and race. She emphasizes that the rhetoric of the prophets emerges from the social location of ancient Israel and from primarily a male audience. Prophets addressed men who were socialized by their context to have particular stereotypes of women, their roles, and their behavior. The promiscuous wife plays havoc with the male fascination with and domination of the female body of his wife. The punishment for deviant female behavior plays out this dominant male role of social control. The society of ancient Israel undoubtedly saw nothing unusual about rape, abuse, and violence toward women who shamed their husbands or heads of the male household. Still, in these prophets forgiveness and the return of romance are told to lure back the unchaste Israel and presumably the unfaithful women in its society.

To break the hold of these and other insidious texts in the Bible defaming women, Weems asserts that we as readers must recognize how dominant they have been in shaping our own social world. All the divine attributes of integrity, courage, love, generosity, and passion are associated with males, while those that are not valued—untrustworthiness, proneness to error, sexual vamping, and wantonness—are attributed to women. This two-edged sword is to be dulled on both sides. Furthermore, we are to move beyond the polarity of rape and romance, two behaviors associated with male domination and the mystery of sexual union. While these texts are to be resisted, there are elements that assist in sustaining women and other marginals, which are not to be discarded. Men and women are to engage intimately in the sharing of a vision that shapes society now and in the future. The prophets' use of sexual metaphors is not to go unchallenged. While they may have led to the "shock of recognition" among men in Israel who saw themselves as faithless women, they also have assisted in insulating a sexist social, political, and religious reality that must be now confronted and rejected.

Weems's well-honed poetic skills and womanist insights are readily used in her commentary on Canticles in the *NIB.* Her interpretative acumen derives from her womanist theological social network that interlaces the corporate experience of black women. Her approach is significantly different from that of Marvin Pope, who focuses on the erotic, sexually explicit, and poetic depictions of art and literature from the ancient Near East in his own infatuation with this book. For Weems, the movement in the Song of Solomon is striking in comparison with the other books of the Bible. This grouping of love songs evokes the intimacy of two lovers, while there are also echoes of other kinship bonds, including mother, sister, brother, and daughter. The book is also strikingly different in that nowhere in the entire collection is God even mentioned (cf. Esther). This collection, unlike Esther, does not point to religious celebration (Purim), but rather to sexual intimacy that leaves unmentioned what many scholars have argued the Israelites cherished theologically: salvation history, the covenant with David, the Torah, and the temple on Zion, God's holy mountain. But most distinctive of all is the recognition that the dominant voice is female—a voice that is almost silent, save through narrative evocations of women characters and their discourse, in the remainder of the Hebrew Bible.

For this collection, lovers revel in the delights and joys of sexual attraction and embrace, enhanced by the affection they exchange. In these songs, one is able to enter into an Israelite woman's heart that is enticed and moved by the experiences of deep desire, dependence, sharing, and vulnerability. The two lovers revel in the pleasures of physical lovemaking in which all of the senses are stimulated, leading to the joyous experience of ecstatic embrace and physical union. Yet the woman is still threatened by the male with imprisonment if she becomes promiscuous (Cant 8:9), and women are abused as they pursue those men whom they love (Cant 5:2-8). The woman of black skin (1:5-6) still pursues the fulfillment of her romantic dreams and her erotic fantasies. Her color invites the audience to shun ethnic prejudice (contrast Moses' Cushite wife), their "Victorian" reserve about the invigorating delight of sensual love, and their class bigotry toward those who are darkened by the sun in their physical labors. Finally, Weems argues poignantly about the risks lovers take in unconventional behavior and sees in their unfeigned familiarity the threat of controlling and manipulative power that comes to cause the lovers potential harm. The woman's lover leaves, and we know not if there is a future consummation. In her reflections, expressed through the writing of her intimate experiences, she (the author) asks the age-old question, "Is love worth it?"

Jeremiah and Womanist Biblical Interpretation

Weems emphasizes that Jeremiah, as was true of Hosea, expected his audience to feel the same contempt for wayward women that they, as spokesmen, felt. We detailed the major social categories and metaphors for women in Jeremiah in the earlier chapter on feminist liberation. Weems points to the graphic and often repugnant metaphors used by the prophet in his description of women. She notes that sexual promiscuity was an activity that Jeremiah despised. Subsequently, he used metaphors of this infidelity and sexually wayward behavior to describe Judah and the city of Jerusalem. The key passages that draw on this imagery are 2:1-3; 2:29-37; 3:1-5; 3:1-11; 4:29-31; 13:20-27; and 31:31-34. In addition, Weems correctly notes that the prophet finds sexual independence in women to be unacceptable. It is in response to this sexual freedom that Jeremiah draws his lewd and disgusting images of the abuse of a sexually promiscuous Judah/Jerusalem in order to describe religious and political apostasy. The majority of this type of metaphor occurs in the first four chapters. He contrasts the people of Judah/Jerusalem now playing the harlot and performing as a faithless spouse with their earlier devotion in the wilderness period before the entrance into Canaan (cf. Hosea). This whore has fornicated wherever and with whomever she can. While Hosea depicts Israel as the faithless wife (Gomer), Jeremiah's female is a slut and a prostitute. In Jeremiah, she is to be punished. Her punishment is to endure the shame of public display of her genitalia when her clothes are raised above her head. This must have been a shocking image, not only in terms of his society's value of chastity and demure feminine behavior, but also in hearing that they are portrayed in this shameful manner.

Yet Yahweh is willing to forgive and take back his faithless wife who is now the woman of pleasure for hire, violating the legal requirements that husbands were allowed to have them executed and were forbidden to take back their wives who had remarried and then divorced again. This, too, must have shocked the audience, accustomed as they were to executing promiscuous women. Thus, reunion with Yahweh and a new beginning, not death, awaits the faithless generation. What troubles Weems is that these metaphors of abuse, left unchallenged, permeate society and culture through the centuries and create a hostile environment for women.

Mujerista Biblical Interpretation

The term *mujerista* is an "invented" word, although it obviously echoes the Spanish word *mujer*, most simply translated as "woman." Thus, *mujerista* theology is Latina "woman's theology," but even more, it is "women's liberation theology." This theology sets forth a theological basis for Latinas to speak their voices from their marginal experience in the United States. These voices cry out for a liberating praxis that enables them to engage in the struggle *(en la lucha)* to bring an end to oppression and to enable Latinas to express as valued human beings in their communities. *La lucha* requires radical struggle to end oppression, not only of Latinas and the larger Latino community, but also of all marginalized persons and groups in the world. This theology provides a model that may be used by all victimized people in obtaining the "space" they need for existence with dignity.

Mujerista *Theology: Ada María Isasi-Díaz*

The term *mujerista* refers to the theology done by Latina women in the United States, which begins with the shared experience of Latinas from a large number of different Latino cultures. This experience has been one of struggle for survival in a racist and sexist world of patriarchy and domination. This oppression began, of course, with the conquistadors who decimated the native populations and enslaved those who survived. And it has continued with Latinas not only exposed to racism and patriarchy from the dominant white-male-controlled social order, but also to the machismo of Latino men.

In their history in America, Latinas have developed through their religious experience, nurtured particularly in the Roman Catholic Church, a popular piety that centers on the heritage of women who have struggled to survive, some of whom became saints, and on Mary in her various appearances (e.g., Our Lady of Guadalupe). The Bible is a second resource, but Latinas knowledge of Scripture has often been limited to what they have heard in their churches. Isasi-Díaz explains that Latinas in America understand the "Word of God" to be not Scripture, but rather the belief that God is in their midst in their struggles. This is the experience, then, that provides the framework for *mujerista* theology. Finally, one finds in some Latina scholarship the combination of rhetorical expertise and social analysis. This is true of Isasi-Díaz.

In her book on *mujerista* theology, Isasi-Díaz sets forth the major features of this woman's theology from a Latina perspective. First, this theology gives Latinas the right to name themselves in ways that provide identity and the conceptual framework used in thinking, understanding, and relating to others. Thus, she invents the word *mujerista*, which expresses Latina theology as differentiated from feminism. Latinas have distaste for feminist theology, because it does not seek to share power among all groups, regardless of differences, and because it seems to promote, at least among white middle-class women, benefits for only some women, often at the expense of other marginalized peoples, including the poor regardless of gender, and people of color. "A *Mujerista* is someone who makes a preferential option for Latina women, for our struggle for liberation." *Mujeristas* engage in this struggle, not as individuals, but as members of a Latino community who are called to bring forth a new anthropology of women and men who are made in the image of God and to repudiate anything that degrades them.

Mujerista theology is not only a systematic articulation of faith, but also a liberation praxis, i.e., "reflective action that has as its goal liberation." This theological praxis enables Latinas to understand and appreciate who they are and seeks to influence mainline theologies that undergird the largely non-Latino churches in the United States. Understanding that struggle is for liberation keeps Latinas from engaging in self-serving actions that seek to benefit themselves and directs them to concentrate on changing the social and theological structures in order to eliminate oppression. This theology seeks to enable Latinas to discover God in their community and especially in their struggles.

Mujerista theology also seeks to enable Latinas to envision their future, their new community, and their common values in ways that lead to its proleptic realization in Latina life. This theology seeks to help Latinas recognize how much they have internalized victimization and thus are obligated to liberate themselves from this sense of being injured by understanding that self-effacement is not a virtue.

Further, *mujerista* theology stresses the importance of social location in the doing of theology. Isasi-Díaz explains that the "place" involves Latinas' *mestizaje* and *mulatez*, i.e., "our condition as racially and culturally diverse people" and as people living in two cultures, Hispanic and Anglo, in the United States. This racial and cultural diversity is reflected in the struggle to live into being a new future, one in which boundaries are removed. Finally, these terms refer to both pluralism and to Latinas' social location in the United States, one that embraces the past and views the future as one in which all people and peoples may participate.

This theology stresses the perspective that issues out of Latino shared experiences and the community in which life is lived. *Lo cotidiano*, meaning the life experiences of Latinas, has not only a descriptive implication, but also a hermeneutical purpose. Thus, Latinas see the world differently than non-Latinas. *Lo cotidiano* has to do with Latinas struggling as marginalized people, who construct both their own meaning and identity and those of the larger world. While it is not normative, liberation becomes the value that construes the legitimacy and truthfulness of certain beliefs and actions over against those that are oppressive and destructive to the community of humankind. *Lo cotidiano* is subversive of oppressive structures, whether social or theological, and serves as a reminder that Latinas are not the object of *mujerista* theology, but rather its subjects and more especially its agents.

Mujerista theology makes significant use of popular religion to express Latina beliefs and praxis. After Spanish as a language, popular religion becomes the most important feature of Latina religious understanding, expression, and action. It is not regarded as heterodox, but as an appropriate means by which Latina theology is shaped and experienced.

Although *mujerista* theology is self-consciously aware of its subjectivity, it strongly rejects the objectivity of reality. Self-disclosure of Latina beliefs and understandings is critically important, yet reality or truth is not objective, existing as an unchallenged understanding. This theology cannot avoid engagement in the struggle for liberation. It is not a passive, disengaged description of some reality that exists outside of life and experience.

While *mujerista* theology is communal in drawing its strength from the mutuality of Latinas living in sisterhood with each other, it also recognizes and values diversity of social location and experiences. This diversity is to be embraced and utilized in effectuating a welcoming reception and embrace of others with different views and understandings.

Finally, solidarity is an important feature of *mujerista* theology. Isasi-Díaz reminds us that solidarity is the "union of kindred persons" that issues from common interests, groups, and goals. It is an important location and expression that initiates and pursues the liberation of oppressed peoples, beginning with Latinas and extending beyond them to include all marginals. Alienation from each other and from God is the major obstacle to this "love" that motivates and brings into being activities of liberation. Effectuating change in the Latina communities results in the transformation of social structures that eliminates racism, sexism, imperialism, and economic exploitation. A strategy emerges out of solidarity, i.e., the conscientization of the oppressed. Once this occurs, the oppressed develop mutuality to engage in actions that will transform the world from one of oppression to one of liberation in which all people, including those silenced by their marginality, may act and exist as humans fully incorporated into the commonality of human dignity and life. There is also the conscientization of the oppressor, who, often unaware of actions that are oppressive, ceases actions that are life-denying and comes to live in harmony with the oppressed.

Mujerista justice involves a variety of factors. The objective of *mujerista* justice is not the construction of theory, but rather acting in ways that will bring about a righteous social order. Isasi-Díaz emphasizes reflective action. Thus, while rational thinking is involved, the goal is to establish justice through actions that are largely communal. Once again, she places her emphasis on contextualization in understanding that justice is a concrete reality existing within the lives of real people. The institution of justice comes through struggle within the Latina context. Thus, sociopolitical and economic understanding of the Hispanic community is essential in understanding and then devising a strategy to obtain justice.

Latina justice is not continuous with the past or accepting of the present. While recognizing the traditions of the Latino experience is an important task, what Latinas emphasize is that the oppression they have known and continue to experience is to be replaced with the realization of their full humanity resulting from their creation in the image of God. At the same time, justice, according to *mujerista* theology, is accepting of differences. This acceptance is needed for interaction between a variety of marginalized groups, Hispanic and others, in order to plot and carry out acts of justice. This view of justice begins, as does all liberation theology, with the grassroots experiences of people who are oppressed and powerless. While oppressive power uses force and coercion to maintain its status and to achieve its goals of self-interest, liberative power transforms the injustice and domination that are life-denying in order to establish a reality in which all may share. Justice begins with the oppressed who tell their stories, moves to solidarity of peoples who share their desire for their liberation, and then culminates in actions that transform the systemic repression that especially subjugates marginals.

Mujerista theology does not permit justice to be achieved at the expense of others' oppression. This understanding rejects the ideas of entitlements, in which all are simply to be given handouts for survival; of meritocracy, in which one achieves and therefore deserves the benefits for which one works; and of utilitarianism, in which justice is understood as the greatest good for the largest number of people. Rather, there is the redistribution of goods so that the well-to-do give of their excess to those who have far less so that all have an equal share in the goods of life. Yet *mujerista* justice requires more than simple redistribution; it seeks restitution in the sense of giving what the poor need to exist and to flourish. It is not restitution in the sense of giving back what was taken, but rather the understanding that humans deserve what they need to exist as people with the goods necessary for life and for hope for the future. This is not a handout, but rather an equalization of power. Otherwise, Latinas and other marginals will continue to be exploited by the rich and powerful. Latinas' rights are socioeconomic as well as political—that is, they have to do with the tangible elements of food, housing, education, and health care, and they include the freedoms guaranteed in the U.S. Constitution. These, coupled with the actions of redistribution of wealth and restitution, make these rights radical in their implications.

In her writings, Isasi-Díaz speaks of "the struggle" *(la lucha)*. Liberation is not simply a theory that sounds good, but rather is a set of actions designed to bring injustice to an end. However, these actions are not simply carried out. They involve intense struggle, because their radical implications would so transform the world that those in positions of domination and wealth are threatened by their loss. Struggle is intimately connected to a *mujerista* anthropology. Struggle means active participation in the goals of self-understanding, the Latinas' own sense of identity, how they value themselves, and the ways they construct themselves. Struggle, being the primary experience of most Latinas, leads not only to survival but also to self-construction, i.e., learning who they are and giving expression to their dreams for the future. Suffering is repudiated as a virtue, or at least is regarded with suspicion, because it has been used to justify poverty and oppression, both their creation and their acceptance. While suffering is a real and active feature of Latina life, it is not idealized. Rather struggle, not suffering, is the key to Latina life and self-understanding. It is a process that is not content with minimal existence, but rather seeks to achieve a full and joyful existence. *Lo cotidiana* (daily existence) includes all features of life—self-identity, self-description, social roles, and ways of action—and struggle becomes the means by which to see these features in their commonality.

Mujerista anthropology also involves discourse and action, both in the past and in the present. Latinas are not to accept being silenced, but go in search of the voices of their sisters before them, to share their experiences and to utter their own understandings and narratives in the present. Historical accounts largely have ignored women on the margins, so they must be rediscovered to allow them to speak their own words. They are not to accept others describing them or speaking on their behalf, either in what historians have written or what others are saying in the present. History usually traces public events, not private ones in the home, where most Latinas live out their lives. Even so, social histories may be written to describe their activities and the social movements they inspired or in which they were active participants.

The Latino family is changing, because increasingly women are no longer willing to live with abusive men. The patriarchal family is slowly dying. The features of *machismo* (patriarchy) and *hembrismo* (passivity projected onto women) are dissolving. In the family, women have been able to claim their voice and to influence Latino society. These family roles are not rejected, but rather are to be respected to give an enhanced status to women. The Latino community is an extension of the family, so as the family changes for the good while maintaining the values of Latinas, the larger society is to be transformed for the better. Latinas' bodies too often continue to be regarded as objects for male pleasure, procreation, and even abuse. They are regarded as objects for exploitation regarding their labor. This understanding of Latinas' bodies must be radically transformed.

How, then, does *mujerista* theology approach biblical interpretation? And beyond that, what would a *mujerista* biblical theology look like? Since the majority of Latinas are practitioners of the religion of their conquerors, the conquistadors, i.e. Roman Catholicism, there is not a strong tradition in the reading of the Bible. However, the fact that more recently Latinos and Latinas are joining Protestant churches where the Bible is read indicates the need for all churches to understand a *mujerista* interpretation of the Bible.

Once again, *la lucha* (struggle) plays a key role in the Latina reading of the Bible. The difficulty of understanding the Bible and the critical methods used to interpret it can be an overwhelming challenge for many Latinas. This is one reason why spirituality, praying to God, and worship have usually taken priority over reading the Bible. Even so, struggle is to serve as the lens through which the Bible is understood. Thus, the struggle of women and other marginalized people in biblical narratives becomes especially important for Latina readers. Also important is the theme of liberation, beginning with stories of survival to the release from the bonds of oppression in Egypt and later in Babylonia. The Bible is understood as inspired only when it contributes to the struggle for liberation. It helps in shaping the *proyecto histórico*, i.e., the desired future in which Latinas will participate as God continues to bring about the "kin-dom" in which all share. This future involves the rejection of the present as a time of oppression and domination by the wealthy and powerful. Biblical eschatology helps Latinas construct a future in which the injustices of the present will give way to a reality of well-being and righteousness.

The Bible also is used by Latinas to discover hope and inspiration, not to find the word of God that tells them what to do. The people in the Bible who struggled, including Jesus, become those with whom Latinas identify. Their struggles and the struggles of their communities allow Latinas to come into contact with those with who have had similar experiences. Latinas learn not to enter into conflict with other oppressed and exploited groups, but to enter into partnership with them to overcome the domination they all have experienced.

However, for *mujerista* theology, the word of God *(palabra de Dios)* is not the Bible, but the faith that God is a participant in daily struggles. It is an incarnation in social life that pursues a transformation of the world and rejects struggle. What Latinas have to say about the Bible is to be heard, not dismissed. Their biblical interpretation allows them to determine what it is that the church believes, in contrast to interpretations of the hierarchical church that are forced upon them.

Mujerista *Biblical Theology for Psalm 137 and Jeremiah*

The biblical approach of Isasi-Díaz may be best understood as a metaphorical presentation of the meaning of struggle in the quest for liberation. But its framing paradigm is that of narrative. Bible stories retold or fashioned anew to give a means of expression to the faith and life of Latinas. Thus, a theology of story also provides the type of biblical/systematic theology that characterizes her understanding.

Psalm 137

"By the waters of Babylon" is a statement from Ps 137 that Isasi-Díaz takes and formulates into a chapter to illustrate how she interprets the Bible. She approaches the text through her own experience of exile. She uses the methods of historical criticism to come to an understanding of the text and its meaning within the exilic community of ancient Babylon longing for the opportunity one day to return home. However, she rejects the position of "disinterested objectivity," a phrase that simply becomes a façade for the domination of the text by Eurocentric interpreters. Rather, she reads this psalm with the subjectivity of her own experience in seeking to discover from the Bible a community like hers (Cuban) living in exile and longing for restoration to the homeland. Even the language of vengeance—and that is what one has, language and not action—can be understood by those who have been refused the possibility of return. Exile is not necessarily a place. It can also be the experiences of domination and injustice. Yet as the psalmist yearns for the return, so does she, a Cuban American, hope one day to go again to the home of her birth.

The Book of Jeremiah

How would an interpretation of the book of Jeremiah look theologically, if written by a Latina using the insights of *mujerista* theology? A *mujerista* theologian and biblical scholar would focus on the struggle for justice in the book of Jeremiah by marginals and the strong criticism of the power of political and religious hierarchies. Jeremiah's "temple sermon" in 7:1-15 (cf. 26:1-6), occurring at the critical period following the death of Josiah and the dreams of national ambition (609 B.C.E.), assaults the theology of security offered by the temple of Yahweh, divine presence in Jerusalem, and the affirmation he will fight to defend it against any and all enemies. This theology the prophet describes as deceptive. Instead, the two pillars of Jeremiah's theology are the religious and social sections of the law (especially demarcated and listed in the Ten Commandments). But what the prophet stresses is a repudiation of the oppression of marginals in Judah's society ("the alien, the orphan, and the widow"). Stealing, murdering, adultery, lying oaths, and the worship of Baal are to be rejected. Unless there is a repudiation of this oppression, the nation will suffer destruction, and its leaders will be exiled.

What is especially important for *mujerista* theology—the struggle for justice against the powers of the state and the church—finds support in not only the preaching of Jeremiah, but also in his own struggles leading to severe persecution. Jeremiah's theology of justice is not only the articulation of its goals in preaching, but also in its actualization in life. Indeed, when Jeremiah speaks of his hopes for the future in chapters 30–31, he tells of the writing of the law on the heart, i.e., the actualization of justice in human existence in community.

Evaluation

The theologies of McFague, Trible, Weems, and Isasi-Díaz point to one important, new journey on which Old Testament theology has embarked. These scholars are quick to remind us that the language of the text must be considered in any effort to set forth its theology. And they remind us of the importance of different associations of women (Anglo, African American, and Latina) in framing and seeking to answer theological questions. Especially the ethnic interpreters are concerned to explicate the social context of the Bible, but even more the interpreter. McFague submits that her own work is intermediary to a larger, systematic rendering. For her, metaphorical theology retains the imagistic character of theological language yet also includes conceptualization. The others move more directly into contemporary hermeneutics, unchallenged by any gulf existing between text and modern life. These scholars have recovered meanings of texts and theological expressions that have been encrusted by many layers of sexist readings. McFague reminds us of the radical theology of Jesus who subverted oppressive social and religious structures. Trible rediscovers the importance of "womb" imagery in Old Testament portraits of God. Weems uncovers the abusive images of prophets that have reinforced mistreatment of women in contemporary culture. Isasi-Díaz sees in the narratives of marginals in the Bible stories that allow Latinas to discover biblical prototypes of their own struggles. Each, in her own way, reminds us that theological language if not critically assessed may be idolatrous or, worse, even oppressive and destructive of contemporary life. They shatter the image of God as male by the use of the Bible's own language for deity and by engaging in strong criticisms of religious and political legitimations of oppression. Sexist readings of texts that lead to a singular portrayal of Israel's God as male, e.g. a Divine Warrior, are indeed undermined. So are the metaphors of abuse and exploitation that have often initiated negative treatments of women. Weems and Isasi-Díaz speak with passion out of the context of their communities to address the text with new meaning.

Indeed, most exciting about the work of these women is that they offer a revolutionary way of speaking about God, marginalized groups, and engagement in the theological enterprise. While McFague's metaphorical theology makes use of classic texts, including Scripture, her work proposes to set forth a new way of speaking about God that is not simply limited to the re-presentation of biblical metaphors, even those neglected or suppressed. Her work is not limited primarily to Scripture. Trible, however, is a Bible scholar who works with Scripture in order to reclaim or rediscover the full range of its variety of metaphors and address them to the contemporary scene. Weems, also a biblical scholar, focuses more on the images of abuse that have directly affected the mistreatment of women due to men's fascination with naked, beaten female bodies. Isasi-Díaz, while recognizing the Bible has not been central in Latina religion, still sees the stories of the struggle of the poor and marginalized in Scripture as important. The work of each suggests a radical reorientation of Old Testament theology that holds much promise.

The understandings of Weems and Isasi-Díaz approach women's interpretations of Scripture from the margins as women of color. In addition to their criticisms of males, both from their own respective social groups and from the dominant white males of American society, they also offer criticisms of white women, including some feminists, for aspiring to the same positions of power and control that white men traditionally have possessed.

The only question I have is what Gadamer calls distanciation.[71] For Trible, the Bible is a "pilgrim" wandering through time that cannot be imprisoned by the past. Yet how is the distance between ancient text and contemporary ethos overcome? I would ask the same of the other three

71. Gadamer, *Truth and Method*.

women. Ancient audiences presumably had less difficulty entering into the linguistic world shaped by the biblical texts that addressed them than do those of the contemporary period, who may be addressed by these texts only through new articulations of meaning. This difficulty is more severe for Trible and Weems than for McFague and Isasi-Díaz, since the latter two are not primarily biblical scholars. One of the advantages of historical criticism is that it provides for distanciation. In any theological enterprise, there needs to be a detailed explication of the world and community of the implied audiences of texts. Doing this would facilitate dialogical interaction with the narrative worlds of the Bible. Entering into these narrative worlds is no easy process and requires some hermeneutical effort that includes the interaction of texts and culture, both those of the past and those of the present opening up to the future.

That said, the potential of metaphor, rhetoric, and social context for explicating the theology of Jeremiah I find to be both exciting and significant. Feminine metaphors, even the shockingly lurid and repugnant ones, and the experience of the struggles of the marginalized are important matters to raise from this prophetic book, and a thorough social history of women and the feminine in the book of Jeremiah would prove very insightful.

6

From Jewish Tradition to
Biblical Theology:
The Tanakh as a Source for
Jewish Theology and Practice

"Why Jews Don't Do Biblical Theology"
— *Jon Levenson*

From his right hand, there emerged a fiery law for the
nation.
— *Deut* 33:2

Introduction

THE FIRST QUOTATION THAT SERVES AS ONE OF THE TWO EPIGRAPHS
for this chapter is the title of a well-known and often cited 1987 essay
written by Jon Levenson. His criticisms of biblical theology, especially that
done by Protestants, have been thoroughly discussed in academic literature and will only be rehearsed here in brief. Nevertheless, in spite of Levenson's assessment in 1987, increasing numbers of Jewish biblical scholars
engage in biblical theology, or at least Jewish theology, as a discipline and
see it as appropriate for practicing Jews to develop and engage.

Levenson and the Rejection of Biblical Theology

In reviewing biblical scholarship that had appeared up to the point he
wrote his essay in 1987,[1] Levenson came to question whether there was
any significant amount of Jewish participation in the discipline of the
theology of the Tanakh. While stating that Jewish scholars have contributed

---

1. See Levenson, "Why Jews Are Not Interested in Biblical Theology." An earlier version
is found in Neusner, *Judaic Perspectives on Ancient Israel.*

various studies to theological themes in the Bible, Levenson notes the omission of any book written by a Jew that calls itself "biblical theology" or "Old Testament theology." This remains true almost two decades after the appearance of Levenson's essay. The question is why. Levenson offers a variety or answers, some convincing, others not so.

First is the recognition that biblical theology is a part of Christian systematic theology, particularly in regard to the constructive dimension of both. This is true, in Levenson's view, in spite of the argument by Gabler two centuries before that biblical theology is a historical discipline that sets forth what biblical writers believed, while dogmatic theology, informed by biblical theology, articulates the faith of the contemporary church. Levenson contends that Christians, especially Protestants, see biblical or Old Testament theology as a constructive enterprise usually revolving around a center that is thought to provide a thematic unity. Perhaps the classic example of this is the two-volume Old Testament theology of Walther Eichrodt, who regarded covenant to be a thematic cross section of the Hebrew Bible. For Levenson, this quest for a unity falsely intimates that the texts of the Hebrew Bible present a common faith, again a questionable argument even twenty years ago. And it is a misleading reading of the Hebrew Bible that distorts the diversity of the texts' various themes and the various ways they are understood. Levenson asserts that Christians are committed to the constructive task of theology, while Jewish scholars are interested primarily in history and philology.

Another factor that discourages Jewish participation in Old Testament theology, writes Levenson, is the recognition that this discipline is Christian in general and Protestant in particular. Protestants in the Reformation developed and have continued to place emphasis on the principle of *sola scriptura,* or "scripture alone," as the single authority for faith and practice. Protestants see the Bible as the norm (canon) of faith, in contrast to Jews, who regard "moral laws" and modern understandings (e.g., the physical sciences) as the instruments of authority. One major implication of this is the recognition that Protestants approach biblical theology from the commitment of their faith and do not differentiate between the Bible and their own theological beliefs. Biblical theology is a Christian discipline that includes the Old Testament and the New Testament as one text of faith. Jews, by contrast, see the Tanakh as important but as only one collection of texts that make up their traditions. These include the Haggadah and Halakakh, the Midrashim, the Talmud, and the Commentaries. When Christians affirm that Jesus Christ is the ultimate fulfillment of the Old Testament, then obviously Jews by definition are excluded.

A third reason for the lack of Jewish biblical theologians is the fact that Jews have found their meaning in history, while Christians have pointed to theology or the "word" of Scripture that is preached to expound Protestant faith and its understanding of practice. Here Levenson has in mind the emphasis by Continental Protestant biblical theologians who were especially influenced by Karl Barth's theological legacy in which the Word of God finds ultimate expression in Jesus Christ. For Protestants, this Word also renews the faith, as seen, e.g., in the Reformation. Reformation is an idea that is rare in Judaism. Protestants, thus, in their understanding of the Word as revelation and as the power of reform, cannot read the Hebrew Bible other than as a Christian book. Jews, by contrast, define themselves as a people existing in history.

The anti-Semitism of some Christian biblical scholars and theologians has also discouraged Jewish participation in biblical theology. Of course, Levenson could have made the same point about biblical studies in general. Nevertheless, this recognition does not diminish the fact that some of the most overtly anti-Semitic Christian scholars have been Old Testament theologians as well as scholars of the Old Testament in general. The misunderstanding of Judaism as a religion of law that is a straitjacket that robs faith of its vitality begins with Paul, continues with Luther, and enters into Protestant biblical scholarship. Eichrodt's views of Judaism and the law are extreme in their anti-Semitic character, while the other great Old Testament theologian, Gerhard von Rad, deals with the Jewish nature of the Old Testament by pretending that Judaism did not and does not exist. Thus, for von Rad, the acts of God in history stop two centuries before the birth of Christ, only to begin again in the "Word made flesh." Old Testament historians often cease their writing with the beginning of the Hellenistic period, reflecting the view that the Hebrew Bible and thus revelation have ended until the coming of Christ and the birth of the early church.

A final factor is the different organization of the canon by Christians and Jews. Protestant Christians read biblical theology through a canon that ends with the prophet Malachi looking to the future as the time of fulfillment, whereas Jews conclude with the Chronicler, which tells of the major tenets of Early Judaism: the Torah, the presence of God in the rebuilt temple and its sacred liturgy, and the observation of the Sabbath. This is one of the most important differences between the two canons that either precludes a common biblical theology or makes it far more difficult to construct (although not as difficult as the imposing problems raised by the differences between the Roman Catholic and the Protestant one!).

Tradition

Levenson sees rabbinic Judaism as the direct continuation of ancient Israelite religion. He often discovers useful insights from the rabbis in understanding the Bible. The Bible, while important for the continuing interpretations in the Midrashim and the Commentaries, still is joined later by the Mishnah, the formulation of Halakhim and Haggadim, and the Talmud. For Jewish scholars, there is no legitimate biblical theology that rejects or ignores rabbinic exegesis and later collections that are postbiblical.

Academic Scholarship

For Levenson, all scholars of any persuasion should approach the biblical text with intellectual honesty. The critical scholar's interests and often his or her results differ from those of scholars who work out of a particular religious or theological orientation. He places himself within the academic community of scholars in his historical, exegetical work. The implication of his argument appears to be that Christian faith eliminates any possible objectivity in approaching the Bible as a historical document. Of course, this is not always true. Even if it were, it would be no more generally true for Christians than for Jews. Both stand within the context of believing communities yet are still capable of working as historians who have put aside their own faith as best they can in historical critical work. The question is whether they should or do interpret the Bible through the lenses of their different faiths. This is the issue that will always be present in research. Indeed, many more recent biblical theologians argue that it is impossible to divest oneself of one's own context and predisposition to engage in reading from the perspective of self-interest.

Tradition as the Formative Crucible for Jewish Thought and Practice

After dispensing with biblical theology as a discipline appropriate for contemporary Jews, Levenson sets forth what is fitting for Jewish reflection on theological understanding and religious practice: tradition, which ranges from the Bible through the Mishnah, the Midrashim, the Talmud, medieval teachers, and modern philosophical, religious, and theological articulations since the Enlightenment. One example of how this is carried out is found in Levenson's essay on Maimonides, the "eighth principle, and the simultaneity of Scripture."

A question that continued to perplex Maimonides was whether the Torah in its present form was of divine or human origin. The heresy that Maimonides opposed was not that Moses wrote the Torah, but that God dictated it. He concluded not only that human beings had tampered with the Torah, but also that it was, nonetheless, a divine compilation. Maimonides held to the unity and divinity of Torah. Maimonides's view continues to hold significance for Jewish theologians today. The Torah is an indissoluble unity and divine revelation, regardless of how its continuous parts came into being. Levenson explains that Jewish scholars today accept the authenticity of historical research but do not allow it to become the basis for theology. For Jewish scholars, contends Levenson, "the modern study of the Hebrew Bible is an evolution out of medieval rabbinic exegesis and not a revolution against it, as the right wing of Orthodox Judaism and others would have it." He adds, "The authority of the Torah does not require faithful exegetes to deny the contradictions within it, but the frank recognition of the contradictions does not allow them to base religious life and practice on something less that the whole."[2] Thus, Jews and Christians can work together on the literal senses and historical meaning of Scripture, but they go their separate ways when articulating their theologies for contemporary faith and practice.

Creation and the Persistence of Evil

In my chapter on creation in *The Collapse of History*,[3] I have previously mentioned Levenson's theology of creation. Levenson's work is one of the best treatments of creation, coming from a former student of Frank Cross who continues to express his teacher's interest in Canaanite myth and the Divine Warrior. Levenson's book *Creation and the Persistence of Evil* grows out of his concern to address the difficult questions posed by the Jewish Holocaust. He asks if, in view of the Holocaust, it is possible to reconcile a doctrine of divine sovereignty with the equally important affirmation of the life-sustaining justice of God. To answer this fundamental question of post-Holocaust thought, Levenson presses forward with three objectives: First, he seeks to demonstrate that *creatio ex nihilo* is an inadequate characterization of creation in the Hebrew Bible. This has led in turn to ascribing "a false finality or definitiveness" to creation that both ignores the vulnerability and fragility of the cosmos and fails to appreciate the drama of God's omnipotence over creation. Second, Levenson detects a general lack of appreciation for the relationship of the priestly creation story with the liturgy of cult. This leads to a common failure to understand the significant role of ritual in the forming and sustaining of the cosmos. Thus, third, he wishes to work out the relationship between cosmos and history, not only

---

2. See three essays in Jon D. Levenson's *The Hebrew Bible, The Old Testament, and Historical Criticism:* "The Eighth Principle of Judaism and the Literary Simultaneity of Scripture," 62–81; "Theological Consensus or Historicist Evasion? Jews and Christians in Biblical Studies," 82–105; and "Historical Criticism and the Fate of the Enlightenment Project," 106–26.

3. See chapter 5, 121-24 in Perdue, *The Collapse of History*.

in understanding God as both creator and Lord of history, but also in appreciating the dialectic of human submission to divine suzerainty and even God's dependence on humanity to effectuate the consummation of salvation history.

In part one of his volume, Levenson points to the basic tension between the mastery of God and the vulnerability of order. While Gen 1 suggests that God has always reigned supreme, other accounts speak of the time when God comes to assume leadership over the divine council. Instead of discounting one or the other portrayal, Levenson develops a model of dialectical theology in which the two poles interact in creative tension.

Levenson argues that it is especially within Israel's historical experience that chaos seemed to have gained the upper hand. Thus, the assertion of Yahweh's sovereignty is often opposed by the contesting of that lordship. Levenson believes that liturgy, by activating divine power, mediates the two contradictory affirmations of God as Lord of creation and history, on one hand, and as the one who is challenged for supremacy and even appears at times to be defeated, on the other. Further, Israel at times projected the combat myth into the future. In the eschaton (cf. Isa 24–27), God will once for all defeat the chaos monster, death will be vanquished, and the cosmos will be ultimately secure. Yet this final mastery over chaos is grounded in hope that issues forth in a confession of faith. Israel stands before, not after, the cosmic victory.

In the second section of his book, Levenson develops the dialectic expressed in the alternation between chaos and cosmos, especially in the priestly account of creation. While Israel may have had a seven-day festival that was the new year's celebration of the reactualization of cosmogony and enthronement, P eventually dissociated creation from the new year and connected it instead to the Sabbath. With Sabbath rest, there was the cessation from the time of opposition to divine rule. Sabbath worship was the way that the cultic community came to participate in the ordering of creation on a weekly basis.

Sacred space is also important, Levenson maintains, for the temple is a microcosm of the perfect and harmonious world as it ought to be. In the ritual building and rededication of the temple, once again humans participate in the divine ordering of the world. In sacred space and time, Israel proleptically participates in the defeat of chaos and the transformation of chaos into order.

Finally, in part three Levenson takes up the dialectic of cosmos and history expressed in the two idioms of creation and covenant. In the mythic battle with the dragon, Israel came to express its monotheistic faith. By monotheism Levenson means that for Israel, there is the exclusive enthronement of God over the divine council and the uncompromising commitment to obey his commands. The other idiom of monotheism, covenant, also requires unswerving loyalty to God. Covenant love is threatened primarily by the seduction of other gods who promise more for less. Even as God's kingship over the cosmos depended on Israel's constant reaffirmation in worship, so God's rule over history required the repetition of the covenant in ritual celebration and loyal but freely given obedience. The actualization of divine power requires the worship and testimony of God's people. God's sovereignty depends on Israel's faithful response, for he sits enthroned on the praises of his people.

Yet, according to Levenson, Israel must be free to recognize and then submit to divine rule. This tension between autonomy and heteronomy, human freedom and submission to God, is explained by reference to Near Eastern suzerainty treaties. The vassal freely enters into covenant with the ruler and recognizes his lordship. Yet behind every treaty is the implied threat that violence will be inflicted on the weaker party. Thus, there is no real alternative to God's suzerainty. Even so, to avoid war, the suzerain must woo the vassal. This element of courtship mediates between autonomy and heteronomy. Likewise, God both woos and commands Israel's faithful response. "Those who stand under covenantal obligation by nature and necessity are continually called upon to adopt that relationship by free decision. Chosen for service, they must choose to serve. This is the paradox of the dialectic of autonomy and heteronomy."[4] The autonomy of humanity makes it possible for people to argue with God and win, but the heteronomy of humankind brings them into submission. Thus, within this "larger, dialectical theology, both arguing with God and obeying him can be central spiritual acts."[5]

Levenson's work represents the Albright school's conservative adoption of the History of Religion in approaching Old Testament theology, as he, similarly to his teachers and their teacher, Albright, uses Near Eastern mythology and Israelite covenant theology to set forth a dialectic in which divine omnipotence and limitation are held together in uneasy tension. At the same time, there are several areas where he may be pressed for further explication. One wonders if Levenson has tended to superimpose the mythic pattern of the battle with the dragon on too much of the Old Testament. One may argue that there are texts with root metaphors of word, aesthesis, and fertility that may not so easily fit his paradigm of combat or eschatological resolution of combat proleptically realized in the cultus.

---

4. Levenson, *Creation and the Persistence of Evil*, 148.
5. Ibid., 153.

Also, the form-critical thesis of a suzerainty treaty used by Levenson to explicate Israel's understanding of covenant and the theological tension between autonomy and heteronomy has come under sharp attack, both as a valid literary construct and as an appropriate analogy for understanding Israelite covenants. Assyrian, Hittite, and Egyptian treaties, to be sure, followed these form-critical features, but for Israel this is extremely doubtful. One has to force the model by searching over separate texts in Exodus, Deuteronomy, and even Joshua. The preamble, for example, so well developed in suzerainty treaties, is limited to the brief prologue to the Decalogue: "I am the Lord thy God who led you out of Egypt, out of the house of slavery" (Exod. 20:2 = Deut 5:6). The "blessings" and "cursings" have to be extracted from Deut 28, while the "witness" is taken from the "stone" in Josh 24. To use this model for understanding Israel's covenant raises serious questions not only about its appropriateness and influence, but also about its implications for the interpretation given to covenant. The argument for this type of treaty as the form for the covenant is strained and unconvincing.

Nevertheless, Levenson's work moves theological inquiry in an important direction. It provides a systematic presentation of the various materials in the Hebrew Bible without negating the plurality of voices that speak, and there is a trace of critical reflection on the hermeneutical value of these voices in the implication that this volume speaks to a world following the Holocaust.

Conventions for Conversation

Levenson offers some important conventions for dialogue by first responding to the earlier study on the topic of interfaith dialogue presented in a volume edited by Lawrence Boadt and others.[6] Boadt begins the conversation by noting that setting forth "the relationship of the Hebrew Scriptures to the New Testament . . . must begin with the premise that each speaks from its own complete integrity."[7] However, Levenson is puzzled by Boadt's argument that Jews and Christians should bracket their religious commitments in the pursuit of biblical studies when they meet. In this setting, they come together not as Jews and Christians, but as something else—something not available in the days of Nachmanides and Pablo Christiani, in days that are long past—that is, as historical-critical scholars. The common ground for conversation is thus the scholarship that is

6. Boadt et al., *Biblical Studies.*
7. Ibid., 3–4.

shared by Jewish and Christian biblical scholars, and not their religious traditions and views. Yet this religious neutrality should not be "mistaken for the key to a genuine and profound dialogue between these two great religious communities."[8] Taken to its logical conclusion, then, there would not be any exchange in the area of biblical theology as it relates to two different historical faiths.

Levenson also refers to an essay by James Kugel,[9] who argues that modern biblical studies have a decidedly Protestant bias. Levenson notes that Protestants have little more than a passing interest in cult and Torah, and this is even more evident in their Old Testament theologies. Some tend either to ignore or caricature the Second Temple period of Jewish history, regarding Judaism in this period as a marked decline from its earlier heights of understanding, especially in the texts of the classical prophets of the monarchical period.[10] Noth even concludes that with the defeat of Bar Kochba, Jewish history came to an end. Levenson contends this claim was motivated by theology: Jews forfeited their right to be Israel at the time of the emergence of Christianity. Noth's view even intimates that the

8. Levenson, "Theological Consensus or Historicist Evasion?"

9. Kugel, "Biblical Studies and Jewish Studies."

10. It is obvious that many Protestant scholars, including Germans (e.g., Wellhausen, *Israelitische und jüdische Geschichte*), have engaged in a caricature of post-Exilic Judaism as stultifying legalism. There is no doubt that a great deal of anti-Semitism appeared in German Old Testament scholarship in the nineteenth and twentieth centuries. However, while not trying to cover up or excuse anti-Semitic interpretations of late biblical Judaism, Levenson should check more carefully his sources before leveling the accusation of anti-Semitism. For example, Levenson argues that the conclusion (last sentence) of Martin Noth's history (*Geschichte Israels*) is anti-Semitic: "Thus ended the ghastly epilogue of Israel's history." Even if the English translation of this sentence is taken as an expression of anti-Semitism, this would be an incorrect reading. The sentence follows Noth's summary of the devastation of Jerusalem by the Romans, the slaughter of many of the population, the slavery endured by survivors, and the emergence of Judah as a Roman province. Indeed, Hadrian later built a temple of Jupiter Capitolinus on the holy site of the temple and erected a nearby temple dedicated to Venus. Jerusalem became a Roman provincial city, and the Jews eventually were excluded from the very city that had for centuries been the center for their political and religious lives. They had become strangers in their own land. This is hardly an anti-Semitic obituary. Furthermore, the final sentence of the volume reads, "Damit endete das schauerliche Nachspiel der Geschichte Israels." *Schauerliche* signifies nightmarish, gruesome, or ghastly, and *Nachspiel* means postlude, sequel, epilogue, or aftermath. What Levenson takes to be anti-Semitic in this conclusion of a standard German history is actually a description of the appalling end of Israel as a state existing in the land of Israel. I would translate Noth's conclusion, "With the Jews' exclusion from their holy city, the final nightmarish episode of the history of Israel came to an end." This is hardly to be understood as anti-Semitic. Instead it is a statement that concludes the chronicling of the frightful suffering the Jewish people in Israel experienced at the hands of their enemies.

dispersion was viewed as punishment for rejecting Jesus. This is some-thing of an overstatement, as I read Noth. Indeed, Noth does deal with the life and ministry of Jesus and the birth of early Christianity. And he does indicate that in Jesus, whom the Jews rejected as the Messiah, the history of Israel came to an end. But he does not argue that there is a type of divine retribution issued against the Jews that led to their dispersion. In Leven-son's criticism of the Christian, particularly Protestant, use of historical criticism, the results of this method generally have been at odds with the underlying method, and it is clear that numerous Christian interpreters, including a historian like Noth, allow their own Christian bias to color historical and theological judgments. Levenson is correct that at least some Christian historical critics have improperly allowed their religious com-mitments to shape a later "recontextualization," one that often is liberal Protestantism.

Protestants, according to Levenson, have been engaged in the "disman-tling of tradition" indigenous to their own history. It is as though the past is that which truly interests most Protestants. Even so, Levenson still con-cludes, "Jews and Christians can indeed meet as equals in the study of this new/old book, but only because the Hebrew Bible is largely foreign to both traditions and precedes them." The common ground is their work as historians. Historical criticism requires both Jews and Christians bracket their traditional identities.

Evaluation

Levenson's criticisms of biblical theology are occasionally on the mark, even though his sweeping generalizations disallow concrete analysis and do not always betray a clear understanding of what it is he wishes to cen-sure. During the two decades since his essay first appeared, there have been important changes in biblical theology that most certainly silence many of his criticisms. Even many of his claims in 1987 point to someone not knowledgeable of biblical theology pursued by Christian interpreters. For example, his contention that Protestants do not recognize the force of ritual in sustaining the cosmos overlooks the work of many Christian his-torians of religion, including, for example, Sigmund Mowinckel. The ar-gument that Christians (i.e., Protestants) read the Hebrew Bible from the perspective of their own faith dismisses a large number of Christian bibli-cal scholars who go to a considerable length to avoid this. His charges of anti-Semitism, while at times accurate, seem to be overblown and directed against even some Christian biblical scholars who do not deserve this type of villification. I include here his criticisms of Gerhard von Rad.

A more judicious assessment would include an awareness of the following points. First, many biblical theologians recognize that diversity is a major feature of the Hebrew Bible and thus must be recognized in biblical theology. Also, many Protestant biblical theologians allow the Hebrew Bible to utter its own distinctive voices and do not Christianize this part of Scripture. Levenson omits the "battle for the Old Testament" that was waged in the early church in order to claim it as Scripture. Third, there are significant efforts at interfaith conversations between Christians and Jews, with both groups respecting and honoring the other's own faith commitments. Christian scholars have recognized that anti-Semitism exists in the New Testament, in the history of the church, and in biblical scholarship. Strong efforts by liberal Christians have been made to expunge this feature from biblical theology and Christian biblical scholarship. In addition, the approach of the History of Religion as a means of accessing biblical theology is an increasingly important way of honoring the original social location and theological understandings of biblical texts, not the older approaches of those like Eichrodt, who searched for and identified a center for a systematic articulation of Israelite faith. In addition, efforts by some biblical theologians to address their relevance for the contemporary communities of faith (Jewish and Christian) are carried out, not with the objective of proving one religion is true and the other false, but rather with the purpose of engaging their respective communities' faith and practice. However, there are also Protestant biblical theologians who do not engage in constructive theology, Christian or otherwise. While neo-Barthianism has continued in some circles as an important theology for some Christians (e.g., the Yale school of Neo-Barthianism), its emphasis on the theology of the Word does not hold the commanding position it once held. This decline of Barth's impact began in the 1960s, twenty years before Levenson wrote his critique. This means other competing constructive theologies have been undertaken that strongly resist a supercessionist understanding of Judaism and Christianity.[11] Finally, to criticize Protestants for ending the Old Testament with the last of the canonical writings of Chronicles, likely appearing in the Hellenistic period, and not resuming until the emergence of the Christian canon in the second century C.E. does not take into account the fact that the Protestant reformers adopted the Jewish Tanakh as the first part of their Scripture. This position also does not recognize that Catholics and even a number of Protestant biblical theologians hold in high regard the apocryphal/deuteronomical writings and use them to reconstruct biblical theology.

11. Zenger, *Das Erste Testament*, 12–27.

The recognition of these points takes some of the edge off Levenson's critique.

Jews Who Do Biblical Theology

In spite of Levenson's apodictic judgment that Jews do not engage in biblical theology, there are Jews in the past and in the present who write theology, although not the Protestant theology (as though it were ever a unified formulation) against which he directs most of his criticisms. I include some of them in the following discussion.

M. H. Goshen-Gottstein

Moshe H. Goshen-Gottstein has been considered to be the first modern Jewish scholar to propose that Jewish biblical (or Tanakh) theology should become a discipline within biblical scholarship.[12] While his untimely death precluded the finishing of his own Jewish biblical theology, Goshen-Gottstein still set forth several key elements that should constitute this work. He began by discussing the long history of the discipline of Protestant Old Testament theology, beginning with Gabler's address and the later appearance of the Old Testament theology of Wilhelm Vatke.[13] Historically, modern biblical studies have been pursued largely by Christian scholars, who have applied their craft in especially theological faculties. In this setting, the theology of the Old and New Testaments are understood as a discipline within the larger context of contemporary theology.

Goshen-Gottstein observed that biblical theology had only begun recently to be understood as a Jewish area of study in the years leading up to his death. Much of the Jewish resistance to biblical theology and indeed historical criticism itself, at least until well into the twentieth century, has been the anti-Semitism that has characterized some Christian research. He mentioned the statement of De Wette: "das Judentum ist die verunglueckte Wiederhestellung des Hebraismus."[14] And then he noted Wellhausen's view that Judaism in the post-exilic period represented the decline of Israelite religion, when a strong legalism focused on the Torah and its interpretation

---

12. For relevant works by Goshen-Gottstein and other scholars cited in this chapter, see the bibliography.

13. Most of the material for the contribution of Goshen-Gottstein to this lively area of interest I have taken from his essay "Tanakh Theology."

14. Quoted by Perlitt, *Vatke und Wellhausen*, 92.

occurred. On the very first page of his Prolegomenon, he wrote: "Judaism is a mere empty chasm over which one springs from the Old Testament to the New."[15] Further, many Christian scholars, tracing their views back to Luther, himself virulently anti-Semitic, could not read the Old Testament without a view to its elucidation of Jesus Christ. For example, Franz Delitzsch, following the understanding of Luther, argued that the Christian scholar of the Old Testament who ceased for a moment to find the presence of Christ in the Old Testament stopped being a Christian.[16] Even Eichrodt wrote that Judaism in the post-exilic period was not the object of an Old Testament theology, due to its legalistic understanding of law and covenant. This strong anti-Semitism, which is still not totally absent from Christian interpretations of the Hebrew Bible, has been a major stumbling block to Jewish engagement of a theology of the Tanakh and as a consequence to dialogue. When historical criticism and the early moves to develop a Jewish biblical theology did enter into Jewish research, the group that engaged in these efforts consisted of Reform Jewish scholars in North America.

In Christian circles, Goshen-Gottstein noted, the major debate occurred between the practitioners of History of Religion and the writers of biblical theology. Furthermore, the failure of biblical theology in Christianity to achieve a significant place, in his view, had been the inability to develop a hermeneutical relationship between biblical theology and contemporary faith. However, the discussion had moved also to include the conversation between Christians and Jews. He remarks that this conversation is historically a longstanding issue, since the early church decided to make the Old Testament its Scripture. Even when a New Testament canon was concluded, the orthodox position kept both testaments within the same Bible. Traditionally, Christians were educated in theology, at least in their seminary studies, while Jews have been educated as philologists, historians, and archaeologists, but not theologians, even if some of them pursued rabbinical education before their graduate studies. As historians, however, Jewish scholars have generally accepted and used the major methods of biblical criticism. But Jewish biblical theology is not concerned especially with historical and archaeological knowledge. Rather, this interest is in articulating a distinctively Jewish understanding of the Bible and later traditions.

Goshen-Gottstein noted that the reticence to engage in biblical theology and to stay within the bounds of the *Religionsgeschichtliche* investigations

---

15. Wellhausen, *Prolegomena zur Geschichte Israels.*
16. Delitsch, *Messianische Weissagungen in geschichtlicher Folge,* 5.

of Israelite tradition has been well articulated by Yehezkiel Kaufmann.[17] Even his history of Israelite religion, while following in general the interpretative methods of Wellhausen and his followers, still contributed its own distinctive points.

1. Universal monotheism was not a late, but rather an early feature of Israelite faith.

2. Pagan mythology was unknown in Israel. Israel had no real understanding of paganism.

3. There are three collections of laws in Torah: JE, P, and D. However, these are not sequential, but rather reflect separate and distinct literary growth. Torah is impervious to prophetic influence. Priests and prophets are opponents.

4. However, while both prophets and Torah possess a common source in Mosaic monotheism, the prophets did not influence the formation of legal codes.

5. P does not presuppose a centralized cult limited to one locale.

6. P's wilderness tabernacle was identifiable with any Israelite sanctuary, and the camp with any sanctuary town.

7. P is older than D (Josiah and D belong together).

8. Prophets represent a new height in Israelite religion, but they are not the creators of ethical monotheism. Rather, they represent a return to the monotheism of Moses and Joshua, with an added emphasis on the primacy of morality.

9. While there was not a Deuteronomistic History, Joshua and Judges were written in an early Deuteronomistic style.

Kaufmann considered biblical theology to be a discipline for Christian scholars and not a task for Jews, who find this area to be foreign to their understandings of both research and practice.

Goshen-Gottstein is accurate in his assessment that the major theologies of the Hebrew Bible by Christian, largely Protestant scholars often reflected their own traditions of faith. This had been true into the 1980s, when his reflections began to take shape. These Christian biblical scholars chose to recast the Old Testament into the systematic categories of con-

---

17. Kaufmann, Yehezkel, *The Religion of Israel from Its Beginnings to the Babylonian Exile.* This is an abridgment of Kaufmann's original work that appeared in Hebrew in seven volumes. Greenberg's abridgment was reissued by Schocken Books, New York, in 1972. The most useful volume for biblical studies has been vol. 4, *The History of the Religion of Israel: From the Babylonian Captivity to the End of Prophecy,* published in English and issued by Ktav in 1977. See also Krapf, *Yehezkel Kaufmann.*

temporary theology. That being the case, if Jews wish to engage in biblical theology, they will have to develop their understanding out of their own traditions and not Christian ones. While Judaism has most been concerned with the understanding and practice of Torah, a theology of the Tanakh should take into consideration the important themes of covenant, election, and monotheism. On the basis of these three features, other themes could be examined. However, he rejects the postulation of a center for Jewish biblical theology or a systematic formulation resulting from placing various texts together as extrapolations of particular themes. Rather, his approach is both descriptive of the contents of the Bible and literary. Goshen-Gottstein fully expected Jews to enter into the field of biblical theology and to write theologies of the Tanakh on the basis of their own traditions.

Matitahu Tsevat

Matitiahu Tsevsat also has reflected on the prospects of doing a Jewish biblical theology.[18] He notes that the discipline of Old Testament theology is an early part of Christianity, beginning as early as Paul, who saw in the Jewish Bible important witnesses and descriptions to Christ. Jews, of course, have not engaged in theology, but rather in the study, interpretation, and application of the Torah. Yet Tsevat is willing to concede that, if Old Testament theology is objective and seeks to set forth its major ideas— in particular, its understanding of God—then it is a discipline that is legitimate for Jews to pursue. Indeed, it is even indispensable to Old Testament research. But it must be both historical and philological in examining texts within their original sociocultural contexts. The only caveat is that Jews should not Judaize the Old Testament even as Christians should not Christianize it.[19]

Isaac Kalimi

Isaac Kalimi has been one of the most prolific Jewish scholars in arguing for the importance of developing a Jewish biblical theology. To this end, he has written several publications that set forth the parameters of Jewish biblical theology as he sees it. In an essay that establishes clear lines of

18. Tsevat, "Theology of the Old Testament."
19. B. Anderson, in "Response to Matitiahu Tsevat," argues, "The Old Testament, which stands independently from Talmud or New Testament, should be read 'objectively' or in a 'scholarly' *(wissenschaftliche)* manner so that it can make its own literary witness." It is not something that leads to modern causes or ideologies. This essay demonstrates Anderson's misunderstanding of Jewish (biblical) theology.

separation between biblical theology and the History of Religion,[20] he explores the relationship between these two approaches. He argues that the two methods are different approaches to the same corpus of books (the Hebrew Bible/Old Testament). These two different approaches have their own legitimate place, but they are to be clearly differentiated. The first deals with the history of Israelite religion on many planes and notes numerous alterations that occurred during the generations of Israel. This approach is diachronic, carried out with philological and historical critical methods, and points to comparisons with the ancient Near East. Objectivity characterizes this way of proceeding. Old Testament theology, by contrast, seeks to set forth the major themes of the corpus and emphasizes the significant social and human value of the Bible. This approach, in Kalimi's understanding, is pursued with a variety of textual, linguistic, literary, and systematic methods. It is largely synchronic, ahistorical, and generally subjective, at least in the sense of the interpreter's standing within his or her own religious framework of belief. Kalimi notes that there are major differences between Jewish and Christian interpreters. Perhaps most distinctive is his rejection of some unifying center around which other themes are developed.

Kalimi points to three types of theology: the theology of the biblical authors and redactors of individual books, the theology of the redactors of the canon, and biblical theology that sets forth the common message of the Bible. Of course, he recognizes that there is no single biblical theology. In general, he argues that Christian interpreters operate from a christological tradition. It combines the two testaments and goes back and forth between them and then between the Bible and contemporary faith. This view, however, does not allow the intrusion of anti-Semitism to lead to the conclusion that the Old Testament and Judaism have been negated and replaced by Christianity. Indeed, the Christian theologian should be sensitive to and reject the negative views and stereotypes of Jews in some of the New Testament (e.g., Matt 27:12-23, 25, 28-31, 38-41; John 8:37-50; 19:6, 12-16; Acts 2:36; 3:13-15; and 1 Thess 2:14-16). These negative portrayals, allowed to go unchecked, have produced tragic results in the past and threaten to continue unless repudiated. After Auschwitz, the church must read the Hebrew Bible in a different way.

In responding to Levenson's essay "Why Jews Are Not Interested in Biblical Theology," Kalimi seeks to contest his view by arguing that what Jews are not interested in doing is Christian biblical theology. Kalimi

---

20. Kalimi, "Religionsgeschichte Israels oder Theologie des Alten Testaments?" See also "Die Bibel und die klassisch-jüdische Bibelauslegung," and *Early Jewish Exegesis and Theological Controversy.*

demonstrates there are biblical Jewish theologians, beginning even in the formation of the Bible: e.g., the Chronicler.[21] Also, Jewish commentators have issued theological assessments over the many centuries: different aspects of God, the relationship between God and humanity, the election of Israel, the relation between the elect and the other nations, the land of Israel as having religious worth, the special relationship between the land and the people of Israel, creation, revelation, covenant, holiness, sin, and many other subjects.[22]

The Bible is the holiest book in Judaism, notes Kalimi, and it is the basis for later significant texts in the development of Jewish tradition. It is the cornerstone for religious ideas, morality, law, and inspiration in all of Judaism. As it is the foundation of Judaism, all other texts derive from it: the Mishnah, Talmud, Midrash, Aggada, and Halakha, which collectively serve as the oral tradition for interpreting Scripture. The study of the Hebrew Bible without oral tradition is not a proper approach, according to Jewish understanding.

Jewish interpretation includes both intertextual and extratextual methods. The intertextual, which, as we shall see in the description of Michael Fishbane's approach, began to occur before the destruction of the temple in 70 C.E. Later texts referred on occasion to other, earlier ones, providing them new insights. This early intertextual interpretation began in the Bible and then continued in the Pesharim of Qumran, the Apocrypha and Pseudepigrapha, the Septuagint, Philo, Eupolemus, and Josephus. According to Kalimi, the second period occurs after the destruction of the Second Temple with the rise and expansion of Christianity. These are especially found in the writings of the rabbis and the later commentaries of the Middle Ages. This second period includes literature that may be divided into several groups: tannaitic-halakhic midrashim (e.g., the Mekhilta to

21. Kalimi, for example, refers to Ackroyd, "The Theology of the Chronicler," 280.

22. Among the many examples of Jewish biblical theology throughout the centuries up to the present, Kalimi mentions "Durch der Glaubenansichten und Meinungen" of Rab Saadia (ben Joseph) Gaon (882–942 C.E.); "Das Buch der Diskussion und des Beweises zur Verteidigung des verachteten Glaubens" by Rabbi Jehuda Hallevi (1085–1141 C.E.); and "The Guide of the Perplexed" of Moses Maimonides, Rambam (1135–1204 C.E.). In the modern period, there are Neumark, *The Philosophy of the Bible;* Guttmann, "Die Grundzüge der biblischen Religion"; Buber, *Prophetic Faith* and *Kingship of God;* Heschel, *The Prophets;* Muffs, *Love and Joy;* and Greenberg, *Studies in the Bible and Jewish Thought.* Greenberg's book contains numerous examples of biblical theology. Kalimi also notes there are many theologies of various biblical books, including Japhet, *The Ideology of the Book of Chronicles;* Weinfeld, "Theologische Trends in der Tora-Literatur"; "Gott als Schöpfer in Genesis 1 und in Deutero-Jesaja"; Weiss, "Psalm 23"; and Hoffman, "The Creativity of Theodicy." Lamentably, Goshen-Gottstein's "Prolegomena to Jewish Biblical Theology" was unfinished at the time of his death in 1993.

Exodus, Sira to Leviticus, and Sifre to Numbers and Deuteronomy); the Mishnah (c. 200 C.E.), Tosefta, and Beraita; the Jerusalem and Babylonian Talmuds (c. 400 and c. 500 C.E.); the haggadic midrashim like Pesikta de Rav Kahana (c. 3rd–4th centuries C.E.) and Midrash Rabba, e.g., to Genesis, the first part of Exodus, Leviticus, Ruth, Midrash Psalms; the Targumim; and the medieval commentaries (Rashi, Yaakov ben Asher, etc.). In contrast to the commentators, the Karaites attempted to interpret the Bible *sola scriptura.*

Kalimi outlines the major fundamentals of the classical Jewish interpretations of Scripture as follows:

1. God gave at the same time the written Torah and the oral Torah (Exod 10–20; Deut 5).

2. The prophets stood in relationship with the Torah.

3. The writings were inspired by the Holy Spirit and were written by kings, sages, and the righteous.

4. The words and letters of Scripture are fixed and may not be altered.

The laws of the Bible and the halakhot mentioned in them are explained by the sages, whose competence no one may doubt. Their interpretations were always appropriate for changing needs from generation to generation. Thus, not only is the Scripture itself holy and canonized, but so also are the explanations and interpretations of the rabbis in the Mishnah, the Talmud, and the Midrashim and thus fully authoritative for Jews in every generation.

The study of biblical texts alone, without oral interpretation, was not desirable, since, due to the lack of knowledge, humans may give a wrong interpretation that is not appropriate for Halakhah and thereby bring imbalance to the world. To study the Bible has no intrinsic value in and of itself. More valuable is the study of the oral Torah that interprets the Bible and provides guidance for life.

Kalimi contends, then, that Jews should write comprehensive theologies of the Hebrew Bible with their own particular approach. Still, they should do so objectively, i.e., by indicating clearly the meaning of the text in its historical settings. One would imagine, then, that Kalimi would support moving this interpretation through the layers of Jewish tradition to understand it (perhaps in multiple ways) in the present. This movement into the composition of Jewish biblical theology stands in a long and enduring stream of interpretation going back to the Bible itself. It is not, contends Kalimi, only a modern phenomenon.

Tikva Frymer-Kensky

A recent collection of essays by Bellis and Kaminsky outlines some of the significant recent approaches to biblical theology. One of these is in an essay by Tikva Frymer-Kensky.[23] Her approach is that of feminist liberation theology, which I have already discussed. But, because of her important feminist and liberation views that emerge in part from her Jewish background, we have chosen to mention briefly the salient features to which she points when doing biblical theology. She is strongly critical of patriarchal Judaism and sees biblical theology, done with a liberation twist, as a way of combating sexism and elitism in both the church and the synagogue.

Frymer-Kensky notes the collapse of the hegemony of elitist interpretations of Scripture that have been formulated and continued by white males of privilege. Readings of Scripture by marginalized people that include the poor, postcolonial peoples, and some Jews and Christians have rejected the authoritative understandings submitted by those who have dominated interpretation from positions of power and control. She argues that each hegemonic reading of Scripture has its own locus of power and its own directed self-interest. She notes there are multiple readings of the Bible, due to the nature of its own "multivocality." In addition, she affirms that the meaning of the text changes even as the audiences and their locations change. The reader, perhaps even more than the text itself, is the determiner of meaning and authority. Indeed, she challenges the legitimacy of being bound to the views of the rabbis and their interpretations alone. She writes:

> By presenting alternative voices in the central iconic text in Judaism, the study of the Bible helps undermine the authority of any single Biblical voice, any one particular Biblical reading. Biblical theology presents an alternative source of authority to rabbinic thinking and creates a very fertile opportunity for dialogue between Biblical and rabbinic ideas. This is the meaning of Torah, teaching that continues to explore and reformulate without drifting into a new absolutism or nihilistic despair.

Marc Zvi Brettler

Another recent voice in the discussion of Jewish biblical theology belongs to Marc Brettler. He notes that Jewish scholars have typically not examined the chasm between the historical meaning of the text and its interpretation

23. Frymer-Kensky, "The Emergence of Jewish Biblical Theologies."

today.[24] Jewish biblical theology has not begun to undertake, at least until now, what Brevard Childs has called a "fundamentally Christian enterprise," i.e. the articulation of biblical theology, only now from a Jewish understanding.

Many of the difficulties in setting forth the parameters and then articulating a Jewish biblical theology are the same that plague Christian biblical theology. However, Brettler sees biblical theology as linked directly to a critically construed history of Israel. Avoiding the extremes of harmonists like Albright and Bright and nihilists like Thompson, van Seters, Davies, and Lemche, Brettler argues four major points in articulating the basis of Jewish biblical theology:

1. We should not be concerned if the historical veracity of what the text reports did not occur or cannot be proven;
2. we should not harmonize divergent biblical traditions;
3. we must be more sensitive to the genres of biblical history texts;
4. and we are to understand what stands behind these texts that are presented as depictions of the past.

In Jewish biblical theology, historical veracity is of no significant consequence. The command to remember the past has little to do with the events of the past, but rather with the legal and moral features that biblical narratives contain. The rabbis themselves had little interest in history for its own sake, but they were concerned with discovering meaning that gives direction to life. Harmonizing divergent understandings of the past and its events is contrary to rabbinic thought. Divergent interpretations are to characterize Jewish biblical theology, even as the rabbis set forth diverse views about the meaning of texts or teachings. Brettler argues that a Jewish biblical theology is to recognize the identity and purpose of the variety of genres present in the Bible and to admit that an ideology stands behind the text and is present in the views of the interpreters.

In his presentation of the theology of the Psalms in a recent SBL meeting (2003), Brettler admits that he is not all that sure what a Jewish biblical theology constitutes. However, this questioning is not due to his lack of serious thinking about or interest in Jewish biblical theology. He notes that he participated in the first conference on Jewish biblical theology that was put together by Michael Fishbane and Tikva Frymer-Kensky at the University of Chicago in May 1996, at which he read a paper entitled "Biblical History and Jewish Biblical Theology."[25]

---

24. Brettler, "Biblical History and Jewish Biblical Theology." His 2003 SBL presentation is entitled "Psalms and Jewish Biblical Theology."

25. See Brettler, *The Creation of History in Ancient Israel.*

In his SBL paper, Brettler is especially concerned to determine what role the Psalms may play in helping to define and exemplify what Jewish biblical theology is. While eschewing harmonization as wrongheaded, Brettler seeks to understand selected Psalms through the tradition of the rabbis in much the same way that Christian theologians interpret the Bible in its engagement with contemporary theology. Tsevat, in his essay just mentioned, and James Barr suggest a similar approach. In the words of Barr, "Jewish Biblical theology . . . could be, as Tsevat suggested, a theology of the interlinkage between the Hebrew Bible and the later authoritative sources and interpretations."[26] However, Brettler limits this larger approach to his four points listed earlier in this section. His essential argument is that polydoxy and polyphony are part and parcel of the teachings of the Psalms. Harmonization goes against the grain of the Psalter even as it does the traditions of the rabbis.

For Brettler, the ongoing quest to discover a "center" *(Mitte)* in the Old Testament and biblical theology has emerged out of the emphasis placed on harmony. Brettler argues that the diverse nature of the Bible itself precludes discovering any unifying center. Instead of a *Mitte,* he points to the diversity of collections, including the Psalter and the Book of the Twelve. He notes by way of example the rabbinic statement (Shir Hashirim Rabbah 1:1, 10) concerning Solomon: Solomon is represented in the Canticles as a youth, in Proverbs as a man of maturity, and Qoheleth as a person approaching death. The fact that this is not a historical observation is irrelevant. Rather, what is important is the fact that the rabbis concluded that even the same person, at different stages of his life, may have very different understandings about human experiences.

The superscriptions of the Psalter, thus, point to separate Psalms that may reflect different moments in communal life and thus at times have a different theology (cf. especially those attributed to David). Thus, Psalms attributed to Korah or Asaph suggest the Psalter is a diverse collection that possesses no *Mitte,* but instead contains a number of sub-collections with divergent understandings. To bring us back to the rabbinic analogy, the Psalter with its ubiquitous introduction, למזמור, allows different theological voices to speak. The Psalter is not characterized by a common theology. Rather it contains "theologies."

Benjamin D. Sommer

Benjamin Sommer and Michael Fishbane offer significant work in Jewish theology. Sommer's recent essay on canon is an important beginning

---

26. Barr, *The Concept of Biblical Theology,* 585.

point in entering this discipline, while his new book outlines its major features and indicates elements that are distinctive for a Jewish approach. Because in Judaism it would be incorrect to speak of a biblical theology as a self-contained entity, considering the continuing stream of tradition over the centuries, he opts for the more general designation of Jewish theology.

The first issue concerns the canon and, in particular, the oral and written Torahs. In defining canon, Sommer points to two major understandings. The more narrow understanding of canon is simply "the closed list of books that make up the Bible." A broader view is to understand the term to refer to texts that are accepted by a religious community as sacred and important. Judaism, of course, adheres to the second understanding while Christians understand the term as a closed list, whether the shorter canon of Protestantism or the larger one of Roman Catholicism due to its inclusion of the Deutero-Canonical literature. The fact that Judaism leans in a different direction in its understanding leads to the question of the impact this has on Jewish theology.

It is especially the case that a much larger canon undermines the case of many Old Testament theologians who have searched for a unity of Scripture (only) on which to build a portrayal of faith and practice in ancient Israel and the consequential application of this theology to the modern communities of faith. Instead, the broader, Jewish view elevates "tradition" to the same status as the Bible. Scripture cannot assume a position of greater importance in faith and practice than tradition. This makes the Jewish understanding much closer to that of Roman Catholicism than to Protestantism. The tensions between the Bible and tradition essentially disappear in this understanding of their role. Catholics regard tradition's claim to importance and authority on the basis of what Sommer calls "three pillars": teachings not in the Bible but handed down and found to be genuine by the believing community, the status of scholars whose interpretations have been honored and acknowledged as truth, and the continuation of divine activity in the forming of tradition. Judaism embraces unquestioningly the first two pillars, but is hesitant about the third.

The matter of the broader canon becomes especially important in the Jewish understanding of the two Torahs, written (תרה שבכתב) and oral (תרה שבצלפה). The first is the tripartite Tanakh (not simply the five books of Torah), while the second is rabbinic literature. The rabbinic works of the early sages (the Tannaim, who date from the beginning of the first century C.E. to the middle of the third century C.E.) and the later sages (Amoraim and Saboraim, mid-third to mid-sixth centuries) include the completed Mishnah, the two Talmuds (or Gemaras), and the Midrashim and Aggadah.

Oral Torah typically refers to later works that are post-Talmudic: the Geonic period (sixth through eleventh centuries, C.E.) and the Middle Ages.[27] Of course, while the oral Torah may have been formed originally by spoken words that were committed to memory and transmitted by word of mouth, it also existed in written form as it developed. This is likely true of the formation of the Tanakh, which was written after a period of orality. What it especially conveys is the relationship between teacher and student and the durative, changing quality of tradition that allows for later oral and then written texts. Oral Torah developed through the teachings of later scribes, sages, and rabbis who developed new laws and interpretations. For Judaism, both Torahs are filled with God's presence and are the basis for normative behavior. For some rabbis, the oral Torah even took precedence over the written Torah. Some do not distinguish between them, while others do, but the duality is unimportant. Thus, for many rabbis, all authoritative teachings are Torah, whether that of the Bible or of the rabbinic tradition. Thus the overlap between the two indicates that "the boundary of the canon does not delimit the extent of canonicity for rabbinic Judaism."[28]

Sommer then asks the important question: Since both written and oral Torah are canonical, is there any distinction in how they are viewed as canon? What is important to the understanding of Judaism is the fact that legal questions are referred to more recent texts and not to the tannaitic or amoraic (much less the biblical) ones. The principle of Halakhah follows the later authorities in stating what the law as practiced is (הלכתא כבתראי). The written Torah and much of the oral Torah are formative in shaping faith and practice, but they are not authoritative, at least in later Judaism.[29] It is true that the written Torah achieved a type of iconic status in Jewish ritual that was not acquired by the oral Torah. There is a difference in the fact that the written Torah is closed, whereas the oral Torah or tradition is not. Finally, there is a difference in Judaism concerning written and oral canons in that the former is attributed entirely to God who alone is responsible for its words, whereas the oral Torah combines divine and human words in that teachers have interpreted and supplemented the divine words and, at times, even forgotten or perverted some of them. Thus, written Torah was directly revealed by God, whereas the oral Torah mediates

27. See Schäfer, "Das 'Dogma'"; Neusner, *What, Exactly, Did the Rabbinic Sages Mean?*; and Jaffee, *Torah in the Mouth*.

28. Benjamin Summer, "Revelation at Sinai in the Hebrew Bible and Jewish Theology," *JR* 79 (1999) 422–51.

29. Of course, many Christians accept this view, since they do not consider a good deal of the written canon (both testaments) to be authoritative for modern faith.

through human teachers the divine words. This explains why rabbis at times will openly disagree with the oral Torah but only indirectly through commentary with the written Torah.

Sommer then deals with the modern Jewish approach to canon. More liberal Jews regard even the written Torah as the result of meditation and see it as humanity's response to God's revelation. Sommer argues that there is no real distinction, then, between the written and oral canons for liberal Judaism. This is true in the development of the Bible where earlier teachings are supplemented or reinterpreted by later ones. The Bible itself has multiple understandings of Torah ranging from static to dynamic. In general, however, Torah was understood not only to refer to a Pentateuchal text but also to its interpretations, or those that are based on it. For Sommer, in modern Judaism there is a canon, but it continues from the beginning of the biblical period until today by the development of unbroken tradition.

Finally, Sommer points to the implications of this understanding of canon for biblical theology. While Protestant Old Testament theologians have often searched for a unifying belief that brings together the diverse views of the Bible, modern Judaism is not engaged in the quest for a center. Indeed, the entire notion of the oral Torah points to diversity, not unity. This suggests that revelation does not end but continues throughout history and is eventually written down in later texts. There is a canonical unity in Judaism, but it is found in the durative journey of interpretation. The exegesis of biblical texts recovers as far as possible the earliest voices in the ongoing development of oral Torah. But this means that, for modern Judaism, there can be no real biblical theology, but only Jewish theology. Religious teachings concerning what is believed and practiced are ongoing, meaning there is no qualitative (i.e., authoritative) difference between the Tanakh and the later oral Torah. This does not mean that Jewish scholars cannot seek a greater clarity regarding the Bible and its teachings and how they compare with later tradition. Thus, Jews could even set forth a dialogical biblical theology that could eventually lead to new oral Torah. One of the results is that canon (in the broader sense) continues to be revitalized.

Perhaps I should note here my response to Sommer's treatment of Protestant theology and Protestant biblical theology. My quarrel with Sommer includes two minor concerns. First, in the manner of Levenson, many Protestant scholars have abandoned the quest for a unifying factor and instead recognize that the protean views in the Hebrew Bible do not allow any unifying factor to bring together its various traditions and different understandings. Indeed, one might even argue that the unifying factor that has long been sought was a constructive, not a descriptive, enterprise.

The second has to do with the failure to recognize that Protestant biblical theology, while having a particular revelatory and authoritative status, still is but a step toward a modern hermeneutical theology. Protestant systematic theology in no way is obligated to give priority to the biblical view as Sommer suggests. Indeed, systematic theology may directly reject a biblical view, and often does, and at times even ignores the Bible as an important resource in developing a theological understanding of various teachings of faith and practice. Protestant theology, whether biblical or systematic, is not the monolithic structure and content that Levenson and Sommer tend to make it.

An excellent example of Sommer's understanding of the process of Jewish biblical theology and Jewish theology is articulated in his essay "Revelation at Sinai."[30] Indeed, this article serves as an exemplar for doing Jewish theology and determining the role of the Tanakh in that process. In answering the question as to whether or not both the Bible and biblical criticism have a place in contemporary Jewish theology, Sommer deals with the matter of the Bible as Scripture. He poses the question in the following way: how may a Jew understand the Bible as sacred and yet also as consisting of human words? His entrance into this issue takes up two related questions that may be examined in both the Tanakh and the later tradition: what did Israel experience at Sinai, and did they receive there the Ten Commandments?

The key Sinai text, found in Exod 19 (also see 20:15-19 and Exod 24), depicts Israel gathering at the sacred mountain to receive the revelation of God. These texts are filled with inconsistencies and ambiguities, complicating the interpretation. First, what did Israel experience? The term *qôl* (קוֹל) may be interpreted in v. 19 to mean "noise." Thus, the NJPS translates the key verse in 19:19, "The blare of the horn grew louder and louder. As Moses spoke, God answered him in thunder." This translation understands *qôl* to be the noise of the horn and thunder as the divine answer to Moses, a possible interpretation that suggests the biblical imagery is associated with theophany. However, also possible is the OJPS translation: "And when the voice of the horn waxed louder and louder, Moses spoke and God answered him by a voice." Thus, the question is whether there is a nature theophany that is an overwhelming revelatory experience of Israel or a revelation in understandable words that is uttered. If the latter is the case, is it the Ten Commandments or at least some of them that are issued for Israel's instruction? The first commentary on this text is Deut 4–5, especially Deut 4:10-14. Deuteronomy explains that the *qôl* is a *qōl děbārîm* (קֹל דבוים), i.e., a "voice of words." And v. 13 makes it clear that what the

---

30. Sommer, "Revelation at Sinai."

people heard is the Ten Commandments. This text in Deuteronomy functions like a *midrash* or *Miqra'ot Gedolot*. By contrast, Exod 24 does not present the people as hearing a thing, sound or words.

Later biblical commentaries suggest that Israel heard either the Ten Commandments or the first two commandments. Rabbi Joshua, in following the line of thought of Rabbi Azaria and Rabbi Judah (Talmud, b. Makkot 23b-24a attributes this to Rabbi Hamnuna), understands Deut 33:2 to mean that Moses taught the Jewish people 611 commandments (= the Torah), indicating that the first two were heard from the voice of God at Sinai (= 613), the traditional number of laws that constitute Torah.

Thus, the two questions are answered differently. Some of the rabbis understand that Israel heard nothing at all; thus, there were no words to hear. What this view emphasizes is the presence of God. Others suggest Israel heard the entirety of the Ten Commandments, while still others argue they heard only the first two, since the experience was so overwhelming.

Sommer presents his own theological perspective on this and the entire Torah within Jewish theology when he argues that all Jewish tradition, including the Bible, which is an important part of it, should be understood as commentary and reflection. The Torah is both noumenal (i.e., divinely expressed) and phenomenal (i.e., the human words that compose the tradition, commentary, and reflection of the early Torah). This leads him to his culminating position. If the true revelation is that which consists of a commanding divine presence, standing behind the voice that speaks or makes an inaudible sound, then the written and oral Torah serve as *midrash*. Through continually changing traditions of understanding, learning, and practice, Jews respond in their own generations to what they perceive to be the primordial word of God at Sinai. God commands, but what he commands is stated by each generation, and this understanding requires obedience. What makes the Torah Scripture is the divine presence that stands behind the human experience of the sounds heard first at Sinai.

Most important to Sommer's work is his overview of Jewish history and theology that he has shared with me in outline form. He continues to distinguish biblical theology, at least in any authoritative sense for Judaism, and Jewish theology that takes into consideration the Bible, later rabbinic work into the Middle Ages, and contemporary Jewish thinkers. In an upcoming volume, he plans to set forth the ways the Hebrew Bible, as critically studied and understood by historical critics, may be viewed as Scripture for contemporary Judaism. This objective is at one with that of Protestant biblical theologians who are usually interested, not only in understanding the religious faith and practice of ancient Israelite texts that are a part of the larger Christian canon, but also in regarding this collection of texts as Scripture that addresses questions of modern import.

Sommer acknowledges that many contemporary Jews, including Jewish scholars of various types, regard historical-critical work as "excavative" and thus irrelevant to understanding the Bible as addressing contemporary faith and life. Thus, the voices allowed to speak by biblical criticism are placed alongside those of the medieval rabbinic scholars whose commentaries are called the *Miqra'ot Gedolot*.

In Sommer's view, the view of some modern scholars essentially silences the voices of the past. If dialogue is the appropriate model for understanding the means by which meaning in the present is achieved, then those who engage the Bible should not only be present students of Judaism, whether modernist or postmodernist, but also those who lived in the past, whether in the periods of the Tanakh or later rabbinic literature. He disagrees with Childs in understanding the canonical approach. In contrast to Childs, Sommer argues that the voices of the Bible should not simply be those unknown redactors who placed books into their canonical form, but also earlier ones who spoke words and traditions that entered into the biblical texts and are recoverable in part by means of historical-critical research.

The themes Sommer will address include the nature of Scripture in the Bible and postbiblical Judaism, revelation, divine manifestation, sacred space, and divine election. He points to several factors that unify the theological discussion. These include his view that modernist theories of history are helpful in recovering the voices of the past in the Bible. In addition, the diversity of internal interpretations of the writers and redactors of the Tanakh is paralleled in postbiblical Judaism, as may be noted in the history of Jewish exegesis. However, making a connection between biblical sources, writers, and redactors with those who contributed to the history of interpretation will permit the construction of "overarching trajectories" that demonstrate how ancient faith is engaged and given new life in the ongoing stream of tradition.

Sommer identifies three models to explain the process of traditioning. The first is *masoret,* meaning "tradition," which is the nominal form of a verb meaning "to pass on." In this model, the receiver is passive. The second model is *kabbalah,* also meaning "tradition" or "reception." This term connotes the active and creative role of those who receive what is handed down to them. The third includes a variety of features involving the receiving of tradition. One is *moreshet* in which *masoret* "masquerades" as *kabbalah* that emphasizes the receiver's creative role. Yet this feature also conveys *yāraš,* i.e., "to inherit." But the related verb *hôrîš* points to the notion of "causing to inherit, to bequeath" as well as its opposite, "to dispossess." Thus *yĕrušâ* points to the occasionally hidden power of those who bestow the legacy. This process occurs when newer understandings of tradition are displaced in allowing room for older ones. This later process indicates that earlier meanings, at times concealed by later redactors, may be recovered in postbiblical interpretation.

Finally, Sommer will argue that one goal of contemporary Jewish biblical scholarship is to "point out the implicitly theological nature of allegedly empirical undertakings of modern Biblicists."[31] While most Jewish scholars deny or at least do not make explicit the theological implications of their work, these are often present. To point this out is important, but even more so is the awareness that Jewish biblical scholarship, while often analytic, often has an important constructive dimension that may well stimulate the articulation of Jewish theology.

Marvin A. Sweeney

The most sanguine and certainly most persistent call for Jewish biblical theology comes from Marvin Sweeney.[32] Sweeney is well aware of the breakdown of theological consensus that emerged in the Enlightenment and reached its culmination in the neo-orthodoxy of Karl Barth. Today, especially in a global world and in increasingly diverse nations like the United States and United Kingdom, multiculturalism, pluralism, and competing epistemologies clamoring for followers have spawned a host of different theological approaches, ideologies, and understandings. While a certain richness has accompanied this phenomenon of diversity, so have confusion, competition, and the loss of dialogue that is directed outside a particular group committed to and convinced by the approaches and conclusions of its own self-generated system of meaning and evaluation of truth. Biblical criticism and biblical theology have certainly not escaped this present fragmentation.

Without rehearsing these developments, let us look at Sweeney's own contributions to the formulation of a Jewish biblical theology. He begins, as does Richard Rubenstein in Jewish philosophical thinking, with the Holocaust (the *Shoah*).[33] This monstrous evil emerged from the heart of the land of the Enlightenment, something almost unbelievable for those who were committed to its humanism and its affirmation of the primacy of reason.

The impact of the Holocaust on Christian theology and Christian Old Testament theology has been dramatic. The repudiation of anti-Semitism

---

31. Sommer's volume, *Artifact or Scripture? The Jewish Bible in the Fifth–Eighth Century,* is in preparation. I am in his debt for having sent me a rough draft to peruse.

32. Sweeney, "Reconceiving the Paradigms of Old Testament Theology," in *Jews, Christians, and the Theology of Hebrew Scriptures.* This is a slightly revised version of an earlier essay found in *Biblical Interpretation.* Sweeney's other writings on this topic include the important essay "Tanak versus Old Testament."

33. See Sölle, "God's Pain and Our Pain."

inherent in some of the New Testament and earlier Christian biblical scholarship has been perhaps the most important development in recent years, even though aspects of this malevolence have continued to cast a long shadow. Christian scholars of the Old Testament have been forced to recognize the existence of this evil present within their own work, especially when it devalues the beliefs of others.[34] Most scholars, save for fundamentalists, would agree with Sweeney that supersessionism is theologically indefensible and repulsive. This does not mean that biblical theology precludes Christians from affirming their Christocentric faith in moving in the direction of hermeneutics. But it does mean that the Hebrew Bible is Scripture, not only for Christians, but also for Jews who see the text as a whole and not simply as a part of a Bible with two testaments.

Other positions with hues of anti-Semitism have been rejected. Thus, the Protestant stereotype of prophetic Israelite religion as the high point of Israelite religion and Old Testament theology and the caricature of postexilic Judaism as a descent into legalism have been largely discarded. Indeed, the devaluing of Judaism signaled by the lack of attention given it in many older Old Testament theologies has been exposed and primarily rejected. Sweeney also notes that the Protestant hermeneutic of promise and fulfillment culminating in Jesus Christ also faces difficulty when it in effect eliminates the Jews from their own story.

Sweeney asks then, "What is the task of Old Testament theology in a Post-Shoah world?"[35] Sweeney notes that, of late, the interests of many scholars in biblical studies has shifted to other areas than biblical theology. The social, anthropological, political, and literary disciplines have provided methods that have captured the interests of the great majority of Old Testament scholars since the 1970s.[36] Epistemological debates have involved deconstruction and the issue of truth, while diversity has characterized even those theologies that have appeared. Scholars have also come to realize the import of social institutions and roles, economics, and ideology on the shaping of theology, while some have attributed more importance to the final form of the text than was done previously.

As for Jewish biblical theology and the involvement of Jews in the larger discipline of Old Testament theology, Sweeney notes that Jews increasingly are engaged in biblical theology in shaping their theology both for their own communities and for conversations with Christians. These

34. See especially the writings of Rolf Rendtorff, including "The Impact of the Holocaust *(Shoah)* on German Protestant Theology" and "Toward a Common Jewish-Christian Reading of the Hebrew Bible."

35. Marvin A. Sweeney, "Reconceiving the Paradigms of Old Testament Theology in the Post-Shoah Period," 155–72.

36. See the first chapter of my volume *The Historical Theology of Wisdom Literature.*

conversations enrich the total enterprise of biblical studies. Each maintains its own distinctive features and traditions out of which it operates yet at the same time provides insights that enable a better understanding both of the Hebrew Bible and of the two different communities who regard it as Scripture.

Ziony Zevit

A review of the issues of Jewish biblical theology and some of its Jewish practitioners has been put together by Ziony Zevit, although his conclusions are rather sobering in considering the possibility of this type of study as an ongoing discipline. Zevit, also a participant in the 2003 SBL discussion of Jewish biblical theology, shared his recent research with me and made several trenchant observations that deserve mention at this point.[37] He considers the subject of a Jewish biblical theology under five headings: the semantics of Jewish biblical theology, typologies of Christian biblical/ Old Testament theologies, calls for Jewish biblical theology and their typologies, reasons Jews should undertake projects in biblical theology, and future directions for this type of study.

Beginning with the matter of semantics, "Jewish" in the academy means those who master one or more bodies of knowledge associated with Judaism. For some, any effort to set forth the theology of the Tanakh would have to include the corpus of classical rabbinic literature that is a precursor to the study and understanding of the Jewish Bible.[38] But are non-Jews able to participate in this endeavor? Furthermore, is Jewish biblical theology restricted only to the Tanakh, or may it include other texts, including Ben Sira, the sectarian writings of Qumran, the literature of Philo and Josephus, and the collections of the Talmud and the Midrash? In addition, what of translations such as the LXX or the Aramaic Targums? And should the cultural worlds of the ancient Near East and the Greco-Roman empire be a source of both understanding and trenchant parallels? Finally, in regard to semantics, how should the term *theology* be understood? While there are numerous definitions, most scholars think of four or five things: God, people in a community, revelation (spoken or in and through a text), an interpreter or exegete who is able to communicate the meaning of a theme or text, and academic disciplines that aid in setting forth the importance and meaning of economics, politics, sociology, anthropology, ecology, and so on. Theology has to do with the present, which in its labyrinth of constant changes requires also new understandings. Theologians

---

37. See Zevit, "Jewish Biblical Theology."
38. See Frerichs," The Torah Canon of Judaism," 13–15, 19–21.

attempt to bridge the gap between past and present to present a divine word to today's community. Even so, the term *theology* is rare in the curricula of Jewish graduate and rabbinical schools.

Christians approach biblical theology in a variety of different ways, including confessional, scientific, biblical that is inclusive of both texts, descriptive, prescriptive, thematic, and systematic. To work through this mass of approaches, Zevit sets up a variety of typologies. The first comprises those who see biblical theology as the combination of both testaments that produces themes that address an "eternal present," although contemporary theologians are needed to explain their relevancy. The second works within a tradition that determines what the meaning of the biblical text has continued to be. The third allows for historical and religious development, distinguishing between the descriptive and the proscriptive. Finally, a fourth allows for development and then uses any variety of methods to allow for Christian appropriation.

After providing his assessments of Jewish scholars who have dealt with the discipline of Jewish biblical theology, all of whom have been examined earlier in this chapter, Zevit offers his conclusions. While Christians have invited Jews to engage in the discipline, they are more interested in gaining insights into their own efforts. This is "spade" work, not real theology that is done by systematic theologians. While theology is a discipline and plays itself out in particular in the Christian faculties of theological schools of European universities and in seminaries in various other settings in the world, theology is not really an academic theology. Rather, it is both descriptive and prescriptive. It is not appropriate, as such, in a secular or humanistic university. It is not a subdiscipline of critical, academic biblical studies. While there is no reason not to engage in this type of study, no one is clamoring for it; certainly not the people in the synagogue or the pulpit rabbis. It is unlikely to have much of a future in Judaism.

Tamar Kamionkowski

Tamar Kamionkowski, who teaches in the Reconstructionist Rabbinical Seminary, expresses a very different view. She sets forth the major parameters of what she describes as the "dialogic model" of Jewish biblical theology. She notes the following in her 2003 SBL address, which she kindly provided me in written form:

> Among the handful of Jewish scholars interested in this area of study, there is no consensus regarding the long-standing contentious issues of Biblical theology. Debate continues regarding: 1) the relationship between Biblical theology and the history of Israelite religion, 2) the

possibilities for a common ground between Jewish and Christian Biblical theologies, 3) the role of rabbinic texts as a guide for Biblical interpretation, and 4) how we define contemporary Judaism.[39]

She explains that Jews, like Christians, are beset with the many different meanings given to biblical theology. The critical issue has been the relationship between biblical theology and historical criticism. While she understands her own role to be that of a historical critic, her identity as a Jew leads her to develop the insights obtained by this type of student in a decidedly Jewish understanding. In this regard, she disagrees, for example, with Kalimi's dichotomous assertion that the history of Israelite religion is diachronic and uses historical-critical tools and strives for objectivity, while theology "is a close study of the different religious messages in their entirety."[40]

Kamionkowski argues differently. According to her definition, Jewish biblical theology is the partnership that exists between historical criticism, what she tentatively calls the *peshat*, and contemporary Jewish questions and concerns. The results are subjective, not objective. But they begin with listening to the voices of the Bible through the means provided by historical criticism. Jewish scholars, she asserts, will never reach a consensus on the definition of biblical theology, for the very same reasons that have beset Christian scholars. Definition, however, is not the fulcrum of the issue. Rather, a theology of any type, Jewish as well as Christian, should be the coherence between a definition provided and the actual work of constructing a theology.

Jews, also like Christians, face the challenge of diverse understandings of their traditions. There are many Judaisms today. And, following the dictum of her reconstructionist founder, Mordecai Kaplan, Judaism is a civilization in constant evolution and growth. While the past has a vote, it cannot issue a veto. Thus, to take the tradition seriously and to engage it in all of its insights means that teachings are important, but they are to be revaluated in light of the present. A dialogue between past and present is at the heart and soul of Jewish biblical theology.

Kamionkowski disagrees with Levenson, because he follows an understanding of religious faith according to Halakha. Yet there are many Judaisms today, and she opposes privileging any particular one. Indeed, she writes that Levenson is one of the Jewish biblical scholars who note that dialogue and debate are at the center of Jewish tradition. In Levenson's words:

39. Kamionkowski, "Jewish Biblical Theology."
40. Kalimi, *Early Jewish Exegesis*, 101.

> Whereas in the Church the sacred text tends to be seen as a *word* (the singular is telling) demanding to be proclaimed magisterially, in Judaism it tends to be seen as a *problem* with many facets, each of which deserves attention and debate.... It is not only that Jews have less motivation than Christians to find a unity or center in their Bible; if they did find one, they would have trouble integrating it with their most traditional modes of textual reasoning. What Christians may perceive as gain, Jews may perceive as a loss.[41]

What Kamionkowski sees as significant is the fact that the Jewish canon places different understandings of matters, including even of truth, side by side, suggesting that while truth may be unobtainable, it is still to be sought. Thus, she contends, "Debate and dialogue are the essence of Jewish theology. The sacred is to be found not in the actual words of the texts but in the dialogue and debate between the texts. It is the spirit of debate and diversity of opinions that I believe to be most significant in a Jewish Biblical theology."[42] Only when we make faith propositional or to be understood as the "correct" articulation of a doctrine do we distort the theology of the Hebrew Bible.

Kamionkowski envisions a Jewish biblical theology as looking something like a page of Talmud. The Jewish scholar sets forth the topics for discussion and is the final editor, but the raw data for the debate would come from the Bible itself. At the center of the page would be the modern scholar's questions that interact with the concerns of modern Jews.

From *Traditum* to *Traditio:* Michael Fishbane

Approaching Jewish Biblical Theology

The recent emergence of Jewish biblical theology or, as some Jewish scholars prefer, Jewish theology, beginning with the writings of Moshe H. Goshen-Gottstein some quarter century ago, has led to the question of approach. Typically, the large part of Jewish biblical scholarship, like that in the academy in general, has been philological and historical. Historical criticism has predominated in all but the strongly orthodox circles of Jewish scholars. Yet it is clear that Jewish biblical scholars participate in every type of approach outlined in this book. For example, Tikva Frymer-Kensky[43] utilizes a feminist approach to Jewish biblical theology that brings into judgment the patriarchy and sexism not only of the Bible, but also the

---

41. Levenson, "Why Jews Are Not Interested in Biblical Theology," 55.
42. Kamionkowski, "Jewish Biblical Theology."
43. Frymer-Kensky, *In the Wake of the Goddess.*

rabbis. David Penchansky[44] is a postmodernist in his interpretation of the Hebrew Bible, and so on. Even so, the question emerges as to what may be distinctive in Jewish scholarship that allows it to carve out its own niche in the discipline of biblical theology. As noted in the preceding survey, the strong emphasis placed on tradition by Jon Levenson, Benjamin Sommer, and Isaac Kalimi, to mention three scholars, suggests that tradition, beginning in the formation of the canon and continuing through the composition and redaction of the Mishnah, the Midrashim, the Talmud, and the Commentaries, is the Jewish matrix out of which theology emerges and is hermeneutically appropriated. This dependence on tradition is quite similar to the theological work in Christian circles in which scholars shape their understandings by reference to their own theologians and writings, from Aquinas to Luther to Calvin, to name only a few. Many have quarreled with the adjective *biblical* to describe Jewish theology, since the emphasis in Judaism is on tradition, beginning, of course, with the Tanakh but moving on into the present through the examination of the enduring stream of interpretation.

The Jewish Tradition and Methodological Study of the Bible

The best approach to Jewish theology is taken by Michael Fishbane.[45] Fishbane opens two doors to this area of study. The first we examined under the previous category of imagination. The second, which uses tradition and traditioning as the hermeneutical key to theology, also requires careful consideration. In his insightful study, *Biblical Interpretation in Ancient Israel,* Fishbane outlines the distinctive features of Jewish interpretation that are at work in the biblical text and that continue into the present.

For me as a Christian, not a Jewish biblical theologian, it would still seem that a distinctively Jewish theology would best proceed along the lines developed by Fishbane in his understanding of tradition and imagination. While the features of Jewish interpretative tradition are well known,

---

44. Penchansky, *The Politics of Biblical Theology.*
45. Also, for a historical review of Jewish biblical exegesis, see the collaborative work by Dohmen and Stemberger, *Hermeneutik der jüdischen Bibel and des Alten Testaments.* While Dohmen investigates Christian theological interpretation, Stemberger provides a clear and incisive overview of Jewish exegesis from the time of the Second Temple to the end of the Middle Ages. Among the rabbis, he examines the seven rules of Hillel, the thirteen rules of Yishmael, the thirty-two rules of Rabbi Eliezer, allegorical interpretation, and the relationship between interpretation and liturgical reading of Scripture. The teachers and approaches he considers in the Middle Ages include the Karaites, Saadya Gaon, Rashi and his disciples, Abraham Ibn Esra, and the relation between literal and allegorical interpretation, including the Kabbala and the fourfold meaning of Scripture.

the contribution of Fishbane's studies is twofold: first, he demonstrates that these features have their origins in the Hebrew Bible, and second, his work suggests how these interpretative features may be used in creating and shaping the whole of Jewish theology.

Biblical Interpretation in Ancient Israel

Fishbane begins with the commonplace that Jewish biblical interpretation assumes that the Bible is both comprehensive and adequate in directing life and understanding. However, the teachings of the Hebrew Bible and their understandings are not always transparent. Thus, the task of exegesis is to make the Tanakh clear, either through determining the meanings of ancient texts or through legitimizing a practice or custom by reference to a text. Thus, two sources come into play in the interpretative enterprise: the inspired Scripture and the community that lives according to its dictates and seeks direction for old questions made new by changing circumstances. The interpretations that were especially valued were preserved, first orally and then in writing, achieving a nobility and authority because of their associations with the sacred texts. Among the Pharisees who became the forerunners of what became modern Judaism, both areas, written and oral teachings, held places of esteem. Indeed, they both were dignified by receiving the status of inspiration and authority. Not only Scripture, but also tradition were divinely revealed and continued through the chain of interpreted meanings that began at Sinai. And equally significant to both was the received tradition and the procession of traditioning in which the teachings of written and oral Torah were handed down through the generations. Together they provided the corporate memory that guided the community into the future.

What Fishbane contends in this remarkable study is that both *traditum* and *traditio* (i.e., tradition and traditioning) are central to inner-biblical exegesis. However, there is one difference. Tradition history, as a method of contemporary biblical scholarship, begins with a written *traditum* and moves backward to trace out the various phases of *traditio*, both oral and then partially written down. Inner-biblical exegesis, by contrast, begins with a relatively fixed *traditum* (although biblical manuscripts continue to give evidence of a certain fluidity) and then interprets it through the stages of oral commentary, until it too becomes written down.

Fishbane notes that examples of the existence of tradition, tradents, and traditioning are not limited to the Hebrew Bible and to later Pharisaic teachings that eventually were written down in the Mishnah and later collections. Other lines of tradition and traditioning were in existence quite early in the history of early Judaism: Qumran, the Tannaitic materials, and the New Testament. Indeed, this process is noticeable in some of the postbiblical Jewish texts, including, for example, the numerous references and allusions to the Hebrew Bible in the early-second-century B.C.E. Book of Ben Sira, the Book of Jubilees, and the *Liber Antiquitatum Biblicarum* of Pseudo-Philo. What is unique in the exegesis of the Hebrew Bible, however, in Fishbane's view, is the presence of "textual comments and clarifications, scribal remarks and interpolations, and theological reactions and revisions."[46] However, this makes it difficult on occasion to distinguish between the *traditum* (the received tradition) and *traditio* (the reactions and comments that were also passed along). The *traditio* at times comments on a tradition in order to clarify it, at other times "annexes" it, and on occasion "submerges" into it. Indeed, it may even be reshaped into a new "anthological form." Yet without *traditio*, *traditum* becomes sterile and dies. The process of commenting, adapting, and reshaping the tradition makes it viable for new circumstances. Yet the recovery of this process and the reconstruction of the various social and cultural developments that required these changes are difficult. Then, after issuing his preliminary warnings, Fishbane enters into an elucidation of each of his four sections: the scribal, the legal, the aggadic, and the mantological. Each section follows the pattern of issues that pertain to the type of exegesis under investigation, the articulation of exegetical examples with a predilection for their types, styles, and sociohistorical features, and then a comprehensive synthesis of the variety of examples.

The Roles of Scribes in Transmission

Fishbane rightly remarks that scribes did more than simply copy the tradition and hand it down to the next generation. They also commented on texts from time to time and made corrections. This activity is noticed even in the Masoretic Text and other texts of the versions that not only serve as translations, but also contain occasional comments and corrections (LXX, Samaritan, and Peshitta texts).

The class of scribes (סֹפְרִים, *sōfĕrîm*), or tradents, engaged in the process of redacting, writing, and handing on tradition is found clearly for the first time in the Second Temple period.[47] These scribes, purportedly under the leadership of Ezra in the fourth and fifth centuries B.C.E., had a significant part in the formation of early Judaism by developing the final stages

---

46. Michael Fishbane, *Biblical Interpretation in Ancient Israel*, 23–43.

47. See J. Collins, *Seers, Sybils, and Sages in Hellenistic-Roman Judaism*; Schams, *Jewish Scribes in the Second-Temple Period*; and my forthcoming book, *The Sage*. Also see my edited volume, *Sages, Scribes and Seers*.

of biblical books that entered eventually into the canon and by establishing the important features of the interpretation of Torah and the other precanonical writings. These scribes did not constitute a new social class, but rather were the direct descendants of sages who traced their steps back into the distant past of the civilizations of Israel and the other nations of the ancient Near East. Indeed, their origins can be found as early as the third millennium B.C.E. in Egypt and the Fertile Crescent.[48] While there are numerous enigmas concerning these scribes (their social location, education, and roles), it is clear that they were involved significantly in the creation of knowledge, the formulation of tradition, its crystallization, its preservation in archives, and its transmission. Some scribal colophons are even preserved that suggest some of the important roles of scribes (cf. Ps 72:18-19; Qoh 12:9-12; and Sir 50:25-29). The addendum of Qoheleth is particularly important because, as Fishbane notes, scribal colophons regularly contain not only summaries and references to the scribe who wrote or transmitted the text, but also the scribal activities in which the writer and/or copyist was involved. The verb עשׂה (ʿāsâ), in a scribal context involving writing (Qoh 12:12), refers to the activity of "composing or compiling" texts, something that is clear from the Akkadian verb uppušu and the Aramaic צבד (ʿăbad). The verb תקן (tiqqēn) in Qoh 12:9 likely means "to edit" or "arrange," as is the case in Aramaic of the period and the later rabbinic term. It is not necessary to trace the numerous examples of scribal redactions of texts in books like Proverbs' seven major collections, since I have done this in detail in other writings. However, it should be clear that the scribes of ancient Israel and early Judaism had a long history, helped to shape the tradition, participated in its transmission, and set forth certain principles of interpretation and corrections that partially are recoverable.

The scribes who copied, corrected, and transmitted the received tradition were the direct descendants of those who shaped and transmitted it in the earlier generations. Since there are numerous studies of the specifics of this process, Fishbane does not stop to discuss them in detail.[49] However, he makes the general point that in the transmission of the texts, errors, corrections, emendations, and interpolations were made. Even the authoritative MT had numerous mistakes and was frequently corrected by scribal notes in the margins. The important point is that there was no attempt to change the text substantially. The corrections and collation of variants are the primary extent to which these scribes would venture in noting the differences and difficulties of the language of the text. However, occasional emendations offered to clarify meaning were interpretations, regardless of

---

48. See especially Gammie and Perdue, *The Sage in Israel and the Ancient Near East.*
49. See Delitzsch, *Die Lese- und Schreibfehler im Alten Testament.*

how minute. The lack of marginalia complicates the discovery of these corrections and emendations, leading some biblical scholars to think they have a free hand in proposing their own changes, often without any established set of regulations to guide them. Fishbane proposes rules in determining the scribal activities, including their corrections and emendations. These include scribal sigla that alert the reader to these comments, examining parallel MT texts, comparing MT texts with major versions, and noting the problems that may require alternative readings, due to redundancies, conflations, dittography, parallel literary strands, and other features that are disruptive. Of course, one should recognize, as Fishbane does, that this last rule, emendation, is the most subjective. It requires extreme care in application, and then only when the other two rules do not offer adequate explanations.

Legal Exegesis

It is clear that no single law code or even all of them together cover the entire gamut of legal matters for ancient Israelite society. Fishbane agrees with Daube, who argues against the view that the absence of laws covering many issues is accidental or due to loss. Rather, "many ancient codes regulate only matters as to which the law is dubious or in need of reform or both."[50] Gaps and contradictions also are present in law codes, as well as the frequent noninclusion of sanctions. In addition, even more problematic is the lack of interpretation. Thus, it seems clear that the written law codes are but elements of a much more comprehensive oral law. Nevertheless, the legal traditions in ancient Israel are viewed as divine revelation and form the basis of covenant life. These law codes were subjected to continual revision so that later ones are in part presented as clarifications and adaptations of earlier ones in order that the laws may continue to be viable.[51] Thus, the lack of comprehensiveness of written traditions required oral interpretations to supplement, clarify, and amend them. This made the legal sphere a dynamic and living one. If the text is clear, interpretation is not needed. Thus, there is never a fixed, resolute meaning that does not change when circumstances and new occasions arise requiring re-

50. Daube, *Studies in Biblical Law,* 94–95.

51. Fishbane summarizes, "The combined effect of these textual references, citations, and citation formulae is thus formally to distinguish the inherited legal identification and analysis of the exegetical processes involved." Narratives reflect the social-historical events and changes that were occurring so that they allow one to see the "dynamic relationship which obtains between laws and social processes, in consequence of which laws are interpreted or transformed." *Biblical Interpretation in Ancient Israel,* 106.

interpretation of the law to meet these situations. The tradition reemerges in a variety of texts, including legal corpora, wisdom, and prophecy. Those in charge of the traditioning process are undoubtedly scribes, who likely were trained in the law. This reinterpretation received the aura of inspiration and revelation. These reformulations bore the status of authority, as did their legal predecessors in an earlier time when the law and its interpretation varied from later explanations. Of course, those who looked to the law and used it as the basis for their actions and understandings clashed from time to time. Yet the exile and the writing down of the laws resolved the conflicts. This did not mean that interpretations did not vary, but much of the debate was quieted by a law, now incorporated into the Pentateuch, that was written. The *traditum*, at least, was finally closed. The *traditio* then explored the full meanings possible of this written tradition. Finally, with the Pharisees, even the *traditio* became ultimately closed so that written law and its interpretation in oral law became fixed. Both, then, were regarded as authoritative.

Aggadic Exegesis

Fishbane explains that the term *aggadah* is "comprehensive in scope" and "applied to moral and theological homilies, didactic expositions of historical and folk motifs, expositions and reinterpretations of ethical dicta and religious theologoumena, and much more."[52] Another way of viewing aggadah is that it refers to all interpretations of Scripture that are non-halakhic. Instead of interpreting the law, aggadah was theological, reflective, moral, and practical. While legal exegesis was concerned with the law and thus was inner-biblical, aggadic exegesis covers the entire range of Jewish literature, ideas, and genres. While legal exposition sought to make relevant the law to new situations, aggadic exegesis seeks to gain theological and moral insights and even speculation. Finally, while legal exegesis sought to clarify gaps and ambiguities in the law, aggadic interpretation took what was known about a tradition and sought to extrapolate from it, making use of literature, ideas, and insights from the entirety of Jewish culture and religion. These were written down in the Midrashim and other types of new literary modes.

Aggadic exegesis occurs in the contexts of crisis that affect the endurance of the community and its covenantal tradition as a whole. The concern was to restore the community's covenantal relationship and to enable it to recapture its heritage. Usually the concern was not with the whole of the

---

52. Fishbane, *Biblical Interpretation in Ancient Israel*, 281.

tradition, but rather with a part of it that stood in danger of being lost to cognitive understanding and lack of assent. Texts in the tradition that tended to alienate a later generation or appeared to be outdated were renewed through transformative exegesis that made them more amenable to a later generation's understanding and views. Historical memory is preserved, but the tradition takes on a radically new meaning that calls for assent. Indeed, the effort is made through aggadic tradition to maintain continuity between past and present by means of memory, imagination, and actualization in faith and living. In Fishbane's words, the goal is "to envisage the future in the light of the past, and thereby affirm continuity between past and present as the sure link between memory and hope."[53] The technique often used for this achievement is typology: e.g., a new exodus and return as articulated by Second Isaiah. Yet, memory is also reshaped in light of present experiences, understandings, and values. Subsequently, this denotes not only that the past affects future vision, but also that future vision and the present shape the meaning of past tradition. This "exemplary version" of the past establishes a durative relationship between the divine and human actions and admonishes the present and future generations. And this process reinvigorates the tradition as a continuing process of faith and practice. The tradition has become "decontextualized" from its earlier moorings and placed into new settings that allow it to speak yet anew.

Fishbane articulates the key techniques and logic of aggadic exegesis. The first is "lemmatic deduction," or inference. In using this technique, the interpreter cites and summarizes the *traditum* and then infers from this a conclusion. A second technique is "correlation," which consists of two types: polarity and analogy. In polarities, a *traditum* is offset by, made less important than, or even replaced by a new *traditio*. Even when there are analogies that positively construe the *traditum*, the new *traditio* still exceeds the old in value and importance. A third technique of aggadic exegesis is "interpolation and supplementation." In this process, the rabbi inserts a new element into the *traditum*, by placing after or beside it a new or revised version. Related to this third technique in historical narratives is that of סמוכי. Thus, textual sections not related to the historical *traditum* are connected to it in order to draw new conclusions. This practice may not necessarily be tendentious, but rather may seek to make explicit what the exegete considers to be implicit in the *traditum*.

These techniques involve shifting from one genre or style to another. Fishbane points to three types of transformation of the *traditum* in this

---

53. Fishbane, *Biblical Interpretation in Ancient Israel,* 281f.

rhetorical shift. First, there is what he names the "spiritualization of content." This means that laws or regulations may be given a spiritual sense; older formulas may be recontextualized so as to transform earlier commandments, e.g., into spiritual strength and obedience; new understandings of older content may be transformed into spiritual understandings; and the didactic or purification of content involving such things as demythologizing or spiritualizing the meaning of past practices. In the second category, the "nationalization of content," legal-covenantal transgression is used as a synecdoche for covenant violations in general, while the violation of the law and/or covenant may be rhetorically identified with activities of the nation. Finally, in the "nomicization and ethicization of content," the interpreter either inserts precepts, values, and relationships into a text or reinterprets a tradition by means of a particular moral position. In these classifications, the interpreter reshapes the rhetoric and content of a tradition to speak to his or her audience and issues. A variety of tools may be used in aggadic exegesis, including irony, subversion, didactic exhortation, new emphases, and so forth.

What is important in this process of adaptation is the opportunity for the audience to participate in the process in order to reshape not only textual meaning, but also to give forth its own views, values, and understandings. The audience does so, not simply by looking at the past, but also by new visioning of the future that leads to transformation. In haggadic exegesis, there is thus not always only continuity with the *traditum,* but also challenges to established beliefs and values, leading to the creation of new understandings. These interpretations of aggadic exegesis may involve summary and application of the *traditum,* a more hidden tradition, that is applied, and a new combination of its elements. These types of aggadic exegesis already present in the Bible are taken up and developed by postbiblical interpreters. Thus, there is a direct continuity between the biblical and postbiblical methods and forms of aggadic exegesis. The contexts for this type of exegesis are sociohistorical (i.e., the location of the interpreter), textual-narrative that focuses on the present literary setting of an interpretation, and mental, i.e., visionary or exhortative (e.g., return to the covenant), revisionary or radical. Those who practice this type of interpretation are aware of belonging to the historical *traditum,* even though they are latecomers. Finally, this type of exegesis affirms the divine voice at work in the tradition and its continuing interpretations, whether it is called God's, or Moses', a prophetic or lay voice. There is the voice of the narrator, who is indistinguishable from the tradition. While they are not revelations in the traditional sense, the new voices that speak through interpretation have a revelatory intention.

Mantological Exegesis

According to Fishbane, mantological exegesis in the Bible involves two categories: first, the elucidation of dreams, omens, and visions, and second, the interpretation and reinterpretation of oracles. These categories demonstrate close links with the tradents of the ancient Near East and the Greco-Roman world.

Biblical mantological language incorporated into a *traditum* was esoteric, meaning that its symbols and codes had to be interpreted. Sages and angels in particular were those who provided the understandings of these esoteric materials. They were provided divine insight to achieve these interpretations. Prophetic oracles, especially those that did not contain mysterious features, were interpreted or reinterpreted and were applied to specific events, times, and people. The prophets and their disciples gave a comprehensible interpretation to a "word of the Lord." However, with the passage of time, new interpretations or reinterpretations were called forth that addressed new situations. The presence of mysterious features that needed decoding further induced scribal reflection and interpretation.

Of course, cognitive dissonance was an accompanying problem for dreams, visions, and oracles, thus requiring adaptations and new meanings to allow them to continue. At times, this "failure" of the content of mantological sayings may be reconstructed by the exegete. But a convincing adaptation and new interpretation could solve this incongruity between prediction and fulfillment. This led to the development of rational frameworks to transcend the irrationality of history and predictive failures. One was promise and fulfillment in the sense of a continuing series of fulfillments that became even more noteworthy and pronounced as the process continued. Sociohistorical contexts could be changed by the relocation of mantological sayings into new narrative contexts or even new mental constructs that allowed for spiritualization, ethical transformation, or reference to the future by providing a new form and new interpretation of the content. What drove these mantological interpretations was the belief that the words of the Lord, whether ensconced in dreams, visions, or oracles, were revelation. These had to be true and thus explained in a way that made sense.

Conclusions

Fishbane asks the question, "Is it possible to trace interbiblical exegesis, its presence, modes, and types of interpretation, through the Bible and into postbiblical circles of interpretation?" In his view, while undoubtedly much of this has been lost, enough survives to allow the demonstrable transition to the rabbinic *traditio.*

Intrinsic in early Judaism was the fundamental belief in two Torahs that were given to Moses, the written and the oral, both bearing the same authoritative status and through Moses made known to the community and eventually available even for the global communities to access. However, as the Qumran community and other apocalyptic groups demonstrate, another principle of interpretation continued into early Judaism. This was the belief in a new revelation to a select few who alone knew the meaning construed by the visions and dreams. In both cases, however, there is the firm conviction in what Fishbane calls "innovative and continuous revelations." These may occur in legal, aggadic, and mantological approaches to interpretation.

There is also the phenomenon of pseudonymity where the revision of the *traditio* is done in the name of a recognized, inspired person, whether Moses or Isaiah. This underscores the belief that the continuous stream of tradition and its interpretation and reinterpretation was inspired and authoritative. It supposes that if the prestigious personality of the past were present in this present situation, he would adapt his teaching in just this way.

Of course, some of the new interpretations are obviously tendentious. New values and beliefs, not belonging to the original text, are read into it. This underscores the freedom that exegetes had to set forth new theologies and values even when they conflicted with those of the past. However, these are subject to new evaluations by the communities that hear them. Thus, one may argue, says Fishbane, for the possibility of what became understood as "revealed exegesis" in the postbiblical period. As sages like the psalmist in Ps 119 (cf. v. 18) or Ben Sira at a later time would contend, they saw themselves as inspired in the same manner that the law and visions were revealed to Moses and the prophets. They understood their interpretations as both revealed and authoritative.

Exegetical Imagination: Midrashic and Mythopoeic Images

While his earlier book was characterized by careful examination of texts and is formative in laying the groundwork for the hermeneutical process of interbiblical exegesis, Fishbane's more provocative book deals with what he chooses to call "exegetical imagination." The second epigraph for this chapter, a quotation from Deuteronomy, provides an image for encapsulating Fishbane's work on imagination, as will become clear along our journey.

Introduction: Midrash and the Nature of Scripture

For Judaism, words and Torah of God are the center of Jewish theology.[54] Midrash is the means by which these are understood.[55] At Sinai, the instruction of God was total and complete in this "paradigmatic" moment, so that later interpretations simply provide historical and human expressions. This understanding is at the core of Midrash. Ezra is its first master. Midrash contains a lengthy line of separate voices, starting with the Scripture, passing through a protracted series of teachers, and concluding with the editor. This process is a chain of memory in which each level is remembered, from Scripture to the teachers mentioned by names and their teachers, and ending with the representation of the past instruction. Yet every interpretation, each new midrashic word *(parole)* participates in the wholeness of the divine revelation *(langue),* making it live for new generations. These continuing interpretations are the reenactment of the divine revelation at Sinai. The image of fire associated with the divine word in texts like Jer 20:9 (cf. Ps 29:8) recalls the fire of God's revelatory presence in the cloud at Sinai (Exod 24:17). Even as God's words give shape and life to nature, so sin causes them to return to heaven, producing the loss of revelation.

Citations are at the heart of the interpretative enterprise of Judaism. Fishbane explains that the exegetical imagination of Midrash is characterized by two major features that are entwined: *poesis,* signifying that every act of exegesis is a conscious construction of meaning that is derived from the verbal character of Scripture, and similarity, in which one biblical interpretation of a text is explained by another. In *poesis,* meaning is never predetermined but rather is the result of creative interpretation of its possible construals. Through this interpretative process, the world is created anew over and over again. It is thus the human imitation of divine creation. In similar fashion, the process of interpretation is ongoing as each new meaning is paralleled to others but always spiraling upward to newer understandings that do not end. This feature is a recognition of intertextual connections within the entire canon. This process is the exegetical creation of human culture. Through a two-level process, past acts of exegetical creation are recaptured and understood so that one can reimagine with the earlier exegete the meaning construed, while the new voice of the contemporary interpreter is the amalgamation of the prior voices. Taken together, these become the cumulative expression of the divine voice.[56]

---

54. Fishbane, *The Exegetical Imagination,* 9–21.

55. For detailed studies of midrash, midrashic exegesis, and intertextuality, see Boyarin, *Intertextuality and the Reading of Midrash;* Fishbane, *The Midrashic Imagination;* and Stemberger, *Midrasch.*

56. Fishbane, *The Exegetical Imagination,* 1–8.

Mythopoesis and Midrashic Imagination

Fishbane is not convinced that the oft-mentioned argument that Israel broke with the world of myth is supportable.[57] Indeed, he notes that the Bible is filled with mythic images and dramas that find their earlier home in ancient Near Eastern cultures. The language of Scripture is replete with references to and images of the gods and their mythologumena (Baal, Anat, Asherah, El, Yam, Marduk and Tiamat). Even more striking is that these images and stories, often given different twists and turns, continue into rabbinic literature, the Pseudepigrapha, Midrash, Babylonian Talmud, and texts penetrating deeply into the late Middle Ages. Fishbane underscores the point that mythopoesis has been a central feature of Jewish theological imagination from its beginning.

Divine Drama: From Creation to the End-Time
(The Battle of the Great Dragon)

The myth of the Great Dragon has been one of the most common ones in Judaism, from the days of the writing of biblical texts well into the Middle Ages.[58] Ancient myths like this one have been adapted into Jewish religion even after the development of monotheism. This particular myth, in many variations, continued through Jewish literature into the Babylonian Talmud.

Israel and the Mystery of God

What Fishbane calls the "measure and glory of God" is an interesting reference to midrashic imagination in which the wondrous nature of God and divine power in Scripture on occasion is shifted to refer to Israel.[59] Furthermore, observations of the Torah and righteous living bring the divine glory nigh, whereas sin keeps one from knowing the divine glory on high. The divine glory, made possible through obedience to the revelation of Moses, may not be directly known but only imagined.

Theologies of Messianic Pathos

Messianic hope is found throughout Judaism and is present in many places in the Midrash.[60] While these expectations filled the mouths of the poets of Israel and were given voice once again through skillful acts of interpretation, they were often placed in the context of suffering and the questioning laments that asked when King Messiah would come to bring about deliverance and put an end to the suffering of God's people. Yet there also

57. Ibid., 22–40.
58. Ibid., 41–55.
59. Ibid., 56–72.
60. Ibid., 73–85.

emerges the theme of the pathos of the Messiah, which God forewarns him to expect even as early as the first days of creation. However, it is through his suffering that the redemption of Israel will come to pass. Humans participate in this divine suffering.

Five Stages of Jewish Myth and Mythmaking

For Fishbane,[61] myth is an act of the imagination reverberating between two poles, one cultural and the other personal, that is a "creative representation of existence as divine actions described in human terms."[62] Gods, through various avenues of revelation, may be addressed and may speak, but only through the imaginative feats of the human conscious or subconscious. Yet they also reposit themselves from self to culture, where they enter into the traditions of literature and temple. It is myth, says Fishbane, that initiates and constitutes tradition, which then, like its literary and spoken context, is retold, refashioned, and reinvented, ever renewing personal and cultural life. In Israel, the myths of older cultures are refashioned by their new monotheistic context (see Ps 74:12-17). Indeed, for Israel, while God is involved in human history, this does not exclude divine activity in the heavenly regions, including, e.g., the battle with the Great Dragon. The dichotomy between myth and history, says Fishbane, is falsely made. Myth involves both primordial and historical acts that are paradigmatic for later ones. Actions take on the characteristics of mythic portrayal, but so does the personality of God.

In the making of myth, Judaism brings into consideration the entire Bible. Due to its privileged position, Gen 1 becomes the fundamental lens through which to understand the entire Scripture. All further texts had to be construed in some fashion by looking at them through this first story of creation. God's power over the forces of reality is construed in mythic images, and these are constantly reshaped. Other mythic images, including those that are obscure, are illumined by the paradigmatic, mythic portrayal of Gen 1. For the kabbalists there is present in the Zohar a grand overarching Myth of the various myths of divine personality in which there are three archetypal triads and a final tenth gradation that interact in a variety of ways, both internal to the triads and in combination with each other. Thus, the highest triad consists of Thought, Wisdom, and Understanding, the second of judgment, mercy, and their synthesis, splendor, and the third tells of their eternity, majesty, and foundation. In kabbalistic mysticism, the divine personality is revealed in the various biblical narratives and laws. The symbols are both personal and impersonal, i.e., they may be fea-

---

61. Ibid., 86–104.
62. Ibid., 87.

tures of human nature and action or natural forces like streams of water or trees. Thus, for the Kabbalah, exegesis and mysticism become inseparable.

The spiritual depth of the teachings of the Zohar and its mythical quality reveals its remarkable vitality. The mystics did not think that the totality of Scripture could be summarized and reshaped into a system, for each sentence of the sacred texts contains insight and creativity that directs and gives life to teachers and others seeking wisdom. Through their exegesis of biblical texts, the mystics sought to open passages into God and the divine world. In the imaginative reinvention of the text through the reconfigurations of its language, divinity (as far as it becomes eye-opening to the nature of reality) becomes the means by which the making of myth achieves the revelation of Divinity.

Finally, there is the steady decline of mythic potency where the poet becomes the creator of words, not the writer and teller of myths. There may be a poetic use of mythic images, but these no longer contain the vibrancy of personal and cultural drama. Even so, now the poet shapes images and allows a culture to experience anew the "sights and sounds" of existence. The power of mythology has been replaced with the potency of poetry.

The Zohar and Exegetical Spirituality

The final four chapters of Fishbane's provocative book speak of a "Jewish practical theology." Thus, theological attitudes and ideas are actualized through the forms of meditation or right attitude. The seventh chapter is titled "The Book of the Zohar and Exegetical Spirituality."[63] The Zohar, of course, is the book of Jewish mysticism that serves as a commentary on the Torah but also reflects a spiritual path that ascends to God through exegesis. The Torah is the vitality and wisdom of God and to the religious seeker offers its heavenly illumination. Words may be read at different levels, from the literal meaning to exegetical explanations, to speculative references, to numerical associations, and to mysteries both hidden and unknowable.

Nevertheless, the approach is inevitably exegetical, regardless of the level of meaning sought by the reader. It is a spiritual process that engages the hermeneutics of texts. The three types of understanding leading to teaching are the benefits of the study of the Torah for humanity and the effects of this exegetical piety upon God; the spiritual counsel for the worshiper, which includes also warnings of dangers encountered; and the understanding of the nature and dynamism of the Godhead. Through

63. Ibid., 105–22.

this exegetical work, the exegete is spiritually transformed, including, e.g., the removal of impurity and natural desire. Fishbane summarizes this process: "The seeker's quest for divine truth is bound up with the myths of God imagined through the work of exegesis—an achievement that puts him in mind of the hidden mysteries, and in connection with them. In turn, these esoteric myths are enacted in liturgical recitation and mystical contemplation—for the sake of God and man."[64] Through the stream of tradition and proper exegesis, one comes to know the teachings of the masters and the mysteries of the divine. The test for authenticity of the interpretation comes from the assent of the community of the faithful who express their joy over hearing an insight into divine truth.

Substitutes for Sacrifice

It is noteworthy in Judaism that exegesis became a substitute for sacrifice following the destruction of the temple and the ending of the rituals of offerings.[65] The masters reshaped the rituals of sacrifice into new acts and understandings by means of substitutions. These substitutions were not only expressions of personal piety, but also eventually became priestly acts in divine service.

In the Hebrew Bible, the sacrificial cult continued to exist in spite of prophetic and sapiential criticisms. This system offered the means by which reparation for private and national sins could be effectuated. Divine blessing resulted from faithful ritual observation. The specific offerings and duties associated with particular festivals, fast days, and temple support are clearly enumerated. Later, after the destruction of the temple, there originated acts of piety in remembrance of the temple that included prayers and other acts of piety in pointing to the equivalence between acts of sacrifice in the temple and the ritual substitutes that developed. "Mimesis" became a significant dimension of religious imagination. Various acts of ritual substitution in addition to exegesis and prayer included fasting and acts of righteousness and mercy toward others, Torah and rabbinic study, which was comprised of recitation and exposition, scriptural teachings, and the recounting of the scriptural paragraphs dealing with incense offerings. These activities, performed by lay people, came to be viewed as being as efficacious as the priestly rituals that had been performed in the former temple.

Fishbane points to two ideals that have guided divine love in Judaism: the quest for spiritual perfection that requires dying to the self and the

---

64. Ibid., 121.
65. Ibid., 123–35.

world, and martyrdom.[66] In the latter, the one who seeks God spiritually desires to or actually commits his or her life to the love of God. The first is a daily regimen of spiritual acts of piety, worship, and study, while the second is a commitment of the will to pursue this spiritual quest. Thus, the sages imagined their labors and commitment to be death to this world in order to pursue spiritual perfection.

One of the strongest features of Jewish spirituality is its connection to joy. Joy is seen as a characteristic of worship that results from participation in divine service and is the proper attitude of the worshiper (cf. Ps 100:2). In addition to being a religious experience that comes from worship and characterizes the attitude of the worshiper, two particular elements are occasions of the piety of joy: the attitude toward the law in regard to its observance and study (Ps 19:9; cf. Ps 119) and the culmination of personal piety (see Ps 16, esp. v. 11) when the worshiper exists within the compassionate presence of God.[67] What is especially emphasized in the rabbinic teachings is the joy associated with religious behavior, the observance of the commandments, and the study of Torah. Thus, it is first of all the association with Torah and its teachings that is the greatest resource of joy, in particular when they are studied and followed. Finally, dance, an act of elation, produces "a series of homologies that coordinate the human world of action and divine worlds of blessing."[68]

Biblical Myth and Rabbinic Mythmaking: Introduction

Fishbane expands his chapter on myth, just summarized, into a penetrating book that explores the richness of myth and mythology in biblical and rabbinic texts.[69] As we shall see, this study has important ramifications for exegesis, biblical theology, and hermeneutics. He begins with the Western Greek tradition that views myth in a variety of ways and ends with the conclusion that there is *logos* (rational coherence) within *mythos*. A broader definition is underscored with the following description: "We shall understand the word 'Myth' to refer to sacred and authoritative accounts of the deeds and personalities of the gods and heroes during the formative events of primordial times, or during the subsequent historical interventions or actions of these figures which are constitutive for the founding of a given culture and its rituals."[70] This broad definition of myth accompanies him

---

66. Ibid., 136–50.
67. Ibid., 151–72.
68. Ibid., 184 (see the chapter on dance, pp. 173–84).
69. Fishbane, *Biblical Myth and Rabbinic Mythmaking.*
70. Ibid., 11.

through a variety of texts that are present in Jewish culture. Jews who have visited mythic texts have asserted that there is a rational core within myth that points to eternal truth. It is specious to argue, says Fishbane, that myth is somehow demythologized or that it somehow is linked to polytheism and thus could not be associated with biblical and later Jewish monotheism. This view is but a modern effort at apologetics to "rescue" the Bible and Midrash from themselves.

Monotheistic myths include those of divine combat against chaos, divine wrath and sorrow (or compassion) as two polarities within divine nature, and sympathetic identification in which the heavenly and earth spheres are separate to the extent that the only relationship between them exists not in divine actions imitating human ones or vice versa, but rather in the pathos that links humans with the divine. For Fishbane, the making of myth (or mythopoesis) involves a number of interpretative moves by biblical and later Jewish writers that often encumber efforts to know what a myth signifies. Fishbane's hermeneutic concentrates initially on the relationship between context and meaning that embraces a myth. The memory of the myth is evoked by a variety of literary genres (psalms, proverbs, prophetic sayings, and so forth), where it is used as a paradigm of primordial or desired future actions of God. Further, there is the recognition that myths are reused and therefore move from context to context. This latter dynamic leads to the creation of multiple variants of a myth and its images that are to be interpreted in view of their uniqueness and not as derivatives of some species of a "metamyth."

In the transmission of myth, Fishbane rehearses his earlier explanation of *traditum* and *traditio*. However, his discussion of the role of Scripture in tracing the movement from references to myth and from mythmaking through Midrash, other traditions, and the culmination in the mystical literature of the Zohar develops a schematic of expansion that is as intriguing as it is insightful. The composers and redactors of Scripture drew on myth and mythological images that pointed to the origins of Israel and then to its future in apocalyptic vision. The Bible contains no particular collection of myths, but the shapers of the canon drew from their cultural worlds in developing their worldviews. However, in the midrashic texts, the writers are dealing with a closed canon, the words of which become the inspiration for any number of expressions, including myth, of the fertile imagination. The biblical myths and mythic images are expanded and related to other biblical texts to describe imaginatively, for example, creation, primordial history, the exodus, Sinai and Torah, temple, and exile and return. These are given mythic qualities of language and meaning, developing a tradition that leads toward the shaping of Jewish myth in the Zohar. Thus, we have what Fishbane often calls a protean mythopoesis developing in Judaism along the lines just mentioned. With the Zohar, all words and images may be mythically coded in order to contain powerful and secretive teachings even about divine mysteries. These are appropriated by wandering teachers, who reshape them on the basis of context, audience, and active imagination in order to speak about God and the divine innermost self. This process eventually leads to fantasy in which unusual images and notions are released in symbolic codes.

Biblical Myth

Fishbane points to two features in the disposition of biblical myth. One is that myths were a part of the oral tradition in which writers and shapers of biblical texts either drew directly from their cultural environment or developed ones that fit their conveyances of creation, divine presence and action, and revelation. A second was the connection of biblical passages with myths through a kind of exegetical process. When the rabbis took over biblical myths, they used a variety of formulations to connect Scripture with interpretations of faith and practice. This connection gave authority to the rabbinic myths, since Scripture was heavily weighted as an authority. Rabbinic myths also received a revered status from being at times linked to a chain of tradition that strings together many well-known rabbis and the mythic tradition that they formulated.

The two examples of myth and mythmaking on which Fishbane focuses are those of the divine battle with the sea in creation, at the exodus, in the temple tradition, and in the redemption at the end-time, and divine involvement in the history of redemption, from Egyptian bondage to the time of the final salvation of the people in apocalyptic imagination. His methodology combines typological analysis and concerns for comparison and context. Last of all, he turns to the topic of these two mythic traditions from the side of human participation in myth and ritual. In this later feature, Fishbane looks at the power of myth and ritual to enhance and decrease the elements of divine might and compassion. Through myth and ritual, humans contribute to the maintenance of the cosmos and the expression of divine majesty and power. From this biblical base, the rabbis develop a mythic theology that is at the very center of their piety and understanding. What one discovers in the Bible is not an expression of a complete myth, but only features that point the imagination of the audiences in the direction of what a myth involved in its entirety. And these elements are placed within a variety of literary forms, ranging from songs to sayings.

The biblical mythic materials point to a hierarchy of spatial and temporal dimensions in which both the heavenly sphere and the world are the recipients of divine will and work. God dwells and is active in the heavenly sphere, which is eternal, whereas the human sphere is finite, is often strictly separated from the world of heaven, and is the recipient of divine actions of creation and providence. Of course, there are occasional exceptions to this hierarchy when God is present in the temple or appears in human form and when humans ascend to the heavens, at least in the prophetic and especially apocalyptic ascensions. In addition, the commandments concerning ethics and ritual are connected to divine rule, meaning the heavenly world may be affected by human action. God may respond, for example, to the cries of the oppressed in coming to deliver the faithful and penitent worshippers from their troubles. Mythic interpretations, furthermore, are given to historical actions—for example, the exodus from Egypt or the new exodus from Babylon, both depicted in part as the defeat of chaos.

Conclusion

Fishbane's substantial study of myth in the three corpora of the Bible, the Midrash, and the Zohar is a prime demonstration of what I would call Jewish theology or, at least, an aspect of this theology that begins with the Tanakh and is carried through later traditions. What are especially important in these corpora are not only their literary and theological connections, but also their richness in mythological diversity. Myth is formed, received, reshaped, and transformed for a period of some two millennia. These mythic elements are filled with vitality and insight that discredit any effort, especially by some biblical scholars, to regard them as merely literary embellishments or as an example of a biblical process of demythologization. Indeed, the bond between the Bible and myth points to the concealment of "a deeper dimension about the acts and nature of God, and thus the language of the readable text is but the surface of another narrative about divine deeds or divine feelings hidden from immediate view."[71] Finally, Fishbane concludes that one passes from myth to mysticism in the Zohar when the mythic realities of God are internalized in the spiritual existence of the righteous. This means, then, that every human act and thought may actualize the modalities of divine being and action. The interiority of the human soul becomes one with the reality of the divine.

Especially important is the recognition that later corpora, the Midrash and then the Zohar, at times express teachings and understandings without a biblical precedent. Indeed, in the case of the Zohar, there are mythical elements that do not have previous expression in either the Bible or

---

71. Fishbane, *Biblical Myth and Rabbinic Mythmaking.*

the Midrash. This shows the creative imagination of writers and teachers that operates in mythical categories without the necessity to find some earlier source from which these were borrowed. The presumption of influence from external sources is not substantiated. These mythic elements may well have been created by the imagination of Jewish writers and tradents without any historical precedent in other literatures and religions. With the Zohar, one has the view of Scripture itself as the myth of God, for the Bible manifests the nature of God even in its most secret dimensions.

The Myth of the Return to Chaos in Jeremiah

For the examination of Jewish biblical interpretation and (biblical) theology as it relates to Jeremiah, perhaps one of the best examples is Fishbane's interpretation of the mythic images and pattern of creation found in Jer 4:23-26.

Fishbane's understanding of this first-person mournful poem (4:23-26), positioned within the context of one of the oracles (4:5-31) concerning the "Foe from the North" (Jer 4–10), skillfully demonstrates through his intertextual method that this prophecy of impending doom "serves as a counterpart to the first chapter of Genesis."[72] Fishbane also points to the significant artistic and thematic correspondences to Job's soliloquy in chapter 3 (especially vv. 3-13). In addition, there are parallels with other creation texts, including Prov 8:22-31 and Ps 8. The traditional creation theology, attested not only in Old Testament texts, but also in those from the ancient Near East (in particular, from Sumerian, Assyrian, and Babylonian cultures), is the potency of the spoken word within the cultus to effectuate the renewal of the cosmos. In both Jeremiah and Job, however, the language of creation myth is used to reverse the order and vitality of the cosmos in order to depict in striking imagery the return of the darkness of chaos and the obliteration of life. The artistic character of Jer 4:23-26, with its use of rhetorical structure, selected imagistic verbs, and paronomasia, unleashes the rhetorical power of language to bring about the negation of the life and light of creation.

Fishbane discusses in detail the utilization of myth, including combat myths in which the forces of chaos (mythical beasts like Leviathan, the sea, and darkness) are defeated in creation.[73] This myth is found in the

---

72. Fishbane, "Jeremiah IV 23-26 and Job III 3-13."

73. See Fishbane, *Biblical Myth and Rabbinic Mythmaking*, 112–31, for a discussion of the myth of the primordial waters in rabbinic traditions. In this chapter, he directs his attention to the normal presentation of God's power over the waters of chaos, and not to the return of chaos found in Jer 4:23-26.

rabbinical teachings in regard to the defeat of Leviathan (and other mythical representations), the separating of the sea, the temple's foundation
stone that is the foundation of the earth and serves to plug against the surg-
ing of the waters of chaos to inundate the cosmos, and the Torah, which
restrains the powers of the ancient waters. The Torah especially becomes
the cosmic force to repel chaos, and the events and location of Sinai are
the sacred acts and place that keep chaos at bay until, in the eschaton, there
is its final abolishment. This mythical imagery is coupled with the theological affirmation of the justice of God and the rule of the order of righteousness throughout the cosmos.

On the basis of this discussion of Jeremiah, I suggest that Jewish theological interpretation has two facets as it relates to the Hebrew Bible. The
theological dimension of the Tanakh is shaped by the intertextual method
in which texts draw directly and/or implicitly from each other. In addition,
theological themes move beyond the Bible into the ever-widening stream
of Jewish tradition. The Bible, as important as it is in Jewish faith, is not
the end of the authoritative tradition, for ever-developing understandings of God, humanity, Israel, and the world wind their way through the
various levels of later tradition, developing new adaptations necessary to
meet the ever-changing religious and intellectual climates. Thus, understanding the theology of Jeremiah is not simply a biblical undertaking. It
also is to be filtered through the varieties of later traditions that provide
different understandings of the themes present in this biblical prophet.

Conclusion

In Jewish theology, the divine fire of Sinai is present in each new interpretation of the Tanakh, when it is shaped and reshaped through the centuries of imaginative construal. Inspiration is not locked in the words of
the past, but rather continues to offer creative insights to the sages throughout the ages.

In spite of Levenson's now outdated assertion that Jews are not interested in biblical theology, this brief survey has demonstrated an increasing output of theological work among a small but growing number of
Jewish biblical scholars. What Levenson may have intended to say was
Jews were not interested in pursuing Christian biblical theology and, in
particular, the work carried out by Protestant biblical scholars. However,
one wonders if he is not simply tilting at windmills in his sharply polem-
ical essay.

If one were to summarize some of the common and distinctive features of Jewish biblical theology, a number of key points emerge. First, the
Bible and then Jewish tradition have placed significant emphasis on the

legal and ethical directions for life, both among Jewish communities in the past and those in the present, which are expressed especially in, though not limited to, the Torah. The clear articulation of duties and responsibilities based on the meaning of the teachings of the commandments is only part of this emphasis. The other is the actualization of obedience to the legal and ethical teachings in life. Further, there is the fundamental understanding of both the written Torah and the oral Torah, both of which go back to Sinai, giving authority to each. Subsequently, later generations develop insights that permeate the lives of ongoing communities.

In addition, aggadic interpretation is the process by which new insights into the teachings of Judaism are offered. This type of interpretation, which begins in the Bible itself, considers the entire realm of knowledge, culture, and tradition. Thus, the tradition does not remain static, but through traditioning by teachers over the centuries, becomes a dynamic and reinvigorating process ever offering new insights, all the while honoring the past understandings. Thus, beginning with the Bible, there is an unbroken chain of memory in which each level of interpretation is remembered and new insights are developed. Reason and knowledge of both the text and the tradition become the means by which to judge the authenticity of the continuing interpretations. This process of traditioning is especially important in approaching Jewish theology.

Third, the imagination is fundamental in the shaping of tradition, both in the Bible and later teachings and reflections. And finally, Fishbane's approach of interbiblical exegesis, *traditum, traditio,* and the process of imagination allows one to trace the weaving of tapestries of meaning for countless themes through the many layers of tradition.

If one were to understand the Protestant principle of *sola scriptura* as the authority of Scripture alone to instruct the generations of the church, then, of course, it has no parallel in Judaism. But if one understands *sola scriptura* as the continuing hermeneutical engagement of Scripture as the primary, though certainly not exclusive, means of revelation through insight and the application of clear and commanding interpretations, then Jewish theology is quite similar to Christian theology, including that of Protestants. Biblical theology is a discipline that borrows heavily from the insights of historical criticism in presenting the worldviews of the ancient Israelites and early Christians. However, it is not the intent of biblical theology to suppose that the biblical views, protean as they are, somehow directly address later generations. Rather, biblical theology is only a step in the direction of hermeneutics to address the issues of each generation of faith. It seeks to determine—within limits, of course—what the early generations of Israel believed. Tradition, while also certainly diverse in Christianity, is equally important in the construction of faith, as are the reason and experience of continuing communities and present interpretations. The foil that has been set up to dispute and discredit so easily is one that views simplistically biblical theology as the beginning and the end of theological understanding in the church. This is not, and never has been, the intention of biblical theology.

Jewish (biblical) theology eschews the notion of theological unity and systematic presentations that presuppose a single Old Testament faith. Further, this lack of unity grows even more noticeable after entering into the waters of Jewish tradition. However, this is not different from biblical theology whose practitioners during the past twenty years have recognized the protean character of biblical faith and later traditions and then the multiple traditions by which theology is formulated and expressed in the present. The distinctive features of Jewish theology have been traced in this brief essay. They richly enhance the presentation of faith as an ongoing process. In spite of the protean character of theological themes and understandings, this diversity offers a richness that should be embraced, not repelled. It offers us multiple ways of engaging in the construction of faith and practice in our own times and places.

7

From History to Cultural Context: Postmodernism

> There is no power relation without the correlative constitu-
> tion of a field of knowledge, nor any knowledge that does
> not presuppose and constitute at the same time power
> relations.
>
> —*Michel Foucault*

Postmodernism: Tenets and Theorists

THE DOMINANCE OF THE HISTORICAL PARADIGM, REGARDLESS OF the philosophy of history used as its framework, whether positivism, neo-Marxism, or feminism, has been fundamentally challenged episte-mologically and linguistically by newer paradigms, including structuralism, poststructuralism, deconstruction, and now, postmodernism, an illusive and elusive term that has a rather extensive array of evocative modula-tions.[1] The central feature of postmodernism is its understandings (or

---

1. The literature on postmodernism is vast. Several introductions offer entrees into this complex, comprehensive approach to the reading of texts. These include Hutcheon, *A Poet-ics of Postmodernism;* Jameson, *Postmodernism;* McGowan, *Postmodernism and Its Critics;* Touraine, *Critique of Modernity;* Harvey, *Justice, Nature and the Geography of Difference;* Frow, *Time and Commodity Culture;* and Hutcheon, *The Politics of Postmodernism.* Among the helpful postmodernist introductions to theology and the Bible, see Postmodern Collec-tive, *The Postmodern Bible;* Ward, *The Postmodern God; The Blackwell Companion to Post-modern Theology;* Carroll, "New Historicism and Postmodernism"; Bartholomew, "Reading the Old Testament in Postmodern Times"; Clines, "The Postmodern Adventure in Biblical Studies"; Segal and Ryba, "Religion and Postmodernism: A Review Symposium"; and B. Long, "Ambitions of Dissent." See also Watson, *Text, Church and World.* A beautifully written and insightful volume is Keller, *Face of the Deep,* which sets forth a theology of cre-ation from chaos. A provocative volume by Beal, *Religion and Its Monsters,* also is required reading. Beal points to the omnipresence of monsters in the texts of Christianity and Judaism, especially the Scripture, and indicates that religion and monsters are bound together in ways that provide insight into human nature and existence.

is it denials?) of epistemology. Thus, the attack of the postmodernists launched against modernism is essentially an epistemological one, in that its meaning, sources, claimed objectivity, and assumed veracity—derived from historicism, in particular, positivism, and its locus in the Enlightenment—are challenged and negated. In place of historical meaning, postmodernism has constructed a model, or better yet, models (one might even say "metaparadigm"), that places the source of understanding within the interaction of the mind of the interpreter, his or her multiple locations, networks of identities, and the linguistic-cultural expressions of the text. The quotation taken from Foucault directs itself to a paradigm shift in current epistemology and its basis for cultural expression. Postmodernism seeks to deconstruct prior meaning-structure and to think of things differently than before. Many new approaches claim legitimacy from the outset by characterizing themselves as involving a paradigm shift followed by a self-proclaimed fanfare with trumpets blowing. Yet the advocates of postmodernism point, not to a single paradigm, but to multiple ones that have in common a rejection of modernist epistemology that originated in the Enlightenment.

Tenets

Postmodernism is a comprehensive term that in effect might best be understood as a metatheory that takes into account most aspects of reality: metaphysics, epistemology, nature, anthropology, sociology, psychology, anthropology, art, architecture, and language. Postmodern approaches, in essence, possess the common feature of deconstructing the epistemologies of the Enlightenment and any theory based on them (save, one might observe with interest, the obvious: the fields of the physical sciences and mathematics, where consistencies and theories of deduction are verifiable). Any attempt to define this term with specificity faces major hurdles impossible to climb. This is because it embraces a variety of points of view, understandings, and arguments, many of which are in opposition to each other. What seems to hold these various and, at times, competing approaches to knowledge, literature, and in our case, the Bible is that they aim their deadliest thrusts at the heart of the formative views of identity, unity, and knowledge that have provided the foundation of Western civilization since the Enlightenment and to replace them with countless expressions of heterogeneity. Even as the Enlightenment arose in response to the collapse of a medieval worldview in Europe, so, postmodernists argue, we are in the midst of the death of the Enlightenment and its strategies for knowing followed by the emergence of many new ways of understanding reality. Among postmodern scholars are those whose insights are creative, provocative, and stimulating. Unfortunately, too many less erudite and thoughtful interlopers have distorted the method into a harangue against other approaches to biblical interpretation and different epistemologies. My strong criticisms are directed against the latter category and not the former.

One definition, the vastness of which makes it completely resistant to understanding, much less criticism, has been offered in the following:

> The Postmodern has to do with transformation in the local ways we understand ourselves in relation to modernity and to contemporary culture and history, the social and personal dimensions of that awareness, and the ethical and political response that it generates. The postmodern as unruly, nebulous, elusive, decentered, and decentering needs to be engaged creatively and critically rather than summarily dismissed or fetishized as the latest intellectual fashion.[2]

Of course, one may ask, transformed from what to what? Or what is it that is "engaged creatively and critically"? There are no answers. To suppose there are means one is still trapped in the outmoded thinking of modernism. As Graham Ward has stated succinctly, "Postmodernity promises neither clarification nor the disappearance of perplexity."[3] I would add only that it offers no possibility of rational understanding, since reason is now an outmoded epistemology. Thus, resistant to concrete definitions, a fact that makes it nearly opaque, the term does appear to contain a number of features or affirmations, some catechetically, even apodictically set forth, that provide some clues in grasping a modicum of understanding. Obviously, diversity characterizes the views of postmodernists, so that a simple catalogue of points may be misleading. Even so, these understandings appear frequently in postmodernist writings. My limited responses to these points are not aimed at debunking the approach, but rather at asking questions that a novice like me raises in the quest to understand a puzzling "intellectual" phenomenon.

First, postmodernism has to do with cultural translation. One type is a reformulation of what is already present in the culture. Features of a culture are taken and rethought. Thus, Marxist economic ideology is taken and transformed in postcolonialism, so the understanding of a global market and goods owned by the workers who produced them is reshaped into a new view in which the desire for goods cannot be realized, since this would mean the end of desire itself.[4] Another type of cultural transformation is

---

2. Postmodern Collective, *Postmodern Bible,* 9.

3. Ward, "Introduction," xii.

4. Ward refers to this view of enjoyment as deriving from not possessing what one desires, or pleasure that comes from absence. Ibid., xx–xxii.

more deep-seated by contravening the logic of a culture or dispensing with the views and actions of modernity.[5] This is the more common aspect of postmodernism that is set forth in present literature.

In addition, there is the unqualified rejection of the epistemology and theories of modernism that have their roots in the Enlightenment. The former modes of knowing no longer command the almost universal assent they once enjoyed, at least in the West. Modernism is characterized by a variety of dualisms that are intrinsic to its understanding: universal-particular, nature-culture, mind-body, reason-passion, subject-object, and public-private.[6] This binary system is repudiated by postmodernists as simplistic, dichotomous, and constrictive. Indeed, for postmodernists, these dichotomies have disintegrated. Ironically, however, Enlightenment thought, including these polarities, is intrinsic to the very methods used by historical critics in the formulation of their understandings.

Postmodernism also seeks to thrust objects of culture back into the maelstrom of human existence to grapple with things that truly matter. The results of modernism have been to sterilize the products of culture in order to rid them of the issues and concerns of everyday life. Of course, I am not sure how a postmodernist would determine what truly matters, except that he or she simply says it does. Are the values of life, freedom, love, joy, or their opposites things that matter? To assert the value of something is to make a judgment rendered on one of two bases: the relationship between a variety of human experiences and affirmations (although this would involve analysis, dialogue, and agreement) or solipsism. Yet, value judgments are rendered by analysis, criticism, and the engagement of debate. These are mental activities that smack of rationalism.

Following up the prior concern, postmodernism seeks to overcome the gap between the products of culture and culture's creators, on one hand, and those who experience these products of culture in their interaction with the vicissitudes of their own culture, on the other. The temporal notion is effectively eliminated in hermeneutics. There is no past, present, or future in the engagement of the subjective knower and the object known. This is one "reason" for the antipathy postmodernism has toward historiography and historical criticism.

Postmodernism understands epistemology as the process by which the knower and the known are together involved in human understanding. Thus, the position is false that argues for the objectivity of the interpreter. Not only is the interpreter involved in formulating the meaning of something, but so also are the listener/reader/witness of the process.

5. Ibid., xiii.
6. Ibid., 17–18.

Postmodernism opposes linear thinking, that is, thinking that moves from the origins and their cause to the conclusion or result of what they precipitate. There is the typical denial that one cannot get "behind" the text to ascertain what really happened and then to trace its developing translation through history. The text does not allow the interpreter to use it to see the world that gave it birth and then the worlds of the communities of redactors, tradents, interpreters, and believers who engaged it and passed it on into the present. Even the boundary of "what happened" (history) and "what is invented" (fiction) dissipates.[7] Conventional historians have argued that the proper social context for reading a text is the one out of which it first emerged and that later redactions also have a social setting that must be reconstructed to understand their new meanings derived from their reinterpretation of texts. In contrast, postmodern interpreters argue that there are many contexts from which to read texts, including in particular, those of their contemporary interpreters. Why, they ask, should one focus on the original setting of the composition or later settings of redactions? Why not look at the settings and locations of the variety of readers and their readings?

Postmodernism further denies that anything is objective or that something exists "out there," apart from the human mind when it comes to the knowing process. How can one know for sure that something exists objectively? This is, for postmodernists, a rhetorical question.

Truth for postmodernists does not exist as an objective, one-dimensional understanding, value, or way of behaving. There is hermeneutical truth in the sense that there is meaning that comes when the object known is engaged by and understood by the objective knower.

Postmodernism intimates that all elements of culture betray features of oppression and/or transformative struggle—an interesting claim to

---

7. Postmodern historiography, known as "New Historicism," reshapes the historian's task to divert it from understanding his or her role as objectively discovering the meaning of a text as part of a point in time, thus claiming that the historical context is the major key to interpretation. New Historicism rejects objectivity as a false claim impossible to achieve in order to emphasize that the connotations of the past suggested by data are integrated with contemporary assumptions about what this past must have been like. While postmodernists are in search for the various cultural, political, and social factors at work at the time of the composition of a text, they also are much more open about their own imaginative interactions in historiography. Adam, *What Is Postmodern Biblical Criticism?* 46–47. See Hens-Piazza, *The New Historicism;* Veeser, *The New Historicism;* Hamilton, *Historicism;* and Brannigan, *New Historicism and Cultural Materialism.* Of course, most of these observations have long been a part of the historicist tradition. Yet historians, in the more traditional sense, have not allowed these questions to subvert historiography to the extent that it is reduced to an unsustainable construct of the imagination of the individual and reflective largely of his or her context, status, and power.

say the least, especially if the original context cannot be exposed or known. The claim for absolute knowledge or for the truth of a particular system of knowledge is but a grasp for power, an explanatory arrangement that ultimately is designed to legitimate an artifice and support those who profit from it. Modern historical criticism that limits proper interpretative strategy to the elite, educated, Western academic is but one form of domination and control that creates oppressive social systems. Those who represent other ways of approaching interpretation are stigmatized as lacking knowledge and pushed to the margins of the world of interpreters. Of course, here we find postmodernists making value judgments about the nature of cultural products, for example, writing. But if this assessment of elitism and self-interest is true of some literature, why not all? And if true of some interpreters, why not others? Is postmodernism not guilty of the same elitism it finds in modernist views and interpretations? And what is the basis upon which to render judgments of good and bad?

Postmodernism also completely rejects metanarratives or any kind of holistic, foundational affirmation, narrative, or system. There is no unifying vision that brings all things together into a common whole either culturally or transculturally. Rather, there are many narratives with significant differences in content.[8] Grand narratives have been intrinsic to modernity and represent a variety of foundational stories for different *Weltanschauungen*, whether it is Christianity's unrealized apocalyptic dream of the approaching kingdom of God, Hegel's gradual self-revelation of *Geist* through time, old liberalism's articulation of human progress, or Marx's understanding of a dialectical movement toward the paradise of the workers. These grand narratives and their intrinsic values and affirmations have provided the grounding and orientation of ways of living and support totalities that claim the embodiment of truth. But their claims to encapsulate the real truth are bogus. Of course, designating anything as truth or true is impossible, according to postmodernists.

Postmodernism includes the recognition that individuals exist contemporaneously in a variety of localities (social realities, cultures, geographical settings, etc.) so that no single explanation or "lesson" may be transferred from one locality to another. All things, affirmations, institutions, and facts are demystified, i.e., removed from the pedestal of unassailability. Yet one wonders if postmodernists have not placed themselves on this same pedestal.

Perhaps the most common affirmation is that diversity or plurality characterizes all things, people, objects, and interpretation. There is no com-

---

8. This is one of the important assertions of Jean-François Lyotard, *The Postmodern Condition*. See also Lyotard, *The Postmodern Explained*.

monly held understanding of anything. Heterogeneity is preferred over homogeneity. This is true of voices as well as forms, since they are varied and mixed. This diversity embraces views that transcend any criticism. One view may not be placed hierarchically over another. This approach denies to anyone, any group, and any culture the lordly position of privilege in determining what is or what is not real and true. The academic and the minister have no special claim to knowing the true meaning of a text. Nothing may legitimate a particular understanding or view. Rather, there are many views and many interpretations that arise from the collage of localities in which readers exist. Postmodernism is antifoundational in denying that anything may be considered the basic truth upon which all theoretical claims must be based. No such principle has commanded universal assent, because there is none. This argument is central to deconstruction, when it approaches literary criticism, including biblical texts. Deconstruction insists there is no reference point for interpretations of texts: not the author, the event, the supposed meaning, not anything.

Finally, the postmodern interpreter does not simply accept the text as it comes to him or her, but engages in the process of the construction of the text. The text is ever an unfinished product requiring the creativity of the interpreter to shape it into new and compelling directions, providing a fullness of language that, at least for the interpretative moment, construes incisive meaning in which text, interpreter, and context come together through imaginative rendering.

Jacques Derrida

What drives Jacques Derrida's philosophy of deconstruction is his strong opposition to authoritarianism, whether political, epistemological, social, or religious.[9] This being recognized, one understands the rationale for his fundamental thesis whereby he denies there are core truths, which may be universally accepted by reference to rational analysis. Literature by its very nature involves "indeterminacy." This means simply that texts defy one single meaning and subvert any or all efforts to impose on them one definitive understanding (hence, the word *deconstruction*). Derrida is strongly opposed to criticisms of deconstruction as nihilistic of meaning, values, and social institutions. Deconstruction is not destructive in its intent, procedure, or results in order to reveal or reduce things to their interior essence, but rather asks questions about this essence, i.e., about its interior and exterior scheme. This is his assertion, but is it accurate in describing his argument?

9. For relevant works by Derrida and other scholars discussed in this chapter, see the bibliography.

For Derrida, there is a fundamental difference between *écriture* ("writing") and *parôle* ("spoken word"). A written text does not have an author present to interpret his or her meaning, answer questions raised by readers, or define the text's implied readers. Thus, texts become, as it were, liberated from their origins in time and space as well as authorial control and allowed to continue existing freely with meanings continuing to be attached, much like redactional additions, through their enduring history of interpretation. Texts thus do not have a meaning created and guaranteed by the author. There is also a difference between *parôle* and *langue*. This means that the speaker may not be understood as the free authority in the creation of meaning. Rather, the speaker is determined by the conventions of the language that he or she must use to convey the spoken text. These cultural codes embedded in language control and determine one's speech. So the speaker is not present in speech, even as the author is absent from the written text. If one grants these two factors are correct, then it follows that the search for the single meaning of a text is futile. It would mean the end of historical criticism that seeks to discover *the* meaning of a text by discovering its origins. Yet, while the gain from this method, if true, would mean the death of authoritarianism based on some view of literature, it is countered by a substantial loss: it denies the basis for any real dialogue between human beings.[10] And what authoritarian system, if institutionalized in any variety of entities, cares if its "meaning" is negated? Authoritarianism is grounded in power, not legitimation through literary ideology. Finally, deconstruction means that texts and any other form of communication lose their determinacy.

Jean-François Lyotard

In opposition to structuralism, Jean-François Lyotard denies that difference can be reduced simply to oppositions in which a text signifies by means of binary oppositions, since literature and other elements of culture are intrinsically complex and lack any significant degree of specificity.[11] Most important in theological circles has been his longstanding, vociferous argument against modernity's penchant for and creation of "meta-narratives," meaning that texts are particularized by their locales and cannot be constructed into a composite of grand narratives that interpret accurately the nature and movement of reality. Thus, he opposes the meta-narratives of modernism and revises them into a series of "little narra-

---

10. This is perhaps the major criticism raised by Watson, *Text, Church and World*, 105.
11. Lyotard, *Le defférend; The Inhuman;* and *Toward the Postmodern*. See also Fish, *Is There a Text in This Class?*

tives" that claim no finality or end to narration. Indeed, narration continues to be important. However, individual communities in their different and various localities create their own specific narratives that are not binding on those outside their boundaries. Theologically, this would mean, then, that any grand scheme of story (e.g., salvation history) or of core themes issuing from a center (e.g., systematic theologies, including Eichrodt's covenantal exposition) cannot be applied universally to the canon or to the Christian faith that commands assent by all believing communities.

Michel Foucault

Early in his intellectual development, influenced especially by the student revolution of 1968, Michel Foucault developed a new type of social domination, i.e., "technologies of power," whether in politics or sexual behavior.[12] He later added to this political affirmation his view that humans are constituted by discourse and actions, a view that not only shaped his own thinking, but also directs critical readers in engaging texts and their literarily embodied ideologies of self-interest. Instead of looking to the author for the meaning(s) of a text, the reader should examine hierarchies of power and meaning, intertextualities, the associations of texts with each other, and their multiple contexts. The reader is to be especially sensitive to the political power that shaped a text and attempt to determine its meanings. Foucault rejects universalizing tendencies in interpretation, since these distort individual features of texts.

Rejecting all conceptual theories, Foucault advocates in their place two methodological elements: archaeology and genealogy. Archaeology provides a synchronic analysis of statements in discourse. This analysis comprises "rules of formation" that both limit and shape what may be said. These rules come into play in the producing of a text. This analysis sets forth the complexities of texts. Genealogy, by contrast, is diachronic and seeks to set forth the origins and development of textual discourse. There is no absolute basis to which one may point to determine what is true. Rather, there are only the associations of things in relationship. From the absolutist perspective, this appears to be nihilistic. Foucault rejects this assessment by arguing that the authoritative principle seeks to have an absolute ground. This absolute ground of truth is what Foucault rejects as false. There is no absolute ground of meaning or understanding, even as

---

12. For an introduction to Foucault, see Poster, "Foucault, Michel." Foucault's most substantial writings include those listed in the bibliography. For a helpful interpretation of Foucault, see Merquior, *Foucault*.

there is no authority possessed by any view or position. Meaning and truth are determined by the variety of interactions of associations a person experiences in his or her context, which itself is infinite in number and nuances.

Foucault teaches us to read texts with suspicion that alerts us to the exclusions of people and ideas and/or their silence. These related factors may well suggest an ideology at work in the text that it seeks to shape and sustain. The same may be true of readers who negate the interpretations of others. Of course, his understanding that power largely shapes discourse often in an authoritarian direction is a keen insight. And most importantly he suggests that texts have networks and frameworks of larger institutions, narrative worlds, and other literary constructions leading to a plethora of possible understandings. The same is true of the interpreters of texts.

Postmodernism and Biblical Interpretation

Since the nineteenth century, historical critics have recognized that interpreters have read their own views and values in the construal of the meaning of a text. Interpreters do not simply read their cultural and theological perspectives into texts, but are active participants in the shaping of what texts mean. Recognizing this, historical critics have attempted to establish objective strictures that resist simply making a text mean what they themselves think and believe. Even so, they have recognized the difficulty of avoiding the slanting of meaning in the direction of their own views, since their views are formed, at least in part, by their own culture and are present in the act of interpretation. Historical critics also have long recognized that there are no objective events, no one-dimensional people of the past, and no text that has not been formed by multiple factors that include the faith and value of the composer, the sources, the editors, and the cultures in which they exist. Indeed, historical criticism developed in order to discover these dimensions.

More recently, some scholars, including postmodernists, in their eagerness to posit something new, have maligned, at times unfairly, the practitioners of historical criticism by attributing to them an interpretative naïveté that blinded them to the issues mentioned in the preceding paragraph. This stereotype of their scholarly ancestors does not diminish the importance of some of their new work. But it has left something of a sour taste in the mouths of those who are well familiar with historical criticism over the past two centuries, especially when the criticisms are often unjustified.

The important difference is one of degree. How involved is the reader in interpretation? The dividing line, broadly put, is between those who argue that they can be aware of their own views and interests and attempt to lay these aside in the act of interpretation and those who argue that all interpreters inevitably read themselves and their views into the text, especially due to self-interest. But what of a wealthy interpreter who articulates the exploitation of the poor by condemning those who violate justice and deny to marginals human dignity? Or consider a man, if his gender necessarily makes him a sexist, who interprets Jael as a hero in her murder of a defeated, sleeping Sisera who sought hospitality from his host. If these interpreters set forth these acts as virtuous undertakings and point to them as contributing to a modern code of ethics, where is the self-interest in this? The simplistic argument of postmodernism is the all too frequent argument that interpreters explain texts to support their own self-interest, and that the same social and psychological principle of self-serving expediency is present in the acts of individuals and groups in the Hebrew Bible, who inevitably seek to advance their own power and control. The card of social conflict deriving from group self-interest has been so overplayed that it has become a panacea for determining the cause of human behavior and borders on acute naïveté.

Sometimes historical criticism has been distinguished from postmodernism in the consideration of objectivity. Does objective knowledge—that is, knowledge that has not been formed by context and diluted by self-interest—truly exist outside the knowing mind? Postmodernism, of course, responds with a definite no. Historical critics have recognized that knowledge is not objective. Rather, they develop arguments to suggest something occurred or that a series of factors may have been responsible for an act or result. But this results from argumentation, interpretation, and debate, nuanced by imagination. Perhaps historical critics would posit the theoretical possibility of objectivity, but its achievement resides outside their capacity to acquire.

The Bible and Culture Collective

Ten essayists in 1995 wrote an introduction to a variety of newer methods that dispense with historical criticism and named their "semi-anonymous work" *The Postmodern Bible: The Bible and Culture Collective.*[13] Indeed, in the introduction, there is the obligatory denigration of historical criticism for its failure to allow the issues of contemporary culture to be engaged.

---

13. *The Postmodern Bible* contains essays that approach a variety of literary and ideological criticisms: reader-response, structuralism and narratology, poststructuralism, rhetoric, psychoanalysis, feminism, and womanism. Taken together, these essays are postmodern in their rejection of Eurocentric Enlightenment thought.

Yet they do not allow that this engagement was an objective that historical critics understood as the consequence of their work. They also fault
historical critics for attempting to find *the* correct meaning of a text or
event. This, of course, is a caricature of the approach, since historians have
operated with the principle of multiplicity in pointing to plausible and
implausible explanations. Some of the essayists have also failed to analyze
their own assumptions and ideologies and sociocultural contexts that
shape the meanings they seek to derive. While the collective argues against
dispensing with historical criticism and its traditional methods, this
does not seem at all to be the case in reading through many of these
essays. The same features of reasonableness, argument, and conclusions
that are central to rational inquiry since the Enlightenment are present in
these essays.

By contrast, the collective argues for a "*transformed*" biblical criticism
that understands that our present context is shaped by aesthetics, a variety
of epistemologies, and multiple politics different from those of Europe in
the eighteenth and nineteenth centuries, when the Enlightenment and
historical criticism emerged. The collective also seeks methods and approaches that benefit from a variety of new understandings of language,
epistemology, rhetoric, and power, along with the conflicts of race, class,
gender, and sexuality, that have shaped the discourse of the Bible's impact
on modern culture. The essays in this collection have in common a suspicion of claiming supremacy for the traditional readings of historical-
critical scholarship; a questioning of the self-interests of the interpreters
in proposing their interpretations; doubts of the correctness of the readings of historical criticism; an emphasis that meaning is constructed by
text, reader, and context; a rejection of claims that particular interpretations are to be regarded as universal and superior to other interpretations;
and a conclusion that historical criticism's position of superiority is an
enactment of the ideology of power and domination.

The members of the collective argue that their postmodern leanings
do not advocate political destabilization or moral relativism. Rather, the
concern is to analyze critically what a theoretical move or interpretation
authorizes and what it excludes. This process of inclusion and exclusion is
thus a political process that seeks to impose meanings and values supported by and sustaining the interests of the interpreter and to exclude
those that do not. Thus, postmodernists assume that there is a politics of
reading inherent in every school of interpretation, ranging from historical
criticism to feminism to liberation theology. A question, in regard to any
interpretation, is, Who benefits? For the postmodernist, it is the ideologues
who compose the text or who later interpret it. Behind this question is the
recognition that the Bible has had enormous influence in shaping cul-

ture, society, and political arrangements. Thus, any interpretation cannot claim to be an innocent reading devoid of self-serving ideology. The Bible has been misused to legitimate colonialism, imperialism, enslavement, misogyny, homophobia, and racism. These distortions originate in the orientation of the interpreter. Postmodernists recognize that Scripture has been used and abused to be an oppressive weapon against humanity. Yet human interpreters have added to these abuses by arguing positions to be objective that in actuality are self-serving.

Walter Brueggemann

Walter Brueggemann's essay, succinct volume, and detailed Old Testament theology provide a clear summary of his major views of postmodernism.[14] There are postmodern intonations in his theology, although I have chosen to place it under the category of imagination. I have done so because he does not adopt many of the fundamental assertions of postmodernism. Thus, while Brueggemann clearly accepts some of the principal views of postmodernism, he does not embrace other rather significant ones. Writing as a theologian of the church, Brueggemann sees postmodernism, not as a threat to mainline faith, but rather as a much-needed vehicle to challenge what he calls "regnant" and "conventional" theologies and epistemologies and their dominant modes of power. He argues this was the *raison d'être* of historical criticism. This approach was designed, at least in large part, to challenge and diffuse the authoritarianism of the church. However, Brueggemann is troubled by the "tyranny" of positivism that has assumed ideological control of political and economic institutions and the intellectual centers of human knowledge, in particular, the academy. He is especially concerned to determine in this "postcritical" age how the church may respond faithfully to the crises that have been occasioned by positivism's coopting of economic, cultural, and academic traditions that deny and undermine the authenticity of humanness. Even so, he does not dismiss the utility of historical criticism, something that many postmodernists have done, since the method is wedded to the epistemology of the Enlightenment. He continues to affirm the value of this approach to textual interpretation but recognizes its excesses wrought by historicists. This and other differences in his work make it abundantly clear that Brueggemann has not sold himself totally to postmodernism. However, he sees in some of its affirmations elements to take seriously in the interpretative and theological process.

---

14. Brueggemann, "Biblical Theology Appropriately Postmodern"; *Texts under Negotiation;* and *Theology of the Old Testament.*

Brueggemann readily confesses he is a Protestant and one who has enjoyed the status of being Western, white, and male. Yet he speaks as a troubled soul, not so much thinking he is personally guilty for the unfair distribution of wealth and power, but as one who is deeply concerned to assist in recharting the course of the church into new channels that will reinstitute the humanity of all people. His vehicle for this transformation is, for him, the Bible, which contains a word of God that demands to be heard. This cry of the Reformation, *sola scriptura,* filtered through a blending of Barthian theology and Recoeur's imagination, is heard reverberating time and again like an operatic libretto performed for a sometimes recalcitrant and unhearing church. Brueggemann is especially compelled to enter into some of the features of an epistemological shift in a postmodern era, because of what he sees as the breakdown of many important modes of theological interpretation. This has been precipitated, in his view, by the "end of modernity" or of "scientific positivism" that drank heavily from the elixir of ebullient optimism that all challenges could be met and all problems solved by the rigorous application of scientific method. Even scientists have drawn back from the aromas of that heady climate to admit there are mysteries that escape the ability of humans to fathom and control. In the social sciences, the arts, and the humanities, this epistemological crisis has been even more keenly felt with the breakdown and reconstitution of forms of human interaction, creativity, and morality.

Brueggemann contends that our epistemologies are by nature contextual, meaning that one's reasoning and experiencing are significantly affected by one's location in the world, including politically, socially, and geographically. These contexts are local, meaning that generalities or universal truths cannot be imposed upon them. Epistemology, itself multifaceted, leads to pluralistic meaning, claiming assent only within the locality in which it is used and its results adopted. Objectivity has been revealed to be what the dominant group within a society has wanted the entire society to believe and unquestioningly accept.

Yet Brueggemann, approaching a little too uncomfortably to the edge of relativism with his examination of the rudiments of postmodernism, chooses instead to draw back. He is willing to give his assent to the position that interpretation, including constructive theology, is contextual, local, and pluralistic. He is even willing to recognize that we have often claimed too easily that our views are objective, whereas they are objective only to us in our own context where we seek to speak with shared knowledge and recognized authority. And our views, he asserts, often are expressive of our self-interests. Yet in explaining his understanding of objectivity, Brueggemann qualifies his position by recognizing the authenticity of the term and what it represents. However, much like the disputant Job, he also notes that there is no final arbiter to adjudicate between opposing positions. Furthermore, while truth indeed exists, there is no one to assert unquestioningly what is or what is not true. He also qualifies his view of objectivity with the comment that rarely does one face the reality of any and everything being espoused as true, even things in opposition, but rather the decision over what is or is not true normally involves only a very limited number of claims. Indeed, unvarnished objectivism that is ensconced in certainty is far more threatening, in his judgment, than relativism. Brueggemann chooses instead to approach hermeneutics from the position of "perspectivism," the idea that reality is filtered through and interpreted according to one perspective that makes sense of it. Of course, postmodernists do not argue that all things are relative, since this would make relativity an absolute. Rather, they argue that we cannot say one interpretation of a text, for example, is the final one, since texts continue to be interpreted over and over again.

For Brueggemann, we know then what is at stake in our interpretation and what it costs to undertake its articulation and implementation. In addition, what we as interpreters of the Bible are required to do is to recognize the shortcomings of a worldview and the epistemology on which it is based. What has been seriously challenged by the postcritical age is the status and power of white, male, Western colonialists. The new worldview establishes bases of support, ranging from economical and political to social and theological, to challenge elitism. Thus, our readings of the Bible must be new and fresh, not disbanding historical criticism, but also not shackled by the worldview that gave it birth and continued to nourish and nurture it.

While acknowledging his debt to postmodernism, Brueggemann readily announces his commitment to theology as imagination.[15] Indeed postmodernism is one type of view that involves imagination, but it is only one of many. Imagination is far more comprehensive, characterizing the way humans interpret sociocultural experiences, transcend the limitations of time and space, shape ideas, and engage both the entire thought process and resultant behavior. As noted in the chapter on imagination in *The Collapse of History* and in observations made throughout this volume, all thinking, including theological assessment, involves the ability to imagine and project what then activates what is imagined in the reality of human experience and knowledge of the world.

Brueggemann announces the end of the supersessionist model of von Rad and Eichrodt and to a lesser extent Childs, who vowed not to engage in this process. This contradiction of the facts has been underscored by

---

15. Brueggeman, *Texts under Negotiation,* 13–18.

Jon Levenson, among others, in his essay, "Theological Consensus or Historicist Evasion?" Many Old Testament theologians have the view that Christianity has superseded Judaism and formulate their own different ways of proceeding to construct a single, comprehensive model of Old Testament theology based on transcendence. Brueggemann emphasizes what has been explicitly admitted by biblical scholars themselves. Christian biblical theology and any specific expression of it must recognize it is but one view among the participants in a discourse in which many different faiths and philosophies engage. Christians do not enjoy a privileged perspective. This recognition allows Christians to engage in authentic dialogue with Jews, who claim the same Hebrew Bible. Levenson's view of why Jews are not interested in biblical theology is on target when he criticizes Christian Old Testament theology for denying, in effect, the Tanakh and its interpretation to the Jewish community.

In his postmodernist leanings, Brueggemann emphasizes that biblical theology is constantly in process. This sounds very much like von Rad, who contended that each generation of Israel has the responsibility of determining what it means to be Israel. Added to this point of entry into the discussion is the statement that the text and the process of interpretation are "plurivocal," a fact that has weighed on the minds of Old Testament theologians since the origins of the discipline in the latter part of the nineteenth century. However, truth claims, normative claims, and substantive claims (i.e., that a theme or view is more important than others) ultimately fail, contends Brueggemann, because the text is endlessly deconstructive. Furthermore, Brueggemann affirms what many other Old Testament theologians have long recognized: it is impossible to find a substantive thematization that is sufficiently comprehensive. Consequently, the seemingly endless quest to find a "center" for the theology of the Old Testament inevitably fails. Brueggemann does add the interesting twist that interpretative thematization is not substantive but processive:

> The theological substance of Hebrew Scripture is essentially a theological process of vexed, open-ended interaction and dialogue between the Holy One and all those other than the Holy One. In this dialogic transaction it is not possible to specify in large categories much substantive about the Holy One, though one may enumerate the usual inventory of actions and attributes. Conversely not much can be said in large categories about the other party to the transaction (variously Israel, creation, human persons, the nations).... The *hermeneutical claim* that interests me is that dialogic transactions offer a crucial alternative to Cartesian positivism.[16]

16. Brueggeman, "Biblical Theology Appropriately Postmodern," *Jews, Christians, and the Theology of the Hebrew Scriptures,* 100.

As already noted, Brueggemann's own approach is to process the content of the Hebrew Bible through the lens of an active metaphor: testimony. He positions the text imaginatively within the setting of a courtroom in which there are both core and counter testimony, which form a continuing, unresolved dialectic. The core witness refers to the numerous claims made for the Holy One that frequently appear throughout the text. The counter witness criticizes these claims. Unlike the Hegelian dialectic, this process has no final resolution.

Brueggemann selects three significant rubrics that are involved in this dialectic and process of testimony: covenant and exile, hymn and lament, and presence and theodicy. The first dialectic, covenant and exile, centers on the enduring relationship between the trustworthiness of God and a community responsive to his requirements. However, the exile destabilizes the assurances of covenant. This is an ongoing dialectic that continues throughout the Hebrew Bible in various forms. Following up these affirmations with the second dialectic, Brueggemann notes that goodness, faithfulness, and power are the central characteristics of God in the hymns that Israel sings in praise. However, the lament subverts these claims by speaking of remoteness, mystery, and caprice. This dialectic continues and does not come to resolution. Finally, divine presence in the traditions of the ancestors, the exodus, and the temple effectuates blessing and redemption is countered by absence and questioning of divine justice.

In the final analysis, interior witnesses of the Hebrew Bible resist and refuse closure, a factor that should become one of the key features of Old Testament theology. Israel's conversation with the Holy One is endlessly dialectical. Even the Christian view of the revelation of God in Christ, a view that seeks closure, is rejected, for the dialectic never ceases. Brueggemann concludes with the following statement:

> It is clear to me that the deconstructive dialectic of the Hebrew Scriptures is indeed characteristically and intransigently Jewish in its openness to ambiguity and contradiction, as is reflected in midrashic interpretation. . . . God is present with but also absent from, a God to be praised in full adoration and assaulted as an abuser. . . . By accenting such a deconstructive dialectic, I mean to give no comfort to dismissive skeptics who have given up on the theological seriousness of the Hebrew Scriptures. One would end in such easy skepticism if the deconstruction were only one step toward negation. But of course it never is only one step in Hebrew Scriptures. Because in turn the negation is also regularly deconstructed with new affirmation. And it is the full dialectic that Israel endlessly enacts in its testimony.[17]

17. Brueggeman, "Biblical Theology Appropriately Postmodern," 103–5.

Mieke Bal

A prolific and gifted writer, Mieke Bal uses a variety of theories, which, taken together, broadly may be termed feminist postmodernist. Her interests are as wide ranging as her theories. However, each volume she composes offers a methodological twist that makes it almost impossible to place her within any particular category of theory. Due to this variety and her almost inexhaustible productivity, I shall concentrate only on three major works that have become exceptional contributions to biblical studies in the area of more recent literary criticism with a postmodernist orientation: *Lethal Love, Murder and Difference,* and *Death and Dissymmetry.*[18]

Like any penetrating writer, Bal chooses to pursue primarily readings of text, rather than outline in detail complex and infinitely boring analyses of theoretical assumptions and principles. These three volumes largely deal with the Book of Judges, a book, she notes, that "is about death. It is one of those numerous monuments of antiquity that celebrate death and that we celebrate."[19] Her early work especially was known for its explanation of focalization in literature, that is, the identification of who sees and who or what is seen in literature, or simply the "point of view" in storytelling.[20] Yet she is also a feminist interpreter whose readings are often reversals of what male scholars have pursued in their interpretation. Indeed, her argument concerning patriarchy is telling: its attraction is the "possibility of dominance," because it provides social cohesion and authority. Also important is her emphasis on the interaction of narrative and social history. The biblical stories are not understood as history, but they do reveal the social history of ancient Israel from which they sprang.

Lethal Love comprises a series of biblical love stories that emphasize the feminine gender of some of its major actors who indeed are wicked or tricky women. But these texts also are engaged by her narrative theory and by the modern rewriting of them in popular fiction. Thus, she gives powerful readings to the stories of Adam and Eve, Ruth and Naomi, and Samson and Delilah. She weaves into these readings of love stories typical biblical interpretations by traditional scholars with her own views of narratology and psychoanalysis. What is striking about her work, even at this early stage, is her ability to find meaning even in seemingly trivial details. These insights often undermine patriarchal readings that have characterized modern interpretation. Particularly insightful is her reading of the ambiguous tale of Samson. Many modern scholars and theologians have

18. See also her important work *Narratology.*
19. Mieke Bal, *Death & Dissymmetry,* 1.
20. A clear explanation of Bal's earlier work within the context of feminist interpretation is provided by J. Anderson, "Mapping Feminist Biblical Criticism."

"morally" rescued this tale by making Delilah the primary villain, in spite of the fact that the story does not portray her as a villain or as a deceitful liar. She is clever, far more than the witless Samson. However, to turn her into an evil schemer makes the tale not only uninteresting, but also misunderstood. According to Bal, the tale undermines male dominance (the strong man, Samson, lacking the wits to understand the wily Delilah's betrayal but still arrogant enough to think his brawn will somehow allow him to prevail). Samson's women—his "mother," "concubine," and "whore"—share the hostility and possessiveness of the man who tries to dominate them, yet they escape him. Also challenged is the patriarchal reading of this text that fails to recognize the ignominy of male physical supremacy and its contrast with the conniving deceit of a woman far more intelligent than he. In examining the gender code of the Deborah story and song, Bal notes that the gender code, entrenched in the psyche of humans, often enters into the interpretation of the story to portray Deborah as a great savior of her people but to treat wrongly Jael as a villain. Both depictions of women by many modern interpreters are reflective of male readings that are guided by their intrinsic gender code.

Her reading of the Adam and Eve story illustrates the key theoretical principal of the "retroactive fallacy." This is when a character is invented or has his or her character or role expanded to explain the story and its plot. Thus, we are not even introduced to Eve's name until the end of the story, when the writer seeks to place blame on the woman for the violation of the commandment prohibiting eating of the tree of life. This principle leads to a patriarchal story that attempts to vilify the woman and to rescue the man from bearing full responsibility for the violation of the divine commandment.

The Emergence of the Lethal Woman

Bal explains that her book, *Lethal Love,* is essentially an examination of the interactions of men and women as characters in a story. In the initial chapter, Bal examines a variety of hermeneutical models at work in biblical interpretation from a variety of literary perspectives. The different dimensions of these models include the use of form, frame-theory, narratology, text, symmetry, frames, subject, and competition.

She examines some of these, for example, in the story of David and Bathsheba. On one level, 2 Sam 11 is a love story, yet because of what transpires, it is a love story with an ironic twist, making it into a story of rape. Indeed, the two aspects of sex, love consummated through the passion of the man and the woman and rape involving violence, force, and power, become so entwined that they cannot be separated. Bal begins by focusing on the interpretations of Perry and Sternberg, on one hand, and Fokkelman, on the other. The interpretation of Perry and Sternberg uses primarily the narrative approach of frames that are structured linearly. They pose questions that careful readers should ask, for example, does Uriah know that Bathsheba was the victim of David's lust? Fokkelmann is more concerned with the formal structure of the text and seeks out chiasmus, parallelism, and concentric, not linear, construction. He considers important the correlation of adultery plus concealment (vv. 1-13) with murder plus concealment (vv. 15-27) and also the centrality of v. 14, which portrays Uriah as the messenger who takes David's instructions to Joab to do in the husband of Bathsheba.

While Bal begins with the intrigue of sex and murder in chapter 11, she limits her study to Bathsheba and her interactions with three men: Uriah, Joab, and David. She concentrates especially on Joab's odd saying to the unnamed messenger to go and tell David of the account of the battle to take Rabbah, that many of his servants were killed when they drew near to the city walls. Anticipating that David will become angry, Joab tells the messenger to then inform David that Uriah was dead. Thus, Joab has executed David's order to draw back his forces and allow Uriah to die. This Hittite mercenary ironically was the same warrior whose solidarity with his fellow warriors in the field was such, that even with the urging of the king, he refused to go home to his wife when the king, through Joab, had summoned his warrior back to Jerusalem. In the midst of Joab's instruction of the messenger, there is the seemingly irrelevant, incoherent question to be offered to David prior to the information that Uriah had died: "Who killed Abimelech? Did not a woman with a millstone when he drew too near to the wall?" These questions become the central one of the entire story of chapter 11. Fokkelmann sees it as a less than flattering comparison of David to the foolish king, Abimelech, who died at the hands of a woman. But Bal strikes home with the explanation that the question compares the unfortunate Uriah, an innocent victim, to Abimelech: both died at the hands of a woman. Thus, within both the brief story of Joab and the larger narrative of chapter 11, the woman is lethal. She signifies danger and death.

Even less important is the question that Perry and Sternberg pose: "Does Uriah know?" This is not at all the meaningful question posed by the narrative. The interpretation offered by Perry and Sternberg is inherently sexist, while the second interpretation, that of Fokkelman, resolves the problem of tension between Joab and David by blaming the king and by letting his commander off the hook. Joab is forced to still his anger that David's lust and desire for concealment led to the death of an innocent man and blaming the woman, Bathsheba. But in removing the conflict of this tension, Fokkelman succeeds only in eliminating the major force behind patriarchy, male solidarity, by siding with David against his general. Bal's insight involving "lethal love," is then used to explain the story of Samson, his wife, and Delilah, and the narrative of Tamar.

Bal's early studies in the 1980s are largely informed by structuralism (binary opposites that include mind and body, public and private, and, of course, male and female). This literary approach examines semiotic codes as "implicit rules on the basis of which scholars attribute means to texts."[21] *Murder and Difference* is an intriguing semiotic interpretation of the poetic account of the song of Deborah in Judg 5 as it contrasts with the narrative story told in the preceding chapter. In this study, Bal confronts the meaning of these chapters given by biblical scholarship in order to show that literary theories, including those operative in biblical studies, are the outcomes of academic "codes" that are not always revealed by scholars in their analysis of texts. At times, these codes may be unknown, at least on a conscious level, to the scholars themselves. The major code of biblical scholarship in the stream of tradition active in the academy and the realm of faith for the church has been interpretation that is heavily historical and theological. Interpreters even bring their own moral codes to the text and render judgments on the behavior of characters. Two other codes, those of theme and gender, also are used. The first of these two codes usually operates by pointing to a single theme that is the "moral" of the story by which all the characters and twists of plot may be charted, thus forcing a literary coherence and structure that is overplayed and ignores difference. The gender code emphasizes difference.

Thus, when Bal contrasts Judg 4 and 5, she does so in terms of the gender of the implied storyteller in chapter 4 (male) with the song of Deborah in chapter 5 (female) in order to relate the social code of honor and shame (feminine; chapter 5) and the division of labor (male; chapter 4). While this analysis is suggestive, I am not convinced that Bal succeeds in making her specific case about Judg 4–5. However, her more general thesis of different codes at work in interpretation is extremely insightful and aids in the understanding of the variety of meanings given to one text.

Her most engaging volume of the trilogy that focuses entirely on the book of Judges is *Death and Dissymmetry: The Politics of Coherence in the Book of Judges*. She outlines in clear and cogent fashion various levels of "positions" in narratives. In her critical method, a "position" is defined as who does what in the story. On one level, position has to do with the spoken word within the narrative world. Speech is demonstrative of power, so that whoever speaks has access to power, whereas the silent do not. The silence of the Levite's concubine is telling: she—the one raped, sacrificed,

---

21. This is discussed with clarity and cogency in her book *Murder and Difference*.

and dismembered—cannot even protest. Her husband is the one who speaks in a monologue to her and then about her. He is the powerful agent. The final act of the story is rife with symbolism. The men of Benjamin who have no wives kidnap the young women of Shiloh, who come out to dance in the annual festival, and force them to be their wives, an event they are made to endure without protest. This final speech-act involving male words and female silence only underscores the unutterable silence of the violence done to the Levite's concubine. She endures this savage treatment without the recourse even to voice her dissent. The later heinous act of kidnapping is legitimated, because it secures the future of a tribe and preserves its culture. The dismembered concubine and the young women of Shiloh are portrayed as powerless, not mindless, victims, an important element of what Bal calls counter-coherence. Only the men are entitled in Judges to exercise power, including the domination of women by accepted social authority, "heroic" acts (they are the *gibbôrîm*, or "mighty men" of valor), and speech.

Another level points to speech-acts of women that limit the power of men. Sometimes they have more information than the "mighty men." For example, Jael responds to the question of Sisera, "Is there a man here?" with "none," knowing that she, a woman, would bring about his death. What is intriguing is that the women's limiting of men is not often picked up in the later story worlds that hand on the story.

A third level involves the readers of the stories and their evaluations. The success of these stories is not because of their restoration of order, but rather is due to the evaluation of the narrative's distribution of power. Thus, Sisera issues an order to Jael, which she carries out due to social custom. Yet he, as a defeated warrior in search of refuge, is in no position to issue a command. By her knowledge and action, she is the one who comes to have power, while Sisera, already defeated in battle, now loses everything in his, unexpected for him at least, humiliating death at the hands of a woman.

In her volume, which teases out with skillful insight meaning from even what seem to be minor details and vagaries of the text, Bal gives attention to the four key terms in her volume's title: death, dissymmetry, politics, and coherence. As already noted, the book is primarily about death and its fascination, especially for men. For example, three women fall victim to male frivolity and patriarchy: the first (Jephthah's daughter) does not question but simply accepts her death, the second (the "concubine") never speaks, and the third (Samson's wife) is burned to death along with her father by the same men to whom she introduced her husband. In addition, she observes not only the symmetry of the relationship between male characters and power, but also the dissymmetry between women and political power. The narratives of the three murders of women by men are recounted in the private sphere, while the three killings of men by women play out in the public domain. This demonstrates the powerlessness of women. Bal's insight here plays a substantial role in her counter-coherence model of interpretation of Judges. The three murdered women do not even receive names. The most damning of the three episodes, the murder and dismemberment of the Levite's concubine, is relegated to the marginal status of serving as an appendix to the book (chps. 17–21).

Bal articulates a counter-coherence to the one developed by the Deutero-nomistic historian and followed largely by traditional scholarship. The book of Judges has largely been interpreted as a text that values history (military in particular) over anthropology (male and female), the public arena (military escapades, thus the world of men) over the private (which allows for an examination of women in the story), change over continu-ity, culture over nature, and theology over social construction. Learned scholars have seen this story, not as real history, even though their approach is a historical one that eventually leads to the narrative's theological mean-ing (divine retribution and deliverance), beginning with their introduc-tion of a chronology that argues for a coherent depiction of history-like narrative stories. History for male interpreters is primarily militaristic and political with a center of attention that is strongly androcentric. But is this the best way to understand this biblical book? Bal notes what appears obvi-ous but is often overlooked or simply passed by to get at the reality of his-tory suggested by the book. She examines the question of lineage, moth-erhood, the lives of young girls, virginity, violence, sex, obedience, death, and the conflicts generated by the quest for power. Her approach consis-tently points to all matters of the text, from the seemingly fundamental to the obscure, oblique, and "trivial," in order to open the literary scholar's careful eye. In addition, it is here that she develops most fully her under-standing of "counter-coherence." Her counter-coherence involves a rever-sal of this traditional reading and its preferences: conflict that is domestic (i.e., family) over conflict in history (i.e., military). At stake is the conflict between the woman who marries and moves to her husband's family's household (patrilocal) and men who marry and move to the wife's fam-ily's household (verilocal).

In rejecting traditional interpretations that concentrate on history, she focuses on other matters, including especially the role of women in these narratives. Whenever traditional readings attempt to obscure or fail to mention the impact of women on history, this results from the patriarchal code of the interpreter. Yet Bal does not attempt to replace men with women in the importance of their respective roles in the text. Rather, she wants to see the impact of both genders. Women are not to be left in the margins by the interpreter when they play substantial or even seemingly minor roles in the text itself. The literary character of the text is a part of its history, just as much as historical events, social institutions, and comparisons to the ancient Near East are considerations of history.

Virginity is also a topic of interest in this volume in two separate chapters. There is a double understanding of virginity, one male and the other female, explored in the text and also reflected in contemporary understanding. Bal eviscerates Freud's interpretation of virginity (his writings are a *subtext* and not an authority by any means) and views it as a result of the anxiety expressed by male concerns. A part of this male anxiety about virginity and contradiction of male domination is found in the tragedy of Jephthah (the "hero of might" — *gibbôr ḥayîl*) who kills his own daughter. Caught by his frivolous vow and fearing to become suspect in regard to his male control of his virgin daughter, if he does not carry out her sacrifice, he murders her. Bal's own approach turns to several key terms for women *(naʿărâ, betûlâ,* and *ʿālmâ)* and interprets them as essentially women who are in transition from the authority of the father to the consummation of marriage and the authority of the husband. Purity is a major concern in Israelite religion, but it is a social issue for Israelite men who seek to control women and for the women themselves who are in transition, i.e., a time of danger when they are betwixt and between male authority figures. Two other terms come into play in the conflict shaped by the story: *pilegeš* refers to the wife who is patrilocal and not to one who is a concubine or secondary wife, while *zānâ* refers to a woman's status of one who has entered the wrong type of marriage from the view of a male, either the father or husband. For Bal, the term does not suggest a prostitute. It is interesting that God identifies with both the husband and the father, never the woman. This view of divine contradiction and lack of sympathy for the woman bring into question the nature and character of God. The view of sacrifice, according to her fascinating interpretation, is the contrast between regular sacrifice (Gideon and Manoah) and extreme sacrifice (the rape, killing, and dismemberment of the Levite's concubine).

Bal also makes use of the theory of speech-act in her interpretation of Judges. She particularly notes the violent conflict of speech-acts of riddle (Samson) and vow (Jephthah). These are both exaggerated for effect and come into play in the story of Samson and his Philistine (unnamed) wife and Jephthah's unnamed daughter. Language, Bal notes, becomes in Judges the instrument of violence, in male speeches, in the vow and riddle, and in the silence or private words of women. In addition, her analysis of spatiality and perception centers on the household in Judges, not as the typical place of safety and security, but rather as a location of violence, which exploits the modern experience of domestic abuse (in German, the household is *unheimlich*—not a typical home but rather transformed into its opposite, a kind of "anti-home"). Finally, she notes the absence of what is a major theme in Greek tragedy, the presence of the mother. There is no mother who takes vengeance on the murderer(s) for the brutal killing of her daughter. Only the nuanced views of Jael, the woman with the mill-stone, and Delilah assume characteristic features of avenging mothers.

Bal openly points to her differences with biblical scholars primarily in two other areas. One is the approach of multiple sources (something she does not question but also recognizes as often speculative) as contrasted with her view of the text as coherent narrative. Thus, her focus is on the final text, regardless of its origins and variety of reshaping. The other approach is historiography. This does not imply historical naïveté on the part of biblical scholars, but they do, as we have argued throughout this volume, tend to view the book from the idea of history and especially the theology of history as captured in the Deuteronomistic History (e.g., Robert Boling's AB commentary on Judges).[22] Boling, she concludes, simply carries forward the highly questionable view of Ben Sira that these men were heroes. While they had daughters, the storytellers leave them largely nameless. And rarely did the male characters of note have sons, save one who had seventy-one but lost all but one, certainly a tragedy in the ancient world of Israelite values. Thus, she does not celebrate with Ben Sira and with Boling the memories of these judges. Instead, she offers counter-readings that, suffice it to say, are the opposite of what these males have understood. This interaction between narrative and social reality is a major insight of how to move forward with this approach that would combine narrative/literary theory, the History of Religion, and social context into a new and compelling way of going about biblical theology. Biblical scholars have questioned some of her views as historically naïve or as philologically suspect, and she does make some glaring errors. But her insights are so striking that they far outweigh the limitations of her knowledge of biblical studies and Northwest Semitic languages.

Postmodern and Culture

More recently Bal has been more interested in theories of culture and the products of culture that certainly include literature, but also other elements, to say nothing of art and media. She even ventures into the arena of theology. In a recent essay, "Postmodern Theology as Cultural Analysis,"[23] she provides substantial insight into what she considers postmodern theology to be. After noting the importance of Christian theology in

---

22. Boling, *Judges.*
23. Bal, "Postmodern Theology as Cultural Analysis."

contemporary Western culture, Bal offers a succinct, but important definition: "*Postmodern theology is the study of this presence of the past within the present.*"[24] Culture today in the West would be impossible to imagine without understanding and affirming three foundational ideas:

1. Christianity largely dominates the cultural world, particularly the West.

2. Christianity is a "cultural structure" that informs the imagination of culture.

3. Christianity is not the only religious structure.

These provide the foundation for postmodern theology, meaning that Christian theology must be a "cultural discipline" that joins with others in the overall understanding of human art. No privilege is granted to any religion or to any particular religious tradition over any others.

Bal explains that the rejection of privilege is based on additional principles. First, history is not the reconstruction of the meaning of the past, but rather the study of the meaning of the present. This signifies that the "knowledge of the past derives its relevance from the ongoing presence of the past within the present."[25] Religion is ever present in human culture and therefore helps to shape all areas of culture, from politics and education to ethics and law. In addition, since culture is all-pervasive and to be understood through the interlocking areas of cultural products, interdisciplinary work is a necessity. This means, consequently, that religion and theology are to be analyzed by interdisciplinary work. The continuing presence of religion is to be investigated as an intrinsic part of culture and cultural studies. It teaches us how to live the past within our present. Religion, or more specifically theology, is an integral part of contemporary culture, meaning then that the religious past "lives" within it. Theology is called upon to interpret and interact with the political, social, literary, and artistic products of culture. This would be true, in my judgment, of biblical theology as well.

While Bal is not a biblical scholar, her theoretical analysis coupled with stunning insights offer a variety of stimulating readings not usually found in books on biblical theology. The issue of feminism, of course, should play an important role in these theologies, especially as she contends and then demonstrates that it can provide a critical interdisciplinary reading of the Bible that overturns some of the traditional views. But also important are her views of conflict and counter-coherence, her dethroning of

24. Bal, "Postmodernism as Cultural Analysis," 4.
25. Bal, "Postmodernism as Cultural Analysis," 5.

the male position of dominance through the telling of history, and her emphasis on interdisciplinary study that provides theoretical advances and that, as is often the case in biblical studies, keeps us from continuing to generate historical analyses that are, to use Thomas Carlyle's understated parody, "dry as dust."

Postmodernism, Biblical Theology, and Jeremiah: Walter Brueggemann

Walter Brueggemann's Old Testament theology incorporates numerous features of postmodernism. However, his emphasis on the viability of historical criticism separates him from the more radical, ahistorical postmodernists. In his volume on postmodernism, he chooses a text in which the poetry of Jeremiah focuses on a myth that has to do with the return of chaos (4:23-26). This text, by means of its mythical content and imagery, allows for a postmodern interpretation that does not depend completely on an historical reconstruction. However, he still points to the historical setting of the Babylonian conquest of Judah as the context for its interpretation.[26]

Brueggemann uses the same imagery of imagination that has provided the hermeneutical lens he has often employed in his writings on the prophets and in his Old Testament theology. In looking at the imminent sacking of Jerusalem he writes, "Jeremiah looked deeper and saw farther than most. He matched his uncommon sight with his uncommon tongue. He gives us a poem, a poem at the edge of being a vision."[27] This poet gives a new reading of Gen 1:1—2:4a. Only this time, instead of creating out of nothingness, it is nothingness that eclipses creation. "The poem assaults our usual view of a fixed, stable, safe world, a world majestic in its coherence, functioning with such regularity and predictability."[28] Yet, in addressing our context that embraces this vision of the prophet, Brueggemann points to our own world of the return to chaos, in Eastern Europe, terrorism, and the inner cities: "The fundamental cause for the return of oblivion is what it always is in the prophetic corpus: disobedience, greed, injustice, false security, and the lack of compassion. The terms of the poem itself invite us into the realm of the precariousness, push us back to the preordered voices of Genesis."[29] What God has described as "very good," we have desecrated by our uncaring stance that sends life, including creatures and humans, as well as the environment, into the abyss of uncreated darkness.

---

26. Brueggemann, *Texts under Negotiation*, 83–85.
27. Brueggemann, *Texts under Negotiation*, 83.
28. Brueggemann, *Texts under Negotiation*, 84.
29. Brueggemann, *Texts under Negotiation*, 85.

Brueggemann brings to life an ancient text, filled with terror for its original hearers in Jerusalem and with threat to a world of injustice. Both faced and face the lifeless void. He demonstrates how the much-decried failure of historical criticism to speak to the present can prove hollow when a text is skillfully interpreted in both past and present context.

My own postmodern reading is best described as Jeremiah's deconstruction of Judah's metahistory and its themes of election, sacral kingship, and the assurance of temple theology. Yet even the prophet's deconstruction is replaced with future vision and transformed into the dreams of apocalyptic's movement beyond history. The election of Israel, set forth in the image of groom and bride in chapters 2–6, leads to divorce and retribution, especially when the groom is cuckolded by her dalliance with the gods of Canaan, particularly Baal. This ultimately culminates in the destruction of the "foe from the north," finally identified with Babylon. The ideology of the inviolability of the temple in Zion, due to divine presence, is rejected and replaced by a call to the obedience to the commandments (7:1-5). Finally, the theology of the just descendants of David as the chosen of Yahweh by means of an eternal covenant is negated by the prophet, who points not only to their continuing injustice but also to the institution's final dissolution. Jeremiah's deconstruction of Judah's metanarrative is replaced by a prophetic vision of a new covenant and a return to the homeland that will precede the coming of the nations to Zion to acknowledge Yahweh in worship. But even this new metanarrative is disassembled by its failure to materialize and is transformed into apocalyptic dreams that are to be realized, not as the culmination of history (an idea of old liberal theology that should be discarded), but as beyond history in the creation of "a new heaven and a new earth." Even so, this apocalyptic metanarrative has broken into fragments as a "dance of the absurd." Thus, metanarrative, followed by deconstruction, leading to new vision, is an ongoing process that has no final culmination.

The Value and Limits of Postmodernism

Criticism of Modernist Epistemology

The major difficulty I have with some postmodern criticism is the reductionism inherent in some of its most extreme adherents' presentation of modernism and particularly its origins in the Enlightenment. Even a cursory reading of important philosophers of the period leading up to and including the Enlightenment demonstrates there is anything but a monolithic epistemology practiced by all during this formative period of Western thought. For example, Leibniz's rationalism that the principles of reason allow us to form an accurate understanding of the world without the invasion of our own perspectives, Hume's skeptical empiricism affirming that all rational ideas are acquired through the senses, thus eliminating anything that intimates the metaphysical, and most importantly, Immanual Kant's differentiation between phenomena and noumena opened the epistemological door to a differentiation between "things as they appear" and "things as they are." To summarize Kant briefly, his three most important works set forth a shift in epistemology from earlier understandings of rationalism. Kant's critique of "pure" reason denies we can know rationally and objectively metaphysical concepts, his critique of practical reason concentrates on morals, and his critique of judgment engages aesthetics with teleology. Kant thought that reason could understand its own limits as well as investigate critically all cherished beliefs in order to reject illusion. Indeed, Kant refuted the argument that knowledge derives from associating our mental concepts with the category of independent, objective facts. For Kant, we construct our world by means of a transcendental analytic that allows us to synthesize things that we see or hypothesize. In dealing with morality, Kant noted that there appears to be a world that is regularized by physical laws. Yet human behavior resists this regularity, for it is free from the constraints of physical laws. Subsequently, there are two worlds in which we exist: one in which we are determined and one in which we are free. These two worlds are separate, so that in his understanding of aesthetics, he begins to move to the reconciliation of these polarities through literature, art, and other cultural forms that are to be examined apart from the social and political realities from which they emerged.

I offer this brief review of a much more complex Kant to demonstrate that Enlightenment epistemology is heterogeneous and not the simplistic, one-dimensional configuration that is frequently asserted; that philosophers of the eighteenth and early nineteenth centuries discussed and presented different views on whether the world was objective or something constructed by the human mind of the interpreter; and that context, both historical and social, was a matter of contention as to its shaping of concepts and worldviews. Some of the astute postmodernists are well aware of these factors of epistemology arising in the Enlightenment. But the less sophisticated often are not. If some of these last-mentioned postmodernists are going to malign rationalism and historical critics, it is incumbent upon them to delve more deeply into the richness and multiplicity of their expressions, understand their intricacies, and avoid misrepresentative caricatures.

Theoretical Critics: Habermas, Jameson, and Said

Perhaps the best known and most strident critic of postmodernism has been Jürgen Habermas.[30] His penetrating censure aimed directly at the heart of postmodernism in what some would consider to be a mortal blow is that the complete immersion of the individual or theory or point of view into localities makes it impossible to judge its veracity or that of any of its arguments and conclusions. Indeed, complete immersion leads to the inescapable accommodation with the culture or the givens that constitute the culture. Habermas continued to affirm the modernist vision of the emancipation generated by the Enlightenment.

Jameson, a Marxist literary critic who has appropriated postmodernism into his schema of the stages of society, with multinational capitalism encapsulated in neocolonial culture, has lamented the postmodern position of so advocating and legitimating heterogeneity that cultural products are rendered incapable of issuing meaning-laden metaphors, images, and ideas that possess the capacity to set forth the vicissitudes of a global order and that are intent on exposing and opposing the exploitation of the marginalized.

Said contends that the critic is obligated to diffuse the power of culture that legitimates the dominant and controlling entities within its field of social operation, but he has been less than enamored with Derrida and postmodernism that denies the ability to decide between alternatives and to shape a new semantic vision that liberates the downtrodden. Thus, he has criticized the inability of the postmodernists to establish a politics of struggle against oppression due to its heterogeneity, removal of the basis for all criticism, and affirmation of multilocality that renders any unified transcultural criticism of exploitation as vapid and unsubstantiated. For Said, political struggle requires negating dominant cultural symbols that dehumanize ethnic and social groups and then retelling the history of these groups in a more authentic way.[31] Diversity is one thing, but an amoral affirmation of the legitimacy of diversity that rejects any criticism of the value of a cultural product and its effects becomes at best useless and at worst counterproductive in human resistance to exploitation. The true scholar cannot abandon the responsibility of being a critic of culture by relinquishing all responsibility for what a culture, as oppressive as it may be, becomes.

---

30. Habermas, *The Philosophical Discourse of Modernity; Die Moderne; The Liberating Power of Symbols;* and *Truth and Justification.*

31. Said, *Orientalism; The World, the Text, and the Critic;* and *Culture and Imperialism.*

While some postmodernists go beyond Derrida to seek to enable themselves and the "exploited" to transcend the constrictions of cultural products and images so as not to be dominated by them, they lack the cohesion necessary to formulate a political agenda for struggle. Without narrative retellings, marginal peoples are left to combat racist and other dehumanizing features of dominant culture myths without an alternative vision and its unifying cultural power. Some postmodernists have tried to argue that they speak for the marginals and the oppressed, but upon what basis could this be done, when, in the final analysis, nothing is ultimately true, and nothing may be judged as patently false? How can they speak for those who have no legitimate metanarrative articulating their marginalization and forming a new horizon for human existence? Indeed, how can elitists speak for the subalterns? To say that they can is the worst example of effete arrogance. As we shall see in the following chapter, subalterns are to speak for themselves, an activity that should not be coopted by Western pretension. The arrogance leading to this unwarranted and unsustainable condescension of claiming to speak for the oppressed is unforgivable.

Biblical Critics: Mary Ann Tolbert

Mary Ann Tolbert has achieved notoriety in literary studies of Mark and in feminist interpretation of the New Testament.[32] Thus, there are several other chapters in this volume where her work could be described. However, I have placed her here, because she gives a sympathetic, although penetrating criticism of postmodernism that is one of the clearest expressions of both the contributions of the approach (or multi-approaches) and its shortcomings.

Tolbert, like many of the postmodernists we have mentioned in this chapter, is critical of the discourse of modernism that has its origins in the Enlightenment. Objectification of "reality," the goal of modernist thought, is, in her judgment, no more than the reification and projection of the cultural and social ideologies of privilege that emerged from the West. She explains that postmodernism is not to be seen as antimodernism, but as a critique of its assumptions. Postmodernism, then, is best seen as a criticism developing within modernism. Yet, at the same time, historical criticism that emerged from Enlightenment epistemology brings to clear view the importance of social location in the writing and interpreting of biblical documents. Without historical criticism applied in order to reveal the presence of ideologies and the social locations of texts and meaning,

---

32. See Fernando F. Segovia and Mary Ann Tolbert, *Reading from this Place*, 1.

postmodernism itself would lose much of its force. Of course, models of societies are social constructions and not the reflection of immutable patterns of reality, and postmodernism enables us to recognize this fact.

However, she articulates criticisms of postmodernism that many other reviewers also have made. First, postmodernists collude in the very ideologies of power that they seek to critique. When this recognition of liability leads some postmodernists to withdraw into the safe havens of theory building and not to engage in transformations of culture and its power relationships that marginalize particular groups as the "other," then their musings are of little more importance than interesting or laborious reading that leads nowhere except to nihilism. This nihilism essentially argues that there is no ultimacy. This means that the multiplicity of views, even concerning human rights, leads into the opaque darkness of meaninglessness. Yet, for Tolbert (and here I strongly agree with her), to set forth visions of human existence as having to do with mutuality and reciprocity and the negation of marginality is a necessary implication of what it means to be human. The argument, made by some postmodernists, that the cultures and social systems that embrace and practice oppression cannot be countered, since there is no real basis for this opposition, becomes a destructive ideology. For postmodernism, opposing fascism, for example, has no authentic basis on which to assert any criticism.

Second, postmodernists have argued that the self is fluid and not static. Since identity is shifting, the notion of a common human essence also has no basis on which to stand. Diversity of identities denies any singling out of one—say, a selfhood liberated from the intolerance of racism—for there are many competing ones. Once again, nihilism is the result.

For Tolbert, the solution is to recognize the importance of social location and its political reality that shape human existence in the world and provide identity and meaning to those who seek to end marginalization based on race, color, sexual preference, and economics. Every person, she explains, speaks from the politics of locations that are entwined. But the final arbiter of appropriate human action is liberation. Solidarity comes from the shared experience of oppression, and it is upon this common experience that struggle must be engaged. The passivity that immobilizes this struggle, a passivity that is found among some of the postmodernists, cannot be allowed to prevail. Otherwise, the common result is indifference to the suffering of the "other." Language, itself a form of power, must be located within responsible and accountable groups that come together to gain empowerment to move forward in the struggle. This does not eliminate diversity, but it provides a means by which to unify the vision of struggle and the activation of efforts to achieve a successful outcome.

Biblical Critics: James Barr

In his usual bold manner, James Barr takes postmodernism to task for enjoying debunking the positions and ideas of others, while refusing to allow itself to be subject to criticism.[33] In his chapter on ideology, a term that possesses a confusing variety of meanings and resonances, he is especially critical of current biblical theologians who seek to explain every approach to biblical exposition and every biblical text as generated by social self-interests in general and social conflict in particular.[34] He is not supportive of those who censure historical criticism. Barr asserts that what is happening in the use of postmodernism, not only in biblical studies but also in all areas of human knowledge, and its irrefutable claims (irrefutable because there is no basis on which to criticize, assess, or even debate issues or assertions) would spell the death of human knowledge and the affirmation of anything being true. However, what one typically has is the intrusion of postmodernists' own meaning and self-interest into any corpus of presumed knowledge. Or, in the words cleverly expressed by Mark Brettler, "The understanding of ideology... has become highly ideological."[35] In rejecting postmodernism, Barr notes that postmodernists themselves are guilty of formulating and applying ideology in the very same way they are critical of nonpostmodern views:

> The postmodernist has no defense to offer. He cannot appeal to truth or rationality. He cannot say that he is not swayed by unconscious ideological drives, because his whole case is that everyone is so swayed, all the time. All he can say is that his ideology is as good as anyone else's, or better; or, perhaps, that he, unlike others, is fully conscious of his own ideological being. But there is no reason to accept this latter claim.[36]

While Barr certainly is not opposed to the use of the concept of ideology criticism or *Ideologiekritik*,[37] he emphasizes that postmodernism should be clearly explained and analyzed. And the term should not be so reductionistic in its meaning that it becomes little more than intellectual blather.

---

33. Barr, *History and Ideology in the Old Testament.*

34. See *History and Ideology of the Old Testament*, 132–34, his rather impressive criticism of David Clines's argument that ideology arises out of social conflict. "Biblical Interpretation in an International Perspective."

35. Brettler, *The Creation of History in Ancient Israel*, 12–14.

36. Barr, *History and Ideology in the Old Testament*, 139–40.

37. *Ideologiekritik* is central to the sociology of knowledge, which engages in the analytical assessment of philosophies and their epistemologies. All understandings and views have developed out of human experiences of life and the interests of the self or the group to which one belongs. See L. Bailey, *Critical Theory and the Sociology of Knowledge.*

Barr chides the "aggressiveness and bellicosity" of Gary Phillips's article on "poststructural criticism" (based largely on deconstruction) appearing in 1990. Phillips boasts that poststructural criticism is able to unmask (his term is "demystify") any criticism's claims of objectivity, the natural, the intuitive, and the abstract by demonstrating it is nothing more than "institutionalized, cultural constructs which articulate very specific arrangements of power and control."[38] Phillips announces confidently that he and other like-minded nihilists have delivered the Bible from the church and the academy, both bastions of privilege and power. Barr interjects that it is useless to raise arguments against Phillips, at least in the latter's thinking, because he "has already explained that they cannot be anything but false."[39] In addition, I would also note that the starting point for Phillips is the position that every theory has its grounding in arrangements of power and control. Of course, if this is true, then one would expect Phillips to come clean and *clearly* express his own ideology and not take refuge in the abstruse language of his narcotic prose.

A volume that portrays a great deal of postmodern bravado and self-congratulatory fanfare, to which Phillips contributes, *The Postmodern Bible*, is heralded by its essayists as announcing a new day in interpretative theory, a kind of key to all "nonknowledge," if you will (my characterization). Barr agrees with Robert P. Carroll's assessment of *The Postmodern Bible* as containing "a highly authoritarian and totalizing ideology of its own (made up of so many parts race and gender and so many parts egalitarianism)."[40] Carroll notes that the intellectuals to whom they give their allegiance almost totally escape criticism in this volume, with the end result being a book that is "didactic (I prefer the term catechetical) as well as deadly dull." Ironically, the book actually deconstructs itself, if its affirmations are granted and applied to its own positions.

Yet Barr also finds fault with Carroll and others who think that the new literary methods are now dominant in gaining access to the construal of meaning and that there are no privileged readings. Barr, in effect, asks, "For whom are they gaining in importance?" Barr offers an interesting comparison between fundamentalists and many biblical postmodernists who are united by the bond of contempt for the Enlightenment. Postmodernists share with fundamentalists the antihistorical critical attitude that leads to the same conclusion: the Bible can be read without critical methods bugging it up. Yet fundamentalists differ from postmodernists in the matter of objective, absolute truth. The former, of course, assert it, while the

38. G. Phillips, "Introduction," esp. pp. 33–36.
39. Carroll, "New Historicism and Postmodernism."
40. Ibid.

latter, just as passionately, deny it. For the postmodernists, there may be "truth" self-defined, but it is a personal truth that is a combination of the object known, the knower of the object, and the listener or reader, without one having priority over the other. Fundamentalists want historical fact, and postmodernists deny any exists. What is particularly striking is the absolute confidence each group has about the veracity of its positions. And just as striking is the common commitment to a particular cause or belief that is inherent in both systems. For reasons never justified or explained, some postmodernists are committed to political and social views that are based on radical egalitarianism, the rejection of academic elitism, and the repudiation of any aggrandizement of a group's special claims and pleading for the superiority of its affirmations. Postmodernism, says Barr, can be just as anticritical and intolerant as fundamentalism. Ridding the academy and the church of their "pretentious" claims to authority and power, argue the more extreme postmodernists, would allow endless numbers of new views and understandings of the Bible to be articulated without having to endure criticism. If biblical criticism and church dogma are denuded of any adjudicatory role of what is true or false and right or wrong, then the way is paved for any meaning, any value, and even any affirmation, no matter how repugnant or absurd, that may be made by anyone.

The fascination with new interpretations that do not submit to criticisms, the disconnection with academic or churchly traditions, and the eagerness to overturn what only a short time before were viewed as the "assured results" of scholarship are common in postmodernist works. The assumption is that criticism has to begin with the negation of the very concepts of truth, the absolute, the normative, and traditional readings promoting the self-interest of the interpreter and the groups to which she or he belongs, before any liberation from oppressive cultural symbols and values may occur. There do appear to be starting points, or endemic values, for most postmodernists. They tend to be egalitarians, who repudiate any differentiation based on any conceivable criteria. Yet, applying their own understanding, the question is "why?" For example, why should I embrace a social utilitarianism in which I am interested in the well-being of others? If I cannot refer in actuality to an external authority that exists outside my own system of thinking, then any value derives from my own personal ideology.[41] And if I am hopelessly mired in the muck of my own self-interest, why should I seek release in order to act in ways that counter what serves me so well?

However, Barr is in agreement with postmodernists in one particular, yet critical view. In referring to Peter Hodgson's *God in History*, Barr

---

41. Ward, "Introduction," xix.

underscore's his former colleague's argument that "there is no triumphal march of God in history, no special history of salvation, but only a plurality of partial, fragmentary, ambiguous histories of freedom."[42] Thus, postmodernist criticism of "metanarratives" or grand schemes and stories that inevitably lead to cultural imperialism is a point well made. I would only ask, however: do we really need postmodernists and the zestful elaboration of unfathomable theory to tell us the obvious?

A Postscript

Postmodernism, especially that of its more sophisticated practitioners, has much to teach and remind us. It is only when the true believer seems set on negating the contributions of others, especially historical critics, that the argumentation becomes arrogant, condescending, and on occasion, infuriating. But the writings of the more judicious interpreters, for example, Mieke Bal, are nothing short of delightful. Postmodernism's recognition of the partial and the fragmentary character of human knowledge and understanding is important to hear once again, but to posit it as a new epistemological insight is simply not true. This same view has come over the generations from many who confess that their insights and understandings are incomplete and often reasonable, but unprovable postulations. This is true of historians, including biblical ones, who are especially aware that the information about the past is only fractional and that their own stance within the modern world separates them from the ancient times. Yet modernists have argued that there are enough elements in common, including rationalism, experience, and method, that make dialogue possible. In this regard, then, postmodernism has simply affirmed a truism in intellectual discourse since the beginning of the Enlightenment: objective truth resides beyond our grasp. But the children of the Enlightenment have not concluded that truth is a fabrication of a witless mind.

Indeed, many of the objections postmodernists have raised against historical criticism have themselves been voiced and considered by both the tradition and its tradents. We have simply forgotten to read carefully the ruminations of historical critics, and instead have chosen to make them collectively into a distorted icon, which is nothing more than an example of a *reductio absurdum*. To think that historical critics are as naïve and simple-minded as some postmodernists have portrayed them is not only reductionism at its worst, but also a distortion that is belittling, unfair, and false. One sometimes has the feeling that some postmodern critics have not even read the works of the historical critics they have assailed for

---

42. Hodgson, *God in History*, 233.

postulating a scientific objectivity. How many have actually taken the time to read De Wette, Vatke, Wellhausen, Gunkel, and the host of their successors? Biblical scholars, even from the beginnings of modern historical criticism, raise the concerns of objectivity, diversity, and pluralism.

Postmodernism's denial that objective truth exists (since interpretation involves both the knowing subject, the object known, and the readers, listeners, or overhearers of the dialogue), that truth can be defined, that interpretations may be counterpoised and argued on a common basis of assent, and that objectivity may be practiced by assayers of knowledge are scarcely new insights. Yet, they have been reissued as though they were. There are been many denigrations of rationalism and empiricism throughout the history of epistemology. For example, the Athenian New Academy posted a similar criticism of rationalism and the objectivity of truth by means of philosophical discourse involving debate, beginning as early as the third century B.C.E.[43] Romanticism's strong reactions against rationalism and empiricism, the twin pillars of the epistemology of the

---

43. For an introduction to and summary of skepticism, see A. Long, *Hellenistic Philosophy.* An important Skeptic, Pyrrho of Elis (c. 365–272 B.C.E.), taught that humans must suspend judgment on the reliability of data derived from the senses and live in reality as it appears, not necessarily as it is. The external world, and more specifically things-in-themselves, cannot be known by either reason or the senses. Thus, we should suspend judgment about the world. This does not preclude making decisions in the everyday world of human existence for which common sense can give direction, but it does deny there is any certainty about the world, moral values, or the existence of God. His teaching strongly influenced the thinking of the Middle and New Academies of Athens. The philosophical orientation of the New Academy (c. 269 to the early to middle first century B.C.E.) continued to flourish for approximately two hundred years. The most significant philosopher who headed the New Academy and shaped the major contours of skeptical approach to theory and life into a major philosophical system was Arcesilaus, scholarch from c. 265 to 240 B.C.E. His epistemology, following the Socratic method, required the suspending of judgment about the veracity of everything. His criticism of Stoic epistemology provided the basis for the conflict between the Stoa and the Academy for two centuries. Largely, his contention with the Stoics resided in the area of epistemology. The latter argued that sense perception has the ability to provide the basis for affirmations that are certainly true, while Arcesilaus denied there was any way of obtaining certain truth. New Academy philosophers set forth the teaching of *akatalepsia,* the idea that absolute knowledge or truth is impossible to obtain. Thus, they aimed their criticisms directly at the epistemologies of the Stoics and Epicureans, who affirmed that truth, reasonably demonstrated, can be known through the senses, since it is through them that the world as it is may be understood. Sharing many of the features adopted by postmodernism, Romanticism was a philosophy that shaped historiography, architecture, and art from the late eighteenth to the mid-nineteenth century. Directed against the concepts of order, idealization, rationality, and empiricism emphasized by neoclassicism, the Enlightenment, and materialism, its major emphases were placed on imagination, irrationalism, emotionalism, and the creation of knowledge and truth by the subjective self.

Enlightenment, also has contested the ways human thought has sought to determine knowledge and truth.[44] Indeed, Romanticism continues to express itself in art and literature and is partially reborn in postmodernism. There are elements of Schopenhauer in some of the extreme forms of postmodernism. In the nineteenth century, Schopenhauer's rejection of his teacher Immanuel Kant's emphases on reason and moral oughtness produced an extreme pessimism that eventuated in a denial of desire and even the will to live. His descent into the oblivion of "senselessness" is an earlier example of some expressions of postmodern denial of objective truth in favor of predilection, if not blind will.[45] In my judgment, some forms of postmodernism are yet another descent into the irrational oblivion of nonmeaning in order to return, *redivivus,* as unbounded subjectivity.

In spite of the strong criticisms I have voiced against some of the less-informed postmodernists, hermeneutical insights of accomplished scholars, writers, historiographers, and artists who are self-described as postmodern are many and varied. There are three to which I would point as important, although hardly new. As feminists and postcolonialists also have seen, the pretense of the so-called objective and scientific approaches of the unaccomplished practitioners of historical criticism have been exposed. It is not only the case that texts are shaped by their composers' and editors' ideology on the edifice of self-interest, for contemporary interpreters also have their own agendas to push. Present-day interpreters stand within the milieus of multiple contexts that make it difficult to point to only one or two dominant themes that form their own ideologies. The rejection of an objective approach as postulated by the more naive practitioners of historical criticism indicates there is no "best" or superior reading of a text. There are many contexts, of both the composers and their interpreters, that shape meaning.

The second contribution of postmodernist interpretation consequently follows the first: meaning is the interaction of text, interpreters, and contexts. Interpreters participate fully in the "meaning" of texts. Added to this awareness is the understanding that there is no particular interpretation that is by objective canons of analysis necessarily privileged or superior to others. I am not suggesting that "any old interpretation will do." But I do think that the awareness of multiple possibilities of informed and well-argued interpretations wrests the text and its meanings from the hands of self-described experts and allows people in a variety of social settings to

44. See, e.g., D. Brown, *Romanticism;* and Eldridge, *The Persistence of Romanticism.*

45. Schopenhauer, *Die Welt als Wille und Vorstellung;* Janaway, *The Cambridge Companion to Schopenhauer;* and Peron, *La philosophie de volonté.*

become interpreters/shapers of import. However, since postmodernists dispense with any "objective" truth, there can be no claim that a theological or ethical view is true or, for that matter, untrue. To say that something is true is only an assertion that cannot be grounded on objective meaning. However, this is a troubling claim, especially in the world of moral affirmation and behavior where things often really do matter.

Another important insight is the objective of history. The writing of history is not simply the reconstruction of the past, but also the "understanding of the present." According to Bal, history enables us to understand the present culture. This is why it is relevant to pursue. The past of religion is also its presence in the present. It informs all aspects of culture, ranging from theological conviction to politics to education to ethics and to law. Because of the multiplicity of cultural products, we have, argues Bal, a second principle. This is the rudimentary requirement of interdisciplinary cultural studies. Religion is a pervasive presence in these products and thus is to be investigated by means of interdisciplinary research from many angles and within an uncountable host of locations.

However, some of the poorly read postmodernists in biblical studies have leveled false charges against the interpretative discipline of historical criticism. The most common accusation is that the method is not capable of hermeneutical construction of meanings. This is a puzzling charge, since any overview of the history of the methodology from its inception in the Enlightenment to the present clearly demonstrates that its objective is the historical reconstruction of the past, and not the construction of hermeneutical meaning for the present. Yet historians suffer the charge of a methodology sufficiently jaundiced toward the nonelite and knowingly prostituted to fashion ideological self-interests. A second frequent criticism that also lacks veracity is that historical critics in their analysis argue that their interpretation is the "true" one. Biblical historians argue for the plausibility of their views, at times aggressively and at other times reservedly, but they are only that, plausible. Only sheer arrogance would lead a historical critic to claim, on the basis of often very fragmentary data, that his or her reconstruction is the "true" one. The heart and soul of historical criticism is debate, not some obscurantist view that this or that scholar has the true meaning.

August claims are made about the various methods that make up postmodernist interpretation of Scripture. For example, we are supposed to have entered a postmodern period when the old ways of thinking that have their origins in the Enlightenment (rationalism and empiricism) no longer prevail. Once again, we hear the language of a "paradigm shift" that Thomas Kuhn described in his now "classic" volume published in

1970.[46] The devotees of every new hermeneutic always seem to think it is required of them to introduce their "new" approach that will revolutionize epistemology by reference to this phrase. I am reminded of the first-person self-praise of new deities in aretalogies, who, not established theologically and cultically, are presented as making imposing claims for their prowess and greatness simply through self-attestation.

The losses to human thinking and understanding, should the post-modern agenda be fully implemented, would be enormous. Perhaps the most debilitating one is dispensing with any affirmation as true in any sense of the word. Postmodernists in religion are quick to deny this and reject the claim that they advocate nihilism. But one is hard pressed to see their arguments as anything but nihilistic, similar to the anti-Kantian view expressed by Schopenhauer in his understanding of blind will:[47] there is no meaning whatsoever that may be claimed and attested as objectively and representationally true. For Schopenhauer, the human will seeks to represent the world experienced through the senses in orderly forms through which knowledge may be obtained that is objectively true. Yet we simply construct our world through self-interest with intent to realize immediate goals that inevitably become conflicting and contradictory. Try as they must, humans cannot escape or abolish this will in the attempt to know what is objectively true. Ideas are nothing more than the epiphenomena of a blind and irrational will that expresses itself through self-constructed ideas and actions based on self-interest.

If the postmodernists and their intellectual predecessors, including the philosophers of the New Academy, the Romanticists, and possibly even Schopenhauer, are correct, then the interpreter, located in multidimensional contexts, determines meaning. Thus, there is no objective reality, and all assertions are ideological construals of self-interest. Nothing may be affirmed as true whether theological or ethical. There is no basis on which behavior may be judged as ethical or unethical. Yet if we abandon ethics, do we not allow marginals to continue in the squalor of degrading, humanity-denying subsistence or fail to oppose authoritarian regimes in their pillaging, destroying, and controlling, without so much as uttering even a whispered protest?

The most significant concern I have with postmodernism is that it is as tendentious as the ideologies of texts and interpreters that it strongly criticizes. While no text or interpreter is capable of transcending self-interest, the biased character of much postmodernism is clear. Thus, the criticisms postmodernists raise about texts and interpreters, especially historical

---

46. Kuhn, *The Structure of Scientific Revolutions*.
47. Schopenhauer, *Die Welt als Wille und Vorstellung*.

critics, are just as partisan, if not more so, since they operate with the deception that their approach transcends ideology. Historical critics may be suffering from self-delusion in attempting to interpret the text as "objectively" as possible, but at least they make the effort. Postmodernists do not. They choose, rather, to reify their own political, social, sexual, and theological affirmations in every text that is interpreted without any accountability to critical scrutiny. They have attempted to construct an approach to biblical interpretation that is "beyond criticism."

8

From the Colonial Bible to the Postcolonial Text: Biblical Theology as Contextual

Growing up
in my father's house
at the missionary's feet
I saw you as a
grey-bearded white man from far
a large all-seeing
all-knowing
EYE.

—Betty Govinden

Postcolonialism

BETTY GOVINDEN'S POEM,[1] EXPRESSED THROUGH THE IMAGINATION of an African child, is a poignant rumination of how missionary religion has legitimated the exploitation and dehumanization of colonialism and imperialism, i.e., through the portrayal of an all-knowing, all-seeing, bearded, white, male deity "from far." Even now, with the collapse of most empires (save for the recent attempt of the United States to forge a Middle Eastern realm as a central part of its policy of universal domination) and the return of the land and national sovereignty to its indigenous inhabitants and the establishment of native nation-states, neocolonialism has become an even more insidious policy of the European Union, Japan, and the United States to control African markets and natural resources, even while tribal genocide is allowed to occur unchecked, AIDS is threatening to decimate the black populations of many African nations, and starvation generated by famines is responsible for shocking numbers of malnourished,

---

1. Govinden, "Re-Imaging God," 148–50. I have recently been commissioned by Blackwells to write a postcolonial interpretation of the history of ancient Israel.

dying, and deceased children.[2] Japan, Europe, and North America have done little officially to combat these disasters, except to monitor them from "far," while Western churches have engaged in only very modest efforts to relieve the suffering and end the exploitation. Indeed, evangelical and fundamentalist churches have largely ignored social issues in order to proclaim a white, male, supremacist deity who offers eternal life in the next world. And the liberalism of mainstream churches is a thin veil covering an entrenched self-satisfaction with a comfortable life. Africa is only one of the many geographical settings for the rise and development of postcolonialism that has affected many intellectuals and defiant opponents of not only the "Two-Thirds World," but also of the West. However, if this understanding of culture and religion is to have any positive results in dealing with the misery of the oppressed and to allow the haunting, often silent voices of marginals to speak, it must move outside the books and the classrooms into the arenas of national policies and international struggle.

2. As a member of the Chickasaw Nation, I have developed a strong personal interest in postcolonialism that resonates well with my own thoughts and feelings, formed during my childhood and youth spent in the former "Indian Territory" of Oklahoma. Certainly the history of some of my indigenous ancestors in America is a tragic one of genocide, diaspora, exploitation, marginalization, and humiliation. The colonizers of Europe have come close to erasing the memory of the Chickasaws by negating the study of its culture and marginalizing even more those who sought to participate in and keep alive its traditions. Many of the experiences of my forebears, including my maternal grandmother in Oklahoma, were degrading and close to debilitating. My own solidarity with postcolonial peoples in the Third World is extremely strong. Few Chickasaws have undertaken to tell their narrative history, and it is one I hope one day to write.

In addition, I am particularly indebted to three of my postcolonial doctoral students, Aliou Niang, Royce Victor, and Makhosazana Nzimande for their many insights into biblical theology and its relationship to religion, political structures, racism, multiculturalism, and postcolonialism. Indeed, the first two students have shaped the outlines of their own approach, which I have chosen to include in this chapter. Nzimande, my graduate assistant, has provided me invaluable scholarly and experiential views of postcolonialism, based on her life in South Africa, her home country.

The literature on postcolonialism, including writings in theology and biblical studies, has proliferated in recent years. Postcolonialism has penetrated all major disciplines in the humanities, the arts, and the social sciences. For an entrée into postcolonialism's histories and actualization in the human experience of the Third World, I recommend McLeod, *Beginning Postcolonialism*, which has a very fine select bibliography (pp. 261–68) of important works divided into the areas of general introductions, reference books, general readers, texts on postcolonial theory, collections of essays, and journals. Also see his select bibliography at the end of each of his chapters. Another fine introduction is Ashcroft, Griffiths, and Tiff, *Key Concepts in Post-Colonial Studies*. The standard history of postcolonialism is R. Young, *Postcolonialism*. His bibliography is immense and lists the standard works in this area up to 2000 (pp. 429–72). Sugirtharajah's important survey of postcolonial biblical studies has a select bibliography that includes many of this discipline's most seminal writings. *Postcolonial Criticism and Biblical Interpretation*, 208–24.

Colonialism and Imperialism

From a historical perspective, postcolonialism embraces largely the aftermath of the demise of European colonization by empires and trading companies that had grown rich in profits of exploitation beginning in the sixteenth century and continuing into the post–World War II period. Thus, while there is a long history of writings and other data that issue from both the colonizers and their critics, postcolonialism marshaled its major forces after the end of imperial colonies following the Second World War. The history of colonialism has been documented in great detail by a variety of scholars, including a comprehensive volume by Robert J. C. Young that provides one of the most detailed surveys. Imperialism is best defined as the economic and military control by one nation over another.

The driving force in European and other geographical centers of colonialism, including especially America, has been profit. States established political control over other lands and people by means of military force, thereby gaining land, natural resources, trade, and cheap labor, including slavery, and gathering the harvests of this decimation of peoples, cultures, and natural resources for the ever-expanding barns of wealthy nation-states. The British, French, Dutch, and Spaniards were especially successful in building and expanding empires from the sixteenth well into the nineteenth and early twentieth centuries, to be followed by the American and the Soviet imperialists since the end of World War II. Imperialism is thus a political policy that, once effectuated, led to the establishment of colonies designed to enrich the national center and the capital of the empire. To homogenize the empire, the instruments used to socialize colonial populations were a common language, the empire's dominant religion, and imperial schools. Citizenship in the empire, of course, varied, but it was purposefully withheld from all but a few who could add to the empire's stability and growth.

The empire builders carried out indoctrination in the "superior" nation's history, form of government, and culture, in order to produce a more unified group of nations who rejected their own cultures and languages and adopted those of the new power. The goal was not to offer colonials an equality of status or the same type of legitimate citizenship as their dictators, but to establish a common identity that "civilized" them with the new traditions and established a new unity and allegiance centered on enhancing and assuring the power and control of the dominant state. The internalization of these ways of seeing the world through the images and representations of the colonial power became the major tool in achieving stability throughout the empire's colonized world. The fundamental doctrine of colonial propaganda was that it was a divinely ordained right for the empire's ruling nation to control "barbaric peoples." Its values were to be accepted as the proper and correct ones in the construction of a worldview. This is but one example of the recognition of the capacity of language to create new realities.[3] This inculturation into the empire's worldview is sometimes presented as the "competition of ideas," but in actuality it is the use of propaganda by the West to bring weaker nations into their orbit of control. The dehumanization of the colonized is presented in a variety of settings, ranging from the imperial schools to government propaganda to belittle people of color and represent them as the "other," the uncivilized who, while capable of a limited education, could never be regarded as equals. They were marginalized, and those who wished to escape life on the margins and to obtain some advancement in the new world of the empire had to embrace the ideals, values, and worldview of the conqueror and to repudiate their own cultures, languages, values, and beliefs.

Postcolonialism and Intellectuals

For the period following the Second World War, an increasing number of Western scholars have joined those who recognize that Europe and North America no longer dominate the intellectual disciplines of the Western universities, including biblical studies, even as their countries may no longer claim ownership of colonies. The interpreters of the Bible in Africa and Asia, including a very large number of scholars from the so-called Third World, have undertaken their studies from very different cultures and histories than those of the Eurocentric or American West. It is safe to say that these communities of faith have nourished new understandings of biblical theology and will continue to do so.

Furthermore, not only in North America but increasingly also in Europe, scholars pursuing their craft in a variety of cultural, social, religious, and academic contexts now approach their work from different gender, sexual, racial, and cultural identities. Thus, they cannot simply dispense with these and the worldviews, understandings of religion, and cultural locations that shape them when interpreting the biblical text and other objects of potential meaning. Objectivity may be a goal, and criteria designed to limit specious interpretation may be used to restrict subjectivity in interpretation (at least, this is the modernist position), but identities and locations play an undeniably fundamental role in shaping the readers and the interpretation of biblical texts. These various identities have led to the creation of a variety of traditions of interpretation, as diverse as

3. McLeod, *Beginning Postcolonialism*, 19.

feminist and womanist understandings; gay, lesbian, bisexual, and trans-sexual approaches; and ethnic readings of African Americans, Latinos and Latinas, and Asian Americans. Since the end of World War II and the breakup of European empires in Africa and the East, many studies have originated in former colonies and represent a diversity of cultural and geographical contexts, academic approaches, and identities. Consequently, biblical theology is becoming now a multicultural, multivocal enterprise that all the more requires not only the understanding of different cultures, peoples, and methods, but also serious conversations and open engagement.

The response to the captivity of the mind imposed by colonialism has involved two or three major stages: exposure, deconstruction, and the creation of new theoretical knowledge in the former colonies themselves. Exposure has to do with examining the classics of Western literature that depict the colonial world and debating whether their representations are accurate or not. Deconstruction has been used by several postcolonial writers to develop new understandings of old texts. Some postcolonial readers, although certainly only a limited number, have used the writings of poststructuralists, including Derrida, Lukan, and Foucault, in the effort to take the representations of both the colonizer and the colonized and reread them so as to shape new understandings. These postmodernists are used to remind readers that the reader participates in the structuring of meaning and the context is essential in understanding the text and the interpreter. While these are not new concepts, they serve to remind us of the importance of ideology, context, and reader participation in shaping the meaning of a "text." Important issues also concern particularity, diversity, and gender in the use of language and both its construals and shaping of values and views.[4] New knowledge emerges from the meaning derived from or given to texts when postcolonial readings occur. These new insights provide rich and provocative understandings that allow the text and its meaning world to expand in new and diverse directions.

Postcolonial reading involves several important features that coalesce in the process of interpretation. One of these involves the emphasis that literature must be placed within its own social, cultural, and historical contexts. Removal of texts from their multiple settings renders literature and its potential meanings impotent, makes interpretation a useless exercise in intellectual abstraction, or gives it a very different meaning. In addition, a postcolonial reading reveals how thoroughly colonial values and the history of Western exploitation permeate art, literature, and music. These must be identified and at least their ideologies revealed and possibly even expunged. Finally, a postcolonial reading provides a powerful

---

4. See P. Childs and Williams, *An Introduction to Post-Colonial Theory.*

weapon of resistance against neocolonialism and its prostitution of local culture and language to perpetuate its presence and expansion through-out the "Two-Thirds World."

Postcolonialism as a General Approach to Knowledge and Experience

Defining postcolonialism is a complicated task, since the term covers so many fields of study and particular ways of proceeding. However, I offer a brief attempt, with the realization that this understanding and approach to human knowledge and experience is decidedly more complex.

A major factor in understanding postcolonialism is the economic theory of capitalism. When colonies were established, the owners of capital inevitably came from the citizenry of the nation-state, while colonials in the colonies were the laborers whose profit in these enterprises was limited or denied. Indeed, the drive toward imperialism was aided by the establishment of global trading companies, e.g., the Dutch West Indies Company, which set up colonies that produced substantial wealth in countries ripe for exploitation. These global companies required the protection of the national center's military to stabilize and carry out profitable ventures. This capitalistic effort is sometimes given the name "colonialism," since it depends on the establishment of foreign settlements in native lands or colonies, viewed primarily in terms of profit. Through these settlements, the establishment of schools and churches, and the teaching of the features of the national center's culture, including particularly its language, metahistory, and worldviews, the colonizing of much of the "Third World" occurred. Thus, colonialism is particularly defined with reference to three factors: settlement, capitalism, and the unequal distribution of power.[5] Of course, the reactions of the colonized to the colonizers varied, but resistance movements began to take root that successfully brought colonialism to an end.[6]

While postcolonialism joins in the struggle to resist the economic exploitation of the "Two-Thirds World" by the West and Japan, there are other issues at stake that are just as important. Part of the victory over colonialism, its aftermath, and its rebirth as neocolonialism has been to expunge the notion of the superiority of Western culture, including technology, which now is used so effectively in the propaganda distributed by

---

5. See Boehmer, *Colonial and Postcolonial Literature.*

6. Definitions of imperialism, colonialism, postcolonialism, and neocolonialism may be found in P. Childs and Williams, *An Introduction to Post-Colonial Theory;* McLeod, *Beginning Postcolonialism,* 6–36; and R. Young, *Postcolonialism,* 13–69.

mass media, and the inferiority of the cultures of the former colonies. This continues to be a goal of postcolonial thinkers, and it is necessary if the "Two-Thirds World" is to build its many diverse understandings of identity, self-worth, and independence from the exploiters. Returning to their own culture's roots and regenerating their national identity as the basis for achieving a new definition of people and nation are an essential undertaking.

Although old-style colonialism may be at an end, it has been replaced by neocolonialism, i.e., the effort to bring under economic control the peoples and resources of a "Third World" country through the establishment and expansion of transnational corporations, so powerful that even the nation-states of the "First World" become the tools of these powerful businesses.[7] While providing the military and technological services needed to maintain world order, the national interests play only a secondary role in the boardrooms of these powerful corporations. Indeed, the leaders of the corporations and those of the powerful nation-states are often the same people with common interests: economic control that knows no limits. Even worse, these transnationals have the economic clout to control political elections and agendas of nations. Thus, neocolonialism is even more insidious than its predecessor, and it strongly opposes the realization of the desire of the nations of the Third World to have their integrity recognized and their own humanity actualized.

It is possible, of course, for enlightened governments to regain their control of the market economy and subsequently regulate the unlicensed greed of transnationals. After all, it is in the self-interests of world governments and peoples to do so. The place to start is with collective efforts through the reforming of the policies and strategies of the International Monetary Fund, World Bank, and World Trade Organization. The destabilizing forces of poverty, the exploitation of the environment, and in-

---

7. My brother, a political sociologist, and I are currently at work on a volume on postcolonialism that not only advocates the urgent need for new nation-states to engage in social and economic liberation, but also levels its criticism toward neocolonialism and its new captivity of the "Third World." Efforts for Third World nations to gain economic freedom have been stymied by reactionary forces of First World states and multinationals concerned to harness power and control for their own self-interest. In our view, it is necessary to move beyond the expunging of Western values and worldviews in order to shape indigenous traditions into new narratives of meaning to engage the even greater threat of neocolonialism. W. Perdue and L. Perdue, *The Fourth Paradigm*. These new narratives require overt action for their actualization. It also is imperative that the corruption of global economic institutions designed to maintain the status quo of rich and poor nations be exposed. These institutions include especially the World Bank, the International Monetary Fund, and the empires of technology, including especially Microsoft.

adequate health care can be checked through international agreements and collective efforts. But to do so requires visionary and committed leadership from the major capitals of the globe, particularly in the European Union and Japan, and most of all the United States of America. It is clear this leadership is lacking at present among national governments of the G-8. As long as the boardrooms of transnationals are filled with capitalist members who often are the finance ministers, central bank governors, and trade ministers, primarily from Europe, Japan, and the United States, who do not make a place at the table for the voices of marginalized countries and peoples whose lives are directly affected by the policies set by these managers, there is little hope for change that will address issues of global proportions.[8] With the composition of these boards, it is no wonder why the pressing issues of poverty, the environment, and health are largely ignored.

One of the major forces in postcolonialism is the recapturing of tradition and the retelling of history. The replacement of the metanarratives of the imperialist countries requires the return to indigenous traditions and the retelling of national histories. This is made difficult not only because of the pervasive integration of colonial stories told as history and fashioned under the guise of civilization, but also because of the diversity of traditions and histories emanating from ethnic groups and tribes that come together to form a nation-state. In addition, nationalist groups within the same state often have engaged in persecution, marginalization, and even genocide of other groups, leading to a basic disenchantment in many quarters with nationalism.[9]

An additional factor in understanding postcolonialism is the emergence of a new elitism of the intellectuals in former colonies. One of the complexities of postcolonialism is its theoretical development by an intellectual class, often educated in the West, which speaks in an esoteric discourse that is beyond the ability of many less-educated persons to understand and put into practice. This new elitism often has not taken into its set of perspectives the experiences of the "ordinary readers," including both their oppression and their hopes and dreams. If this is so, then how can intellectuals claim to recover the subaltern voice and consciousness that they wish to portray?

There also has been a general failure to take into consideration the questions of patriarchy and gender. Marginal peoples often are presented as male. At times women are not even present in the writings or recognized

8. See in particular Stiglitz, *Globalization and Its Discontents.*
9. See Gikandi, *Maps of Englishness.*

as the creators of postcolonial literature. Thus, their marginalization has continued at the hands of a new, indigenous male elite.[10] While some Western women—although restricted by the patriarchal nature of their own governments, which placed them in subordinate roles—were involved in opposing the processes and activities of imperialism as a patriarchal system, colonized women who had the possibility to do so were more engaged in the activities of education and the active struggle for liberation, including civil rights.[11] Even with emancipation from the empires, indigenous women have not often achieved liberation. Ironically, the males who have assumed leadership of newly independent states have often reinstituted structures of domination and control of women. Male postcolonial intellectuals have often ignored this travesty. Women in the new nation-states have yet to achieve the goals of liberation that were central to their anticolonial struggles.

Finally, postcolonial thinkers continue to emphasize the importance of place and context. As they have frequently noted, the subaltern experience cannot be extracted from its location and made into a generalized abstraction. It must be understood in terms of its specific social and cultural setting. This location is usually the colonial or former colonial role within an empire or former empire. However, one of the tragedies of colonialism was the displacement of peoples to other lands and unusually strange conditions. This is the "diaspora" experience that must be kept in mind for certain peoples and their experience of marginalization, whether they are the slaves of Western trade or the native communities taken from their homelands to new places to exist and attempt to survive.

Major Theorists in Postcolonialism

Numerous scholars in a variety of disciplines have shaped postcolonial thinking in recent years. The list includes such important figures as Edward Said, Frantz Fanon, Homi K. Bhabha, Gayatri Chakravorty Spivak, Paul Gilroy, Anne McClintock, Neil Lazarus, and T. Minh-ha Trinkh. Of course, many others could be added to this shortened list. For brevity's sake, I shall discuss only two of these: Edward Said and Gayatri Chakravorty Spivak.

---

10. See especially Jayawardena, *Feminism and Nationalism in the Third World; The White Woman's Other Burden;* Ware, *Beyond the Pale;* and Midgley, *Gender and Imperialism.*

11. See R. Young's helpful discussion in his chapter "Women, Gender and Anticolonialism," *Postcolonialism,* 360–82.

Edward Said

For Said, texts, like their authors, are intrinsically connected to their time, space, culture, language, social world, and political reality.[12] They cannot be abstracted from these locations without doing violence to their content and meaning. As a native of Jerusalem (1935–2003 C.E.), Said grew up in the tumultuous world of the Middle East that witnessed the end of the British Mandate, the formation of the state of Israel, and the early period of conflict between Arabs and Israelis. Educated in the United States, Said taught at Columbia University his entire academic career until his death in 2003.

Perhaps more than anyone, Said demonstrated that colonialism and imperialism are not simply carried out by military and economic strategies of control and domination, but also by the discourse of knowledge that is falsely asserted to be unquestionably true. Discourse is imbued with power and self-professed knowledge, leading to control and domination of those less equipped to handle intellectual matters so adroitly. The struggle against the domination of the West involves then, not simply military and economic counterrevolutionary activities, but even more importantly, a new discourse that not only dispels the fallacies and misrepresentations inherent in Western metanarratives of superiority and control, but also develops new knowledge that liberates the mind. His own work was not to develop an entirely new theoretical model, for structuralism and poststructuralism had already undermined the certitude of Western models of knowledge. And he readily admits his debt to the discourse theory of Michel Foucault. Rather, within these newly emerging linguistic paradigms, he shaped a version of anticolonial rhetoric that helped to subvert the dominance of Western mythic narratives about the East and to begin to fashion new ones more representative of postcolonial culture in this region. He argues that "orientalism" corresponds only to a Western fantasy world about the Orient. This is a Western projection that produces a strange, mysterious, uncivilized "other" all the more easy to debauch, castigate, and subvert.

Said sought through his prolific writings to set forth a fundamental understanding of location in its multiple forms and meanings that underlies all of his critical work. His most important book that influenced the world of intellectuals and even governments was *Orientalism,* in which he criticizes the colonial powers, Britain and France, in their imperial activities in North Africa and the Middle East from the end of the nineteenth into

---

12. For relevant works by Said and other scholars discussed in this chapter, see the bibliography. In *Postcolonialism* (383–94), R. Young has provided a well-written, succinct introduction to Said.

the early part of the twentieth centuries. He condemns imperialism both as a policy of nations and as a state of mind that seeks to subjugate others by inculturating a Western way of thinking that is falsely described as unquestionably true. These destructive bodies of knowledge that dehumanized other peoples have been at the basis of university education for centuries. He proposes and helped to achieve the infiltration of a new way of viewing the world, a new epistemology, and a new body of knowledge that counteracts the distortion inherent in "orientalism." He exposes repeatedly the use of propaganda by the colonizers and their successors to plant their worldview in the hearts and minds of the colonized. He also advocates recruiting intellectuals to shape by political action the transformation of the present world of power and inhumanity into one of justice that escapes the shackles of controlling imperialism and the shameless exploitation of marginals. Rejecting the cultural politics of the Western academy, his writings deconstruct the mythic structures of imperialism promulgated even in universities. He seeks to disassemble the classic stereotypes of people of the East, who are misrepresented in the media, the political polities, and the literature of the West, stereotypes that have continued even after the withdrawal of Britain and France from colonial occupations. These have essentially combined to form a powerful yet fabricated portrayal of Islam and Arabs (e.g., wrongly imposing upon them the inability to think rationally and thus necessitating acts of passion and violence).

The Western depiction of the Orient is to portray it in oppositional terms, not as partnership, but rather to reinforce the stereotypes of the East to underscore the sense of Western superiority. Stereotype has been fictitiously presented as objective description. In essence, orientalism is a fabrication of Western propaganda to allow the West to assume a posture of innate supremacy over the "other." These stereotypes involve racial mischaracterization, the notion of Eastern "strangeness," and the portrayal of the unyielding concept of timelessness in the East, where progress and change are inimical to native identity. Misogyny often enters into these Western portrayals in that the Orient is presented as feminine, exotic, and seductive. It is a place for the fantasies of Western male power and masculinity that attempt to subjugate the wicked, untrustworthy, and entrancing East. Thus, the East is a world of uncivilized people who pose a threat to Western civility and moral standards.

Said confronts Eurocentrism and imperialism in particular, which exist not only in political policies but also in the subconscious of Western thinking. Indeed, the colonizers even produced vast amounts of knowledge about those they subjugated in order to legitimate their hegemony. Together, these two forces, political policies and the control of knowledge, have been responsible for colonialism and its successor, neocolonialism. The postcolonial thinker is one who not only exposes the fallacy of this collusion, but also intervenes politically through the craft of retelling the history of colonial peoples. Yet the goal of the postcolonial is not simply to effectuate the return of the land and self-rule to the colonized. It is more, in that it seeks to replace the forced stereotypes victimizing the colonized mind with a new understanding of the world and to value its own traditions and understandings. This is the moral imperative of the postcolonial writer. Opposing the powerful colonial world is an imposing but necessary task for postcolonial writers. While influenced by deconstruction, Said remains critical of Derrida's formulation, since in the final analysis, his position eliminates the human freedom and responsibility to decide, in this case, to oppose colonialism.

Said's classic, *Orientalism*, has been the subject of arguments and counterarguments in postcolonial theory since its appearance in 1978. Yet its very criticism has helped to shape the new postcolonial discourse of later writers, even those who sharply censure him. The recognition that the notion of "orientalism" is distorted discourse, both culturally and ideologically, has been the lasting contribution of Edward Said.

Gayatri Chakravorty Spivak

Spivak, a native of Calcutta, India, was born in 1942 and grew up in the politically tumultuous time of the end of British rule and the beginning of Indian statehood. She currently teaches at Columbia University in New York. She has written on the related fields of race, gender, colonialism, and imperialism. She is best described as a Third World Marxist engaged in critiques of feminism, political theory, and deconstruction. In her first major book of essays, published in 1988 *(In Other Worlds)*, Spivak exposes the antiwomen's biases of major metanarratives and literary classics in Western culture, offers an analysis of Marxism's implications for understanding value, delivers a pointed criticism of some forms of Western feminism, reveals the ideological nature of the knowledge taught in major "First World" universities, and offers critical readings of "Third World" texts, including two works of Mashasweta Devi, "Draupadi" and "Stanadayini" ("breast-giver"). Through her emphasis on the responsibility of women to "negotiate" or "redescribe" the "structures of violence" and her critique of the limits of liberal and leftist Western political and feminist thought, she offers her own insights into the difficulties faced by women in the "Third World." Thus, she issues a warning to postcolonialists that should be heeded. Indeed, she advocates the need for subalterns (the economically deprived) to speak with their own voice to break through the code of silence developed by oppressors and even would-be supporters.

However, she is also critical of the uniting of voices of "Third World" intellectuals who eschew the substantial diversity that exists throughout these societies.

Cultural homogeneity, often represented as culture studies in Western university departments, is a misrepresentation of the varieties of cultures among subalterns. If subalterns speak from a cultural unity, they suffer the fate of becoming exactly what colonialist and neocolonialist propaganda has made them: an undifferentiated and indistinct mass. Thus, Spivak is concerned, and includes herself in her critique, that subaltern intellectuals essentially employ the same methods of exploitation that colonialists and postcolonialists have used to dominate and control "Third World" peoples.[13] She also questions the fact that postcolonialism is often male, elitist, intellectual, and privileged discourse even though done by "Third World" writers, at least in their origins, who come to prestigious American and European universities to teach. She warns that the insertion of postcolonialism into Western university departments has an unexpected result: instead of only portraying the travesties of colonialism and neocolonialism, the approach allows for the calcification of the images and symbolism of the "Third World" that become not deconstructed, but rather reified. This reification obstructs the amorphous and creative changes inherent in culture and cultural by-products. Women in subaltern studies are especially combined into a one-dimensional entity so that individuality and difference are lost.

Consciousness, Spivak explains, is not self-created, but occurs outside the self through the process of discourse. Intellectuals wrongly present themselves as the spokespersons for marginals. This is not a reliable expression of subaltern consciousness, but rather a distortion. The search for subaltern women in archival history in order to retrieve their voice means they are only rewritten once more as they are in the narratives of patriarchal or imperialist intellectuals. Rather than trying to find the voice of marginal women, Spivak argues that postcolonial writers need to assail the systemic social, political, racial, and patriarchal structures that render women speechless. Listening to subaltern women confronts and subverts the distortions and structures of oppression that have marginalized them.

The Stages of Postcolonialism and Its Impact on Subaltern Religion

These two seminal thinkers provide us only a glimpse into the critical world of postcolonial thought. What now unfolds is a brief review of the

13. See Spivak, "Can the Subaltern Speak?"

ideas and theorists of postcolonialism who focus primarily on the role of religion in the connection among the various areas of reality and human life.

Justin S. Upkong

Justin Upkong's useful overview of the development of postcolonial interpretation of religion in Africa during the twentieth century provides a point of entry for the current discussion of Old Testament theology from the Third World.[14] Expressing his suspicion of the colonial churches and Eurocentric theological scholarship, Upkong indicates that he wishes "to create an encounter between the Biblical text and the African context." Instead of focusing on the history of Christianity and historical theology in the West as the context for developing biblical interpretation, Upkong points to the shifting of biblical studies to other cultural and geographical contexts in postcolonial criticism. Two other helpful summaries have been provided by Knut Holter[15] and Grant LeMarquand.[16] Like Upkong, they emphasize the location and interpretation of the Bible in the African context.

Upkong's heuristic summary traces and characterizes three phases of African biblical interpretation:

> Phase I (1930s–1970s)—reactive and apologetic: The focus is on legitimizing African religion and culture, and the approach is dominated by the comparative method.
> Phase II (1970s–1990s)—reactive-proactive: The African context is used as a resource for Biblical interpretation, and studies are particularly nuanced by the inculturation-evaluative method and liberation hermeneutics.
> Phase III (1990s)—proactive: This phase understands the importance of the ordinary reader, the African context becomes a subject of Biblical interpretation, and the scholarship makes use primarily of the methods of liberation and inculturation.

The initial phase was essentially a response to Western Christian missionaries who condemned as pagan African culture and religion. The large majority of Western Christian missionaries regarded these cultures and religions as demonic and immoral. However, some Westerners were sympathetic to African traditions and wrote accordingly. This sympathetic regard

14. Upkong, "Developments in Biblical Interpretation in Africa."
15. Holter, "Ancient Israel and Modern Nigeria."
16. LeMarquand, "The Historical Jesus and African New Testament Scholarship."

eventually culminated in comparative studies that pointed to important similarities between the Old Testament and Africa. For example, resemblances between Israelite and African religions were noted. Upkong himself did a comparative study of the sacrifices of the Ibibio of Nigeria and those in Leviticus.[17] Others have pointed to comparisons between African and biblical conceptions of God.[18]

The second phase witnessed the use of the African context as a resource for biblical interpretations, an emphasis that was combined on occasion with Marxism.[19] The two major approaches to biblical interpretation became inculturation and liberation. African Christianity is no longer regarded as incorporating the civilization and epistemologies of the European Enlightenment supported increasingly by Western churches, but now is recognized as shaping its own traditions. Africa became both a valid context for formulating biblical theology and a subject in the Bible to be studied. Now, instead of a comparative approach that still regarded African Christianity as foreign, postcolonial scholars recognized and honored it as a valid expression of religious faith that emerged out of its own culture. Inculturation and evaluation, together, become a method that recognizes both Africa in the Bible and African contributions to the history of Israel and the early church and demonstrates the importance of local African cultural and religious traditions in understanding Christianity and spreading the Christian gospel. From liberation theology came efforts to use the Bible to confront political and economic oppression in the forms of foreign domination in the Western strategies of neocolonialism, poverty, and the marginalization of many people even in their own nations.

Postcolonial scholars have also emphasized the presence of Africa and African peoples in the Bible. Their studies demonstrate African influence on Ancient Israel and Africa's contribution to salvation history and on early Christianity in both the Bible and in the early church. This counters Western European efforts to deemphasize Africa's presence in the Bible and contribution to the development of Old Testament and New Testament theological teachings. Western-generated myths, including the "curse of Canaan" in Gen 9:18-27 to speak of the people of Ham as the ancestors of

---

17. Upkong, *Sacrifice, African and Biblical.* He provides an extensive bibliography that illustrates the important factors of each phase.

18. S. Kibicho, *The Kikuyu Conception of God.* A summary of the thesis may be found in *Cahiers des Religions Africaines* 2 (1968). John Mbiti has argued for similarities between African and New Testament conceptions of eschatology. Mbiti, *New Testament Eschatology in an African Background.* See also Dickson, *Theology in Africa.*

19. Mosala, *Biblical Hermeneutics and Black Theology in South Africa.*

the black race—an argument used to support slavery, subjugation, and exploitation of dark-skinned people—have been rejected through research.

In Phase II, theology takes on a decidedly liberation (or contextual) shape and looks to the Bible as a resource for resisting social oppression, based on greed and racism. The biblical God opposes oppression and is on the side of the oppressed. Especially stressed is the area of economics and freedom from Western governments and corporations that exploit African natural resources and peoples for their own greed. Marxism becomes a prominent socioeconomic tool in the interpretation of the Bible to end economic exploitation, to oppose political oppression from without and within, and to advance political transformation. To become a proper tool for justice, however, the Bible itself must be liberated from the justification of oppression in which Israel engaged.[20] Feminist theology among African scholars also interprets the Bible through this hermeneutical lens. They remove the inferiority of women from the Bible and illuminate significant women, named and unnamed, in ancient Israel and early Christianity.[21] However, African feminists are critical of Western feminists for their involvement in the exploitation of Africa, its people, and its resources, and for seeking the same positions of control, power, and wealth dominated by white Western males. In African feminism, the same two main concerns arise that are found in Western feminist theology: a critique of the androcentrism of both the Bible and its male interpreters and a recovery of the silent voices and their contributions to the faith of Israel and the early church.

Upkong notes that in the scholarship in Phase III, developing since the 1990s, biblical studies in Africa have become much more proactive in making original contributions that no longer simply emulate Western scholarship. Once more the two major areas of interpretation are inculturation and liberation, but now with a decidedly African nuance. Especially important is the effort for scholars to listen to and learn from ordinary readers' conceptions of God and texts.[22] The hermeneutics of inculturation continues to be central, stressing the African context as the hermeneutical purpose of biblical interpretation.[23] In contextual (liberation) biblical theology, the Bible is read against a specific concrete human situation, e.g., racial oppression, poverty, starvation, and AIDS. Ordinary readers are now enlisted not only for their fresh insights into the biblical text, but to

20. See, e.g., Tutu, *Crying in the Wilderness.*

21. The journal *Voices from the Third World* is replete with articles on postcolonial interpretations, including a number by African feminists. See, e.g., Beya, "Doing Theology as African Women," 155–56.

22. G. West, *Contextual Bible Study.*

23. Upkong, "Inculturation and Evangelization"; "Towards a Renewed Approach to Inculturation Theology"; and "The Parable of the Shrewd Manager."

empower them to relate Scripture to their personal and social situations in order to participate in transformation. Scholars and ordinary readers using their life experiences become partners in biblical interpretation and establishment of justice. The use of ordinary readers enables academic scholarship to become relevant to the community of believers.

The inculturation model of interpretation, according to Upkong, becomes a holistic approach in which the religious and secular aspects of culture are interconnected and have implications for each other, and the Bible is read through the economic, social, and political contexts of Africa. This form of interpretation brings together academic and ordinary readers in order to learn both the meaning of Scripture and how to use it in the transformation of the world. Ordinary readers are important, notes Upkong, not only because of their life experiences, but also because they operate with their own worldview and not a Western one that condescendingly presents them as ignorant, poor, and marginalized. This means, then, that theological interpretation results from the interaction of the Bible and the African social context. This hermeneutical approach is shaped to a large extent by African social, cultural, and religious perspectives. The Bible is not read through a Western framework of interpretation that makes it little more than a marginalized discipline in a Eurocentric theology that is based on Western culture and religious meaning.

For Upkong, the basic hermeneutical principle may be summarized as follows: "*The meaning of a text is a function of the interaction between the text in its context and the reader in his/her context.*"[24] This means that interpretation is not a two-step procedure in which the original meaning is ascertained and then applied to the current situation, but rather is a dynamic dialogue in which interpreters engage the text from their context, and in turn the context is engaged by the text. Seen in this way, interpretation has three interacting elements: the historical approach that focuses on the meaning of the text in its ancient context, the literary approach that decodes the text and allows the reader and text to interact, and the reader's context that shapes the meaning of the text even as the text shapes him or her in the contemporary context.

Current State of Postcolonial Biblical Theology

Upkong's study may be extended to other postcolonial, Third World global settings, as a way of proceeding with biblical theology. One of the missing elements, currently, is a complete volume on postcolonial biblical theol-

24. Justin S. Upkong, "Developments in Biblical Interpretation in Africa: Historical and Hermeneutical Directions," 24.

ogy. Thus, we shall have to focus our attention on methodological essays concerning postcolonial biblical theology and individual articles that illustrate a variety of ways it is conceived by present scholars. But key ingredients of this type of theology are already in the brew.

The religious setting for postcolonial biblical theology is no longer that of Western Catholicism, including Augustine, Aquinas, and the Counter-Reformation, as well as modern post–Vatican II theologies, the European Reformation, or the Enlightenment and the scholarly traditions that emerged from them. Rather, the new context is that of former colonies that have gained their independence from colonial powers during the period following World War II.[25] *Postcolonialism* is a social, political, and cultural term that refers to the writing and reading practices of some of the people from the "Third World" who have shared the colonial experience that resulted from European and American expansion and exploitation, beginning as early as the sixteenth century.[26] In regard to modern history since the sixteenth century, colonialism and imperialism both involve the subjugation of a largely non-Western country or social group for the express purpose of domination and exploitation of its resources. *Colonialism* is a term that focuses more on the enterprise of an economic agency seeking to enrich itself and its financial supporters (e.g., the West Indies Company of the Netherlands), while *imperialism* points to an empire's use of force to build an expanding realm ruled at the center of its power in the homeland.

Political expansionism is usually economically driven as states become empires in the quest to increase their markets, exploit natural resources, and develop cheap labor. The imperial state is the beneficiary and uses propaganda through its various media to try to inculcate its metanarrative and values in ruled peoples, who are taught that the domination is

25. The Third World communities of Christianity do not resonate easily with the theologies of the Reformation and Roman Catholicism. Subsequently, biblical theology in the "Third World" takes on very new and rather different formulations. Here, the Bible is engaged with indigenous peoples' own experiences, worldviews, and ways of understanding. Thus, it would be naïve to think that somehow a new biblical theology can be written that takes so many social and cultural perspectives into view. Postcolonial biblical theologies as they are written will take on a variety of distinctively "Third World" views emerging out of very different contexts. The newly developing postcolonial theological views are emerging at a time when liberal Protestant Christianity in the West, particularly in the northern hemisphere, is seriously declining, in contrast to Christianity in the Third World, which is thriving. For a detailed look at this phenomenon with an indication of its important results for politics, society, economics, and the church, see Jenkins, *The Next Christendom*.

26. An important overview is R. Young, *Postcolonialism*. R. S. Sugirtharajah explains that the term *Third World* is a "socio-political designation of a people who have been excluded from power and authority to mold and shape their future." "Introduction," 8, n. 1.

benevolent and seeks to improve their lot. Metanarratives, political and religious ones, were constructed to legitimate expansionism by subjugation and the use of force. Indeed, religion became a tool of the imperialistic state in legitimating its expansionism. Once these older empires crumbled following World War II, a new type of colonialism appeared, simply known as neocolonialism. As a reactionary force to failed imperialism, neocolonialism has emerged in the effort to exploit poorer nations largely for economic profit, status, and power. This includes economic policies that have led the International Monetary Fund (IMF), the World Bank, and the World Trade Organization to place the pressure on developing economies to produce goods desired by First World markets and to open their doors to dominating international corporations. The beneficiaries of these policies are especially the transnational corporations and the advanced industrial nations in which they are headquartered, not the countries of the Third World, where their subsidiaries are placed.[27]

The goal of neocolonialism is to stabilize and secure the current world order for the wealth of these multinational corporations and, not indirectly, the enhancement of money and power of the Western nations. Neocolonialists focus on the world's market economy, which they proclaim in rather vague ways as somehow benefiting all those who take part in the capitalistic drive for wealth. Of course, the ones who benefit are the owners and stockholders of the transnationals, while those who provide the bulk of the labor and their countries that offer major financial incentives

---

27. The 2001 Nobel laureate in economics, Joseph Stiglitz, while noting many positive results in world health, democracy, and justice due to globalization, points to the culpability of Western economic institutions in the staggering increase in poverty in much of the Third World. Indeed, these institutions make decisions and establish policies that "all too often, have served the interests of the more advanced industrialized countries—and particular interests within those countries—rather than those of the developing world" (*Globalization and Its Discontents*). These policies have often issued from a particular, fundamentalist view of economy and society that has blamed the unwillingness of the poor countries to set in motion procedures to solve their problems. The view is that somehow the magic of capitalism will bring wealth, but only if strictly followed and allowed to permeate Third World economies. The international institutions of the World Trade Organization (WTO), International Monetary Fund (IMF), and the World Bank have been far more interested in pursuing the interests of international markets than in stemming the tide of poverty and aiding countries and indeed the world in achieving global economic stability. While the WTO has been interested only in trade, the IMF and World Bank have provided huge amounts of capital to Third World governments and banks, but impoverished countries find it almost impossible to repay these loans without devastating internal economic consequences for their indigenous populations. Poverty and the environment have to become the central concerns of these Western institutions for achieving a stable world order. With the collapse of the Soviet Union, the dominance of the United States has led to the unchallenged supremacy of "free" enterprise, unrestrained capitalism, and the principle of market economy.

and natural resources to these megalithic giants are fleeced and manipulated. Indeed, the captains of industry not only forge strong associations with officials in the positions of power in the large states, including especially the triage of the United States, Japan, and Germany and now the larger European Union, but also participate in a revolving door moving back and forth between these two types of corporate power. There exists a very cozy relationship between the leaders of these Western democracies and the multinational corporations. Even the boards and administrators of institutions that are supposed to shape economic stability throughout the globe (e.g., the World Bank and the IMF) share in this power of relationships. Small wonder that these economic institutions have the interests of the major powers, especially the G-8, in mind when devising strategy and carrying out policy. The United States enjoys a dominant position in the global economy and willingly inserts military power into financially driven efforts at controlling world markets, not only in selling their products but also in acquiring needed resources like oil at a cheap price. Capitalism and the myth of local democratic autonomy are central to the ideology and power of controls exerted by states largely under the domination of international corporations and the G-8. The church has willingly become the vehicle of legitimation of the Western powers and the transnationals in their financial exploitation of the Third World. They too are usually controlled by businessmen and -women from national and international corporations of the First World.

This has not meant that the colonized and their postcolonial successors have not engaged in subversive, subaltern readings of Western texts or that there were no anticolonialists in Europe and America who resisted the dishonorable treatment of the colonized. Indeed, through the many generations and especially of late, a plethora of interpreters in the social sciences and the humanities representing a large number of marginalized and exploited people have been at work to deconstruct the cultural metanarrative that legitimates the small group of nations engaged in a joint multinational control of the global economy. The code word is national *interest*. The increase in these readings and the joining together of these interpretations from a variety of very different cultural contexts has developed dramatically in the past generation. However, postcolonial thinkers have reminded us that the struggles and disappointments of a new state to achieve a desired destiny have also affected this emerging literature. Thus, postcolonialism responds to two developments: the oppression of the imperial powers and the struggles of more indigenous regimes that too often fail because the global economy is controlled by the international corporations and monetary institutions they have spawned to represent the interests of the wealthy Western nations. Postcolonial interpreters focus on the cultures and humanity of indigenous peoples to improve their lot. But the power of the West and the transnationals is so vast that overt resistance seems to have little chance.

This does not mean a naïveté characterizes these writings, since post-colonialists are more than aware of the powerful forces they must combat to achieve their goals of the humanization of social, political, religious, and cultural structures. However, the central concern is to establish a realistic program of change that might be implemented and have a chance to succeed. This program of change and transformation is to be based on a different vision of humanity and the creation than the one that currently drives capitalism. This alternative vision regards life as the central value, joined by the importance of humaneness, brother- and sisterhood, and oneness with the existing world of living creatures and the life-sustaining earth. The competing vision is of relationships based on the mutuality of common interests and the preservation of the creation. As long as the capitalistic definition of the good as power, status, and achievement for the enhancement of the individual continues, a good that understands meaning and value only in production and consumption and power as the control of resources and people, the postcolonial vision will not be obtained. The implementation of a new vision will be won not with weapons and militant revolution, but rather through the capturing of the minds of future generations in both the First and Third Worlds.

Characteristics of Subaltern Writings and Readings in Religion and Theology

R. S. Sugirtharajah

Sugirtharajah, originally from Sri Lanka and now a professor at the University of Birmingham in the United Kingdom, has defined postcolonial or subaltern interpretation of literature as "signifying a reactive resistance discourse of the colonized who critically interrogate dominant knowledge systems in order to recover the past from Western slander and misinformation of the colonial period, and who also continue to interrogate neo-colonializing tendencies after the declaration of independence."[28] Post-

---

28. Sugirtharajah, *Postcolonial Criticism and Biblical Interpretation*, 13. Homi Bhabha adds that the perspectives of postcolonialism "intervene in those ideological discourses of modernity that attempt to give a hegemonic 'normality' to the uneven development and the different, often disadvantaged, histories of nations, races, communities, people." *The Location of Culture*, 171.

colonialism is not a theory or method, but rather a collection of shared attitudes that has as its goal the inclusiveness of all peoples to use their experiences and insights jointly in order to achieve new possibilities for life.[29] Postcolonialism is more of a criticism of Western hegemony and the ideological basis upon which it is structured and more of a worldview that is expressed in different ways by the former colonized than a methodology.

Several general perspectives characterize most postcolonial interpreters engaging in writing, reading, and interpretations of texts. First, postcolonialists seek to question and finally deconstruct the major metanarratives of the colonizing and neocolonizing West. Postcolonialists participate in a direct confrontation with the system of thought and the values of the West in order to achieve emancipation from all dominant, external structures.[30] These narratives normally speak of the so-called superiority of Western moral values and cultural norms. Postcolonialists understand that all social groups that are dominant have paradigms of meaning that are ideological. Ideology has been and continues to be used to dominate marginals by attempting to coerce them into internalizing Western metanarratives as the presumed universal, social construction of reality. In their ideology of resistance, postcolonial writers and interpreters speak out of the conviction of the value of their own cultural heritage and resist allowing it and its people to be stereotyped as cultural and intellectual inferiors.

Postcolonialists also reread classic texts in order either to find their own place within them or point to the questionable assumptions that the dominant cultures engender in and through these narratives. Postcolonialists seek, first, to detect the prejudices of the worldviews that produced them and then, second, to subvert them. Postcolonial writers also construct their own narratives of meanings free of extraneous myths that seek to portray the world in ways that will support the self-interests of dominant groups and cultures who construct them. During times of colonization, the empires that established theories of domination and hegemony often failed to recognize the "hidden transcripts" of meaning composed by the marginalized who sought to undercut the privileged positions of their oppressors and exploiters.[31] In the current world, postcolonialists recognize their task to be the subversion of dominant paradigms of meaning both overtly and covertly by showing the intrinsic linkage between ideas of socioeconomic and political power and the self-interest of the oppressors.[32]

29. Said, *The World, the Text, and the Critic.*
30. Sugirtharajah, "A Postcolonial Exploration of Collusion and Construction."
31. Scott, *Domination and the Arts of Resistance.*
32. Sugirtharajah, "A Postcolonial Exploration of Collusion and Construction."

Postcolonialists use their own cultural values in shaping new world-views that include them and encourage their overt participation. They also realize the multivocal nature of meaning that exists, not only in the global community of cultures, but also in their own cultures. Postcolonialists speak from the margins of the global communities as places of creativity in shaping new realities that are at odds with the dominant cultures.[33] The margin is a place that allows for and encourages critical reflection and new understandings, rather than a place that simply stands in opposition to the center. Postcolonialists further allow the formerly silenced to find and utter their own voices, even though they are at variance with the dominant metanarratives.

Postcolonialists stress readings that are not individualistic but rather dialogical and pluralistic in determining meaning. This dialogue occurs in several directions: colonizer and colonized, colonial and postcolonial, rich and poor, powerful and impotent, those in the center and those on the margins, male and female, and different racial and ethnic groups. This type of reading brings together inculturation (including the culture of the oppressed) and liberation (or contextual theology). Thus, this dialogically derived meaning is not simply between social superiors and inferiors with an eye toward liberation, but also between people who share the peripheries of dominant cultures.

Sugirtharajah has indicted biblical scholarship in the West for its reluctance to engage in critical discourse that seeks marginal voices in the text and allows them to speak. There are several reasons for this bias in Western biblical scholarship. These failures of omission result at times from the fact that Western biblical scholars often enjoy positions of privilege in First World countries, are reluctant to challenge the current world order for fear of the adverse reaction of the Western churches and governments, and are hesitant to question the exegetical and hermeneutical methods of interpretation that they have mastered.[34] In my reading of postcolonial literature and in conversations with its representative biblical scholars, I have been surprised to discover that many have not abandoned the use of historical criticism. However, the essential goal of postcolonial scholars is to discover in the literature and its culture voices of the silenced and to recognize the ideologies at work in the writing of various texts. And, of course, the hermeneutical move follows. Where postcolonial interpreters part company with most Western scholars has usually been in the

---

33. Sugirtharajah, "Introduction," 1–8.

34. This lament is voiced by Sugirtharajah throughout *Postcolonial Criticism and Biblical Interpretation* and other writings.

area of contemporary hermeneutics that applies the teachings of the Bible to present situations in a variety of different sociocultural contexts. How the hermeneutical task in Africa and Asia has been carried out is extremely different from that pursued in the West, due to the widely different contexts of the modern global cultures.

Gerald West

Born and raised in the United Kingdom, Gerald West teaches at the University of Natal in South Africa and has been a major voice not only in opposing the ideology and social disinterest of biblical scholarship produced in the West, but also in writing significant postcolonial studies. During apartheid in South Africa, the *Kairos Document* and its successor, *The Road to Damascus*, were written, in 1986 and 1989 respectively. These documents called for the liberation of black South Africans and challenged the church to engage in the struggle by means of active participation and in producing new readings of the Bible that contain fresh theological insights opposing racism and tyranny.[35] West was among the few Westerners to speak prophetically during the period before the legal collapse of apartheid in 1991 and free elections in 1994 giving the formerly outlawed African National Congress control of the government. Since then, West has continued to write numerous essays and books advocating the major features of postcolonialism and adding his own contributions to the conversation. His volume *The Academy of the Poor* notes that one of the paradoxes in Africa is the joint sharing of the same Bible and faith by the oppressor and the oppressed. While the Bible and its readings by dominant cultures have been used to oppress and exploit indigenous populations, the Bible also has been seen as a resource for life and liberation for the oppressed. Indeed, the Western church in earlier times read the missionary journeys in the New Testament (Matt 28:19; Acts 13–14; 15:40—18:22; and 18:22—21:16) and misused them to convert the "heathen" and to legitimate colonial and imperial expansion. Many missionaries even became willing participants in imperialism and colonization and supporters of economic developments for the good of the dominant power. Missionaries in favor of imperialism coopted the Bible to support efforts to evangelize non-Christians, while other imperialists justified their efforts by pointing to a divine commission to bring Western civilization to the East. On the other hand, the stories of liberation in the exodus and the return

---

35. Kairos Theologians (Group), *The Kairos Document:* and *The Road to Damascus: Kairos and Conversion* (Johannesburg: Skotaville, 1989).

from Babylonian exile and the laments of the Psalter are examples of texts that have provided nourishment to marginals.

West argues for shifting the social loci for interpretation away from the elitist Western scholars to two groups: so-called "ordinary" readers who are indigenous to a non-Western culture and educated often in many different traditions than the metanarratives of the West, and socially engaged biblical scholars who collaborate with the marginalized and pauperized to give old texts new meanings. This, of course, requires a shift in epistemology away from the modernist ways of knowing, stretching back to the Enlightenment, to new understandings that emerge from non-Western cultures and are grounded in very different worldviews and human experiences.

West refers to the 1976 statement of the Ecumenical Association of Third World Theologians (EATWOT):

> The theologies from Europe and North America are dominant today in our Churches and represent one form of cultural domination. They must be understood to have arisen out of situations related to those countries, and therefore must not be uncritically adopted without our raising the question of their relevance in the context of our countries. Indeed, we must . . . reflect on the realities of our own situations and interpret the word of God in relation to these realities. We reject as irrelevant an academic type of theology that is divorced from action. We are prepared for a radical break in epistemology which makes commitment the first act of theology and engages in critical reflection on the praxis of the reality of the Third World.[36]

West asks, "Who are the interlocutors of theology?" He answers with the argument that the conversation partners are those most affected by what is articulated. In the theology shaped in the dominant Western cultures, however, the point of view and the major beneficiary are those who comprise the Western church. However, West argues that the Western church must learn to assume a prophetic role and engage in strong criticism of the status, wealth, and power of the Western church and the First World cultures in which it thrives. West agrees with the liberation theologians who have argued that the primary voice in the conversation should belong to the poor and marginalized. These are the "nonpersons" who constitute the exploited poor of all races and despised cultures. As socially engaged

---

36. See G. West, *The Academy of the Poor*, 12. The statement is found in Frostin, *Liberation Theology in Tanzania and South Africa*, 6–11.

scholars, we must accept, according to West, "the epistemological privilege of the poor."[37] He writes, "All theology is knowingly or not engaged for or against the oppressed."[38] They, and they alone, are to be the interlocutors of theology whose views are to carry the most weight.

But to read with "nonpersons" requires a conversion of Western biblical scholars to assume the position of those who strive for social justice. The first step in this conversion is the recognition that biblical interpretations have significant social features at work in the world of the text, the culture of the reader, and those who are affected by these readings. According to West, "Ours is a context in which Biblical interpretations do matter; they do shape our world. As the South African context reminds us, Biblical interpretations have life and death consequences: They shape the type of response the state, the Church, and ordinary people make to particular social realities."[39]

Actual work with marginalized communities provides a language that allows conversation and understanding to take place. Unfortunately, the marginalized have often accepted the interpretative paradigms of the dominant cultures so that change is not even contemplated as necessary, much more envisioned as even remotely possible.[40] This "false consciousness" becomes embedded in the self-understanding of the marginalized through education, laws, social customs, and stigmas going back to colonial times and continued through the Western media.[41] The "false consciousness" of the privileged is resistant to change due to the fear that a situation will deteriorate from the lack of social networking that permits contrary views to be expressed. West suggests that one way to overcome "false consciousness" is to establish a group of comrades in social circles that will allow marginals to reclaim their dignity and escape the humiliation imposed by the dominant groups. No longer will they be forced to feign compliance to the worldview of the powerful. In a nonpaternalistic way, the socially engaged scholar participates in these social groups and helps marginals claim their self-worth and value their own and their culture's

37. G. West, *The Academy of the Poor*, 14.
38. Schüssler Fiorenza, *Bread Not Stone*, 45. While pointing to many significant features in liberation theology, Sugirtharajah is also critical of what he sees as several shortcomings of much biblical theology. It stresses too much the interpretation of texts, disregards indigenous religions and their role in interpretation, homogenizes the poor, and does not take into consideration the experience of marginals. *Postcolonial Criticism and Biblical Interpretation*, 117–22).
39. G. West, *The Academy of the Poor*, 35.
40. Ibid., 40.
41. Cormaroff and Cormaroff, *Of Revelation and Reason*.

contributions to shaping new meanings for justice and biblical interpreta-tion.[42] The scholars also learn from the marginals new insights into their hermeneutical efforts and their biblical interpretations.

West also values postmodern and poststructural readings that chal-lenge the dominant epistemology of the West. In the conversion process, then, these subversive readings need to be used to create a new epistemol-ogy that is conducive to liberation. In addition, the conversion of biblical scholars involves acknowledging colonial misrepresentations, including contrived biblical interpretations, which have contributed to colonial sub-jugation. Finally, conversion involves the recognition that we are both constructed by the context and epistemology of the poor and active partic-ipants in the creation of meaning that includes the marginalized. These new understandings emerge from a partnership and not from paternalism.

Most biblical scholars who are postcolonialists have been educated in the universities of the West. They are taught to read critically, but inherent to this critical method is the recognition that all interpretation emerges out of an ideology. Itumeleng J. Mosala has argued that the Bible is not an innocent text that contains messages of truth.[43] Rather, the Bible is a prod-uct of ideology or ideologies that the reader must learn to recognize in the interpretation of texts.[44] Just as valid is the recognition that there is no innocent reading or innocent interpreter of the text. All readers and their readings are grounded in ideologies that must be understood and identified. While scholars need to recognize both the tremendous suffering and humiliation to which Western interpreters have exposed marginals and their complicity in the legitimation of Western metanarratives, they also must become aware of the potentially liberating and invigorating effects

---

42. Scott, *Domination and the Arts of Resistance.* Scott indicates that the subjugated groups often engage in the language of the dominant group in order to foment revolution. This language becomes subversive to its own paradigm in the telling of tales and jokes, the singing of songs, and the performing of theater (pp. 101–03).

43. In a fashion similar to postmodernism, Pui-lan Kwok has argued that one must ask a series of questions regarding truth, not only in regard to what it is, but who owns it and who has the authority to interpret it. She notes that many Chinese Christians reject the position that the Bible contains all truth and is forever closed, positions that would deny any authenticity to sages like Confucius, Mencius, and Moti. She argues that once we have freed ourselves from the wrong position that the Bible contains all truth, then we can test it and reappropriate it for other contexts. In addition, the formation of the canon is an issue of power. But why do we need a Bible that excludes many voices and the stories of others? She indicates that those who read the Bible must use their imagination to generate more truths: "In the end, we must liberate ourselves from a hierarchical model of truth which assumes there is one truth above many. This biased homogeneity excludes multiplicity and plural-ity") "Discovering the Bible in the Non-biblical World," 289–305.

44. Mosala, *Biblical Hermeneutics and Black Theology,* 40.

of sensitive readings of biblical texts. Scholars of Western universities and the Western-trained indigenous scholar must learn to shape the Bible to become a powerful weapon in fighting oppression and dominant cultural paradigms.[45] Or to state it in anecdotal African language, marginal readers who have become educated in the West must learn to use the master's tools to tear down the master's house.[46]

Nevertheless, postcolonial interpreters and readers cannot allow uncritical readings "to substitute for a theoretically well-grounded Biblical hermeneutics of liberation."[47] In addition, we scholars of the West constantly must remind ourselves that we are persons of privilege. What we may offer indigenous groups of the marginalized are resources and conversation partners in the quest to find forgotten and neglected narratives of liberation and life in the biblical text.[48]

Voices from the Third World: Male and Female

Itumeleng J. Mosala

The South African scholar Itumeleng Mosala, who serves in the South African government, has applied a neo-Marxist paradigm to the social settings of South Africa and the biblical prophet Micah to render a strikingly different reading of this biblical text than has been typical in Western scholarship. His articulation of social materialism demystifies and delegitimates Western scholarship and neocolonial domination, opening one door to postcolonial theology in South Africa. As I have argued elsewhere,

> Social materialism is both an ontological and an epistemological theory, ontological in that it asserts that the data of the world are in their essence material and epistemological in affirming that knowledge derives from understanding the social nature of ideas. These two features, ontology and epistemology, are entwined. Social and historical experiences of human beings represent an encounter with

45. Mofokeng, "Black Christians, the Bible and Liberation."

46. Sugirtharajah points to the process of coding and decoding in postcolonial biblical interpretation. He notes that four different codes are encountered in the Bible. The hegemonic code legitimizes the self-interests of the ruling aristocracy, the professional code advocates social order and hierarchical authority through law and instruction, the negotiated code seeks to allow texts and experiences to meet new situations that call for readjustments of understanding, and the oppositional code represents the voice of the marginalized. Thus, Jesus is a countercultural prophet who seeks to protect the weak and to promote an egalitarian world in opposition to Roman imperialism. *Postcolonial Criticism and Biblical Interpretation*, 74–102.

47. Mosala, *Biblical Hermeneutics and Black Theology*, 30.

48. G. West, *The Academy of the Poor*, 108.

the materials (both data and ideas) of the physical world and become their embodiment.[49]

Culture develops out of political, social, and economic spheres of human reality. Literature, including the Bible, personifies the social materialism present and functioning in a society. But what can be particularly seductive is the idea that the worldview of a text is naturally true. This allows ruling classes, who normally control the media of a society, to create and maintain a metanarrative and their privileged role within it. Mosala recognizes that what is said to embody "truth" is created and does not enjoy an objective existence outside the world of the truth makers. This creation of truth and its embodiment in metanarratives become propaganda by which the ruling class and its artistic minions intentionally justify their own elitist positions. Artists, writers, and priests coopted and rewarded by the ruling class become cultural prostitutes paid handsomely with positions of status and goods for their legitimation of the present order. They shape the jaded ideology of their culture's self-expression. The major features of this ideology are presented as self-evident to the various groups and classes in a society. These wielders of power profit from the economic system of a society that controls the modes of production supporting the economic interests of their ruling social classes.

Neo-Marxism has become one important ideological tool of the marginalized as their intellectuals have realized that the primary means for social change regarding power, wealth, and status is class conflict pursued by the workers against the owners who own and are in control of markets and products. Thus, literature—in this case, the Hebrew Bible—may become an important lens through which to view class struggle and provides some of the material for revolution. In addition, it is not to be forgotten that some biblical literature, which escapes the constraints of its own confining ideology, is critical of the prevailing consensus, bringing into question many assumptions of an oppressive ruling class. This questioning of and opposition to many of the prevailing social values and beliefs reflects their contestation in the larger society.

Musa W. Dube

There are also significant women's voices who speak to us from the Third World, including Africa, Central America, Asia, and the Western countries

---

49. Social materialism is not only a theory of being, but also an epistemology. According to Jürgen Habermas, "Labor or work is not only a fundamental category of human existence but also an epistemological category." *Knowledge and Human Interests,* 28.

to which some have migrated. I have necessarily limited my examples to a few, keenly aware that other voices have been and continue to be heard.[50] Among African feminists who are biblical scholars, one of the most provocative has been Musa Dube.[51] In her contributions to postcolonial readings of the Bible, she has argued that too many Western biblical interpreters read the Bible as a text that relates to and has meaning for the past. In many cases, these boundaries between past and present become barriers incapable of being crossed. Yet these must be crossed. In doing so, she advocates postcolonial readings that decolonize imperialist tendencies in the Bible that have been wittingly or unwittingly used to support colonization.

> For me to read the Bible as an African woman and from my experience . . . is to be inevitably involved with the historical events of imperialism. Indeed, to read the Bible as an African is to take a perilous journey, a sinister journey, that spins one back to connect with dangerous memories of slavery, colonialism, apartheid, and neo-colonialism. To read the Bible as an African is to relive the painful equation of Christianity with civilization, paganism with savagery.[52]

"This melancholic assertion made by the Motswana woman, Musa Dube, the doyen of postcolonial feminist Biblical criticism in Africa, is indeed an irrefutable truism that speaks for the multitudes of African women in the African continent."[53]

Dube uses a postcolonial interdisciplinary approach and employs "a strategy of resistance" aimed at opposing the colonizer's interpretation of the canon, in particular how the Bible has been abused to support Western views that include imperialism.[54] Like West, Dube posits the challenge of ethical responsibility to Western and non-Western biblical scholars, urging that issues of land, race, power, international connection, contemporary history, and gender need to be given serious consideration on the hermeneutical agenda. She cautions that the term *postcolonial* does not denote that colonialism has come to an end; it refers to an overall analysis of the methods and effects of imperialism as a continuing reality in global relations. According to Dube, postcolonial biblical hermeneutics entails an examination of the assimilation or colonization of the mind. Dube explains that postcolonialism is a very complex phenomenon that "propounds a

50. Just one notable example is the introduction of Kwok, *Introducing Asian Feminist Theology.*
51. See Dube, "Savior of the World but Not of This World."
52. Dube, "Towards a Postcolonial Feminist Interpretation of the Bible," 13.
53. Nzimande, "Towards a Postcolonial *Imbokodo* (African Women's) Hermeneutics."
54. For a detailed discussion on postcolonial feminist biblical interpretation, see Dube, "Savior of the World but Not of This World."

myriad of methods and theories, all of which examine literature and its participation in the building, collaboration, or subversion of global imperial relationships."

As a woman, Dube contends that although both colonized peoples and colonized women are categorized as oppressed and equally affected by patriarchy, colonized women suffer more because they have two patriarchal systems superimposed on them, that of the colonizer and that of the postcolonial, largely male government. As beneficiaries of the political, social, economic, and high class benefits of colonialism, "the colonizing women, too, partake of its colonial harvest," although men remain its major beneficiaries.[55] Yet Western feminists are also culpable. Like Sugirtharajah, she proposes a syncretizing reading strategy whereby the colonized reread the master's canon for decolonization using intertextual dynamics and their social location.[56] However, the neocolonizing tendencies of globalization and its implications for African women in particular remains high on Dube's hermeneutical list of concerns.

Mercy Amba Oduyoye

The African scholar Mercy Amba Oduyoye of Ghana, active in the World Council of Churches, initiated the "Decade of Churches in Solidarity with Women" and, in addition to her own writing, has mentored a growing community of African women in theology. These women, and their colleagues in training, operate from the social location of the background of colonization and slavery, the continuing effects of racism, misogyny, and poverty within the frameworks of African patriarchy, globalization, and neocolonialism. For Oduyoye, African feminists make important contributions to theology, especially through the power of story, construed by contemporary scholars as narrative theology. This storytelling tradition activated by African women draws heavily on African traditions of myth, culture, and women's creativity. She recognizes, along with many other Third World feminist scholars, that there are problems unique to the feminine gender that must be addressed theologically. Like many other women scholars, she notes that the Bible has been used to oppress women, but at the same time it serves as a resource for women to use in their resistance

---

55. See Dube, *Postcolonial Feminist Interpretation of the Bible.*

56. Dube, *Postcolonial Feminist Interpretation of the Bible,* 106. For additional insights on Dube's hermeneutics, see her essays "*Batswakwa:* Which Traveller Are You?" and "To Pray the Lord's Prayer." In a recent publication, Dube uses African storytelling and divination methods to interpret biblical texts (see Dube's essays, "Fifty Years of Bleeding" and "Divining Ruth for International Relations").

to the violence perpetrated against them. Female circumcision, AIDS, rape and abuse, and genocidal murder have been experienced by women as a result of living in their own tribal societies. The narratives of women in the Bible who survived in spite of patriarchy and abuse provide a much-needed resource for encouragement and hope. The Bible is read as a text that points to the liberation of women and their brothers from the destruction of violence and oppression. Thus, like many other feminist scholars, Oduyoye sees biblical interpretation and contemporary theology in dialogue in order to address the plight of marginalized women.

Women's theologies in Africa point to the history of women participating in the travails of colonialism and missionary activity yet also in liberation movements inspired by postcolonialism. Oduyoye emphasizes the common and shared experience of these women that gives rise to ways of addressing women's understanding of the meaning of the Bible and their theological views that take seriously the issues that emerge from what they have undergone and continue to endure in contemporary life. These African women are required to reflect on their shared experiences and to determine their meanings for their own lives. Thus, theology involves more than knowing and believing certain things. Rather, this discourse must contribute to and take shape within the context of social locations of women seeking liberation and the dignity of humanity.

Central to Oduyoye's approach is a twin-pronged theology: biblical hermeneutics and theological understanding that are shaped by the experience of women who speak by creating and telling narratives, not only of the Bible, but their own that they use to reshape scriptural stories. The basis for this interactive theology of two different narratives is the social context of each. She defines theology as "an expression of faith in response to experience." Biblical narratives are studied, not in order to reconstruct historically the life and thought of ancient Israel, but rather to point to the presence of God in the lives and experiences of people, both past and present. This theology begins with a criticism of the mission theology of churches at work in Africa for three hundred years but then moves into the present human culture and seeks to shape it in the direction of liberation from oppression and the formation of a new sociopolitical world in which God dwells among all humans who exist in mutuality.

Several features of the feminist theology of Oduyoye should be mentioned in any entrée into her work. The first deals with life lived in Africa, in the midst of global challenges that must be addressed. This is its context. The theology is that of the living women of this continent in the form of a story that is told, a song that is sung, and a prayer that is uttered. This narrative tells who Christians in Africa, especially women, understand God to be.

A second feature is the recognition that theology does not bifurcate life into the secular and the holy. Rather, this understanding regards all of life as the context for reflection and articulation. The economic exploitation of the people of Africa leading to pauperism in large numbers, the political instability of its nation-states that makes life all the more uncertain, large-scale epidemics and famine, and the militarism of its leaders and groups competing for control that leads to war and even genocide are experienced and become the grist from which theology originates. Thus, the obvious theological question asks how God is present in these areas to offer consolation, support, and empowerment in the struggle, not only for liberation, but for current life. How can human dignity be achieved in the midst of this chaotic, impoverished life? Not all theologies of women are born of the innate desire for liberation from patriarchy, since some teach the domestication of women within the male-dominated household and larger society. In addition, the African world is one in which Muslims and Christians engage in sharp conflict, while a highly developed globalization presents images of the values of capitalism and the "good life" that renounce any traditional ones that have provided direction and shaped character for centuries.

Oduyoye also acknowledges that women in Africa engage in the mothering not only of families and children, but also of those who are more destitute than they and in the combating of the evils of marginalization, including discrimination based on sex, color, and tribal identity. This image of "mothering" has become the dominant one in African feminist theology.

Oduyoye looks at the religiocultural context of Africa as primary for the development of women's theology. She observes that "Africans live in a spiritual universe." Traditional culture and religion that see the spiritual essence of life are inextricably bound. All values, customs, and beliefs are connected to religion. This religion does not claim to be a revealed one, since divine presence includes nature spirits and the spirits of the ancestors, while well-known myths tell of humanity's place in the scheme of things. The question is how communication with these controlling and directing spirits may be obtained. Religion in a broad sense (ancestors, worldviews, traditions, spirits, etc.) is much more important than "Scripture" in teaching men and women about God. God is the one who has established the traditional laws, ways of behaving, and means of community and harmony in collective life. Especially significant is the concept and practice of communal life. Humans are born into community and live out their existence within its institutions and customs. This community extends into the past to include the ancestors and into the future to include those yet to be born. This is one reason why marriage is central for women, since their status and existence focus on child bearing and rearing. They provide the link between past and future generations. Finally, there are the important celebrations of life concerning health, well-being, and abundance. Festivals become the religious means of institutionalizing these celebrations in the community, while hospitality extended to ensure life continues is at the heart of religious practice.

African Christianity began as the religion of missionaries, both Catholic and Protestant, but it has developed its own distinct forms of expression. The missionaries came and expressed an intolerant attitude toward African religion, an attitude not foreign to the fundamentalist and evangelical forms of Christianity that are increasingly prevalent in Africa today. This intolerance in religion has also continued in elements of imported culture from both Christianity and Islam. The power of patriarchy has entered into the religious understanding of much of African religious expression through these two imported religions. This has led to the diminishment of women's place in society, making them largely subject to the patriarchal family system. In addition, African culture has been assaulted by globalization with its technology-deifying Western culture, its traditions, and its values as those that should replace traditional African ones. African women who see beyond the enticements of Western values and the undermining of traditional life point to the cultural plurality that should operate in society, but not at the expense of subjugating groups, including women, to domination. African feminists oppose the suppression of past values that honor women and resist new ones that diminish women's dignity. This resistance takes the form of women's solidarity as the source for mutuality and support. They work together in the hope that women's likeness in the image of God will be acknowledged and achieved through active struggle.

While multiculturalism prevails in Africa as elsewhere, the most powerful tool for shaping identity and values is cultural education through the various processes of socialization. Stories convey important values and gender roles that people are expected to assume. The difficulty is that nonconformity to sexist traditions leads to a variety of sanctions unpleasant to experience.

African feminist theologians note especially the importance of rituals attendant to the important phases and aspects of women's lives, including marriage and motherhood. In addition, African women by tradition are socialized to nurture others, much to the good of their own identity, but leading at times to the distortion that they are to please their men at all costs. Language and rituals are replete with this notion of subservience of women to men. Dispelling the power of this mythic structure of subservience is one of the greatest challenges to the struggles of African feminists.

The emphasis on *koinonia* has permeated feminist theology as together women struggle for justice. These features of life and faith are central to the narratives African women tell.

Traditional theological language in Africa points to the myths in which those of creation take special importance. They point to the communal nature of human existence in which God, the spirits, and humans exist together in a harmonious whole. Through mutuality people find their lives are sustained and their existence given a direction for just action. The native stories of women are also filled with expressions of hope that the struggles in which they engage will lead to greater wholeness among human beings. Living in harmony with community, God, and nature, including the spirits of the ancestors and of nature, is central to life, as is integrity in which humans respect the realities in which they live and their features held in common. Integrity is shaped by the ethos of the local manifestation of community in which one lives. This sense of integrity comes from nurturing the severely disadvantaged in society: the old, the sick, children, strangers, and widows. This sense of wholeness leads to the experience of well-being and consequently to the celebration of life both formally, through festivals and ritual occasions, and informally in the sharing of what one has with others, e.g., in a meal.

Africans also have a sense of communion with nature, so ecology and environmental concerns hold considerable importance. Mythic relationships with the people and nature are especially important and enter into the narrative worlds of women storytellers. A sense of a spiritual relationship with nature pervades African worldviews.

Africans have the sense of reciprocity and justice that operates in their social worlds. This ensures that communities will address themselves the needs of others. Traditional governments are more representative than the dictatorships of the earlier colonialists. But the influence and the imposition of individualism from the West have led to difficulties by destabilizing the strong sense of community that traditional African values had taught. In addition, women have found the strong prevalence of patriarchy within their own societies to be debilitating. They are underemployed and often hold jobs that are far below their skill levels. In addition, they are often the victims of blame for whatever evil that occurs. Thus, their self-worth and justice are doubly difficult to assert and to obtain. Social transformation is a driving force in the efforts of feminist theologians in Africa.

The key to feminist theology in Africa, of course, is God-talk, and the primary narrative that presents the nature and activity of God in relationship to humanity, the spirits, and the environment is the creation myth of origins. In narratives of origins, God is the Source Being who has initiated all of life, thus making the entirety of existence sacred. These creation narratives depict reality as consisting of God the creator, the world (environment), humanity, and the spirits (ancestral and nature spirits) mediating between heaven and earth. While the creator is known by many terms and names in African religions, the one Oduyoye prefers to use is that of "Source Being." Divine presence gives life to all that exists, but its withdrawal, which leads to theological questions, is used to explain the devastations that afflict humans.

In Oduyoye's theology, the dominant mythical metaphor for God is "mothering." In viewing the theological repository of African mythology, God at times is male and at other times female who creates all humans, regardless of the divine or human gender. Indeed, characteristics normally associated with males in tribal customs are given to God even as the divine nature also comprises those that are thought to be typically female. All people, male and female, are made in the image of God. One of the roles for women in Africa is that of the mother who nurtures and cares for her children and all who need compassionate treatment. Thus, for all Africans, male and female, God is typically viewed as a mother who gives to and cares for the needy, who extends hospitality to all, regardless of who they are, and who exists in a loving relationship with humans and with the environment.

For Africans, explains Oduyoye, all of life is sacred, meaning then there is a holistic reality in which its constituent parts are in harmony. Disharmony is a distortion of this sacred order normally caused by human sin. Too often in African thinking, this disturbance is interpreted as deriving from willful sins of women or from the failure to engage in rituals of female purity. And from this theological explanation derives patriarchy and the abuse of women in family relationships, especially by their spouses. This is the challenge for feminist theologians in Africa: the removal of sexism by advocating a social ethic based on the metaphor of "mothering" that points to the interdependence and mutuality of all life. Too often the African social constructions are disempowering to women. The way to change these into empowerment is theologically presenting God as the Source Being who either is both male and female or even beyond gender.

The sacredness of life, encapsulated in the mythologies of creation, are also a means by which feminist theologians may use African traditions to develop an eco-theology that points to the importance of humanity as being to serve as the stewards of God's good earth and not to become its exploiters. The development of a theology of creation that regards its elements as sacred is necessary to resist a destructive capitalism intent on raping the environment for short-term profit. Again, the mothering image of God and the faithful is important to Oduyoye in caring for and nurturing all of life.

The biblical narratives are taken by African women, lay and theologian, to describe woman's hospitality (e.g., Rebekah and the servant of Isaac in Gen 24:15-27) and to criticize men who fail to do the same (e.g., Lot's offering of his virgin daughters to save his male guests from abuse in Gen 19:1-8). These stories are given new life in the experiences of African women.

This mothering image derives from the sociopolitical, cultural, and religious location of Africans in their societies. Women are to join men at the table in making policy decisions in the maintenance of all of life and in the efforts to protest injustice that is even more devastating to them. This mother God is also then the God of liberation, freeing those who are exploited and devalued by their societies.

Oduyoye's final point brings home the same objective of Schüssler Fiorenza: the mutuality of women's experience of oppression leads them to take strength from each other. The "way forward" is the togetherness of women that is extended in due time to men as well. She argues that women theologians and women in general need to remove the boundary of gender by returning to the religious and cultural heritage that is so powerfully portrayed in stories, whether those of the Bible or of new fiction writers. All voices are allowed to speak and not fear ostracism by unpopular views. Oduyoye is sure that what will emerge is a community that does not regard gender as a line separating human beings into competing factions.

Samuel Tinyiko Maluleke

The South African missiologist Samuel Tinyiko Maluleke has noted the diversity that exists among postcolonial interpreters, making it difficult for their voices to be heard. He agrees with Upkong that inculturation is an important feature of African hermeneutics, since African culture and traditional religions are the "womb out of which African Christian theology must be born."[57] Even so, it is not enough to limit interpretation to an exclusively Christian African theology, since plurality requires an interreligious approach that includes the variety of Christian churches and the traditions and beliefs of native African religions. Among the emerging theologies in Africa, according to Maluleke, are the theologies of the African Independent Churches;[58] African charismatic/evangelical theology that requires dialogue and debate, not polemics; translation theologies inherent in the vernacular languages of Africa into which the Bible is being

---

57. Maluleke, "Half a Century of African Christian Theologies," 4-23.
58. See Maluleke, "Theological Interest in African Independent Churches." According to Maluleke, the theologies of these churches may no longer be dismissed in a cavalier fashion.

rendered; African feminist/womanist theologies;[59] and self-critical analyses. However, for Maluleke, liberation and inculturation paradigms are no longer up to the task of shaping African theology, especially after the conclusion of the cold war. In place of these paradigms, he argues for a proactive theology of reconstruction that allows serious dialogue to take place in regard to the vital issues of democracy, human rights, nation building, and economics.[60] Thus, he advocates for a strong emphasis on social justice as the primary purpose of biblical theology, directed not only to the global powers but also to the internal regimes.

R. S. Sugirtharajah

As noted already in this chapter, Sugirtharajah has articulated clearly the important concepts necessary to understand and apply a postcolonial reading of texts. His fundamental thesis is that postcolonialism is a posture of reading intended to criticize the various forms of totalitarian, Eurocentric thinking. This means that postcolonialism represents "a discursive resistance to imperialism, imperial ideologies, imperial attitudes and their continued incarnations in such wide-ranging fields as politics, economics, history and theological and Biblical studies."[61] It acknowledges the points of coalescence and convergence between the colonizer and the colonized and tries to provide a new perspective by critically and profitably syncretizing ingredients from both vernacular and metropolitan centers.[62] It encourages "contrapuntal reading," a reading strategy in which the experiences of the colonizer and the colonized are studied together, thus obliging readers to be simultaneously aware of both mainstream and peripheral scholarship, the latter of which is often sidelined and domesticated by the dominant discourse.

Further, postcolonialism is an engagement of praxis that takes seriously the related political and cultural issues like poverty and patriarchy. To engage in postcolonial discourse, asserts Sugirtharajah, biblical interpreters should create contemporary identities. They should position themselves in the "interstitial cultural space...between and betwixt cultures and countries and engage in a processual hermeneutic."[63] This positioning of the interpreter amidst the variety of human cultures allows for all groups

---

59. See Kanyoro and Njoroge, *Groaning in Faith.*
60. See Mugambi, *From Liberation to Reconstruction.*
61. Sugirtharagah, "A Postcolonial Exploration of Collusion and Construction."
62. Ibid.
63. Sugirtharajah, *Asian Biblical Hermeneutics and Postcolonialism,* 108–09.

to express their views and concerns and to engage in conversation about contemporary meaning.

Sugirtharajah provides a heuristic survey of different approaches to biblical interpretation, including dissident readings, heritage readings, nationalistic readings, and liberationist readings.[64] Dissident readings, which set forth the corrupt character of colonialism throughout its insalubrious history, are made by both colonized critics and Western anticolonialists. These readings also are directed against the leaders of newly independent states for the silencing and abuse of their indigenous populations ironically by using the same means of colonialism in which discrimination is based upon class, gender, and ethnicity. These readings give expression to prophetic voices of protest fortified by examples of God's intervention on behalf of the poor. Heritage readings stress the recovery of a culture's memory and make use of indigenous religions and philosophies to understand and interpret Christianity. Nationalistic readings focus more on the ravaging of countries and cultures by colonialism and seek to establish economic equalities to address the challenges of education, medicine, industry, employment, and agriculture. The Bible is used to point to the belief that the land is not privately owned, but rather belongs to the community for its total benefit. Liberationist readings look to the biblical exodus and the prophets to address the evils of oppression of the poor and to chastise the wealthy for exploitation and pauperization of the marginalized. All in all, the purpose of postcolonial biblical criticism is to put the evils of colonialism at the center of biblical scholarship and contemporary interpretation, to deconstruct their power and influence, and to replace them with life-enhancing values and activities that return dignity to all human beings.

Sugirtharajah challenges the missionary translations of the Bible into Asian languages and vocalizes the need for "textual cleansing," i.e., a retranslation of biblical texts into Asian texts that employ wider intertextual hermeneutics that allow for the "chutnification of language and history." These retranslations should rid biblical translations of their "ideological trappings" and seek "a radical remolding of the text to meet new situations and demands."[65] Sugirtharajah vehemently criticizes condescending, Western, exegetical efforts for undermining the role of Oriental and Third World biblical interpretations by regarding them as "vague and practical" in comparison to Western interpretations that are considered to be "cerebral and intellectual." Sugirtharajah observes that the biblical academy assigns all historical, exegetical, and intellectual activities to Western scholars, to the

---

64. Sugirtharajah, *Postcolonial Criticism and Biblical Interpretation*, 43–73.
65. Ibid., 97.

dismissal and denigration of "the other interpreters" who are forced to draw from their experiences and heritage due to their assumed lack of incisive mental acuity.[66] He has pointed to numerous misuses of the Bible by imperialists, including both clergy and scholars, to provide theological sanctions for colonial expansion. He also has noted the general ignoring of Eastern contributions to biblical interpretation, including not only the work of biblical scholars, but also the influence of Indian, Buddhist, and Hindu understandings and practices on Christian culture. He is also critical of Western scholars who disregard the important hermeneutical moves to explain Christianity to non-Christians by reference to their own cultural contexts and metanarratives.

Recently he has joined Segovia in advocating a "diasporan" interpretation of the Bible.[67] The term *diaspora* connotes the meaning of displacement, hardship, suffering, and victimization of those who are forced into geographical and spiritual exile. In postcolonialism, Christianity relinquishes its position at the center, its territories, and its cultural homogeneity. As noted in an earlier chapter, Segovia searches for the elimination of colonialism in the study of the Bible and proposes its movement into a global context where all peoples speaking from their own locations and otherness may participate in the discourse and interpretation of texts.[68] This approach also seeks to uncover experiences of uprooted experience in the Bible in order to make use of the global literatures of those who live in an alien place. Since marginals have no dwelling place, they must reside betwixt and between cultures, and therefore are required to reinterpret traditions through their own hermeneutical lens. In the diaspora, they learn to oppose and subvert the agents of hierarchy, hegemony, and monolithic understanding.

Postcolonial Biblical Theology in Geographical Settings: The Case of Senegal

Aliou C. Niang[69]

Historical Setting

Senegal has a long history of colonialism. Precolonial Senegal shared a rich cultural symbiosis with three great civilizations: Ghana, Tekrur, and

---

66. Ibid., 104–5.
67. Ibid., 179–99.
68. Segovia, "Toward a Hermeneutics of the Diaspora."
69. Aliou C. Niang, a Senagalese Christian completing doctoral studies at Brite Divinity School, wrote this section of the chapter.

Mali.[70] Subsequent displacements of the empires of Ghana and Tekrur by Almoravid incursions led to the rise of the Jolof Empire, which dominated much of the Senegalese territory by engaging in trade, including the commodities of slaves and various goods, with Arabs, other Africans, and the Portuguese. Contacts with European slave traders (especially the Portuguese) eventually led to the division of the Jolof Empire into small and independent empires (Wolof, Serer, Walo, Kajor, Bawol, Sin, Salum, etc.).[71] The subsequent colonization of Senegal further disrupted the unity once enjoyed by pre-European culture.[72]

In 1444, the Portuguese, under the leadership of Dinis Diaz, sailed to an uninhabited island, about two miles from the shore of what is now called Dakar, where they later built trading posts.[73] The strategic location of this island was so attractive that it generated fierce conflicts between European traders. The Dutch seized this island from the Portuguese and by 1588 renamed it Goede Reede, a name that evolved into Gorée.[74] The British succeeded in displacing the Dutch and occupied the island from 1664 to 1667 but were finally forced out by the French, who controlled it from 1677 throughout much of the colonial era.[75] Early stages of the trans-Atlantic slave trade, or *Commerce Triangulaire,* contributed to precolonial Senegalese and European economies alike in that it was traditionally directed and implemented by ratified treaties guaranteeing the rights of both parties.[76] The eventual abolition of slavery limited the trade to gum and peanuts in return for "manufactured goods from France." The colonial conquest was

---

70. The term *Tekrur* is sometimes spelled Takru, Tekrour, or Tikrur. The precolonial economy was based on slavery, trans-Saharan gold, and the Arabic-gum trade.

71. Colvin, *Historical Dictionary of Senegal,* 2–3.

72. Crowder, *West Africa under Colonial Rule,* 15. Although there were interethnic wars before colonial rule, there were clear traces of precolonial moves to statehood initiated by various ethnic groups.

73. The Portuguese named the island Palma.

74. Crowder, *West Africa under Colonial Rule.*

75. Colvin, *Historical Dictionary of Senegal,* 184–86.

76. Vaillant, *Black, French, and African,* 35–36. Most traded slaves were war prisoners captured during skirmishes between kingdoms or tribes. Colvin notes that slaves were sent to various parts of the globe (to Portugal and to its conquered islands in the fifteenth century). By the sixteenth century, the Portuguese sent their slaves to Spanish colonies in the Americas. The Dutch in the seventeenth century shipped their slaves to sugar cane (Caribbean) and tobacco (North America) plantations (pp. 184–86). It would be untrue to think Senegalese people were readily submissive to French colonization (Crowder, *Senegal,* 3–4). Further, one ought not to view Senegal's precolonial caste system, which included nobles, artisans, and slaves, as being as detrimental as colonialism. This picture might mislead the outside observer to conclude that this type of social structure is a recipe for social unrest. In contrast to Western hierarchy, in the Senegalese caste system, the noble acts responsibly toward artisans and slaves. So Marxism would not work in this context, in that revolution is

a poignant and unpredictable phenomenon in that it reduced most Senegalese people, except the Four Communes dwellers, to objects.

Colonial Themes: The Influence of Association and Assimilation

French colonial rule in Senegal was differently nuanced in comparison to that practiced by other European imperialists. The French were convinced that it was their responsibility to convert Senegalese people to French culture, a responsibility that, if need be, would be carried out by the sword. Their duty was to show indigenous people "all that they gain by becoming French."[77] This was true, of course, of the British colonial rule. However, the Senegalese were viewed as French, and those who resided in the Four Communes were French citizens, not simply members of a commonwealth. The process of acculturating Senegalese people was carried out through two crucial themes: assimilation and association.[78] The former was a pilot program first tested in the Four Communes.[79]

French civilization was to be the quintessential paradigm for the colony to ensure that the Four Communes of Senegal were governed through French-style municipal councils controlling their own budgets. The communes elected representatives to a *Conseil-Général* similar to those of the *Départment* of France, and, during the Second and Third Republics in France, they were allowed to elect a deputy to the French National Assembly.[80] This advocacy and practice of assimilation was bolstered by sociological conclusions suggesting, "Les races africaines sont aptes au progrès et qu'ils n'y a aucune preuve de douter de leur facultés à cet égard" (The African Races are suited for progress, and there is no proof that would question their faculties in this regard).[81] Consequently, indigenous people were "educated to assimilate French culture."[82] The Enlightenment affirmation of human equality led to the theoretical equality of all people. Hence, any intellectual differences resulted from nurture—a deficiency that could be corrected by assimilation[83] and interaction with metropolitan institutions, particularly those found in the city and culture of Paris.[84] French

---

not carried out by lower castes. The likelihood for revolution or social unrest rests on the shoulders of the nobles. See Diop, *Precolonial Black Africa*, 1–3.

77. Michelet, *Introduction à l'histoire universelle*, 221.

78. McNamara, *France in Black Africa*, 33. This policy was carried out from 1880 to 1960.

79. Crowder, *Senegal*, 1–2.

80. Ajayi and Crowder, "West Africa 1919–1939," 514.

81. Ibid., 201.

82. Crowder, *Senegal*, 1–2.

83. Ibid.

84. O'Brien, *White Society in Black Africa*, 45.

citizenship was then granted to all who lived in the Four Communes of Senegal: Saint Louis, Rufisque, Dakar, and Gorée—a process proudly called by the French "*la paix Française*" or "*l'oeuvre civilisatrice*"[85] ("the French peace" or "the work of civilization").

In distinction to assimilation, the policy of association was introduced as a result of the realization that the colonized significantly outnumbered the French population living in the colonies and that those to whom French citizenship was granted knew little if anything about French civilization.[86] The new policy "*tient essentiellement à respecter les traditions et les coutumes des indigènes*" (holds in essence the position of respecting of the traditions and the customs of the indigenous people)[87] in the hope that, through association, the people of Senegal would progressively acculturate French civilization.[88] So by the eve of World War II, association became the policy for the *Protectorat,* but assimilation remained the ultimate "goal" for the Four Communes dwellers and "French-educated elites."[89]

In summary, assimilation and association were the twin themes that dominated French homogenization. Whereas through assimilation the French ruled directly, "associationism" was an attempt to rule indirectly, as in British colonization.[90] It is important to note that most Senegalese and French preferred the policy of assimilation. For the Senegalese, assimilation helped promote equality, provided political power, and led to citizenship.[91] These rights and privileges were partially undermined by the shift to the association policy.[92] Senegalese traditional leaders and Muslim clerics were not passive in regard to the French occupation. The abrupt disruption of and blatant disregard for Senegalese culture generated at times

---

85. Crowder, *Senegal,* 25.

86. McNamara, *France in Black Africa,* 34. General Faidherbe applied this policy when he realized the apparent contradiction embedded in the process of turning indigenous people into French citizens. He signed treaties with local rulers respecting traditional leadership, while at the same time upholding French sovereignty.

87. Péter, *L'effort français au Sénégal,* 197–98.

88. Colvin, *Historical Dictionary of Senegal,* 126. Behind this imperialistic philosophy is the conviction that Africans are not civilized. African contacts with Muslims are regarded by the French as an introductory phase in the civilization process, which reaches it apex with that of becoming French. This is understood as an indirect way of leading the colonized.

89. Ibid. It is interesting to note that illiterate citizens of the Communes still can appeal to French or Muslim laws.

90. Crowder, *West Africa,* 116–39, 169–71, 217–33. Although direct rule was never part of the British colonial rule, they appeared to have tried it. However, British colonizers never entertained the idea of equality with Africans.

91. G. Johnson, *The Emergence of Black Politics in Senegal,* 217.

92. Ibid.

fierce resistance. However, the assimilation policy required that Senegal adopt a French education system and that French become the national language of the country.

Resistance to Colonialism in Senegal

As mentioned above, French colonization was stymied by resilient strategic resistance that was intense. Militants opposed French efforts to penetrate the interior. The refusal to pay taxes and enlist in the French army were the longest-standing forms of passive resistance against French colonial policies.[93] Subsequent movements of resistance emerged from educated Senegalese elites instead of from traditional rulers and clerics.

Negritude and Socialism as Intellectual Modes of Resistance

Although assimilation was preferred over association, the success of the former was crucial.[94] The Senegalese culture that once received people of diverse ethnic backgrounds was somewhat divided between French citizens of the Four Communes and those of the protectorate, often referred to as *indigénat*. The former belittled the latter—a contemptuous relationship expressed by a fictional character in Ousmane Sembène's novel this way:

93. Ibid. By the mid-nineteenth century, French colonists encountered and subdued the powerful Wolof kingdoms, which were no match for the French military. Subsequently, they attacked the Serere and Saloume and defeated them along with southern kingdoms of the Casamance. Afterward, inland kingdoms of the Walo were conquered by 1865 by General Faidherbe, whose strategy was to use Algerian troops and draft mainland Africans to reinforce his army. New leaders (Lat Dior Ngoné Latir Diop of Kajor, Albory Ndiaye of Jolof, and Abdou Kane of Fouta Toro), based on Islamic convictions, nobility, and prowess, arose to step up the resistance in the form of sporadic violence mitigated by diplomacy. The French determination to rule by force led to the extermination of all these leaders between 1886 and 1890. Clerics such as Ehadji Omar Tall (1845–1852) resisted corrupt traditional dynasties as an indirect opposition to French rule. Ma Ba, Shaixu Amadou Ba, and Lamine Drame claimed that Elhadji Omar Tall authorized them to wage jihad against the French. In the south, similar clerical resistance took shape (Moussa Molo and Fode Kaba Dumbia, who were rivals). Military resistance ended in north and central Senegal in 1890 and in the south (Casamance) by the early twentieth century. This defeat led to yet another phase of resistance: withdrawal from the French, noncooperation, and cultural defiance. Leaders of this phase were Amadou Bamba Mbake and Elhadji Malik Sy. By World War II (1939–1945), these leaders conceded that French rule was inevitable and counseled their followers to pay taxes and serve in the French army, but warned that they should avoid full assimilation with deference to their traditions. They even financed and supported educated elites like Blasé Diagne and Galandou Diouf, who later launched a new dynamic kind of resistance, African Nationalism.

94. Senghor, *Liberté* 1.

> Look at the inhabitants of the towns of Saint-Louis, Dakar, Rufisque, Gorée. Because of their long period of contact with Europeans, they thought themselves more "civilized" than the other bush Africans living in forest or savanna. This arrogance grew when they alone were given the vote and considered French citizens. People from these four *Communes* and their descendants, were proud of being the equals of Europeans. They began to parody them, and acquired a pretentious mentality. . . . How many times have we heard a man from Dakar, Gorée, Rufisque or Ndar (Saint-Louis) saying contemptuously to his country cousin: "I was civilized before you were."[95]

This deplorable attitude of the citizens of the Four Communes is indicative of their profound alienation,[96] a phenomenon that also deeply affected educated elites of the protectorate, including Léopold Sédar Senghor and Cheikh Hamidou Kane among others.[97]

Léopold Sédar Senghor

Senghor was born October 9, 1906, attended Catholic missionary school at Ngasobil,[98] completed his secondary school education at Lycée Van Vollenhoven, and then traveled to France to study at the Lycée Louis le Grand in 1928.[99] He earned his *Licence ès Lettres* in 1931 and his *agrégation* in 1935, and became a French citizen, even serving in the French Army.[100] While in France, Senghor met European, black American, and West Indian writers, including, in particular, Aimé Césaire. The reciprocal influence that arose from those encounters was so crucial to Césaire and Senghor that it became the catalyst for their self-discovery as blacks of the diaspora.[101]

---

95. Sembène, *The Last of the Empire,* 134. Sembène is another prolific Senegalese writer whose works of fiction often convey strong political messages despite his disclaimers.

96. Ibid.

97. Other crucial Senegalese writers are Cheikh Anta Diop, Ousmane Socé Diop, Ousmane Sembène, Mariama Bâ, and Aminata Sow Fall.

98. Biondi, *Senghor ou la tentation de l'universel,* 14–19. As a poet, Senghor was a prolific author whose writing focused on colonial and postcolonial issues. Only to list a few, his works include: *Liberté* 1; *Liberté* 2; *Liberté* 3 (see bibliography); and *The Collected Poetry* (Charlottesville, Va.: University of Virginia Press, 1991).

99. Biondi, *Senghor,* 20–21. As a young Senegalese whose father was not a French citizen, Senghor through education became a French citizen. This was the goal of the French assimilation policy.

100. Ibid. During World War II, Senghor fought for France along with Senegalese recruits called *les Tirailleurs Senegalais.* He was captured by German troops. After his release in 1942, he taught and then entered politics. He eventually negotiated the independence of Senegal with General De Gaulle in 1960 and became the country's president.

101. Colvin, *Historical Dictionary of Senegal,* 258.

This encounter along with the European surrealist movement paved the way for the idea of negritude,[102] a groundbreaking concept aimed at debunking the colonial assumption that Africans have no civilization.[103] Rather than succumbing to the contradiction inherent in being black and French, Senghor developed a mode of existence characteristic of exilic life sustained by his Christian faith.[104] As an exilic ideology, negritude is a black consciousness and the sum and substance of sociopolitical, economical, intellectual, and artistic values shared by all dehumanized black people of any country.[105]

The implications of negritude run deeply in Senegalese culture, for it took root and sprang forth a distinctive socialism that is situated in common rural life. It is a context where one finds individuality in the various interrelationships of communal life.[106] One may appreciate and enjoy the self in the "other," for it is in the "other" that individual existence is given its identity and meaning.[107] Characteristic of village or tribal life, important social relations are regulated by religion instead of Marxist, neo-Marxist, or capitalistic ideology.[108] The African is a social being who is at home with nature, because "he lives of the soil and with the soil, in and by the cosmos."[109]

Postcolonial Hermeneutical Clues

The move from colonial to postcolonial contexts in Senegal calls for a serious theological jousting between history and the indigenous writings mentioned. First, Hans-Georg Gadamer's fusion of the horizons[110] cannot be overlooked, because negritude was a response to confusions generated by the duality created by colonial policies. Senghor reminds the reader that duality has its advantages and drawbacks in that it is a sphere of life

102. Césaire, *Discourse on Colonialism*, 83–85.

103. Crowder, *West Africa*, 16–17.

104. Ibid., 137–38.

105. Crowder, *West Africa*, 88. Negritude was a concept born in exile—a profound quest for identity and a way out of cultural alienation in the early 1930s.

106. Senghor, "The Spirit of Civilisation," 52–54. Senghor believed that intuition is the most crucial element of human consciousness.

107. Senghor, *On African Socialism*, 73, 93–94. Existence cannot be reduced solely to one's ability to think (as in Descartes) or love (as in Augustine) or hope (as in Moltmann), but in the experience of the being of the "other;" namely, the neighbor.

108. Ibid., 132–65; Colvin, *Historical Dictionary of Senegal*, 122–23. Colvin rightly observes that Senghor does not hesitate to link Senegalese socialism to his concept of negritude.

109. Senghor, "The Spirit of Civilisation," 52. The idea of living off the soil is a crucial hermeneutical key I will address later.

110. Gadamer, "The Historicity of Understanding," 267–73.

where self-understanding could be reached and appreciated. France was wrong. Africans have their own indigenous cultures and civilizations, a fact even some descendants of the colonizers have learned once to appreciate.[111]

In addition, life between worlds compels one to construe a culture-centered language with pertinent symbolism,[112] since the art of self-reinvention calls for a poetic voice[113] that seeks to create a new world in which negritude is operative.

Postcolonial hermeneutics cannot ignore the political nature of religion. It must give voice to "the inclusive horizon of human life"[114] by revitalizing *Freiheitsgeschichte*.[115] This posture advocates and exercises human equality in order to dismantle oppressive theological doctrines,[116] tradition, and institutions.[117] This effort will liberate the poor and advocate the kind of praxis that creates a universal justice.[118] African philosophy is both practical and intuitive.[119] Like African traditional religion, African philosophy will remain a practically lived experience assessed, taught, and exercised by living libraries: the elders.[120]

Postcolonial Hermeneutics: A Proposal

The question is, where should a Senegalese hermeneut begin? Postcolonial theological interpretation from Senegal has yet to appear in academic discussions and writings. Here are several suggestions. After realizing that colonization had turned him into an awkward being, Césaire described colonial experience as that which reduces the colonized to an object instead of a human person.[121] Frantz Fanon has used a geological term depicting the colonized as being frozen in time by a slow racist process of fossilization initiated by the colonizer.[122] Decolonization, he argues, is the sole way out of this deleterious condition—a violent turn of events.[123] These

111. Vaillant, *Black, French, and African*, 122–26.

112. Ricoeur, *Interpretation Theory*, 1–43.

113. Vaillant, *Black, French, and African*, 128–29.

114. Moltmann, "The Cross and Civil Religion," vi–x.

115. Ibid., 83–86.

116. Moltmann, *On Human Dignity*, 98; Moltmann, "Communities of Faith."

117. Moltmann, *On Human Dignity*, 99.

118. Moltmann, "Communities of Faith," 248.

119. Senghor, "The Spirit of Civilisation," 52.

120. Baum, *Shrines of the Slave Trade*, 16–17; Senghor, "The Spirit of Civilisation," 64; and Linares, *Power, Prayer and Production*.

121. Césaire, "Between Colonizer and Colonized," 340.

122. Fanon, "Racism and Culture," 24.

123. Fanon, "Decolonizing, National Culture, and the Negro Intellectual" 359. Violence, in my opinion, is not the answer.

two intellectuals agree that the culture that will precede decolonization will include old and new elements.[124] This means there will be some discontinuity in the midst of the usual continuum of certain elements that the colonized must securely preserve.

Senghor has shown that the African is a social being, a force among other forces of creation.[125] This force, like others under the universe, is extrinsic because it owes its being to God. In other words, Senghor's cosmological pyramid has God at its apex, ancestors and tribal founders ("demi-gods"), "the living who are . . . ordered according to custom," and last of all the fauna, flora, and minerals.[126] This primordial unity of creation is "centered on humans" and "inspires" the harmony found in a civilization. Religion unifies creation through the various sacrificial aspects of the cultus. This unity is reflected by the African family, which, in turn, relates to other families that compose the clan, which includes the living and the dead united by a common ancestry leading eventually to God.[127]

Senghor also stresses the pertinence of language. For Senghor, language is "the major instrument of thought, emotion and action."[128] Language is inherently powerful in that when spoken, it becomes "the supreme expression of vital force." Granting that this power belongs to God who creates through the word, human language also creates.[129] This creative capacity of spoken words is also inherent in humans whether African or European. For Senghor, speech is expressed through poetry and concrete representational arts (sculptures and paintings) that reflect surrealist images conveying stories. He then ties all these aspects of human creativity to the word, which, in turn, is divine in origin.[130] Postcolonialism "frees our mind from mental slavery." The centrality of the word, emphasized by Senghor, could well be the reconciling medium for a postcolonial world in which Europe and Africa will dine at the same table without hypocrisy (Gal 2:11-14). Those who champion a mere return to traditional ways may do well to hear Sembène's advice: " 'It would be a dangerous step backwards, to revert to our traditions. . . .' 'That's not what I'm saying, Joom Galle,' she interrupted. 'We must achieve a synthesis. . . . Yes, a synthesis. . . . I don't mean a step backwards. . . . A new type of Society,' she ended, blinking. There followed a brief silence."[131] If what the African experiences in daily communal

---

124. Cesaire, "Culture and Colonization," 207; and Fanon, "Racism and Culture," 131.
125. Senghor, "The Spirit of Civilisation," 53.
126. Ibid.
127. Ibid., 54.
128. Ibid., 58.
129. Ibid.
130. Ibid., 55–63.
131. Sembène, *The Last of the Empire*, 135.

interactions is true of the interrelatedness of various elements in creation and other cultures, acting through the word may be the lasting weapon against any dehumanization. We should strive to utter the word and let it shape and transform lingering injustices that still pervade our postcolonial era.

A Hermeneutic That Is Liberating, Both Theologically and Politically

Africans need to assert the dignity of their traditions and to honor them with open consent. The West cannot and should not be the model for emulation:

> "Exactly," exclaimed Djia Umrel. "What model of society are we offered through the media? We're made to swallow outdated values, no longer accepted in their countries of origin. Our television and radio programmes are stupid. And our leaders, instead of foreseeing and planning for the future, evade their duty. Russia, America, Europe and Asia are no longer examples or models for us."[132]

However, Sembène is right in asserting that we cannot take a step backwards, yet the traditions of the indigenous culture must be formed into a new synthesis with western views. For Fanon, there are two options for hermeneutics: either to part with colonization or to collaborate.[133] Aware of the dilemma that faces most of the colonized world, Senghor counsels that colonialism has drawbacks as well as advantages and says it would be wise for "the colonized of yesterday . . . [to] be more attentive to the contributions than to defects."[134]

That being the case, the Senegalese hermeneut should heed Gadamer's challenge. The contemporary colonized rural people should fuse their horizons with new views that have value regardless of their source of origin. This fusion will then serve as a starting point for the way to emancipation. Abdoulaye Wade, the current president of Senegal, encourages this symbiosis not only between the colonized, but also a synthesis between Senegalese traditional law and that of France.

Worthy and aware of his or her postmodern stance, the postcolonial hermeneut is a member of various interpreting communities who delights in the availability of various religious and secular traditions voiced from below via "visual, oral and aural means."[135] But these are used, not for

---

132. Sembène, *The Last of the Empire*, 135.
133. Fanon, *The Wretched of the Earth*, 59.
134. Senghor, *On African Socialism*, 82.
135. Ibid., 116.

reveling in insights, but rather for religious and political liberation that enables both marginals and centrists to share a common gospel.

A Second Example of Postcolonial Biblical Theology: India and Dalit Theology

Royce Victor[136]

History of Colonialism and Postcolonialism in India

The current quest of Indian Christians to develop a relevant theology that is suitable for their contemporary context began with the Protestant Christian missionary endeavor. However, this Western theology is now being replaced with an indigenous one that draws on Indian resources for a more relevant articulation of the gospel. This does not mean that this theological articulation is being done without consideration of the challenges and contributions of other faiths,[137] or that there have not been important contributions of the sympathetic "Western" missionaries.[138] But this does mean that Indian theologians are reshaping Christian theology in the traditions of their own cultures and not those of the West.

The Christianity offered by Western missionaries, unfortunately, had nothing in common with the local culture or practice of life of people in India. Except for the land on which the church building was placed, everything else was Western in many senses: the style of worship, language, vestments, hymns, musical instruments, architecture, and so on. Christianity remained a Western religion to many in India. In this "second coming" to an Asian land, Jesus could not identify with its people. He became an alien in the continent to which he came. It was difficult for the indigenous people to understand the Westernized message of Jesus and of Christianity. The missionaries could not effectively convey the message of the gospel to Indian minds. Christianity did influence the upper-caste Hindus, the majority people;[139] however, it made little impact on the lower castes and especially the outcast Hindus, the Dalits. The Dalits had hoped that by embracing the new religion, they could change the caste stigma, which was

---

136. Royce Manojkumar Victor, a graduate student at Brite Divinity School pursuing his Ph.D. in biblical studies, is the author of this section. He is from Palakkad, Kerala State, India and is an ordained minister of the Church of South India.

137. See the contributions of M. K. Gandhi, Keshub Chandra Sen, Ram Mohan Roy, and other Indians who have challenged Christianity by arguing for an indigenous expression of faith.

138. For example, Stanley Jones and B. F. Andrews.

139. According to the 2001 census, about 18 percent of the total Indian population belongs to the outcastes.

forced on them by the religion and society, but they have been strongly disappointed.

The Caste System and Indian Society

The caste system is a unique part of Indian society and philosophy. In ancient India, a social system developed in which people were divided into separate closed communities. These communities are known in English as castes. The origin of the caste system is in Hinduism, but it affected the entire Indian society. There are four castes—Brahmins, Kshethriyas, Vaishya, and Sudra—hierarchically arranged. But below them all are the outcastes, the Panchamas or Dalits.[140] Socially the caste system is far more complex, with many more castes and subcastes and other divisions as well.

The caste system is also related to people's economic occupations. Each caste is assigned certain duties, known as Varnashrama Dharma. Varna means predestination of the choice of one's profession. The law of Varna is that a person shall follow the profession of his or her ancestors to have a livelihood. Varna, therefore, is, in a way, the law of heredity.[141] According to the doctrine of Varnashrama Dharma, the Brahmins are to be the spiritual and temporal guides (the priests of the society), teachers and exponents of law. Kshethriyas are the warriors, princes, and kings—in short, the nobility. Vaishyas take on the tasks of agriculture and business; and the Sudras include individuals who perform various types of labor and services: manual and agricultural workers, artisans, masons, and so on. The outcastes, however, have no place in society and exist as marginals. Literally, they are not permitted to participate in village life, not even to enter into a village. Their place is always outside the village, and they are expected to live as servants to the high caste in the society, which is considered their *dharma*. Many still live as slaves or experience slave-like conditions in various parts of the country, because of the practice of Varnashrama Dharma. The ideology of the dogma of Varnashrama Dharma, which comprises the sociocultural, economic, and political elements of human communities, dominates people's lives and legitimizes the hierarchical order and power of the privileged. Some 18 percent of the total population of India are the outcastes, who make up the main body of the poor and oppressed in India.

---

140. See the short etymological discussion and the importance of the word *Dalit* later in this section.

141. Gandhi, *The Removal of Untouchability*, 40ff.

Dalits and Christianity

The Dalits originally joined Christian churches in the hope of achieving upward social mobility. However, the missionaries had thought of their conversion as a purely religious act; they did not understand and respond to their social aspirations. The Western missionaries primarily were interested in preaching the gospel to the upper-caste people. Some of the missionaries even abhorred the prospects of Dalits becoming Christians. They did not wish to "take rubbish into the church." Despite this anti-Dalit stance of many of the missionaries, Dalits still embraced their religion.

As Christianity took root and grew in India's rich soil, it began to absorb the Indian caste system. Separate churches and even burial places were set up for the Dalit Christians.[142] Dalits were disappointed with the attitude of the Christian missionaries and of the high-caste Christians toward them. In protest against this discrimination, the Dalit Christians issued a memorandum: "We remain today what we were before we became Christians—Untouchables—degraded by the laws of the social position obtaining in the land, rejected by the Caste Christians, and excluded by our own Hindu depressed class brethren."[143]

The response was not at all encouraging to them, with the result that there has been no change in the social situation of the Dalits, even to the present. They continue to be treated as marginalized people in both the society and the Christian churches in which they are members. Kappen notes that Christianity in India, in many respects, has tried to identify itself with the culture of the ruling class and the high castes of the society. The ethos prevailing in its religious institutions is, on the whole, one of blind obedience, personal dependence, patronage, and privilege, while its secular institutions (schools, hospitals, etc.) tend to reflect the values of bourgeois society.[144] Even in the early theological enterprises of Indian Christians trying to embrace Christian theology, this tendency to reflect prevailing social traditions has continued to be evident.

Indian Christian Theology

In efforts to acculturate Christianity, many Indian theologians have reformulated its teachings in order to make them relevant to the Indian context.

142. This was not the case of Protestants, but discrimination was strong among the Roman Catholics. For more details of this view, see Fernades, "A Socio-Historical Perspective for Liberation Theology in India," 9–34.

143. Nalunnakkal, *New Beings and New Communities*, 9.

144. Kappen, "Jesus and Transculturation," 173.

While most of them have been attracted to the Indian philosophy of the high caste, they still have integrated the philosophy and social structure of India with Christian theology. This more recent trend is commonly known as "Indian Christian theology."[145]

Indian Christian theology has sought to work out its major tenets in relationship to either Advaita Vedanta or Vishista Advaita, the ancient Indian philosophies of the high castes. There have been many attempts at synthesis, some of which are extremely provocative. However, most of the contributions of Indian Christian theology in the past came from high-caste converts to Christianity. The result has been that Indian Christian theology has perpetuated within itself the high-caste tradition. Nirmal, a prominent Dalit theologian, would call it the Brahminic tradition of Indian Christian theology,[146] while many others refer to it as the "Sanskritization" of Christian theology.[147] Years of coexistence with the dominant communities in the society with its hierarchical values and ideology has had its obvious impact on the theological thinking of the Indian Christians.

However, in the attempt to place Christian faith and practice into the framework of the dominant culture of the society, there was very little concern about the situation of the lowest stratum of the society to which the majority of Christians belong: the caste of the Dalits. The ancient Hindu holy books were not to be read by the Dalits, for these writings embodied brahmanical spirituality. The prescribed punishment for Dalits was the pouring of molten lead into their ears for even inadvertently hearing the recital of the Scriptures. The tragedy is that it was Hindu texts, teaching the caste system, which began to be evoked by Christians of the upper castes to illuminate and enhance biblical texts.

The Theology of Dialogue

There is yet another trend in Christian theology in India, one that has emerged from its ecumenical movement. In the early days of ecumenicity, the concern was to engage in dialogue with people of other faiths. This new approach responded to the predominant characteristic of the Indian

---

145. The significant contributions of Brahmabandhab Upadhyay, A. J. Appasamy, P. Chenchiah, and Vengal Chakkarai are some examples for this trend in Indian Christian theology. This trend is not confined to these earlier thinkers and writers, for it continues. For more recent attempts in this perspective, see Gabriel, *Dharma in the Hindu Scriptures and in the Bible;* and Abraham, *Prajapati: The Cosmic Christ.* The Ashram movement and new experiments in the liturgy and worship, music, architecture, and other phases of Christian life are products of this new movement.

146. Nirmal, "Towards a Christian Dalit Theology," 28.

147. Chatterji, "Why Dalit Theology."

context, namely, religious pluralism and the diversity of secular ideologies. The new movement abandoned the earlier missionary attitude of replacing other religions with Christianity. This branch of Indian Christian theology is continuing to develop, and its expansion into groups involved in social action has led to a significant contribution[148] to communal harmony.[149]

However, this new trend in theological concern again has contributed to Indian Christian theology's obsession with the Brahminic traditions.[150] Often the dialogue has taken place only with the high castes, making this an enterprise of the elite. Moreover, the scope of this trend was limited. It is unfortunate that the Indian church has lacked the inclination to reflect theologically on the faith and life of the Dalit converts who form the majority of Christians.

Indian Liberation Theology

In the early seventies, Indian theologians began to take the questions of socioeconomic justice more seriously. Many Indian theologians were attracted to the "liberation theology" of Latin America and imported its insights into Indian theological and social arenas of study and practice. The main attraction of liberation theology was its theme of freedom, for this is relevant to the Indian situation where the majority people continue to struggle with poverty.

The attempt has faced obstacles, since it originally sought to transplant the theology that emerged in Latin America, an entirely different context. However, the promoters of this enterprise soon came to realize the inability of this theology to meet the needs of the Indian context. The major disappointment was its shallow hermeneutics, which neglected the cultural and theological dimensions of liberation. The advocates of this new trend soon realized that the Marxist social analysis, which is the basis of the new theology, is inadequate to address the Indian context due to its neglect of the caste factor.[151] The Dalits rejected the class concept of this new trend as totally alien and "Western" in orientation and advocated in its place the

---

148. One should consult the contributions to Christian theology of P. D. Devanandan, Raymond Panikkar, Stanley J. Samartha, and M. M. Thomas.

149. I myself (i.e., Royce Victor) had an experience of working with a social action group, which was active among the slum dwellers of the city of Hyderabad, AP, where communal riots between Hindus and Muslims at one time were frequent. After many years of hard work, peace was achieved.

150. Nirmal, "Towards a Christian Dalit Theology," 29.

151. Many studies have been done on the failure of Marxist social analysis in India. Even the promoters of Indian liberation theology were reluctant to use it in constructing new theological understandings. A detailed discussion may be found in Chatterji, 'Why Dalit Theology."

indigenous tool of caste to analyze Indian society. While the economic problem does figure as an important factor in the social situation of India, the caste structure in the society is intimately connected to it. Economics and the caste factor are so intertwined they cannot be treated separately.

Dalit Theology as Contextual Theology

The emergence of Dalit theology has already exerted a significant impact on theology in India. It has inspired a constructive debate among theologians and thinkers as to whether "caste" should have the priority in Indian social analysis.

The word *dalit* means "oppressed" or "broken" in Sanskrit. It is both a noun and an adjective. As a noun, *dalit* can be used for all three genders, masculine, feminine, and neuter.[152] Etymologically speaking, *dalits* are those who are broken or oppressed in the society. Throughout the centuries, the Dalits in India have been subjected to oppression, not only economically but also socially. Therefore, it is right to say that the Dalits in India are twice oppressed. They can rightly be described as the "Dalits of the Dalits"[153] or the "twice alienated."[154] They comprise those who are denied social equality, economic justice, and human freedom. They are made into a "nonpeople" who are strangers in their own native soil, deprived of their human rights as well as their personal dignity. Prabhakar is correct when he speaks about the "fourfold alienation" of Christian Dalits. First, the state does not allow them to receive economic assistance or to secure political representation, even if they claim membership in the recognized caste communities. Second, Dalits look with disfavor upon members of their own caste who seek government assistance, since they are considered to have already been helped by missionary patronage. Third, the so-called upper-caste Christians treat Christian Dalits with contempt. And fourth, the Christian Dalits are at odds with themselves, being divided into subcastes and regional, linguistic, and denominational differentiations.[155] A relevant theology is more likely to emerge from theologians and activists who have inserted themselves into the life of the people as partners in their struggle for justice than from outsiders who only write theoretically about the issues of Dalit Christianity.

Dalit Christian theology challenges the existing "Indian Christian theology," thus becoming a countertradition of faith in the Indian context. In

---

152. For more detailed discussion of the term *Dalit,* see Massey, *Roots,* 9f.
153. Azariah, "Doing Theology in India Today," 40.
154. Chatterji, "Why Dalit Theology," 16.
155. Prabhakar, "The Search for a Dalit Theology," 35–47.

this theological venture, the primacy of the term *dalit* will have to be conceded. In Dalit theology, the Triune God is on the side of the Dalits and not the non-Dalits who are the oppressors. Major theological features include the following.

The Question of God

Dalit Christian theology is based on a faith in a Dalit God, who is identified with the oppressed. This understanding of the ultimate as a Dalit has resulted in the movement of Indian Dalits from Hinduism to Christianity. In addition, this "exodus" of Dalits has been understood in terms of the Israelite exodus. The recognition of the Dalit God in and through the person of Jesus Christ has led the Dalits to reject all other deities, including both those that are non-Dalits and those that are anti-Dalit.

Christology

For the Dalit Christians, Jesus Christ is also a Dalit, an understanding that becomes the key to comprehending the mystery of the divine-human unity in Jesus Christ. Indian Dalits have often been labeled as immoral and illegitimate in ways that parallel the ancestry of Jesus in the Matthean genealogy. These factors have Dalit implications and speak to the existence of Dalits in their oppression. Christ, the servant, is affirmed by the powerless and the poor. Dalit theology affirms that Christology is not to be understood in terms of power, but rather in terms of humility and human weakness.

Ecclesiology

The church as the body of Christ is a basic affirmation in Dalit ecclesiology. As the body of Christ was broken and crushed on the cross, the church, comprising the community of the Dalits, also is torn asunder by the oppressors. The church has the inescapable role and its consequent responsibility for the liberation of the Dalits. "Being in solidarity with the victims" is the role the church has to learn its master, the crucified Christ. All movements and groups, secular, Christian, and non-Christian, who are engaged in the struggles of people for justice and liberation become allies in the fulfillment of the church's mission.[156] Dalit liberation is primarily a struggle to achieve human dignity and to gain the right to live as free people created in the image of God.

The Importance of Pathos

Dalit theology affirms the primacy of pathos over theoretical abstraction. Pathos originates before the participation in struggles for human dignity.

156. Ibid., 46.

Dalits have been deprived of their rights as citizens in their own country throughout the many centuries. Generations of Dalits have experienced pathos and pain in their life. The people of the high castes have been their oppressor. But this experience of pathos and pain allows them to understand both the world and God who participates in human suffering. God lives in and among the Dalits and works to support them in their struggle to be recognized as fully human.

Conclusion

The emerging Dalit consciousness and identity have far-reaching consequences in Indian society. Centuries of exploitation and oppression by the people of the higher castes and the struggle for human dignity and justice led the Dalits to a theology that addresses their suffering, a theology that emerges out of their own context. They reject all theologies, which do not speak to their situation. They have experienced these theologies to be oppressive. They understand that the Dalit theology should challenge the society that consistently denies them their humanity, socially ostracizes them, economically exploits them, and culturally subjugates them. Dalit theology is not only a prophetic theology for identification with the oppression of Dalits and their struggles for equality and justice, but also is a political theology for social action designed to subvert and transform unjust, undemocratic, and oppressive structures. *Doing theology* means living in community with the sufferings and struggles of Dalits. Through dialogue, critical reflection, and committed action, a new life-order will emerge in the society.[157] The Indian Christian's quest for a relevant contextual theology that is capable of addressing the actual life situation of the majority of Indian Christians is occurring in the context of Dalit Christianity.

The Dalits are determined today that their destiny will not be decided by someone else, but rather by themselves. They also understand that their struggle needs to be continued both in society and in the church until they achieve their goal of liberation, defined as human dignity. The far-reaching consequence is that this emerging consciousness, if and when permeating the society of India, will dramatically transform Indian life.

A Postcolonial Interpretation of the Theology of Jeremiah

What would a theology of postcolonial interpretation of the book of Jeremiah look like? A number of texts could illustrate this approach, but I

---

157. Ibid., 44.

point to the two features of postcolonial theology that emerge most often: inculturation and liberation. In both of these, the foundation is the strong emphasis on context. The Assyro-Babylonian policies of conquest were driven by the insatiable desire for power, wealth, and status. To achieve their objectives, the conquerors slaughtered populations that resisted their invasions, made many slaves, and took the elite ruling classes into exile. Jeremiah was a northern prophet in his early life, prophesying in Benjamin and then moving to Jerusalem. In Source A of the prophetic speeches, the images of the "foe from the north" were graphic and fear provoking. Audiences who heard the prophet speak undoubtedly were strongly affected by the earlier tragedy of the northern kingdom, which was annihilated by the Assyrians.

The official response to Jeremiah as his stature grew in prominence following the catastrophe at Megiddo and the death of the "Messianic King" Josiah is presented in both the poetic and the prose tradition as deeply divided. The pro-Egyptian party at court sought to silence him, since he opposed their efforts to achieve liberation from Babylonian suzerainty in effect as a consequence of the victory of the forces of Nebuchadnezzar II over the Egyptians at Carchemish (605 B.C.E.). This group of loyalists still thought it possible for the Babylonian grip on the nation to be loosened by a coalition of Syro-Palestinian states headed by Egypt. Small wonder they regarded Jeremiah's dire warnings of devastation from the north as disloyal and even treasonous. Likely, the narratives of Jeremiah's persecution in the prose tradition were historical. The other party, who looked to Jeremiah and the former officials of the dead King Josiah's court, including the most prominent, Shaphan, along with his family, counseled the king (Zedekiah) to remain a faithful vassal to the Babylonian empire. Undoubtedly, they hoped for the eventual collapse of Babylon as the way to achieve independence in the future.

Conquest and Preparation for Life in Exile

When the city of Jerusalem fell to the Babylonians in 586 B.C.E., followed by widespread slaughter and then exile of leading citizens, Nebuzaradan, the Babylonian captain of the guard, in charge of administering the exile, gave Jeremiah his choice of staying or going under the protection of the Babylonians to Babylon. Jeremiah chose to stay and help to rebuild a ruined nation with the newly appointed governor, Gedaliah, the grandson of his old ally Shaphan. However, when Gedaliah was murdered by Ishmael, the descendant of David, a group of army officers who had been charged with protecting the dead governor decided to flee to Egypt to escape what they expected would be Babylonian retribution. Forced against his will to travel with former army officers to Egypt to find refuge, he disappeared from history.

A Postcolonial Theology of Exile

It was in exile that Jeremiah or, more likely, his disciples fashioned a theology of liberation by which they focused on the destruction of the Babylonians. Two features emerge from these texts shaped by the diasporan experience of exile: inculturation, in which the traditions of the past are remembered and embraced as the basis for future hope, and liberation, in which the destruction of Babylon would occur much to the joy of the victim nations forced into its empire (see the oracles of judgment against Babylon in 50:1—51:58). Inculturation and liberation are joined together in the recovering of the Zion tradition, the transformed understanding of the covenant, and liberation. Once Babylon has fallen and its gods put to shame, the liberated exiles will return with penitence to Zion. There, not only will the old covenant be renewed, but an everlasting one will be celebrated.

The language of holy war permeates these speeches in describing Yahweh's vengeance directed against Babylon to bring about its destruction. The imperial power that had devastated the tiny nation of Judah would meet its just retribution in being laid waste by Yahweh and the nations he has arrayed against her. The earlier Jeremiah's images of the northern foe are now used to describe the cruel enemy from the north that will decimate Babylon. These prophetic voices, likely the disciples of Jeremiah, speak in the words of their prophet judgments against an empire based on conquest, exile, and exploitation. The power of Yahweh is described not only in images of the warrior God, but also, through acculturation of its own theology, in the creation tradition in which God originated the earth "by his power" and "established the world by his wisdom." Through God's providential control, then, of sustaining and directing creation and ruling over the nations, God unleashes his wrath against Babylon and its idol makers, craftsmen who shaped gods in images, gods who can not contest Yahweh's great power. Finally, the cosmic sea, or chaos, will inundate this hated enemy, and its great vestiges of architectural wonder will be decimated.

It was in exile that a diasporan theology emerged, which took this bitter experience of destruction and diaspora, and reshaped it into an anticipation of future deliverance. The context of exile becomes then a creative and formative one in shaping the reformulation of Judaism and in developing a theology of hope that creates a vital vision that draws its believers into the future. There is no final reconciliation between the destroyer of nations and its victims. Rather, their shout is one of joy, expressed over the deserved end of their former oppressor. Inculturation through the reformulation of past tradition and the rejection of Babylonian religion, liberation in the form of return home from exile, and the context of a people in the diaspora, yearning for deliverance and the deserved destruction of its hated conqueror, are forged together in these oracles of Jeremiah and his prophetic successors.

9

The Changing Future of
Old Testament Theology: A Postscript

Si finis bonus est, totum bonum erit.

— *Gesta Romanorum*

Concluding Observations

I END THIS SURVEY WITH SEVERAL OBSERVATIONS, ASSERTIONS, AND a proposed series of steps designed to lead to biblical theology engaging contemporary faith. Old Testament theology, as can be seen in this book and in *The Collapse of History,* has become a vital discipline once again. Its voices are many and disparate, they speak out of different methodologies, contexts, and often conflicting epistemologies, but they should be heard and become dialogue partners in theological conversation that seeks to express both the Old Testament's and the current church's religious understanding. This variety of approaches and interpretations may be characterized as fragmentation or as diversity, implying a richness of insight that offers many opportunities for conversation. In my judgment, the present discussions issue from an enriching diversity that brings life to ancient texts. At times, representatives of these approaches engage in dialogue, but too often they either ignore or criticize each other. When serious conversation does not occur, there is a significant loss for the entire discipline.

The primary question that stimulates all Old Testament theology is the knowledge of God and how it is obtained. And here is a major area of disagreement. Where does the knowledge of God reside: behind the text in the social location of the biblical texts, which in Old Testament theology is only to be described; in the theological approach based on the historical reconstruction of Israel that leads to either a center and a systematic formulation or to a synchronic and diachronic number of understandings of ancient Israel and early Judaism; in the original and then the present community, which interprets the text from its own social location; in the interaction of text and readers, both past and present, that produces meaning; in the dynamic interaction of canon, content, and community; in the experience of the interpreter or the interpreter's group (for example, women's experience); in the narrative world created by the vision of the text; in the imagination of author, or narrator, or interpreter; in the self-interest of the interpreter; in the multivocal expressions that emerge from interconnecting contexts from which each interpreter stands; or in the order and continuation of creation? This theological question resides behind all methodologies and constructions. And it is senseless to think that unanimity will ever be achieved in the securing of a single answer. The days of neoorthodoxy and a consensus of biblical scholar and contemporary theologian belong to a less complex, more simple time. This time is long since past. Due to the diversity of Old Testament theology (not to mention contemporary theology), it is highly doubtful anything approaching an agreement of presentation and understanding will develop. Rather, there are older, more recent, and newly emerging schools of thought. The most one may hope is that the door to dialogue will open wide and not remained closed. It is only through dialogue that a new, changing future of Old Testament theology will emerge.

The survey of Old Testament approaches in this book and in *The Collapse of History* has traced the major developments in theological construction (liberation, creation, canon, feminism, story, imagination, ethnocentrism, Judaism, postcolonialism, and postmodernism), rather than stressing approaches of various elements. Many important perspectives have not been examined, since to do so would create the need for yet a third volume. Even so, what unites the development of the new approaches examined in these two volumes is their incorporation of the two fundamental features of human existence: historicity (including quite broadly questions and matters of cosmos) and language. To deny one in favor of the other or to privilege one while subordinating the other runs counter to what is fundamentally true about what it means to be human. Thus, history and text belong together. While there are important discussions of the meaning of "history" in reference to a field of knowledge about the past and the methods used to recapture plausible understandings of the past, one should not dispense with history in the theological enterprise of reconstructing the major and varied expressions of Israelite and early Jewish faith. To do so is to invent a philosophy (actually revive an old one) in which there is no objective or attainable knowledge and every view is capable of acceptance or rejection. Indeed, theological expressions are beyond criticism. Even the concept of plausibility disappears, since there is no basis for privileging reason and critical inquiry. Once rational analysis is abandoned, we are left with the endless proposals of understandings, some of which are silly and others of which may be dangerous to human existence. I contest directly the view that the diversity of Scripture and theological understandings in the present should begin with a rejection of historical criticism. Rather, the quest to understand the variety of beliefs and the diversity of theological affirmations present in the Bible should be examined and articulated before authentic dialogue leading to modern expressions of faith, also highly diverse, may be articulated. Dialogue cannot occur without understanding the views, traditions, and faith of conversation partners, both past and present. Historical criticism provides a necessary tool to engage the text in conversation. This does not mean that I am naïve enough to think that we do not operate with our own preconceptions of meaning and importance in trying to legitimate them by reference to the text. Yet, at the same time, to abandon history opens wide the gate to "senselessness" and what can only be a theological nihilism expressed within the contours of relativism. However, the question of whether the text, the interpreter, the community, or the context is the major locus for decisions regarding what to believe depends on the theological orientation of a community of faith and its members.

Each of the various approaches to Old Testament theology since World War II has something of value to contribute. However, the power of imagination to create narrative worlds of meaning, whether in history or fiction, provides the greatest potential for conversation between these developing ways of doing Old Testament theology and historical criticism. Narrative history and narrative fiction, as well as theology itself, involve the use of the imagination. And it is the imagination that offers the opportunity both for discourse between historians and literary scholars and for modern readers to enter into the world of the Bible. Of course, I am speaking from my own preference. Others may choose to follow different paths. This should result in conversation, not the avoidance of mutual exchange of understandings.

As I noted in the first volume, the shift to the theme of creation contains at least the recognition that part of the Old Testament cannot be subsumed under the theme of history in any of its understandings. The simplistic view of history and creation as mutually exclusive, long advocated by earlier generations of theologians, is properly discarded for any correct understanding of the Old Testament and contemporary faith. Yet the tension between the two traditions may not be ignored, for it is present in the text itself. The Mighty Warrior of Wright and the Wisdom Goddess of Schüssler Fiorenza both are biblical portrayals of God. The question is whether one wishes to celebrate the pluralism or to attempt to write a more integrative, even systematic, theology that puts these and other understandings of God into critical relationship, for each requires the other for a full explication.

The previous observation raises the question of whether one is content to describe or wishes to relate and then assess critically the various affirmations of the Old Testament texts. I continue to argue that Old Testament theologies may be described by interpreters who recognize there is no single overarching theology, but rather there are many that surface from the depths of the texts. For those who share a common passion for systematic presentation and ultimately constructive theology, these should not eliminate the plurality or too easily place into a hierarchic order protean theological traditions. The world is created through conversation, beginning even in the Bible, not by the imposition of an inflexible order that leads to the suppression of pluralism, and this is true of the canon in the variety of its forms. Theology, to be creative and compelling, needs to retain a tensive quality that produces the regeneration of its spirit. Yet pluralism should not allow theology to descend into the quagmire of relativity and private preference. Also, other understandings present in noncanonical literature and implied by material culture must be given equal weight in setting forth the understandings of theological expression in the biblical world. There are textual indications that these suppressed voices have been all but silenced yet continue to surface in the efforts to construe theological meanings. Careful readings and the examination of material culture allow these silent or barely audible voices to resonate with strong words demanding to be heard.

Biblical theology should take into account the fact that the Bible is at times a patriarchal, racist, and homophobic book that has denied women, ethnic minorities, and homosexuals the right to speak out of their own experiences. This fallen state of the Bible has denied to many their full humanity and has served as an exclusive collection that suppresses a variety of groups. There are ideologies present in Scripture that are demonic. A descriptive approach cannot bring into question and then undermine texts, religious ideas, cultural forms, and social roles and institutions that are stereotypical of and demeaning to marginal and oppressed groups. The necessary step is to use oppressed peoples' experience as a source, even a norm, for the evaluation of biblical theology. But in moving toward a new Old Testament theology, a criteriology is required that includes their experiences as one consideration for constructive work. Hence, the abandonment of reason ends in a mindless void of meaninglessness or unchallenged values and beliefs that belie criticism. Reason and experience, brought to the text, are necessary for the correlation of analysis and evaluation. Thus, liberation theologies of various kinds, ranging from feminism to postcolonialism, provide a significant contribution to new efforts at the reconstruction of theological language, because they open themselves to correlation and judgment.

As noted in *The Collapse of History,* a comparison between narrative fiction and narrative history indicates the two are not so radically different as may have been thought. Both make use of imagination in the presentation of plot, though fiction's imagination is productive, thus leaving to the narrator more license in the telling of the tale, while historical imagination is reproductive. Thus, e.g., a biblical narrative like the book of Ruth may be understood as fiction, while John Bright's *A History of Israel* attempts to be a narrative history that uses reproductive imagination, even though his neoconservative, southern brand of Presbyterianism is unmistakable in his presentation. At the same time, both fiction and history may adopt the same four types of plot: romance, tragedy, comedy, and satire. However, even when one assesses the book of Ruth according to literary methods that include Alter's close reading approach, one cannot ignore the culture that gives rise to the text and the changing contexts, which have shaped it. This is the fatal weakness of Alter's approach, for it eliminates context from the equation. Context, including both text and reader, contributes to and shapes meaning, indeed is inseparable from understanding, just as assuredly as repetitions of types of scenes, words, and motifs. To ignore these multiple contexts is to distort any process of proper interpretation. Historical-critical method and social scientific analysis of modern culture provide access to these various contexts. The search for the synchronic should not negate the equal importance of the diachronic in any new hermeneutic. Theology and culture are intrinsically inseparable.

Serious consideration of issues of text and language does not necessarily lead to an either-or decision for literary study as opposed to historical criticism. Historical criticism, including genre analysis, establishes the necessary distance between the biblical worlds and the modern reader. Distanciation is the critical and needed intersection between first and second naïveté. Yet, once distance is properly secured and narrative analysis takes place, the entrance into the linguistic worlds of the Bible may occur, leading to the engagement of life and faith. Further, religious life is one of faith in the process of becoming and ritual practices that symbolically portray what is theologically affirmed. Narrative theology properly moves one away from the one-sided notion that faith is a system of correct doctrines to be believed to the view of faith as a journey in process that passes through a variety of collapsing and emerging worlds. And it is through the many entrances into the various worlds of the Bible, through conversation with other experiences of the biblical stories, and through dialogues with cultures past and present that the believer's faith is constructed, deconstructed, and reconstructed. This does not mean that conceptualization of symbols, metaphors, and themes in the Old Testament should not take place, at least at the next level of theological discourse. This is a necessary step in order to do systematic theology in the contemporary period, but it is also necessary for biblical theologians, if indeed they wish to move beyond the enormous variety and nuances of literally thousands of texts and distill them into major understandings. Only then can these conceptions be scrutinized critically and ultimately used in constructive theological work in the present.

I have been especially critical of postmodernism, not because of some disguised conservatism or a reactionary concern to hold on to past methods I have learned and practiced. Rather, I have two major concerns with postmodernism. The first is its celebration of "senselessness" and the view that all meaning is constructed by a person shaped by and living within a variety of contexts and issues forth from and captures his or her own self-interest. The second is the cavalier treatment of truth as something that is not objective, but rather is the invention of a person operating out of self-interest. If reason and truth are in effect negated, then there is the moral issue that appears in the question, How do I assess the rightness or wrongness of a position—say, for example, fascism, the denial of humanity to groups not like me, or domination of the weak? One may ask, "What is the basis on which to oppose imperialism, neocolonialism, genocide, sexism, racism, and homophobia?" Postmodernism seduces us into the black hole of nothingness. In its quest to reject authoritarianism, postmodernism ironically has opened wide the gate to this same evil. Postmodernism allows authoritarianism to enter and provide the basis on which to deprecate all human values and any human groups it so chooses.

Old Testament theology in whatever form should address contemporary issues. The very questions that are posed to the text arise out of the contemporary world and the interpreter's community, either religious or secular, or both. To ignore these questions of contemporary meaning and still to claim to engage in Old Testament theology is both impossible and self-deceptive. Indeed, the very effort to produce an Old Testament theology is an antiquated enterprise that is rendered unachievable. The two volumes I have produced are nothing more than curiosities that are lacking in value.

Constructing a Paradigm for Old Testament Theology

Descriptive versus Constructive Presentation

Old Testament theology should be both descriptive and constructive. That is, it should attempt to reflect as accurately as possible the theology of the Old Testament texts but then move on to constructive work that attempts to valorize their ethical judgments and theological representations, if and when these are appropriate for the modern communities of faith in the construction of their faith and moral behavior. No biblical theology can by the very nature of the enterprise be purely descriptive, since the questions that are addressed to the text and the means of interpretation arise from the interpreter and his or her contemporary world. Furthermore, the interpreter's own subjective self, shaped by class, location, and values, is inevitably involved in the knowing process. This does not mean, however, that the interpreter may redescribe tendentiously the content of biblical theology according to subjective whim. Critical reason should provide some limits to the extremes of subjectivism, if the enterprise of Old Testament theology is to take seriously the voices of the text, the cultural data, and their context.

A constructive rendering of Old Testament theology begins with recognizing the importance of Gadamer's articulation of distanciation and second naïveté.[1] According to Gadamer, interpretation is a moral conversation with a classic text, a conversation shaped from the beginning by practical concerns about application that emerge from the interpreter's present culture and its questions. Hence, systematic theology is the fusion of the whole of the past with the present; that is, if interpretation is successful, the visions of the contemporary culture fuse with the visions of the classic text. There are multiple fusions of the horizons emerging from the very practical questions we as human beings bring to the text and the text itself. Yet the process for fusion of horizons is dialogical, for it involves the questions and answers of cultural experience, those of different cultures and social locations, and those of the Bible.

A constructive rendering of the material by necessity requires critical-reflective interaction. Once a systematic presentation and fusion of horizons occur, an evaluation must be given. This reflective, critical rendering allows for choices, based not on the premise of subjective preference, but rather on the grounds of sound and clear criteria. These include the criteria of adequacy, coherence, and the correlation with human experience. These criteria test the validity of the fusion of visions that emerge from the hermeneutical rendering of biblical theology. Obviously, these criteria and their testing are rational discourse, but I am hard pressed to sacrifice Apollo on the altar of Dionysus in order to engage in a bacchanalia of deconstruction that rushes headlong into meaninglessness. Of course, the systematization of the biblical traditions should not eliminate the pluralism inherent in the text. And the alternative visions shaped by the voices of culture, which were not privileged with canonical inclusion, should be heard and included in the conversation. But at the same time, pluralism

---

1. Gadamer, *Truth and Method.*

should not be allowed to paralyze an intelligent rendering of the theologies of the biblical traditions in a way that makes sense and may be compelling.

All of this means that biblical theologians must begin to make the effort to become more theologically literate. As biblical scholars who possess some sense of the importance of public discourse, we must learn to read texts and visions that are not simply within the past domain of history but also that are beyond the Bible and eventuate in the consciousness of modern cultures. This means we must attempt to become theologically literate in order to become familiar with the horizons of meaning that historical and modern cultures produce. Otherwise, the questions we bring to the text and the answers we discover are highly subjective and unavoidably individualistic. And if we wish contemporary theologians to have access to and even use our material, we must assist them to do so, and not continue to hide behind the technical jargon of our complex disciplines. This does not indicate we should replace contemporary theology with a constructive biblical theology, but it is obvious that serious dialogue between the two groups would enrich them both.

A Paradigm for Old Testament Theology: A Proposal

Is Old Testament theology a discipline that originates within theology, or is it more a history of Israelite religion that sets forth the ideas, values, and beliefs of an ancient community? This has been the fundamental question for the past two centuries.[2] But no major approach that has developed since World War II has cast its lot totally with one or the other of these two options. Indeed, new work in the approach to biblical theologies by means of the History of Religion is engaging and promising in assisting the entire enterprise of biblical theology. With the exception of postmodernism, the goal of each new approach has been to allow Scripture to lead into contemporary hermeneutics, without completely sacrificing historical particularity.[3] To accomplish this overall goal, theological work on the Bible should proceed through no less than four successive stages. I readily admit this is a rational construct, but then I know of no other way of setting forth an argument.

Before beginning the task, however, I consider it to be critically important for the theologian to engage in self-disclosure. A candid description

---

2. The variety of factors that are to characterize new biblical theologies have been listed and explicated by Jeanrond, "Criteria for New Biblical Theologies." This entire issue is important in discussing "The Bible and Christian Theology," to state its title. The issue of *Journal of Religion* in which this article appears is edited by John J. Collins.

3. Ollenburger, "Biblical Theology," 50.

of one's own identity shaping values, cultural location, interacting networks of influence, ideological preferences, and social roles should precede the work of description and construction. This disclosure allows the readers to gain some insight into the interpreter and the interpreter some insight into the influences operative in the act of interpretation. Objectivity as an approach to interpretation may be an ideal, but it is hampered by a variety of factors that shape the understanding and meaning of the texts.

The first stage of theological interpretation articulates the more convincing possible meanings, which derive from understanding texts in their historical and cultural context. This produces the diversity of the meanings of implied author, text, and implied audience within their historical and cultural contexts. This task is primarily historical and descriptive and acknowledges the significant diversity and particularity present in the canon and the biblical world in which the canonical texts were created. This stage requires the activation of the imagination of the modern interpreter who follows the canons of exegetical interpretation in offering probable readings of texts.

The second stage is conceptualization of the multiple images, ideas, and themes, which leads to the systematic rendering of the multiple theologies of Old Testament texts within the dynamic matrix of creation and history. The natures and activities of God, the differing understandings of space and time in creation and history, and the natures and behaviors of humanity are conceptualized and then integrated into a narrative or system of themes capable of being understood. The unifying themes for this systematic presentation, in my own approach, include, first of all, the sovereignty and providence of God who shapes and sustains in righteousness and compassion both cosmos and history and the humane and immanent deity who is present in the world. The meaning of human history derives in part from the meaning of creation. And the meaning of creation shapes human history. The second theme is the *imago Dei,* or the view that all humans are made in the divine image and deserving by this inclusion of justice and honor. This does not mean I am advocating a return to a thematic approach that operates with a center. But it does mean that these are the dominant theological themes that emerge in multiple forms from the Bible and the cultures in which the canonical texts assumed their shape. Pluralism should not be eliminated, but through the evaluation of the multiple theologies of the biblical texts by accepted criteriology, an adequate, cogent, and coherent Old Testament theology should emerge.

The third stage is perhaps the most difficult, but it is critically important. This stage envisions the recognition of how biblical texts and their theologies have been construed within the history of interpretation. This process shapes the meaning of texts placed in new settings, and the ever-changing meaning of texts influences the modern interpreter and his or her contemporary setting. We have the responsibility to engage the understandings of the faith of earlier generations who also sought to articulate their faith in dialogue with the biblical text and their cultural contexts and with the generations that preceded them.

Finally, in the fourth stage, hermeneutics requires critical reflection in order to correlate the theologies of the Old Testament and past interpretations with the horizons of meaning that derive from contemporary discourse involving theology, ethics, self-interest, and moral issues of pressing concern. This necessitates serious conversation with contemporary theology and with the interpreter's own theological tradition. It means that the context and identity of the interpreter need to be clearly articulated and set forth as acknowledged components in the conversation. This position requires that the text should enable believing communities to engage in theological reflection on their practical life in the present. And it also means that Old Testament theology should be critically evaluated in the light of modern hermeneutics, even as modern hermeneutics should be open to critical evaluation by Scripture and the history of its interpretation.

To abandon critical evaluation is to obstruct the possibility of dialogue between biblical, historical, and contemporary theologians. While postmodernism has warned us against the possibility of the reification of knowledge as something that is objective and to be comprehended and the dangers of absolutism and the authoritarianism to which it may lead, we are still heirs of the Enlightenment. And we are in part, at least, the products, not simply of an ungrounded culture, but of history. To deny history is to deny a substantial feature of what it means to be human. We cannot pretend the Enlightenment did not take place and hastily move into a major epistemological transformation in all areas of human knowledge, from the sciences to the humanities, to philosophy, and to religion. And we cannot pretend we have not been formed, in a major way, by these epistemologies. We should not attempt to return to a pre-Enlightenment worldview, a first naïveté that is devoid of the canons of reason, or to reject the epistemology of reason to move into to a modern "anti-epistemology" that repudiates, in the final analysis, all ways of obtaining knowledge that may be evaluated. Relativity is not the proper alternative to absolutism. Rather, rational discourse leading to an understanding of the Bible, the traditions of the church, and the views of their multiple contexts through the centuries leads to a variety of possible theological positions articulated in the past. It then becomes our responsibility as believers and practitioners in the present to articulate our views of the faith in conversation with others, past and present, Christian and non-Christian, in ways that become guides to faith and moral discernment. We do so as members of believing communities, where this dialogue continues internally and becomes a matrix that invites conversation with those outside the community.

The stakes are high. For instance, to begin with the acceptance of the value of human life and human dignity that is theologically expressed in the *imago Dei* is fundamental to how believing communities act out their faith and its ramifications in daily existence. The *imago Dei* moves beyond the canons of empirical experience and rational inquiry to an affirmation of faith that, to use Barth's language, involves the encounter with the Word that requires a yes-or-no response. Those who value humanity in all of its expressions will respond with a resounding yes. Reason returns to allow us to make informed judgments about the implications of fundamental beliefs in the faith and practice of the church.

Certainly, we may and should engage critically earlier understandings of faith and practice. The key word is *criticism,* that is, a process of intellectual inquiry, evaluation, and decision grounded in the epistemology of reason and experience. To abandon a combined reason and experience as the mode of understanding leads to obscurantism and/or intellectual chaos that undermines all social constructions of reality, every system of moral behavior, and any attempt to engage in the quest for understanding and discourse with cultures past and present. To abandon criticism also means that the Bible or anything else, for that matter, will contribute absolutely nothing to theological conversation in the present. Indeed, the final result is that nothing "means," except what the individual is disposed to affirm, something I would regard as an unfortunate, debilitating solipsism.

Furthermore, epistemology and the construction of faith may be used together but are not to replace each other. Faith ultimately must move beyond reason and human understanding to an affirmation of important beliefs concerning the nature and existence of God, humanity, and the world. Articulations of faith, of course, are subject to criticism and discourse. I return to the value placed on human life in the divine image that is a theological affirmation. This affirmation cannot abrogate responsibility for respecting and supporting human nature and existence in all of its features. Thus, human life in the divine image repudiates opposing and hierarchical arrangements of people according to gender, sexual preference, race, and cultural contexts. To affirm the *imago Dei* is to reject divisions of human beings, to negate evaluations of superior/inferior based on ethnicity, gender, and sexual preference, and to actualize faithful behavior that respects all human beings and actively works to support and enhance the lives of all human beings. While reason may and should be used to evaluate the intricacies of faith, faith itself moves beyond reason and experience into the category of belief. We begin with faith and then move into theological discourse to establish the ways of understanding and actualizing what we believe.

In spite of the enormous diversity that exists among theologians, historical theologians, and biblical scholars, discourse and dialogue together comprise the *sine qua non* of faith and the ways we seek to understand it. This is the rationale behind the series I am editing, the Library of Biblical Theology, in which biblical theologians, historical theologians, contemporary theologians of the church and Jewish theologians engage in serious dialogue to seek to encounter the faith of their forebears, to engage them in conversation, and then to participate in conversation with others in the contemporary world.[4] Out of this mix emerges a faith articulate.

It is as naïve to think that contemporary theologians have the capacity to move unaided into biblical theology as it is to think that biblical theologians can address questions of modern import without assistance from contemporary theologians. This involves risk for biblical scholars and systematic theologians, but so what? To borrow a phrase from Peter Berger, the plausibility of meaning systems "hangs together by the thin thread of conversation," in this case linking contemporary, historical, and biblical theologians.[5]

Finally, there is, to borrow a phrase from Kant, "the moral imperative." The huge influence of the Bible on world cultures has led to the permeation of its ideas and practices, both humane and destructive. When the Bible presents views that are sexist, racist, homophobic, militaristic, vicious, and neocolonial, in a word, inhumane and thus opposed to the well-being of creation and creatures, then these must be strongly opposed. To sit back in silence, either as proponents of "objective" scholarship or as adherents of a so-called nonobjectified knowledge that is immersed in self-interest or as nihilists who reject ethical ideals by denying they can be transmuted into common values, is to countenance the demonic behavior of racists, sexists, homophobes, militarists, terrorists, and fascists to which an unchallenged Bible, theology, and worldview ultimately lead. This is a silence that we cannot and must not tolerate, if we expect not only to live authentically, but also to exist responsibly. The antiworld of chaos awaits those who refuse to engage in critical reaction to the biblical text and their own interpretations, for this lack of self-criticism can only lead to a vacuous

---

4. I am the general editor of the series, while James Dunn and Michael Welker are coeditors, and Walter Brueggemann is a consultant overseeing this project. The sixteen volumes will be published over the next several years by Abingdon Press.

5. Berger, *The Sacred Canopy.* See especially the chapters "Religion and World-Construction," and "Religion and World-Maintenance," 3–51.

mind that descends into the abyss of oppression, abuse, and destruction of the world and its living creatures.

Theology seeks to understand God, not simply as a part of a compendium of knowledge, but rather as a means of achieving, however imperfectly, a relationship that determines self-identity within the locations in which humans live and carry out their search for meaning. The approaches I have described and evaluated are normally carefully construed and often lead to provocative attempts at this achievement. If they are carried out with skill and hard thinking about life in the cosmos and in the human world, then there can be only a good end. And it is here that the matter comes to its conclusion, as we recognize that in the ever-continuing quest to come to a knowledge of God, we find ourselves once again in the beginning.

Bibliography

Abraham, Koshy. *Prajapati: The Cosmic Christ*. Delhi: ISPCK, 1997.

Ackermann, Susan. "'And the Women Knead Dough': The Worship of the Queen of Heaven in Sixth-Century Judah." In *Women in the Hebrew Bible*, edited by Alice Bach, 21–32. London: Routledge, 1999.

Ackroyd, Peter R. "The Theology of the Chronicler." In idem, *The Chronicler in His Age*, 273–89. JSOTSup 101. Sheffield: Sheffield Academic, 1991.

Adam, A. K. M. *What Is Postmodern Biblical Criticism?* GBS. Minneapolis: Fortress Press, 1995.

Adorno, Theodor W. *Zur Metakiritk der Erkenntnistheorie: Drei Studien zu Hegel*. Gesammelte Schriften 5. Frankfurt: Suhrkamp, 1970.

———. *Zur Metakritik der Erkenntnistheorie: Studien über Husserl und die phänomenologischen Antinomien*. Frankfurt: Suhrkamp, 1972.

Ahlström, Gösta. *The History of Ancient Palestine from the Palaeolithic Period to Alexander's Conquest*. JSOTSup 146. Sheffield: JSOT Press, 1993.

Ajayi, J. F. A., and Michael Crowder. "West Africa 1919–1939: The Colonial Situation." In *History of West Africa* 2, edited by J. F. A. Ajayi and Michael Crowder, 514–41. New York: Columbia Press, 1973.

Albertz, Rainer. "Hat die Theologie des Alten Testaments doch noch eine Chance?" *JBTh* 10 (1995) 177–87.

———. *A History of Israelite Religion in the Old Testament Period*. 2 vols. Translated by John Bowden. Louisville: Westminster John Knox, 1994.

———. "Jahwe allein! Israels Weg zum Monotheismus und dessen theologische Bedeutung." In *Geschichte und Theologie: Studien zur Exegese des Alten Testaments und zur Religionsgeschichte Israels*, edited by Ingo Kottsieper and Jakob Wöhrle, 359–82. BZAW 326. Berlin: de Gruyter, 2003.

———. *Persönliche Frömmigkeit und offizielle Religion: Religionsinterner Pluralismus in Israel und Babylon*. Stuttgart: Calwer, 1978.

———. "Religionsgeschichte Israels statt Theologie des Alten Testaments! Plädoyer für eine forschungsgeschichtliche Umorientierung." *JBTh* 10 (1995) 3–24.

Albrektson, Bertil. *History and the Gods: An Essay on the Idea of Historical Events as Divine Manifestations in the Ancient Near East and in Israel*. ConBOT 1. Lund: Gleerup, 1967.

Alt, Albrecht. "The God of the Fathers." In *Essays on Old Testament History and Religion*, 1–77. Translated by R. A. Wilson. Oxford: Blackwell, 1968.

Alter, Robert. *The Art of Biblical Narrative*. New York: Basic Books, 1981.

———. *The Art of Biblical Poetry*. New York: Basic Books, 1985.

Anderson, Bernhard W. "Response to Matitiahu Tsevat 'Theology of the Old Testament—A Jewish View.'" *HBT* 8 (1986) 51–59.

Anderson, G. W. "Hebrew Religion." In *The Old Testament and Modern Study: A Generation of Discovery and Research*, edited by H. H. Rowley, 283–310. London: Oxford Univ. Press, 1951.

Anderson, Janice Capel. "Mapping Feminist Biblical Criticism: The American Scene, 1983–1990." *CRBR* 4 (1991) 21–44.

Ashcroft, Bill, Gareth Griffiths, and Helen Tiff. *Key Concepts in Post-Colonial Studies*. London: Routledge, 1998.

Austin, J. L. *How to Do Things with Words*. William James Lectures 1955. Cambridge: Harvard Univ. Press, 1962.

———. *Philosophical Papers*. Oxford: Clarendon, 1961.

———. *Sense and Sensibilia*. Oxford: Clarendon, 1962.

Azariah, Masilamani. "Doing Theology in India Today." In *Readings in Indian Christian Theology* 1, edited by Cecil Hargreaves and R. S. Sugirtharaja, 37–45. New Delhi: ISPCK, 1993.

Bach, Alice. "Introduction: Man's World, Women's Place. Sexual Politics in the Hebrew Bible." In *Women in the Hebrew Bible*, edited by Alice Bach, xiii–xxvi. London: Routledge, 1999.

———, ed. *The Pleasure of Her Text: Feminist Readings of Biblical and Historical Texts*. Philadelphia: Trinity International Press, 1990.

———. *Women, Seduction, and Betrayal in Biblical Narrative*. Oxford: Oxford Univ. Press, 1997.

Bächli, Otto. *Das Alte Testament in der Kirchlichen Dogmatik von Karl Barth*. Neukirchen-Vluyn: Neukirchener, 1987.

Bailey, Leon. *Critical Theory and the Sociology of Knowledge: A Comparative Study in the Theory of Ideology*. American University Studies 11. Sociology/Anthropology 62. New York: Lang, 1994.

Bailey, Randall C. "Academic Biblical Interpretation among African Americans in the United States." In *African Americans and the Bible: Sacred Texts and Sacred Textures*, 696–711. New York: Continuum, 2000.

———, ed. *Yet with a Steady Beat: Contemporary U.S. Afrocentric Biblical Interpretation*. Semeia Studies 42. Atlanta: Society of Biblical Literature, 2003.

Baker-Fletcher, Karen. *Sisters in the Wilderness: The Challenge of Womanist God-Talk*. Maryknoll, N.Y.: Orbis, 1993.

Baker-Fletcher, Karen, and Garth Kasimu Baker-Fletcher. *My Sister, My Brother: Womanist and Xodus God-Talk*. Eugene, Ore.: Wipf and Stock, 2002.

Bakhtin, M. M. *Problems of Dostoevsky's Poetics*, 2d ed. Translated by R. W. Rotsel. Ann Arbor: Ardis, 1973.

———. *Speech Genres and Other Late Essays*. Translated by Vern W. McGee. Edited by Caryl Emerson and Michael Holquist. Univ. of Texas Press Slavic Series 8. Austin: Univ. of Texas Press, 1986.

Bal, Mieke, ed. *Anti-Covenant: Counter-Reading Women's Lives in the Hebrew Bible.* JSOTSup 81. Sheffield: JSOT Press, 1989.

———. *Death and Dissymmetry: The Politics of Coherence in the Book of Judges.* CSHJ. Chicago: Univ. of Chicago Press, 1988.

———. *Lethal Love: Feminist Literary Readings of Biblical Love Stories.* ISBL. Bloomington: Indiana Univ. Press, 1987.

———. *Murder and Difference: Gender, Genre, and Scholarship on Sisera's Death.* ISBL. Bloomington: Indiana Univ. Press, 1988.

———. *Narratology: Introduction to the Theory of Narrative,* 2d ed. Toronto: Univ. of Toronto Press, 1997.

———. "Postmodern Theology as Cultural Analysis." In *The Blackwell Companion to Postmodern Theology,* edited by Graham Ward, 3–23. BCR 4. Oxford: Blackwell, 2001.

Barbour, Ian. *Myths, Models and Paradigms: A Comparative Study in Science and Religion.* New York: Harper & Row, 1974.

Barr, James. "Biblical Interpretation in an International Perspective." *BibInt* 1 (1993) 67–87.

———. *The Concept of Biblical Theology: An Old Testament Perspective.* Minneapolis: Fortress Press, 1999.

———. *History and Ideology in the Old Testament: Biblical Studies at the End of a Millennium.* The Hensley Henson Lectures 1997, Oxford. Oxford: Oxford Univ. Press, 2000.

———. "The Problem of Old Testament Theology and the History of Religion." *CJT* 3 (1957) 141–49.

Barstad, H. M., and Magnus Ottosson, eds. "The Life and Work of Sigmund Mowinckel." *SJOT* 2 (1988) 1–91.

Barth, Karl. *Church Dogmatics,* 2d ed. Translated and edited by Geoffrey W. Bromiley and T. F. Torrance. Edinburgh: T. & T. Clark, 1975.

———. *The Epistle to the Romans,* 6th ed. Translated by Edwyn C. Hoskyns. London: Oxford Univ. Press, 1933.

Bartholomew, Craig G. "Reading the Old Testament in Postmodern Times." *TynBul* 49 (1998) 91–114.

Bass, D. C. "Women's Studies and Biblical Studies: An Historical Perspective." *JSOT* 22 (1982) 6–12.

Baum, Robert M. *Shrines of the Slave Trade: Diola Religion and Society in Precolonial Senegambia.* Oxford: Oxford Univ. Press, 1999.

Beal, Timothy K. *Religion and Its Monsters.* London: Routledge, 2002.

Benjamin, Don C., and Victor H. Matthews. "Social Sciences and Biblical Studies." *Semeia* 68 (1994[96]) 7–21.

Bentzen, Aage. *King and Messiah,* 2d ed. Translated by G. W. Anderson. Oxford: Blackwell, 1970.

Berger, Peter. *The Sacred Canopy: Elements of a Sociological Theory of Religion.* Garden City, N.Y.: Doubleday, 1967.

Berger, Peter, and Thomas Luckmann. *The Social Construction of Reality: A Treatise in the Sociology of Knowledge.* Garden City, N.Y.: Doubleday, 1966.

Beya, Marie Bernadette Mbuy. "Doing Theology as African Women." *Voices from the Third World* 13 (1990) 153–74.

Beyerlin, Walter, ed. *Religionsgeschichtliches Textbuch zum Alten Testament.* Göttingen: Vandenhoeck & Ruprecht, 1975. ET = *Near Eastern Religious Texts Relating to the Old Testament.* Translated by John Bowden. OTL. Philadelphia: Westminster, 1978.

Bhabha, Homi K. *The Location of Culture.* London: Routledge, 1994.

The Bible and Culture Collective. *The Postmodern Bible.* Edited by George Aichele et al. New Haven: Yale Univ. Press, 1995.

Biondi, Jean-Pierre. *Senghor ou la Tentation de l'universel.* L'Aventure Coloniale de la France. Paris: Denoël, 1993.

Bird, Phyllis A. "The Harlot as Heroine: Narrative Art and Social Presupposition in Three Old Testament Texts." In *Narrative Research on the Hebrew Bible.* *Semeia* 46 (1989) 119–39.

———. "Images of Women in the Old Testament." In *Religion and Sexism,* edited by Rosemary Ruether, 41–88. New York: Simon and Schuster, 1974. Reprinted in Bird 1997: 13–51.

———. *Missing Persons and Mistaken Identities: Women and Gender in Ancient Israel.* OBT. Minneapolis: Fortress Press, 1997.

———. "The Place of Women in the Israelite Cultus." In *Ancient Israelite Religion: Essays in Honor of Frank Moore Cross,* edited by Patrick D. Miller et al., 397–417. Philadelphia: Fortress Press, 1987. Reprinted in Bird 1997: 81–102.

———. "Women's Religion in Ancient Israel." In *Women's Earliest Records: From Ancient Israel and Western Asia,* edited by Barbara S. Lesko, 283–98. BJS 166. Atlanta: Scholars, 1991.

Black, Max. *Models and Metaphors: Studies in Language and Philosophy.* Ithaca, N.Y.: Cornell Univ. Press, 1962.

Bleeker, C. J. "Comparing the Religio-Historical Method and the Theological Method." *Numen* 18 (1971) 9–29.

Bleich, David. *Readings and Feelings: An Introduction to Subjective Criticism.* Urbana, Ill.: National Council of Teachers of English, 1975.

———. *Subjective Criticism.* Baltimore: Johns Hopkins Univ. Press, 1978.

Boadt, Lawrence, Helga Croner, and Leon Klenicki, eds. *Biblical Studies: Meeting Ground of Jews and Christians.* New York: Paulist, 1980.

Boehmer, Elleke. *Colonial and Postcolonial Literature: Migrant Metaphors.* Oxford: Oxford Univ. Press, 1995.

Boff, Leonardo, and Clodovis Boff. *Introducing Liberation Theology.* Translated by Paul Burns. Maryknoll, N.Y.: Orbis, 1987.

Boling, Robert G. *Judges: Introduction, Translation, and Commentary.* AB 6A. Garden City, N.Y.: Doubleday, 1975.

Bonino, José Míguez. *Doing Theology in a Revolutionary Situation.* Confrontation Books. Philadelphia: Fortress Press, 1975.

Booth, Wayne C. *A Rhetoric of Irony.* Chicago: Univ. of Chicago Press, 1974.

Bourguet, Daniel. *Des Metaphores de Jeremie.* EBib 9. Paris: Gabalda, 1987.

Bousset, Wilhelm. *Die Religion des Judentums im späthellenistischen Zeitalter,* 3d ed. Edited by Hugo Gressmann. Tübingen: Mohr/Siebeck, 1926.

———. *Religionsgeschichtliche Studien: Aufsätze zur Religionsgeschichte des hellenistischen Zeitalters.* Edited by Anthonie F. Verheule. NovTSup 50. Leiden: Brill, 1979.

Boyarin, Daniel. *Intertextuality and the Reading of Midrash*. ISBL. Bloomington: Indiana Univ. Press, 1990.

———. *A Radical Jew: Paul and the Politics of Identity*. Berkeley: Univ. of California Press, 1994.

Brannigan, John. *New Historicism and Cultural Materialism: Transitions*. New York: St. Martin's, 1998.

Brenner, Athalya. *Are We Amused? Humour about Women in the Biblical Worlds*. JSOTSup 383. London: T. & T. Clark, 2003.

———. *The Israelite Woman: Social Role and Literary Type in Biblical Narrative*. BibSem 2. Sheffield: JSOT Press, 1985.

Brenner, Athalya, and Carole Fontaine, eds. *A Feminist Companion to Reading the Bible: Approaches, Methods and Strategies*. Sheffield: Sheffield Univ. Press, 1997.

Brenner, Athalya, and Fokkelien van Dijk-Hemmes, eds. *On Gendering Texts: Female and Male Voices in the Hebrew Bible*. BibIntSer 1. Leiden: Brill, 1993.

———, eds. *Reflections on Theology and Gender*. Kampfen, NL: Kok Paros, 1994.

Brenner, Athalya, and Jan Willem van Henten, eds. *Bible Translation on the Threshold of the Twenty-First Century: Authority, Reception, Culture and Religion*. JSOTSup 353. London: Sheffield Academic, 2002.

Brettler, Marc Zvi. "Biblical History and Jewish Biblical Theology." *JR* 77 (1997) 563–83.

———. *The Creation of History in Ancient Israel*. London: Routledge, 1995.

Brooten, Bernadette J. "Early Christian Women and Their Cultural Context: Issues of Method in Historical Reconstruction." In *Feminist Perspectives on Biblical Scholarship*, edited by Adela Yarbro Collins, 65–91. BSNA 10. Chico, Calif.: Scholars, 1985.

———. *Love Between Women: Early Christian Responses to Female Homoeroticism*. Chicago Series on Sexuality, History, and Society. Chicago: Univ. of Chicago Press, 1996.

———. *Women Leaders in the Ancient Synagogue: Inscriptional Evidence and Background Issues*. BJS 36. Chico, Calif.: Scholars, 1982.

Brown, David Blayney. *Romanticism*. London: Phaidon, 2001.

Brown, Robert McAfee. *Gustavo Gutiérrez: An Introduction to Liberation Theology*. Maryknoll, N.Y.: Orbis, 1990.

Bruce, F. F. "The Theology and Interpretation of the Old Testament." In *Tradition and Interpretation*, edited by G. W. Anderson, 385–416. Oxford: Clarendon, 1979.

Brueggemann, Walter. "Biblical Theology Appropriately Postmodern." In *Jews, Christians, and the Theology of the Hebrew Scriptures*, edited by Alice Ogden Bellis and Joel S. Kaminsky, 97–108. SBLSymSer 8. Atlanta: Scholars, 2000.

———. "Jews and Christians in Biblical Studies." In *Hebrew Bible or Old Testament? Studying the Bible in Judaism and Christianity*, edited by Roger Brooks and John J. Collins, 109–45. CJA 5. Notre Dame: Univ. of Notre Dame Press, 1990.

———. *Texts under Negotiation: The Bible and Postmodern Imagination*. Minneapolis: Fortress Press, 1993.

———. *Theology of the Old Testament: Testimony, Dispute, Advocacy*. Minneapolis: Fortress Press, 1997.

Buber, Martin. *Kingship of God*. Translated by Richard Scheimann. New York: Harper and Row, 1967.

―――. *Prophetic Faith*. Translated by Carlyle Witton-Davies. New York: Harper & Row, 1960.

Burnham, Frederic B., ed. *Postmodern Theology: Christian Faith in a Pluralist World*. San Francisco: Harper & Row, 1989.

Buttrick, George. *Interpreter's Dictionary of the Bible*. 4 vol. 1962.

Camp, Claudia. *Wisdom and the Feminine in the Book of Proverbs*. BLS 11. Decatur, Ga.: Almond, 1985.

Cannon, Katie. *Katie's Canon: Womanism and the Soul of the Black Community*. New York: Continuum, 1996.

Carr, Anne. *Transforming Grace: Christian Tradition and Women's Experience*. San Francisco: Harper & Row, 1987.

Carroll, Robert P. "New Historicism and Postmodernism." In *The Cambridge Companion to Biblical Interpretation*, 50–66. Cambridge Companions to Religion. Cambridge: Cambridge Univ. Press, 1998.

Carter, Charles E. "A Discipline in Transition: The Contributions of the Social Sciences to the Study of the Hebrew Bible." In *Community, Identity, and Ideology: Social Science Approaches to the Hebrew Bible*, edited by Charles F. Carter and Carol Meyers, 3–36. Winona Lake, Ind.: Eisenbrauns, 1996.

―――. "Ethnoarchaeology." In *The Oxford Encyclopedia of Archaeology in the Near East*, edited by Eric M. Meyers, 1:280–84. New York: Oxford Univ. Press, 1997.

―――. "Social Scientific Approaches." In *The Blackwell Companion to the Hebrew Bible*, edited by Leo G. Perdue, 36–57. BCR 1. Oxford: Blackwell, 2001.

Carter, Charles E., and Carol L. Meyers, eds. *Community, Identity, and Ideology: Social Science Approaches to the Hebrew Bible*. SBTS 6. Winona Lake, Ind.: Eisenbrauns, 1996.

Causse, Antonin. *Du groupe ethnique à la communauté religieuse: le problème sociologique de la religion d'Israël*. Études d'histoire et de philosophie religieuses 33. Paris: Alcan, 1937.

Césaire, Aimé. "Between Colonizer and Colonized." In *Social Theory: The Multicultural and Classic Readings*, edited by Charles Lemert, 340–42. Boulder, Col.: Westview, 1999.

―――. "Culture and Colonization." In *Presence Africaine: The First International Conference of Negro Writers and Artists* 8–10 (1956) 193–207.

―――. *Discourse on Colonialism*. New York: Monthly Review Press, 1955.

Chatterji, Saral K. "Why Dalit Theology." In *Towards a Dalit Theology*, edited by M. E. Prabhakar. Bangalore: CISRS, 1988.

Childs, Brevard S. *Biblical Theology in Crisis*. Philadelphia: Westminster, 1970.

―――. *Biblical Theology of the Old and New Testaments: Theological Reflection on the Christian Bible*. Minneapolis: Fortress Press, 1993.

Childs, Peter, and Patrick Williams. *An Introduction to Post-Colonial Theory*. London: Harvester and Wheatsheaf, 1997.

Clifford, Anne M. *Introducing Feminist Theology*. Maryknoll, N.Y.: Orbis, 2004.

Clines, David J. A. "Biblical Interpretation in an International Perspective." Biblical Interpretation 1 (1993) 67–87.

————. "The Postmodern Adventure in Biblical Studies." In *Auguries: The Jubilee Volume of the Sheffield Department of Biblical Studies,* edited by David J. A. Clines and Stephen D. Moore, 276–91. JSOTSup 269. Sheffield: Sheffield Academic, 1998.

————. "Why Is There a Book of Job and What Does It Do to You if You Read It?" In *The Book of Job,* edited by W. A. M. Beuken, 1–20. BETL 114. Leuven: Leuven Univ. Press, 1994.

Coats, George W. "Theology of the Hebrew Bible." In *The Hebrew Bible and Its Modern Interpreters,* edited by Douglas A. Knight and Gene M. Tucker, 239–62. Philadelphia: Fortress Press, 1985.

Collingwood, R. G. *History as Imagination,* rev. ed. Oxford: Oxford Univ. Press, 1994.

Collins, Adela Yarbro, ed. *Feminist Perspectives on Biblical Scholarship.* BSNA 10. Chico, Calif.: Scholars, 1985.

Collins, John J. "Is a Critical Biblical Theology Possible?" In *The Hebrew Bible and Its Interpreters,* edited by William Henry Propp et al., 1–17. Biblical and Judaic Studies 1. Winona Lake, Ind.: Eisenbrauns, 1990.

————. *Seers, Sibyls, and Sages in Hellenistic-Roman Judaism.* JSJSup 54. Leiden: Brill, 1997.

Colvin, Lucie Gallistel. *Historical Dictionary of Senegal.* African Historical Dictionaries 23. Meteuchen, N.J.: Scarecrow, 1981.

Cone, James. *Black Theology and Black Power.* New York: Seabury, 1969.

————. *A Black Theology of Liberation.* New York: Lippincott, 1970.

————. *God of the Oppressed.* New York: Seabury, 1975.

Cormaroff, Jean, and John Cormaroff. *Of Revelation and Reason: Christianity, Colonialism, and Consciousness in South Africa.* Chicago: Univ. of Chicago Press, 1991.

Craven, Toni. *Artistry and Faith in the Book of Judith.* SBLDS 70. Chico, Calif.: Scholars, 1983.

————. "Women Who Lied for the Faith." In *Justice and the Holy: Essays in Honor of Walter Harrelson,* edited by Douglas Knight and Peter Paris, 35–49. Atlanta: Scholars Press, 1989.

Crenshaw, James L. *Gerhard von Rad.* Makers of the Modern Theological Mind. Waco: Word, 1978.

Cross, Frank. *Canaanite Myth and Hebrew Epic: Essays in the History of Religion of Israel.* Cambridge: Harvard Univ. Press, 1973.

Crowder, Michael. *Senegal: A Study in French Assimilation Policy.* New York: Oxford Univ. Press, 1962.

————. *West Africa under Colonial Rule.* Evanston: Northwestern Univ. Press, 1968.

Crüsemann, Frank. "Religionsgeschichte oder Theologie? Elementare Überlegungen zu einer falschen Alternative." *JBTh* 10 (1995) 69–77.

Culler, Jonathan. *The Pursuit of Signs: Semiotics, Literature, Deconstruction,* augmented ed. Ithaca, N.Y.: Cornell Univ. Press, 2002.

Daly, Mary. *Beyond God the Father: Toward a Philosophy of Women's Liberation.* Boston: Beacon, 1978.

Darr, Kathryn Pfisterer. *Isaiah's Vision and the Family of God.* Louisville: Westminster John Knox, 1994.

Daube, David. *Studies in Biblical Law.* Oxford: Clarendon, 1947.

David, Nicholas. "Integrating Ethnoarchaeology: A Subtle Realist Perspective." *Journal of Anthropological Archaeology* 11 (1982) 330–59.

David, Nicholas, and Carol Kramer. *Ethnoarchaeology in Action.* Cambridge World Archaeology. Cambridge: Cambridge Univ. Press, 2001.

Davies, Philip R. *In Search of Ancient Israel.* JSOTSup 148. Sheffield: Sheffield Academic, 1992.

Day, Peggy, ed. *Gender and Difference in Ancient Israel.* Minneapolis: Fortress Press, 1989.

Delitzsch, Franz. *Die Lese- und Schreibfehler im Alten Testament.* Berlin: de Gruyter, 1920.

———. *Messianische Weissagungen in geschichtlicher Folge.* Leipzig: Akademische/ Faber, 1890.

Derrida, Jacques. *Dissemination.* Translated by Barbara Johnson. Chicago: Univ. of Chicago Press, 1981.

———. *L'Écriture et différence.* Paris: du Seil, 1967. ET= *Writing and Difference.* Chicago: Univ. of Chicago Press, 1978.

———. *Of Grammatology,* corrected ed. Translated by Gayatri Chakrovorty Spivak. Baltimore: Johns Hopkins Univ. Press, 1998.

Dever, William. "Archaeology and the Religions of Israel." *BASOR* 301 (1996) 83–90.

———. "The Contribution of Archaeology to the Study of Canaanite and Early Israelite Religion." In *Ancient Israelite Religion: Essays in Honor of Frank Moore Cross,* edited by Patrick Miller et al., 209–47. Philadelphia: Fortress Press, 1987.

Dickson, K. A. *Theology in Africa.* London: Darton, Longman and Todd; Maryknoll, N.Y.: Orbis, 1984.

Diebner, Bernd-Jörg. "Die Götter des Vaters." *DBAT* 9 (1975) 21–51.

Dijk-Hemmes, Fokkelien van, and Athalya Brenner, eds. *Reflections on Theology and Gender.* Kampen: Kok Paros, 1994.

Diop, Cheikh Anta. *Precolonial Black Africa: A Comparative Study of the Political and Social Systems of Europe and Black Africa, from Antiquity to the Formation of Modern States.* New York: Lawrence Hill, 1987.

Dohmen, Christoph, and Günter Stemberger. *Hermeneutik der jüdischen Bibel and des Alten Testaments.* 2 vols. Studienbücher Theologie 1, 2. Stuttgart: Kohlhammer, 1996.

Douglas, Mary. *In the Wilderness: The Doctrine of Defilement in the Book of Numbers.* JSOTSup 158. Sheffield: JSOT Press, 1993.

———. *Leviticus as Literature.* Oxford: Oxford Univ. Press, 1999.

———. *Natural Symbols; Explorations in Cosmology.* New York: Pantheon, 1970.

———. *Purity and Danger: An Analysis of the Concepts of Pollution and Taboo.* London: Routledge and Kegan Paul, 1966.

Dube, Musa W. "*Batswakwa:* Which Traveller Are You (John 1:1-18)?" In *The Bible in Africa: Transactions, Trajectories and Trends,* edited by Gerald O. West and Musa W. Dube, 150–62. Leiden, Brill: 2000.

———. "Biblical Interpretation and the Social Location of the Interpreter: African Women's Reading of the Bible." In *Reading from This Place,* edited by Fernando F. Segovia and Mary Ann Tolbert, 2:33–51. Minneapolis: Fortress Press, 1995.

———. "Divining Ruth for International Relations." In *Other Ways of Reading: African Women and the Bible,* edited by Musa W. Dube, 179–95. Atlanta: Scholars, 2001.

———. "Fifty Years of Bleeding: A Storytelling Feminist Reading of Mark 5:24-43." In *Other Ways of Reading: African Women and the Bible,* edited by Musa W. Dube, 50–60. Atlanta: Scholars, 2001.

———. *Introducing African Women's Theology.* Introductions in Feminist Theology 6. Sheffield: Sheffield Academic, 2001.

———. "Introduction: The Fire of the Smoke." In *Daughters of Anowa: African Women and Patriarchy,* edited by Mercy Amba Oduyoye, 1–16. Maryknoll, N.Y.: Orbis, 1995.

———. *Postcolonial Feminist Interpretation of the Bible.* St Louis: Chalice, 2000.

———. "Savior of the World but Not of This World: A Postcolonial Reading of Spatial Construction in John." In *The Postcolonial Bible,* edited by R. S. Sugirtharajah, 118–35. Sheffield: Sheffield Academic, 1998.

———. "To Pray the Lord's Prayer in the Global Economic Era (Matt 6:9-13)." In *The Bible in Africa: Transactions, Trajectories and Trends,* edited by Gerald O. West and Musa W. Dube, 611–30. Leiden: Brill, 2000.

———. "Towards a Postcolonial Feminist Interpretation of the Bible." In *Reading the Bible as Women: Perspectives from Africa, Asia, and Latin America,* edited by Phyllis A. Bird. *Semeia* 78 (1997) 11–26.

Durkheim, Émile. *The Division of Labor in Society.* Translated by George Simpson. Glencoe, Ill.: Free Press, 1933.

———. *Les formes élémentaires de la vie religieuse, le système totemique en Australie.* 4th ed. Paris: Presses Universitaires de France, 1960. ET = *The Elementary Forms of Religious Life.* New York: Free Press, 1995.

———. *Les règles de la méthode sociologique.* Paris: Flammarion, 1988. ET = *The Rules of Sociological Method,* 8th ed. Edited by George E. G. Catlin. New York: Free Press.

Ebeling, Gerhard. "Was heisst 'biblische Theologie'?" In idem, *Wort und Glaube* 1, 69–89. 3d ed. Tübingen: Mohr/Siebeck, 1967.

Eco, Umberto. *The Role of the Reader: Explorations in the Semiotics of Texts.* Bloomington: Indiana Univ. Press, 1979.

Eichhorn, Albert. *Das Abendmahl im Neuen Testament.* Hefte zur Christlichen Welt 36. Leipzig: Mohr/Siebeck, 1898.

Eichrodt, Walther. "Does Old Testament Theology Still Have Independent Significance?" In *The Flowering of Old Testament Theology: A Reader in Twentieth-Century Old Testament Theology, 1930–1990,* edited by Ben C. Ollenburger, Elmer A. Martens, and Gerhard F. Hasel, 30–39. SBTS 1. Winona Lake, Ind.: Eisenbrauns, 1992. Originally published as "Hat die Alttestamentliche Theologie noch selbständige Bedeutung innerhalb der alttestamentlichen Wissenschaft?" *ZAW* 47 (1929) 83–91.

———. *Religionsgeschichte Israels.* Bern: Francke, 1969.

Eissfeldt, Otto. "The History of Israelite-Jewish Religion and Old Testament Theology." In *The Flowering of Old Testament Theology: A Reader in Twentieth-Century Old Testament Theology, 1930–1990,* edited by Ben C. Ollenburger,

Elmer A. Martens, and Gerhard F. Hasel, 20–29. SBTS 1. Winona Lake, Ind.: Eisenbrauns, 1992. Originally published as "Israelitisch-jüdische Religionsgeschichte und alttestamentliche Theologie." *ZAW* 55 (1926) 1–12.

Eldridge, Richard. *The Persistence of Romanticism.* Cambridge: Cambridge Univ. Press, 2001.

Eliade, Mircea. *Myth and Reality.* Translated by Willard R. Trask. New York: Harper & Row, 1963.

———. *The Sacred and the Profane: The Nature of Religion.* Translated by Willard R. Trask. New York: Harcourt, Brace, 1959.

Eliade, Mircea, and Joseph M. Kitagawa, eds. *The History of Religions: Essays in Methodology.* Chicago: Univ. of Chicago Press, 1959.

Engnell, Ivan. *Divine Kingship in the Ancient Near East,* 2d ed. Oxford: Blackwell, 1967.

Exum, J. Cheryl. "'Mother in Israel': A Familiar Figure Reconsidered." In *Feminist Interpretation of the Bible,* edited by Letty Russell, 73–85. Philadelphia: Westminster, 1985.

Exum, J. Cheryl, and Johanna Bos, eds. *Reasoning with the Foxes: Female Wit in a World of Male Power.* Semeia Studies 42. Atlanta: Scholars, 1988.

Exum, J. Cheryl, and David J. A. Clines, eds. *The New Literary Criticism and the Hebrew Bible.* JSOTSup 143. Sheffield: JSOT Press, 1993.

Fanon, Frantz. "Decolonizing, National Culture, and the Negro Intellectual." In *Social Theory: The Multicultural and Classic Readings,* edited by Charles Lemert, 390–95. Boulder, Col.: Westview, 1999.

———. "Racism and Culture." *Presence Africaine: The First International Conference of Negro Writers and Artists* 8–10 (1956) 122–31.

———. *The Wretched of the Earth.* New York: Grove, 1963.

Felder, Cain Hope. *Race, Racism, and the Biblical Narratives.* Facets. Minneapolis: Fortress Press, 2002.

———, ed. *Stony the Road We Trod: African American Biblical Interpretation.* Minneapolis: Fortress Press, 1991.

———. *Troubling Biblical Waters: Race, Class, and Family.* The Bishop Henry McNeal Turner Studies in North American Black Religion 3. Maryknoll, N.Y.: Orbis, 1989.

Ferm, Deane William. *Contemporary American Theologies: A Critical Survey,* rev. ed. San Francisco: Harper & Row, 1990.

Fernades, Walter. "A Socio-Historical Perspective for Liberation Theology in India." In *Leave the Temple: Indian Paths to Human Liberation,* edited by Wilfred Felix, 9–34. Maryknoll, N.Y.: Orbis, 1992.

Ferré, Frederick. "Metaphors, Models, and Religion." *Soundings* 51 (1968) 327–45.

Finkelstein, Israel. "The Emergence of the Monarchy in Israel: The Environmental and Socio-Economic Aspects." *JSOT* 44 (1989) 43–74.

Fish, Stanley E. *Is There a Text in This Class? The Authority of Interpretive Communities.* Cambridge: Harvard Univ. Press, 1980.

Fishbane, Michael. *Biblical Interpretation in Ancient Israel.* Oxford: Oxford Univ. Press, 1995.

———. *Biblical Myth and Rabbinic Mythmaking.* Oxford: Oxford Univ. Press, 2003.

———. *The Exegetical Imagination: On Jewish Thought and Theology.* Cambridge: Harvard Univ. Press, 1998.

———. "Jeremiah IV 23-26 and Job III 3-13: A Recovered Use of the Creation Pattern." *VT* 21 (1971) 151–67.

———, ed. *The Midrashic Imagination: Jewish Exegesis, Thought, and History.* Albany: State University of New York Press, 1993.

Fohrer, Georg. *History of Israelite Religion.* Translated by David E. Green. Nashville: Abingdon Press, 1972.

Ford, David. *Barth and God's Story: Biblical Narrative and the Theological Method of Karl Barth in the Church Dogmatics.* Studien zur interkulturellen Geschichte des Christentums 27. Frankfurt: Lang, 1981.

Forstman, Jack. *Christian Faith in Dark Times: Theological Conflicts in the Shadow of Hitler.* Louisville: Westminster John Knox, 1992.

Foucault, Michel. *The Archaeology of Knowledge and the Discourse on Language.* New York: Pantheon, 1982.

———. *Death and the Labyrinth: The World of Raymond Roussel.* London: Continuum, 2004.

———. *The History of Sexuality.* 3 vols. London: Penguin, 1990–1992.

———. *Power.* Translated by Robert Hurley et al. Edited by James D. Faubion. New York: New Press, 2000.

Frankenberg, Wilhelm and Friedrich Küchler, eds. *Abhandlungen zur semitischen Religionskunde und Sprachwissenschaft, Wolf Wilhelm Grafen von Baudissin zum 26. September 1917 überreicht von Freunden und Schülern und in ihrem Auftrag und mit Unterstützung der Strassburger Cunitzstiftung.* BZAW 33. Giessen: A. Töpelmann, 1918.

Frazer, James G. *The Golden Bough: A Study in Magic and Religion.* Vols. 1–2. London: Macmillan, 1890.

Frerichs, E. S. "The Torah Canon of Judaism and the Interpretation of Hebrew Scripture." *HBT* 9 (1987) 13–25.

Friedl, Ernestine. *Women and Men: An Anthropological View.* New York: Rinehart and Winston, 1975.

Frostin, Per. *Liberation Theology in Tanzania and South Africa: A First World Interpretation.* Lund: Lund Univ. Press, 1988.

Frow, John. *Time and Commodity Culture: Essays in Cultural Theory and Postmodernity.* Oxford: Oxford Univ. Press, 1997.

Frymer-Kensky, Tikva. "The Emergence of Jewish Biblical Theologies." In *Jews, Christians, and the Theology of the Hebrew Scriptures,* edited by Alice Ogden Bellis and Joel S. Kaminsky, 109–21. SBLSymSer 8. Atlanta: Society of Biblical Literature, 2000.

———. *In the Wake of the Goddess.* London: Oxford Univ. Press, 1991.

Fuchs, Esther. "The Literary Characterization of Mothers and Sexual Politics in the Hebrew Bible." In *Feminist Perspectives on Biblical Scholarship,* edited by Adela Yarbro Collins, 117–36. BSNA 10. Chico, Calif.: Scholars, 1985.

———. "Who Is Hiding the Truth? Deceptive Women and Biblical Androcentrism." In *Feminist Perspectives on Biblical Scholarship,* edited by Adela Yarbro Collins, 137–44. BSNA 10. Chico, Calif.: Scholars Press, 1985.

Gabler, J. P. "An Oration on the Proper Distinction between Biblical and Dogmatic Theology and the Specific Objectives of Each." In *The Flowering of Old Testament Theology: A Reader in Twentieth-Century Old Testament Theology,* edited by Ben C. Ollenburger, Elmer A. Martens, and Gerhard F. Hasel, 492–502. SBTS 1. Winona Lake, Ind.: Eisenbrauns, 1992.

Gabriel, James Canjanam. *Dharma in the Hindu Scriptures and in the Bible.* Delhi: ISPCK, 1999.

Gadamer, Hans-Georg. "The Historicity of Understanding." In *The Hermeneutics Reader,* edited by Kurt Mueller-Vollmer, 267–73. New York: Continuum, 1985.

———. *Truth and Method.* 2d ed. Translated by Joel Weinsheimer and Donald G. Marshall. New York: Continuum, 1993.

Gammie, John G., and Leo G. Perdue, eds. *The Sage in Israel and the Ancient Near East.* Winona Lake, Ind.: Eisenbrauns, 1990.

Gandhi, M. K. *The Removal of Untouchability.* Ahmedabad: Navajivan, 1954.

Gates, William Henry. "Ideology and the Interpretation of Scripture in the African-American Christian Tradition." *Modern Theology* 9 (1993) 141–58.

Gerstenberger, Erhard. *Theologies in the Old Testament.* Translated by John Bowden. Minneapolis: Fortress Press, 2002.

Gikandi, Simon. *Maps of Englishness: Writing Identity in the Culture of Colonialism.* New York: Columbia Univ. Press, 1996.

Goodman, Nelson. "Metaphor as Moonlighting." In *On Metaphor,* edited by Sheldon Sacks, 175–80. Chicago: Univ. of Chicago Press, 1979.

Gorman, Frank. *The Ideology of Ritual: Space, Time and Status in the Priestly Theology.* JSOTSup 91. Sheffield: Sheffield Univ., 1990.

Goshen-Gottstein, M. H. "Christianity, Judaism, and Modern Study." In *Congress Volume Edinburgh 1974,* 69–88. VTSup 28. Leiden: Brill, 1975.

———. "Jewish Biblical Theology and the Science of the Bible." *Tarbiz* 50 (1980–81) 37–64. [Heb.]

———. "Tanakh Theology: The Religion of the Old Testament and the Place of Jewish Biblical Theology." In *Ancient Israelite Religion: Essays in Honor of Frank Moore Cross,* edited by Patrick D. Miller et al., 587–644. Philadelphia: Fortress Press, 1987.

Gottwald, Norman. "Poetry, Hebrew." In *IDB* 3 (1962) 829–38.

———. "Reconstructing the Social History of Early Israel." *Eretz-Israel* (Malamat Volume) 24 (1993) 77–82.

———, ed. *Social Scientific Criticism of the Hebrew Bible and Its Social World: The Hebrew Monarchy. Semeia* 37 (1986).

———. *The Tribes of Yahweh: A Sociology of the Religion of Liberated Israel, 1250–1050 B.C.E.* Maryknoll, N.Y.: Orbis, 1979.

Gould, Richard A., and Patty Jo Watson. "A Dialogue on the Meaning and Use of Analogy in Ethoarchaeological Reasoning." *Journal of Anthropological Archaeology* 1 (1982) 355–81.

Govinden, Betty. "Re-imaging God." In *Transforming Power: Women in the Household of God,* edited by Mercy Amba Oduyoye. Proceedings of the Pan-African Conference of the Circle 1996. Accra, Ghana: Sam-Woode, 1997.

Grant, Jacquelyn. *White Women's Christ and Black Women's Jesus: Feminist Christology and Womanist Response*. AARAS 64. Atlanta: Scholars, 1989.

Greenberg, Moshe. *Studies in the Bible and Jewish Thought*. Philadelphia: Jewish Publication Society, 1995.

Gressmann, Hugo. *Die älteste Geschichtsschriebung und Prophetie Israel*, 2d ed. Göttingen: Vandenhoeck & Ruprecht, 1921.

———, ed. *Altorientalische Texte und Bilder zum Alten Testament*, 2d ed. Berlin: de Gruyter, 1926–27.

———. *Der Messias*. FRLANT 43. Göttingen: Vandenhoeck & Ruprecht, 1929.

Gressmann, Hugo, et al. *Entwicklungsstufen der jüdischen Religion*. Giessen: Töpelmann, 1927.

Griffith, Elizabeth. *In Her Own Right: The Life of Elizabeth Cady Stanton*. Oxford: Oxford Univ. Press, 1984.

Groden, Michael, and Martin Kreiswirth, eds. *The Johns Hopkins Guide to Literary Theory and Criticism*. Baltimore: Johns Hopkins Univ. Press, 1994.

Gros Louis, Kenneth R. R., James S. Ackermann, and Thayer S. Warshaw, eds. *The Literary Interpretations of Biblical Narratives*. Nashville: Abingdon, 1974.

Gunkel, Hermann. *Genesis*, 3d ed. Handbuch zum Alten Testament Göttingen: Vandenhoeck & Ruprecht, 1910. ET = *Genesis*. MLBS. Mercer, Ga.: Mercer Univ. Press, 1997.

———. *Israel and Babylon: The Influence of Babylon on the Religion of Israel*. Philadelphia: McVey, 1904.

———. *Die Religionsgeschichte und die alttestamentliche Wissenschaft*. Berlin: Protestantischer Schriftenvertrieb, 1910.

———. *Schöpfung und Chaos in Urzeit und Endzeit: Eine religionsgeschichtliche Untersuchung über Gen 1 und Apoc Joh 12*. Göttingen: Vandenhoeck & Ruprecht, 1895.

Gunneweg, Antonius H. J. *Biblische Theologie des Alten Testaments: Eine Religionsgeschichte Israels in biblisch-theologischer Sicht*. Stuttgart: Kohlhammer, 1993.

———. *Vom Verstehen des Alten Testaments: Eine Hermeneutik*. Göttingen: Vandenhoeck & Ruprecht, 1977.

Gutiérrez, Gustavo. *A Theology of Liberation*. Maryknoll, N.Y.: Orbis, 1971.

———. *We Drink from Our Own Wells: The Spiritual Journey of a People*. Maryknoll, N.Y.: Orbis, 2003.

Guttmann, Julius. "Die Grundzüge der biblischen Religion." In *The Philosophy of Judaism: The History of Jewish Philosophy from Biblical Times to Franz Rosenzweig*, 3–17. New York: Holt, Rinehart, and Winston, 1964.

Habermas, Jürgen. *Erkenntnis und Interresse*. Frankfurt: Suhrkamp, 1968.

———. *The Future of Human Nature*. Cambridge: Polity, 2003.

———. *Knowledge and Human Interests*, 2d ed. Translated by Jeremy J. Shapiro. London: Heinemann, 1978.

———. *The Liberating Power of Symbols: Philosophical Essays*. Translated by Peter Dews. Cambridge: MIT Press, 2001.

———. *Die Moderne, ein unvollendetes Projekt: Philosophisch-Politische Aufsätze*, 3d ed. Leipzig: Reclam, 1994.

———. *Moralbewusstein und kommunikatives Handeln*. Frankfurt: Suhrkamp, 1983.

————. *Multikulturalismus und die Politik der Anerkennung.* Frankfurt: Fischer Taschenbuch, 1997.

————. *Nachmetaphysisches Denken: Philosophische Aufsätze.* Frankfurt: Suhrkamp, 1988.

————. *The Philosophical Discourse of Modernity: Twelve Lectures.* Translated by Frederick G. Lawrence. Cambridge, Mass.: MIT Press, 1987.

————. *Truth and Justification.* Edited and translated by Barbara Fultner. Cambridge, Mass.: MIT Press, 2003.

Hackett, Jo Ann. "Women's Studies and the Hebrew Bible." In *The Future of Biblical Studies: The Hebrew Scriptures,* edited by Richard Elliott Friedman and H. G. M. Williamson, 19–59. Semeia Studies. Atlanta: Scholars, 1987.

Haldar, Alfred. *Associations of Cult Prophets among the Ancient Semites.* Translated by H. S. Harvey. Uppsala: Almqvist & Wiksells, 1945.

Hamilton, Paul. *Historicism: The New Critical Idiom.* London: Routledge, 1996.

Harries, Karsten. "Metaphor and Transcendence." In *On Metaphor,* edited by Sheldon Sacks, 71–88. Chicago: Univ. of Chicago Press, 1979.

Harris, Marvin. *Cultural Materialism: The Struggle for a Science of Culture.* New York: Vintage, 1980.

————. *The Rise of Anthropological Theory: A History of the Theories of Culture,* new ed. Walnut Creek, Calif.: Alta Mira, 2001.

Harvey, David. *Justice, Nature and the Geography of Difference.* Oxford: Blackwell, 1996.

Hasel, Gerhard F. *Old Testament Theology: Basic Issues in the Current Debate,* 4th ed. Grand Rapids: Eerdmans, 1991.

Hauerwas, Stanley. "The Self as Story: A Reconsideration of the Relation of Religion and Morality from the Agent's Perspective." In idem, *Vision and Virtue: Essays in Christian Ethical Reflection,* 68–89. Notre Dame: Fides, 1974.

Hayes, John H., ed. *Dictionary of Biblical Interpretation.* 2 vols. Nashville: Abingdon, 1999.

Hayes, John H., and Frederick C. Prussner. *Old Testament Theology: Its History and Development.* Atlanta: John Knox, 1985.

Hens-Piazza, Gina. *The New Historicism.* GBS. Minneapolis: Fortress Press, 2002.

Herion, Gary A., ed. *Ancient Israel's Faith and History: Introduction to the Bible in Context. Essays in Honor of George E. Mendenhall.* Louisville: Westminster John Knox, 2001.

————. "The Impact of Modern and Social Science Assumptions on the Reconstruction of Israelite History." *JSOT* 34 (1986) 3–33.

Hermisson, Hans-Jürgen. *Alttestamentliche Theologie und Religionsgeschichte Israels.* Forum Theologische Literaturzeitung 3. Leipzig: Evangelische, 2000.

Heschel, Abraham. *The Prophets.* New York: Harper & Row, 1962.

Heyward, Carter. *Touching Our Strength: The Erotic as Power and the Love of God.* San Francisco: Harper & Row, 1989.

Hodgson, Peter. *God in History: Shapes of Freedom.* Nashville: Abingdon, 1989.

Hoffman, Yair. "The Creativity of Theodicy." In *Justice and Righteousness: Biblical Themes and Their Influence,* 117–30, ed. Henning Graf Reventlow and Yair Hoffman. JSOTSup 137. Sheffield: Sheffield Academic, 1992.

Høgenhaven, Jesper. *Problems and Prospects of Old Testament Theology.* BibSem 6. Sheffield: JSOT Press, 1987.

Holter, Knut. "Ancient Israel and Modern Nigeria: Some Remarks from Sidelines to the Socio-Critical Aspect of Nigerian Old Testament Scholarship." Paper read at annual conference of the Nigerian Association for Biblical Studies, Owerri, Nigeria, October 1995.

Honecker, Martin. "Zum Verständnis der Geschichte in Gerhard von Rad's *Theologie des Alten Testaments.*" *EvTh* 23 (1963) 143–68.

Hooke, S. H., ed. *The Labyrinth: Further Studies in the Relation between Myth and Ritual in the Ancient World.* London: SPCK, 1938.

———, ed. *Myth and Ritual: Essays on the Myth and Ritual of the Hebrews in Relation to the Culture Pattern of the Ancient East.* London: Oxford Univ. Press, 1933.

———, ed. *Myth, Ritual, and Kingship.* Oxford: Clarendon, 1958.

Hume, David. *An Enquiry Concerning Human Understanding.* Edited by Tom L. Beauchamp. Oxford: Oxford Univ. Press, 1999.

———. *A Treatise of Human Nature.* Abridged and edited by John P. Wright et al. London: Everyman/Dent, 2003.

Hutcheon, Linda. *A Poetics of Postmodernism: History, Theory, Fiction.* New York: Routledge, 1988.

———. *The Politics of Postmodernism,* 2d ed. London: Routledge, 2002.

Hvidtfeldt, Arild. "History of Religion, Sociology and Sociology of Religion." *Temonos* 7 (1971) 75–89.

Imen, Richard van. "The History of Religion as Social Science." *Telos* 16 (1983) 20–29.

Irwin, William A. "The Study of Israel's Religion." *VT* 7 (1957) 113–26.

Isasi-Díaz, Ada María. "'By the Rivers of Babylon': Exile as a Way of Life." In *Reading from This Place,* edited by Fernando Segovia and Mary Ann Tolbert, 1:149–63. Minneapolis: Fortress Press, 1995.

———. *En la Lucha / In the Struggle: Elaborating a Mujerista Theology.* Minneapolis: Fortress Press, 2004.

———. *Mujerista Theology: A Theology for the Twenty-First Century.* Maryknoll, N.Y.: Orbis, 1996.

Isasi-Díaz, Ada María, and Fernando F. Segovia, eds. *Hispanic/Latino Theology: Challenge and Promise.* Minneapolis: Fortress Press, 1996.

Isasi-Díaz, Ada María, and Yolanda Tarango. *Hispanic Women: Prophetic Voice in the Church: Toward a Hispanic Women's Liberation Theology.* San Francisco: HarperSanFrancisco, 1993.

Iser, Wolfgang. *The Act of Reading: A Theory of Aesthetic Response.* Baltimore: Johns Hopkins Univ. Press, 1978.

Jackson, Jared J., and Martin Kessler, eds. *Rhetorical Criticism: Essays in Honor of James Muilenburg.* PTMS 1. Pittsburgh: Pickwick, 1974.

Jaffee, Martin. *Torah in the Mouth: Writing and Oral Tradition in Palestinian Judaism 200 B.C.E.–400 C.E.* Oxford: Oxford Univ. Press, 2001.

James, E. O. *History of Religions.* New York: Harper, 1957.

———. *Myth and Ritual in the Ancient Near East: An Archaeological and Documentary Study.* New York: Praeger, 1958.

Jameson, Frederic. *The Cultural Turn: Selected Writings on the Postmodern, 1983–1998*. London: Verso, 1998.

———. *Postmodernism, or the Cultural Logic of Late Captialism*. Durham: Duke Univ. Press, 1991.

Janaway, Christopher, ed. *The Cambridge Companion to Schopenhauer*. Cambridge: Cambridge Univ. Press, 1999.

Janowski, Bernd, ed. *Jahrbuch für biblische Theologie* 10 (1995). Neukirchen-Vluyn: Neukirchener Verlag, 1995.

Janowski, Bernd, and Matthias Köckert, eds. *Religionsgeschichte Israels. Formale und Materiale Aspekte*. Veröffentlichungen der Wissenschaftlichen Gesellschaft für Theologie 15. Gütersloh: Chr. Kaiser, 1999.

Japhet, Sara. *The Ideology of the Book of Chronicles and Its Place in Biblical Thought*. BEATAJ 9. Frankfurt: Lang, 1989.

———. "Periodization: Between History and Ideology. The Neo-Babylonian Period in Biblical Historiography." In *Judah and the Judeans in the Neo-Babylonian Period*, edited by Oded Lipschits and Joseph Blenkinsopp, 75–89. Winona Lake, Ind.: Eisenbrauns, 2003.

Jayawardena, Kumari. *Feminism and Nationalism in the Third World*. London: Zed, 1986.

———. *The White Woman's Other Burden: Western Women and South Asia during British Colonial Rule*. New York: Routledge, 1995.

Jeanrond, Werner G. "Criteria for New Biblical Theologies." *JR* 76 (1996) 233–49.

Jenkins, Philip. *The Next Christendom: The Coming of Global Christianity*. Oxford: Oxford Univ. Press, 2002.

Jeremias, Jörg. "Neuere Entwürfe zu einer 'Theologie des Alten Testaments.'" *VF* 48 (2003) 29–58.

Johnson, A. R. *The Cultic Prophet in Ancient Israel*, 2d ed. Cardiff: Univ. of Wales Press, 1962.

———. *Sacral Kingship in Ancient Israel*, 2d ed. Cardiff: Wales Univ. Press, 1967.

Johnson, G. Wesley. *The Emergence of Black Politics in Senegal: The Struggle for Power in the Four Communes, 1900–1920*. Stanford: Stanford Univ. Press, 1971.

Jones, Major J. *Christian Ethics for Black Theology*. Nashville: Abingdon, 1974.

Kairos Theologians (Group). *The Kairos Document: Challenge to the Church. A Theological Comment on the Political Crisis in South Africa*. Grand Rapids: Eerdmans, 1986.

———. *The Road to Damascus: Kairos and Conversion*. Johannesburg: Skotaville, 1989.

Kalimi, Isaac. "Die Bibel und die klassisch-jüdische Bibelauslegung: Eine interpretations- und religionsgeschichtliche Studie." *ZAW* 114 (2002) 594–610.

———. *Early Jewish Exegesis and Theological Controversies: Studies in Scriptures in the Shadow of Internal and External Controversies*. JCHS 2. Assen: Van Gorcum, 2002.

———. "Religionsgeschichte Israels oder Theologie des Alten Testaments? Das jüdische Interesse an der Biblischen Theologie." *JBTh* 10 (1995) 45–68.

Kamionkowski, Tamar. "Jewish Biblical Theology: A Dialogic Model." "Lecture at the SBLAM, 2003."

Kant, Immanuel. *The Critique of Judgment*. Translated by Werner S. Pluhar. Indianapolis: Hackett, 1987.

―――. *The Critique of Practical Reason*. Translated by Werner S. Pluhar. Indianapolis: Hackett, 2002.

―――. *The Critique of Pure Reason*, 2d ed. Translated by Norman Kemp Smith. New York: Palgrave Macmillan, 2003.

Kanyoro, Musimbi R. A., and Nyambura J. Njoroge, eds. *Groaning in Faith: African Women in the Household of God*. Edited by Musimbi R. A. Kanyoro and Nyambura J. Njoroge. Nairobi: Acton, 1996.

Kappen, Sebastian. "Jesus and Transculturation." In *Asian Faces of Jesus*, edited by R. S. Sugirtharaja, 173–88. Maryknoll, N.Y.: Orbis, 1993.

Kaufmann, Yehezkiel. *The Religion of Israel from Its Beginnings to the Babylonian Exile*. Edited and abridged by Moshe Greenberg. Chicago: Univ. of Chicago Press, 1960.

Keel, Othmar. *Die Welt der altorientalischen Bildsymbolik und das Alte Testament: Am Beispiel der Psalmen*. Zurich: Benzinger, 1972.

Keel, Othmar, and Christoph Uehlinger. *Gods, Goddesses, and Images of God in Ancient Israel*. Translated by Thomas H. Trapp. Minneapolis: Fortress Press, 1998.

Kellenbach, Katharina von. *Anti-Judaism in Feminist Religious Writings*. AARCCS 1. Atlanta: Scholars, 1994.

Keller, Catherine. *Face of the Deep: A Theology of Becoming*. London: Routledge, 2003.

Kibicho, S. *The Kikuyu Conception of God, Its Continuity into the Christian Era and the Questions It Raises for the Christian Idea of Revelation*. Thesis, 1973.

Kimbrough, S. T. Jr. *Israelite Religion in Sociological Perspective: The Work of Antonin Causse*. SOR 4. Wiesbaden: Harrassowitz, 1978.

―――. "A Non-Weberian Sociological Approach to Israelite Religion." *JNES* 31 (1972) 197–202.

Klatt, Werner. *Hermann Gunkel: Zu seiner Theologie der Religionsgeschichte und zur Entstehung der formgeschichtlichen Methode*. FRLANT 100. Göttingen: Vandenhoeck & Ruprecht, 1969.

Kliever, Lonnie. *The Shattered Spectrum: A Survey of Contemporary Theology*. Atlanta: John Knox, 1981.

Knauf, E. A. "From History to Interpretation." In *The Fabric of History: Text, Artifact and Israel's Past*, edited by Diana Vikander Edelman, 26–64. JSOTSup 127. Sheffield: Sheffield Academic, 1991.

Knight, Douglas A., ed. *Julius Wellhausen and His Prolegomena to the History of Israel: Collection of Significant Essays*. Semeia 25 (1983).

Köckert, Matthias. *Vätergott und Väterverheissungen: Eine Auseinandersetzung mit Albrecht Alt und seinen Erben*. FRLANT 142. Göttingen: Vandenhoeck & Ruprecht, 1988.

Kramer, Carol, ed. *Ethnoarchaeology: The Implications of Ethnography for Archaeology*. New York: Columbia Univ. Press, 1979.

Krapf, Thomas. *Yehezkel Kaufmann: Ein Lebens-und Erkenntnisweg zur Theologie der Hebräischen Bibel*. Studien zu Kirche und Israel 11. Berlin: Institute Kirche und Judentum, 1990.

Kraus, Hans-Joachim. *Die Biblische Theologie*. Neukirchen-Vluyn: Neukirchener, 1970.

————. *Worship in Israel: A Cultic History of the Old Testament.* Translated by Geoffrey Buswell. Richmond: John Knox, 1966.

Kugel, James. *The Idea of Biblical Poetry.* New Haven: Yale Univ. Press, 1981.

————. "Biblical Studies and Jewish Studies," *Association for Jewish Studies Newsletter* 36 (Fall 1986) 22–24.

Kuhn, Thomas S. *The Structure of Scientific Revolutions.* Chicago: Univ. of Chicago Press, 1970.

Kwok, Pui-lan. "Discovering the Bible in the Non-biblical World." In *Voices from the Margin: Interpreting the Bible in the Third World,* 2d ed., edited by R. S. Sugirtharajah, 289–305. Maryknoll, N.Y.: Orbis, 1995.

————. *Introducing Asian Feminist Theology.* Introductions in Feminist Theology 4. Sheffield: Sheffield Academic, 2000.

Laffey, Alice L. *An Introduction to the Old Testament: A Feminist Perspective.* Philadelphia: Fortress Press, 1988.

Lagarde, Paul de. *Purim: ein Beitrag zur Geschichte der Religion.* Göttingen: Dieterich, 1887.

————. *Semitica.* Göttingen: Dieterich, 1878–79.

Lakoff, George, and Mark Johnson. *Metaphors We Live By.* Chicago: Univ. of Chicago Press, 1980.

Lanczkowski, Günther. *Einführung in die Religionsgeschichte.* Die Theologie. Darmstadt: Wissenschaftliche Buchgesellschaft, 1983.

Leibniz, Gottfried Wilhelm Freiherr von. *Discourse on Metaphysics; and The Monadology.* Translated by George R. Montgomery. Buffalo, N.Y.: Prometheus, 1992.

LeMarquand, Grant. "The Historical Jesus and African New Testament Scholarship." In *Whose Historical Jesus?,* edited by William E. Arnal and Michel R. Desjardins, 161–80. SCJ 7. Waterloo, Ont.: Wilfrid Laurier Univ. Press, 1997.

Lemche, Niels Peter. *The Canaanites and Their Land: The Tradition of the Canaanites.* JSOTSup 110. Sheffield: Sheffield Academic, 1991.

————. "Warum die Theologie des Alten Testaments einen Irrweg darstellt." *JBTh* 10 (1995) 79–92.

Lenski, Gerhard E. "Rethinking Macrosociological Theory." *American Sociological Review* 53 (1988) 163–71.

Lenski, Gerhard E., and Peter Nolan. *Introduction to Human Societies: A Macro-Sociological Approach,* 6th ed. New York: McGraw-Hill, 1991.

Lerner, Gerda. *The Creation of Feminist Consciousness from the Middle Ages to 1870.* Women and History 2. Oxford: Oxford Univ. Press, 1993.

Leuze, Reinhard. "Möglichkeiten und Grenzen einer Theologie der Religionsgeschichte." *Zeitschrift für theologische Forschung und kirchliche Lehre* 4 (1978) 230–43.

Levenson, Jon D. *Creation and the Persistence of Evil: The Jewish Drama of Divine Omnipotence.* San Francisco: Harper & Row, 1988.

————. "Theological Consensus or Historicist Evasion? Jews and Christians in Biblical Studies." In *Hebrew Bible or Old Testament? Studying the Bible in Judaism and Christianity,* edited by Roger Brooks and John J. Collins, 109–45. CJA 5. Notre Dame: Univ. of Notre Dame Press, 1990.

————, "The Eighth Principle of Judaism and the Literary Simultaneity of Scripture." In *The Hebrew Bible, the Old Testament, and Historical Criticism.* Louisville: Westminster John Know, 1993.

————. "Why Jews Are Not Interested in Biblical Theology." In *The Hebrew Bible, the Old Testament and Historical Criticism: Jews and Christians in Biblical Studies,* 33–61. Louisville: Westminster John Knox, 1993.

Levine, Amy-Jill. "Second Temple Judaism, Jesus, and Women." *BibInt* 2 (1994) 8–33.

————. "Who's Catering the Q Affair? Feminist Observations on Q Paraenesis." *Semeia* 50 (1990) 145–62.

————, ed. *"Women Like This": New Perspectives on Jewish Women in the Greco-Roman World.* Early Judaism and Its Literature 1. Atlanta: Scholars, 1991.

Lévi-Strauss, Claude. *Myth and Meaning.* New York: Schocken, 1979.

————. *La pensée sauvage.* Paris: Plon, 1962. ET = *The Savage Mind.* The Nature of Human Society Series. Chicago: Univ. of Chicago Press, 1966.

————. *Structural Anthropology.* 2 vols. Translated by Claire Jacobson and Brooke Grundfest Schoepf. New York: Basic, 1963–76.

Linares, Olga F. *Power, Prayer and Production: The Jola of Casamance, Senegal.* Cambridge Studies in Social and Cultural Anthropology. New York: Cambridge Univ. Press, 1992.

Long, A. A. *Hellenistic Philosophy; Stoics, Epicureans, Scepticism.* London: Duckworth, 1974.

Long, Burke O. "Ambitions of Dissent: Biblical Theology in a Postmodern Future." *JR* 96 (1996) 276–89.

Lüdemann, Gerd, and Martin Schröder, eds. *Die Religionsgeschichtliche Schule in Göttingen. Eine Documentation.* Göttingen: Vandenhoeck & Ruprecht, 1987.

Lyotard, Jean-François. *Le defférend.* Paris: Minuit, 1983. ET= *The Differend: Phrases in Dispute.* Theory and History of Literature 46. Minneapolis: Univ. of Minnesota Press, 1988.

————. *The Inhuman: Reflection on Time.* Stanford: Stanford Univ. Press, 1991.

————. *The Postmodern Condition: A Report on Knowledge.* Translated by Geoff Bennington and Brian Massumi. Theory and History of Literature 10. Minneapolis: Univ. of Minnesota Press, 1984.

————. *The Postmodern Explained.* Translated by Julian Pefanis and Morgan Thomas. Minneapolis: Univ. of Minneapolis Press, 1993.

————. *Toward the Postmodern.* Philosophy and Literary Theory. Atlantic Highlands, N.J.: Humanities, 1993.

Malina, Bruce J. "The Social Sciences and Biblical Interpretation." *Int* 37 (1982) 229–42.

Maluleke, Tinyiko Sam. "Half a Century of African Christian Theologies. Elements of the Emerging Agenda for the Twenty-First Century." *JTSA* 99 (1997) 4–23.

————. "Theological Interest in African Independent Churches and Other Grass-Root Communities in South Africa: A Review of Methodologies." *Journal of Black Theology in South Africa* 10 (1996) 18–48.

Marcuse, Herbert. *Counterrevolution and Revolt.* Boston: Beacon, 1972.

————. *An Essay on Liberation.* Boston: Beacon, 1969.

————. *Technology, War, and Fascism*. Edited by Douglas Kellner. Collected Papers of Herbert Marcuse vol. 1. London: Routledge, 1998.

————. *Towards a Critical Theory of Society*. Edited by Douglas Kellner. Collected Papers of Herbert Marcuse vol. 2. London: Routledge, 2001.

Markham, Ian S. *A Theology of Engagement: Challenges in Contemporary Theology*. Oxford: Blackwell, 2003.

Marx, Karl. *Capital: A Critique of Political Economy*. 3 vols. Translated by Samuel Moore et al. Chicago: Kerr, 1906–9.

————. *The Communist Manifesto of Karl Marx and Friedrich Engels*. Edited by D. Ryazampff. New York: Russell & Russell, 1963.

Massey, James. *Roots: A Concise History of the Dalits*. New Delhi: ISPCK, 1991.

Mayes, A. D. H. *The Old Testament in Sociological Perspective*. London: Pickering, 1989.

Mays, James Luther. "What Is Written: A Response to Brevard Childs' *Introduction to the Old Testament as Scripture*." *HBT* 2 (1980) 151–63.

Mbiti, John. *New Testament Eschatology in an African Background: A Study of the Encounter between New Testament Theology and African Traditional Concepts*. London: London Univ. Press, 1971.

McCauley, Karen A. "Russian Formalism." In *The Johns Hopkins Guide to Literary Theory & Criticism*, edited by Michael Groden and Martin Kreiswirth, 634–38. Baltimore: Johns Hopkins Univ. Press, 1994.

McFague, Sallie. "God as Mother." In *Weaving the Visions: New Patterns in Feminist Spirituality*, edited by Judith Plaskow and Carol Christ, 129–50. San Francisco: Harper & Row, 1989.

————. *Metaphorical Theology*. Philadelphia: Fortress Press, 1982.

————. "Models of God for an Ecological Evolutionary Era: God as Mother of the Universe." In *Physics, Philosophy, and Theology: A Common Quest for Understanding*, edited by Robert J. Russell et al., 249–271. Notre Dame: Notre Dame Univ., 1988.

————. *Models of God: Theology for an Ecological, Nuclear Age*. Philadelphia: Fortress Press, 1987.

————. "Mother God." In *Motherhood: Experience, Institution, Theology*, edited by Anne Carr and Elisabeth Schüssler Fiorenza, 138–43. Concilium. Edinburgh: T. & T. Clark, 1985.

————. *Speaking in Parables: A Study in Metaphor and Theology*. Philadelphia: Fortress Press, 1975.

McGlasson, Paul. "Barth, Karl." In *DBI* 1:99–100.

McGovern, Arthur F. *Liberation Theology and Its Critics: Toward an Assessment*. Maryknoll, N.Y.: Orbis, 1989.

McGowan, John. *Postmodernism and Its Critics*. Ithaca: Cornell Univ. Press, 1991.

McKnight, Edgar V. *Postmodern Use of the Bible: The Emergence of Reader-Oriented Criticism*. Nashville: Abingdon, 1988.

————. "Reader-Response Criticism." In *To Each Its Own Meaning*, edited by Stephen R. Haynes and Steven L. McKenzie, 197–219. Louisville: Westminster John Knox, 1993.

McLeod, John. *Beginning Postcolonialism.* Beginnings. Manchester: Manchester Univ. Press, 2000.

McNamara, Francis Terry. *France in Black Africa.* Washington, D.C.: National Defense Univ. Press, 1989.

Merk, Otto. *Biblische Theologie des Neuen Testaments in ihrer Anfangszeit.* Marburger Theologische Studien 9. Marburg: Elwert, 1972.

Merquior, J. G. *Foucault.* Berkeley: Univ. of California Press, 1987.

Metzger, Bruce M. *The Bible in Translation: English and Ancient Versions.* Grand Rapids: Baker Academic, 2001.

Meyers, Carol L. *Discovering Eve: Ancient Israelite Women in Context.* New York: Oxford Univ. Press, 1988.

———. "Early Israel and the Rise of the Israelite Monarchy." In *The Blackwell Companion to the Hebrew Bible,* edited by Leo G. Perdue, 61–86. BCR 1. Oxford: Blackwell, 2001.

———. "An Ethnoarchaeological Analysis of Hannah's Sacrifice." In *Promegranates and Golden Bells: Studies in Biblical, Jewish, and Near Eastern Ritual, Law, and Literature in Honor of Jacob Milgrom,* 77–91. Winona Lake, Ind.: Eisenbrauns, 1995.

———. "The Family in Early Israel." In *Families in Ancient Israel,* edited by Leo G. Perdue et al., 1–47. Family, Religion, and Culture. Louisville: Westminster John Knox, 1997.

———. "Procreation, Production, and Protection: Male-Female Balance in Early Israel." *JAAR* 51 (1983) 569–93.

———. "'To Her Mother's House': Considering a Counterpart to the Israelite *Bêt 'āb.*" In *The Bible and the Politics of Exegesis: Essays in Honor of Norman K. Gottwald on His Sixty-Fifth Birthday,* edited by David Jobling, Peggy L. Day, and Gerald T. Sheppard, 39–51. Cleveland: Pilgrim, 1991.

———. "Women and the Domestic Economy of Early Israel." In *Women in the Hebrew Bible,* edited by Alice Bach, 33–43. London: Routledge, 1999.

———, ed. *Women in Scripture: A Dictionary of Named and Unnamed Women in the Hebrew Bible, the Apocryphal/Deuterocanonical Books, and the New Testament.* Boston: Houghton Mifflin, 2000.

Meyers, Carol L., Ross S. Kraemer, and Sharon Ringe. *Gender and the Biblical Tradition.* Louisville: Westminster John Knox, 1991.

Meyers, Carol L., et al., eds. *The Women's Bible Commentary.* Louisville: Westminster John Knox, 1992.

Michelet, Jules. *Introduction à l'histoire universelle.* Paris: Librairie Larousse, 1930.

Midgley, Clare, ed. *Gender and Imperialism.* Manchester: Manchester Univ. Press, 1998.

Miller, Ed. L., and Stanley J. Grenz, eds. *Fortress Introduction to Contemporary Theologies.* Minneapolis: Fortress Press, 1998.

Miller, Patrick D. "The Cross and Civil Religion." In *Political Religion and Political Society,* 11–47. Institute of Christian Thought. New York: Harper & Row, 1974.

———. *The Divine Warrior in Early Israel.* HSM 5. Cambridge: Harvard Univ. Press, 1973.

———. "God and the Gods: History of Religion as an Approach and Context for Bible and Theology." *Affirmation* 1 (1973) 37–62.

———. "Israelite Religion." In *The Hebrew Bible and its Modern Interpreters,* edited by Douglas A. Knight and Gene M. Tucker, 201–37. Philadelphia: Fortress Press, 1985.

———. *On Human Dignity: Political Theology and Ethics.* Philadelphia: Fortress Press, 1984.

———. *The Religion of Ancient Israel.* LAI. Louisville: Westminster John Knox, 2000.

Mofokeng, Takatso. "Black Christians, the Bible and Liberation," *Journal of Black Theology* 2 (1988) 34-42.

Moltmann, Jürgen. "Communities of Faith and Radical Discipleship." Interview by Miroslav Volf. *Christian Century* (16 March 1983) 248.

———. "The Cross and Civil Religion." In *Religion and Political Society,* edited and translated by the Institute of Christian Thought, vi–x. New York: Harper & Row, 1974.

———. *On Human Dignity: Political Theology and Ethics.* Translated by M. Douglas Meeks. Philadelphia: Fortress Press, 1984.

Moore, Stephen. "The 'Post'-Age Stamp: Does It Stick? Biblical Studies and the Postmodernism Debate." *JAAR* 57 (1989) 543–59.

Morgan, Robert. "Gabler's Bicentenary." *ExpT* 98 (1987) 164–68.

Mosala, Itumeleng J. *Biblical Hermeneutics and Black Theology in South Africa.* Grand Rapids: Eerdmans, 1989.

Mowinckel, Sigmund. *He That Cometh.* Translated by G. W. Anderson. New York: Abingdon, 1954.

———. *Psalmenstudien.* 6 vols. Kristiania: Dybwad, 1921–24.

Muffs, Yochanan. *Love and Joy: Law, Language and Religion in Ancient Israel.* New York: Jewish Theological Seminary in America, 1992.

Mugambi, J. N. K. *From Liberation to Reconstruction: African Christian Theology after the Cold War.* Nairobi: East African Educational Publishers, 1995.

Muilenburg, James. "Form Criticism and Beyond." *JBL* 88 (1969) 1–18.

Murry, John Middleton. *Countries of the Mind: Essays in Literary Criticism.* London: Oxford Univ. Press, 1937.

Nakhai, Beth Alpert. *Archaeology and the Religions of Canaan and Israel.* ASOR Books 7. Boston: American Schools of Oriental Research, 2001.

Nalunnakkal, George Mathew. *New Beings and New Communities: Theological Reflections in a Postmodern Context.* Thiruvalla, India: KCC/EDTP, 1998.

Netting, Robert M. *Smallholders, Householders: Farm Families and the Ecology of Intensive, Sustainable Agriculture.* Stanford: Stanford Univ. Press, 1993.

Neumark, David. *The Philosophy of the Bible.* Cincinnati: Ark, 1918.

Neusner, Jacob. *Judaic Perspectives on Ancient Israel.* Philadelphia: Fortress Press, 1987.

———. *What, Exactly, Did the Rabbinic Sages Mean by 'The Oral Torah'? An Inductive Answer to the Question of Rabbinic Judaism.* South Florida Studies in the History of Judaism 196. Atlanta: Scholars Press, 1998.

Newsom, Carol A. "Bakhtin, the Bible, and Dialogic Truth." *JR* 76 (1996) 290–306.

Newsom, Carol, and Sharon H. Ringe, eds. *The Women's Bible Commentary.* Louisville: Westminster John Knox, 1989.

Niditch, Susan. *Ancient Israelite Religion.* New York: Oxford Univ. Press, 1997.

Niehr, Herbert. "Auf dem Weg zu einer Religionsgeschichte Israels und Judas. Annäherungen an einen Problemkreis." In *Religionsgeschichte Israels: Formale und Materiale Aspeckte,* edited by Bernd Janowski and Matthias Köckert, 57–78. Gütersloh: Kaiser, 1999.

Nirmal, A. P. "Towards a Christian Dalit Theology." In *Frontiers in Asian Christian Theology,* edited by R. S. Sugirtharaja, 27–42. Maryknoll, N.Y.: Orbis, 1994.

North, C. R. "Old Testament Theology and the History of Hebrew Religion." *SJT* 2 (1949) 113–26.

Noth, Martin. *Geschichte Israels,* 6th ed. Göttingen: Vandenhoeck & Ruprecht, 1966.

———. *The History of Israel,* rev. ed. Translated by P. R. Ackroyd. New York: Harper & Row, 1960.

Nzimande, Makhosanda N. "Towards a Postcolonial *Imbokodo* (African Women's) Hermeneutics in Post-apartheid South Africa: A Case in Proverbs 1-9 (9:1-18)." Paper presented at the Old Testament Society of South Africa, Stellenbosch, South Africa, September 2002.

O'Brien, Rita Cruse. *White Society in Black Africa: The French of Senegal.* Evanston, Ill.: Northwestern Univ. Press, 1972.

Oden, Robert A. Jr. *The Bible without Theology: The Theological Tradition and Alternatives to It.* San Francisco: Harper & Row, 1987.

Oduyoye, Mercy Amba. "Biblical Interpretation and the Social Location of the Interpreter: African Women's Reading of the Bible." In *Reading from This Place* 2: 33–51.

———. *Introducing African Women's Theology.* Introductions in Feminist Theology 6. Sheffield: Sheffield Academic Press, 2001.

———. "Introduction: The Fire of the Smoke." In *Daughters of Anowa: African Women and Patriarchy.* Maryknoll, N.Y.: Orbis, 1995.

Oesterley, W. O. E. *Sacrifices in Ancient Israel: Their Origin, Purposes and Development.* New York: Macmillan, 1937.

Ollenburger, Ben C. "Biblical Theology: Situating the Discipline." In *Understanding the Word: Essays in Honor of Bernhard W. Anderson,* edited by James Butler et al., 37–62. JSOTSup 37. Sheffield: JSOT Press, 1985.

Ollenburger, Ben C., et al., eds. *Old Testament Theology: Flowering and Future,* rev. ed. SBTS 1. Winona Lake, Ind.: Eisenbrauns, 2004.

Olson, Alan M. "Postmodernity and Faith." *JAAR* 58 (1990) 37–53.

O'Neill, John. *On Critical Theory.* New York: Seabury, 1976.

Overholt, Thomas W. *Cultural Anthropology and the Old Testament.* GBS. Minneapolis: Fortress Press, 1996.

Pannenberg, Wolfhart. "Die Bedeutung des Alten Testaments für den christlichen Glauben." *JBTh* 12 (1995) 181–92.

Patte, Daniel. "Speech Act Theory and Biblical Exegesis." *Semeia* 41 (1988) 85–102.

Pedersen, Johannes. *Israel: Its Life and Culture.* 4 vols. Translated by Aslaug Møller. Atlanta: Scholars, 1991.

Penchansky, David. *The Politics of Biblical Theology: A Postmodern Reading.* SABH 10. Mercer, Ga.: Mercer Univ. Press, 1995.

Perdue, Leo G. *The Collapse of History: Reconstructing Old Testament Theology.* OBT. Minneapolis: Fortress Press, 1994.

―――. *The Historical Theology of Wisdom Literature.* (Louisville: Westminster John Knox, 2005).

―――. "Liminality and the Social Setting of Wisdom Instructions." *ZAW* 93 (1981) 114–26.

―――. *The Sage.* LAI. Louisville: Westminster John Knox, forthcoming.

―――. *Sages, Scribes and Seers.* FRLANT. Göttingen: Vandenhoeck & Ruprecht, forthcoming.

―――. *Wisdom in Revolt. Metaphorical Theology in the Book of Job.* JSOTSup 112. Sheffield: Almond, 1991.

Perdue, William D., and Leo G. Perdue. *The Fourth Paradigm: Postcolonialism and Beyond.* Forthcoming.

Perdue, Leo G., et al. *Families in Ancient Israel.* Family, Culture, and Religion. Louisville: Westminster John Knox, 1997.

Perlitt, Lothar. *Vatke und Wellhausen.* BZAW 94. Berlin: de Guyter, 1965.

Peron, Gabriel. *La philosophie de volonté.* Paris: L'Harmattan, 2000.

Péter, Georges. *L'effort français au Sénegal,* edited by E. De Boccard. Paris: Librairie des Écoles Français d'Athènes et de Rome, 1933.

Phillips, Gary. "Introduction." *Semeia* 51 (1990) 7–49.

Phillips, Vicki C. "Feminist Interpretation." In *DBI* 1:388–98.

Plaskow, Judith. "Anti-Judaism in Feminist Christian Interpretation." In *Searching the Scriptures: A Feminist Commentary,* edited by Elisabeth Schüssler Fiorenza, 1:117–29. New York: Crossroad, 1993.

―――. *Standing Again at Sinai: Judaism from a Feminist Perspective.* San Francisco: Harper & Row, 1990.

Poster, Mark. "Foucault, Michel." In *The Johns Hopkins Guide to Literary Theory and Criticism,* edited by Michael Groden and Martin Kreiswirth, 277–80. Baltimore: Johns Hopkins Univ. Press, 1994.

Prabhakar, M. E. "The Search for a Dalit Theology." In *Towards a Dalit Theology,* edited by M. E. Prabhakar, 35–47. Bangalore: CISRS, 1988.

Preuss, Horst Dietrich. *Old Testament Theology.* Vol. 1. OTL. Louisville: Westminster John Knox, 1995.

―――. *Theologie des Alten Testaments.* Vol. 1. Stuttgart: Kohlhammer, 1991.

Rad, Gerhard von. *Old Testament Theology.* 2 vols. Translated by D. M. G. Stalker. New York: Harper & Row, 1962, 1965.

―――. "Royal Ritual in Judah." In *From Genesis to Chronicles: Explorations in Old Testament Theology,* edited by K. C. Hanson, 167–73. FCBS. Minneapolis: Fortress Press, 2005.

Ransom, John Crowe. *The New Criticism.* Norfolk, Conn.: New Directions, 1941.

Rascke, Carl A. "Fire and Roses: Toward Authentic Post-Modern Religious Thinking." *JAAR* 58 (1990) 671–89.

Rau, Johannes, and Eberhard Busch. *Karl Barth: Gedenkfeier zum 100. Geburtstag am 20. April 1986 in Düsseldorf.* Düsseldorf: Presse- und Informationsamt der Landesregierung Nordhein-Westfalen, 1986.

Rendtorff, Rolf. "Die Entstehung der israelitischen Religion als religionsgeschichtliches und theologisches Problem." *TLZ* 88 (1963) col. 737.

———. "Die Hermeneutik einer kanonischen Theologie des Alten Testaments." *JBTh* 10 (1995) 35–44.

———. "The Impact of the Holocaust *(Shoah)* on German Protestant Theology." *HBT* 15 (1993) 154–67.

———. *Der Text in Seiner Endgestalt: Schritte auf dem Weg zu einer Theologie des Alten Testaments.* Neukirchen-Vluyn: Neukirchener, 2001.

———. *Theologie des Alten Testaments.* 2 vols. Neukirchen-Vluyn: Neukirchener, 1999, 2001.

———. "Toward a Common Jewish-Christian Reading of the Hebrew Bible." In *Canon and Theology: Overtures to an Old Testament Theology,* 31–45. OBT. Minneapolis: Fortress Press, 1993.

———. "Was haben wir an der Bibel? Versuch einer Theologie des christlichen Kanons." *JBTh* 12 (1998) 99–152.

Reventlow, H. Graf. "Modern Approaches to Old Testament Theology." In *The Blackwell Companion to the Hebrew Bible,* edited by Leo G. Perdue, 221–40. BCR 1. Oxford: Blackwell, 2001.

———. *Problems of Biblical Theology in the Twentieth Century.* Translated by John Bowden. Philadelphia: Fortress Press, 1986.

———. *Problems of Old Testament Theology in the Twentieth Century.* Translated by John Bowden. Philadelphia: Fortress Press, 1985.

Richards, I. A. *The Philosophy of Rhetoric.* New York: Oxford Univ., 1936.

Ricoeur, Paul. *Interpretation Theory: Discourse and the Surplus of Meaning.* Fort Worth: Texas Christian Univ. Press, 1976.

———. "The Metaphorical Process." *Semeia* 4 (1975) 75–106.

———. "The Narrative Function." *Semeia* 13 (1978) 177–202.

———. *The Rule of Metaphor.* Toronto: Univ. of Toronto Press, 1977.

Ringgren, Helmer. *Israelitische Religion,* 2d ed. Stuttgart: W. Kohlhammer, 1982. ET = *Israelite Religion.* Translated by David E. Green. Philadelphia: Fortress Press, 1966.

The Road to Damascus: Kairos and Conversion. Johannesburg: Skotaville, 1989.

Roberts, J. Deotis. *Liberation and Reconciliation: A Black Theology,* rev. ed. Maryknoll, N.Y.: Orbis, 1994.

Robinson, Theodore H. *Hebrew Religion, Its Origin and Development,* 2d ed. London: SPCK, 1937.

———. *A Short Comparative History of Religions,* 2d ed. London: Duckworth, 1951.

Robinson, Theodore H., and W. O. E. Oesterley. *Hebrew Religion: Its Origin and Development.* New York: Macmillan, 1930.

Rollmann, Hans. "Eichhorn, Karl Albert August Ludwig." In *DBI* 1:324–25.

———. "William Wrede, Albert Eichhorn, and the 'Old Quest' of the Historical Jesus." In *Self-Definition and Self-Discovery in Early Christianity: A Study in*

Changing Horizons, Essays in Appreciation of Ben F. Meyer, edited by David J. Hawkin and Tom Robinson, 79–99. Lewiston, N.Y.: Mellen, 1990.

Rosaldo, Michelle Zimbalist, and Louise Lamphere, eds. *Women, Culture and Society.* Stanford: Stanford Univ. Press, 1974.

Rubenstein, Richard. *After Auschwitz: History, Theology, and Contemporary Judaism,* 2d ed. Baltimore: Johns Hopkins Univ. Press, 1992.

Ruether, Rosemary. *Sexism and God-Talk: Toward a Feminist Theology.* Boston: Beacon, 1983.

Russell, Letty, ed. *Feminist Interpretation of the Bible.* Philadelphia: Westminster, 1985.

———. *Human Liberation in a Feminist Perspective: A Theology.* Philadelphia: Westminster, 1974.

Sacks, Sheldon, ed. *On Metaphor.* Chicago: Univ. of Chicago Press, 1979.

Saebø, Magne. "Johann Philipp Gablers Bedeutung für die biblische Theologie." *ZAW* 99 (1987) 1–16.

Safran, William. "Diasporas in Modern Societies: Myths of Homeland and Return." *Diaspora: A Journal of Transnational Studies* 1 (1991) 83–99.

Said, Edward W. *Beginnings: Intention and Method.* London: Granta, 1997.

———. *Covering Islam: How the Media and the Experts Determine How We See the Rest of the World.* London: Routledge & Kegan Paul, 1981.

———. *Culture and Imperialism.* New York: Knopf, 1994.

———. *Orientalism.* New York: Pantheon, 1978.

———. *The World, the Text, and the Critic.* Cambridge, Mass.: Harvard Univ. Press, 1988.

Sakenfeld, Katherine Doob. "Feminist Perspectives on Bible and Theology." *Int* 42 (1988) 5–18.

Sanders, Cheryl J. *Living the Intersection: Womanism and Afrocentrism in Theology.* Minneapolis: Fortress Press, 1995.

Sanders, James. *Canon and Community: A Guide to Canonical Criticism.* GBS. Philadelphia: Fortress Press, 1984.

Sandys-Wunsch, John. "The History of Religion and the Religion of Israel." *Religious Traditions* 3 (1980) 22–28.

Sandys-Wunsch, John, and Laurence Eldredge. "J. P. Gabler and the Distinction between Biblical and Dogmatic Theology: Translation, Commentary, and Discussion of His Originality." *SJT* 33 (1980) 133–58.

Sawyer, John F. A. *Sacred Languages and Sacred Texts.* London: Routledge, 1999.

Schäfer, Peter. "Das 'Dogma' von der mündlichen Torah im rabbinischen Judentum." In *Studien zur Geschichte und Theologie des rabbinischen Judentums,* 153–97. AGAJU 15. Leiden: Brill, 1978.

Schams, Christine. *Jewish Scribes in the Second-Temple Period.* JSOTSup 291. Sheffield: Sheffield Academic, 1998.

Scharlemann, Robert P., ed. *Theology at the End of the Century: A Dialogue on the Postmodern.* Charlottesville: Univ. of Virginia Press, 1990.

Schmidt, Werner H. *The Faith of the Old Testament: A History.* Philadelphia: Westminster, 1983.

———. "'Theologie des Alten Testaments' vor und nach Gerhard von Rad." *VF* 17 (1972) 1–25.

———. *Vielfalt und Einheit alttestamentlichen Glaubens 1: Hermeneutik und Methodik, Pentateuch und Prophetie.* Neukirchen-Vluyn: Neukirchener, 1995.

Schopenhauer, Arthur. *Die Welt als Wille und Vorstellung.* Edited by Rolf Toman. Köln: Könemann, 1997–.

Schottroff, Luise. "Wanderprophetinnen: Eine feministische Analyse der Logiaquelle." *EvTh* 51 (1991) 322–34.

Schürer, Emil. *The History of the Jewish People in the Age of Jesus Christ (175 B.C.– A.D. 135).* Edited by Geza Vermes and Fergus Millar. Edinburgh: T. & T. Clark, 1973–1987.

Schüssler Fiorenza, Elisabeth. *Bread Not Stone: The Challenge of Feminist Biblical Interpretation.* Boston: Beacon, 1985. (2nd ed., 1995.)

———. *But She Said: Feminist Practices of Biblical Interpretation.* Boston: Beacon, 1992.

———. *In Memory of Her: A Feminist Reconstruction of Christian Origins,* 2d ed. New York: Crossroad, 1994.

———. *Jesus and the Politics of Interpretation.* New York: Continuum, 2000.

———. *Jesus: Miriam's Child, Sophia's Prophet: Critical Issues in Feminist Christology.* New York: Continuum, 1994.

———. *Rhetoric and Ethic: The Politics of Biblical Studies.* Minneapolis: Fortress Press, 1999.

———. *Sharing Her Word: Feminist Biblical Interpretation in Context.* Boston: Beacon, 1998.

———. *Wisdom Ways: Introducing Feminist Biblical Interpretation.* Maryknoll, N.Y.: Orbis, 2001.

Schüssler Fiorenza, Elisabeth, and Pui-Lan Kwok. *Women's Sacred Scriptures.* Maryknoll, N.Y.: Orbis, 1998.

Scott, James C. *Domination and the Arts of Resistance: Hidden Transcripts.* New Haven: Yale Univ. Press, 1990.

Scullion, John J. "Gunkel, Johannes Heinrich Hermann." In *DBI* 1:472–73.

Segal, Robert A., and Thomas Ryba. "Religion and Postmodernism: A Review Symposium." *Religion* 27 (1997) 101–49.

Segovia, Fernando. *Decolonizing Biblical Studies: A View from the Margins.* Maryknoll, N.Y.: Orbis, 2000.

———. *A Dream Unfinished: Theological Reflections on America from the Margins.* Maryknoll, N.Y.: Orbis, 2001.

———, ed. *Interpreting Beyond Borders.* The Bible and Postcolonialism 3. Sheffield: Academic, 2000.

———. "Postcolonial and Diasporic Criticism in Biblical Studies: Focus, Parameters, Relevance." *SWC* 6 (1999) 177–95.

———. "The Text as Other: Towards a Hispanic American Hermeneutic." In *Text and Experience,* edited by Daniel Smith-Christopher, 276–98. BibSem 35. Sheffield: Sheffield Academic, 1995.

———. "Toward a Hermeneutics of the Diaspora: A Hermeneutics of Otherness and Engagement." In *Reading from This Place: Social Location and Biblical Interpretation in the United States,* edited by F. F. Segovia and Mary Ann Tolbert, 57–73. Minneapolis: Fortress Press, 1995.

Segovia, Fernando, and Ada María Isasi-Díaz, eds. *Hispanic/Latino Theologia: Challenge and Promise.* Minneapolis: Fortress Press, 1995.

Segovia, Fernando, and Mary Ann Tolbert, eds. *Reading from this Place.* 2 vols. Minneapolis: Fortress Press, 1995.

―――. *Teaching the Bible: The Discourses and Politics of Biblical Pedagogy.* Maryknoll, N.Y.: Orbis, 1998.

Segundo, Juan Luis. *Liberation of Theology.* Translated by John Drury. Maryknoll, N.Y.: Orbis, 1976.

Selvidge, Marla J. *Notorious Voices: Feminist Biblical Interpretation, 1500–1920.* New York: Continuum, 1996.

Sembène, Ousmane. *The Last of the Empire.* London: Heinemann, 1981.

Senghor, Léopold Sédar. *Liberté 1: Négritude et humanisme.* Paris: du Seuil, 1964.

―――. *Liberté 2: Nation et voie africaine du socialisme.* Paris: du Seuil, 1971.

―――. *Liberté 3: Négritude et civilisation de l'universel.* Paris: du Seuil, 1977.

―――. *On African Socialism.* New York: Praeger, 1964.

―――. "The Spirit of Civilisation, or the Laws of African Negro Culture." *Presence Africaine* 24–25 (1959) 52–54.

Sharma, Arvind. "An Inquiry into the Nature of the Distinction between the History of Religion and the Phenomenology of Religion." *Numen* 22 (1975) 81–95.

Shklovskii, Viktor. *Theory of Prose.* Elmwood Park, Ill.: Dalkey Archive, 1990.

Smart, James D. *The Past, Present, and Future of Biblical Theology.* Philadelphia: Westminster, 1979.

Smend, Rudolf. *Deutsche Alttestamentler in drei Jahrhunderten: Mit 18 Abbildungen.* Göttingen: Vandenhoeck & Ruprecht, 1989.

―――. "Karl Barth als Ausleger der Heiligen Schrift." In *Theologie als Christologie,* edited by Heidelore Köchert und Wolf Krötke, 9–37. Berlin: Evangelische Verlagsanstalt, 1988.

―――. *Lehrbuch der alttestamentlichen Religionsgeschichte,* 2d ed. Freiburg: Mohr/Siebeck, 1899.

―――. "Theologie im Alten Testament." In *Verifikation: Festschrift für Gerhard Ebeling,* edited by Eberhard Jüngel, 104–17. Tübingen: Mohr/Siebeck, 1982.

Smith, Huston. "Postmodernism's Impact on the Study of Religion." *JAAR* 58 (1990) 653–70.

Smith, Mark S. *The Early History of God: Yahweh and the Other Deities,* 2d ed. Grand Rapids: Eerdmans, 2002.

Sölle, Dorothee. "God's Pain and Our Pain: How Theology Has to Change after Auschwitz." *Remembering for the Future* 3, edited by Yehuda Bauer et al., 2728–44. Oxford: Pergamon, 1989.

Sommer, Benjamin D. "Revelation at Sinai in the Hebrew Bible and in Jewish Theology." *JR* 79 (1999) 422–51.

―――. "The Scroll of Isaiah as Jewish Scripture, Or, Why Jews Don't Read Books." In *SBL Seminar Papers,* 225–42. Atlanta: Scholars, 1996.

―――. "Unity and Plurality in Jewish Canons: The Case of the Oral and Written Torahs." In *One Scripture or Many? Perspectives Historical, Theological and Philosophical,* edited by Christine Helmer and Christof Landmesser. Oxford: Oxford Univ. Press, forthcoming.

Spieckermann, Hermann. "Die Verbindlichkeit des Alten Testaments: Unzeit-gemässe Betrachtungen zu einem ungeliebten Thema." *JBTh* 10 (1995) 25–51.

Spivak, Gayatri Chakravorty. "Can the Subaltern Speak?" In *Marxism and the Interpretation of Culture,* edited by Cary Nelson and Lawrence Grossberg, 271–313. Urbana: Univ. of Illinois Press, 1988.

———. *A Critique of Postcolonial Reason: Toward a History of the Vanishing Present.* Cambridge, Mass.: Harvard Univ. Press, 1999.

———. *Death of a Discipline.* New York: Columbia Univ. Press, 2003.

———. *In Other Worlds: Essays in Cultural Politics.* New York: Routledge, 1988.

Spivak, Gayatri Chakravorty, and Ranajit Guha. *Selected Subaltern Studies.* Oxford: Oxford Univ. Press, 1988.

Stemberger, Günther. *Midrasch: Vom Umgang der Rabbinen mit der Bibel.* Munich: Beck, 1989.

Stendahl, Krister. "Biblical Theology, Contemporary." In *IDB* 1 (1962) 419–31.

Steuernagel, Carl. "Alttestamentliche Theologie und alttestamentliche Religions-geschichte." *Vom Alten Testament: Karl Marti zum siebzigsten Geburtstage,* edited by Karl Budde, 266–73. BZAW 41. Giessen: Töpelmann, 1925.

Stiglitz, Joseph. *Globalization and Its Discontents.* London: Penguin, 2002.

Stolz, Fritz. *Einführung in den biblischen Monotheismus.* Darmstadt: Wissenschaft-liche Buchgesellschaft, 1996.

———. "Probleme westsemitischer und israelitischer Religionsgeschichte." *ThR* 56 (1991) 1–26.

Stuhlmacher, Peter. *Historical Criticism and Theological Interpretation of Scripture: Toward a Hermeneutic of Consent.* Philadelphia: Fortress Press, 1977.

Sugirtharajah, R. S. *Asian Biblical Hermeneutics and Postcolonialism: Contesting the Interpretations.* Maryknoll, N.Y.: Orbis, 1998.

———. "Introduction: The Margin as a Site of Creative Re-visioning." In *Interpreting the Bible in the Third World,* edited by R. S. Sugirtharajah, 1–8. Mary-knoll, N.Y.: Orbis, 1995.

———. *Postcolonial Criticism and Biblical Interpretation.* Oxford: Clarendon Press, 2002.

———. "A Postcolonial Exploration of Collusion and Construction in Biblical Interpretation." In *The Postcolonial Bible,* edited by R. S. Sugirtharajah, 91–116. Sheffield: Sheffield Academic, 1998.

Sweeney, Marvin A. "Reconceiving the Paradigms of Old Testament Theology in the Post-Shoah Period." *BibInt* 6 (1998) 142–61.

———. "Reconceiving the Paradigms of Old Testament Theology in the Post-Shoah Period." In *Jews, Christians, and the Theology of Hebrew Scriptures,* edited by Alice Ogden Bellis and Joel S. Kaminsky, 155–72. SBLSymSer 8. Atlanta: Scholars, 2000.

———. "Tanak versus Old Testament: Concerning the Foundation for a Jewish Theology of the Bible." In *Problems in Biblical Theology: Essays in Honor of Rolf Knierim,* edited by Henry T. C. Sun and Keith L. Eades with James M. Robinson, 353–72. Grand Rapids: Eerdmans, 1997.

Tabb, William K., ed. *Churches in Struggle.* New York: Monthly Review, 1986.

Thistlethwaite, Susan. *Sex, Race and God: Christian Feminism in Black and White.* New York: Crossroad, 1989.

Thompson, Thomas L. "Das Alte Testament als theologische Disziplin." *JBTh* 10 (1995) 157–73.

———. *Early History of the Israelite People: From the Written and Archaeological Sources.* SHANE 4. Leiden: Brill, 1992.

Tigay, Jeffrey H. *You Shall Have No Other Gods: Israelite Religion in the Light of Hebrew Inscriptions.* HSS 31. Atlanta: Scholars, 1986.

Tolbert, Mary Ann, ed. *The Bible and Feminist Hermeneutics. Semeia* 28. Chico, Calif.: Scholars, 1983.

Tompkins, Jane P., ed. *Reader-Response Criticism: From Formalism to Post-Structuralism.* Baltimore: Johns Hopkins Univ. Press, 1980.

Toorn, Karel van der. *Family Religion in Babylonia, Syria and Israel: Continuity and Change in the Forms of Religious Life.* Studies in the History and Culture of the Ancient Near East 7. Leiden: Brill, 1996.

———. *From Her Cradle to her Grave: The Role of Religion in the Life of the Israelite and the Babylonian Woman.* BibSem 23. Sheffield: JSOT Press, 1994.

Touraine, Alaine. *Critique of Modernity.* Oxford: Blackwell, 1995.

Townes, Emilie. *In a Blaze of Glory: Womanist Spirituality as Social Witness.* Nashville: Abingdon, 1995.

Tracy, David. *The Analogical Imagination: Christian Theology and the Culture of Pluralism.* New York: Crossroad, 1981.

———. "Metaphor and Religion: The Test Case of Christian Texts." In *On Metaphor,* edited by Sheldon Sacks, 89–104. Chicago: Univ. of Chicago Press, 1979.

Trible, Phyllis. "Five Loaves and Two Fishes: Feminist Hermeneutics and Biblical Theology." *TS* 50 (1989) 279–95. Reprinted in *Promise and Practice of Biblical Theology,* edited by John Reumann, 51–70. Minneapolis: Fortress Press, 1991.

———. *God and the Rhetoric of Sexuality.* OBT. Philadelphia: Fortress Press, 1977.

———. *Rhetorical Criticism: Context, Method, and the Book of Jonah.* GBS. Minneapolis: Fortress Press, 1994.

———. *Texts of Terror: Literary-Feminist Readings of Biblical Narratives.* OBT. Philadelphia: Fortress Press, 1985.

———. "Treasures Old and New: Biblical Theology and the Challenge of Feminism." In *The Open Text,* edited by Francis Watson, 32–56. London: SCM, 1993.

———. "Women's Studies and Biblical Studies: An Historical Perspective." *JSOT* 22 (1982) 6–12.

Tsevat, Mattitiahu. "Theology of the Old Testament: A Jewish View." *HBT* 8 (1986) 33–49.

Turner, Victor. *Dramas, Fields, and Metaphors: Symbolic Action in Human Society.* Ithaca, N.Y.: Cornell Univ. Press, 1974.

———. *The Ritual Process: Structure and Anti-Structure.* Chicago: Aldine, 1989.

Tutu, Desmond. *Crying in the Wilderness: The Struggle for Justice in South Africa.* Grand Rapids: Eerdmans, 1982.

Upkong, Justin S. "Developments in Biblical Interpretation in Africa: Historical and Hermeneutical Directions." In *The Bible in Africa: Transactions, Trajectories, and Trends,* edited by Gerald O. West and Musa W. Dube, 11–28. Boston: Brill, 2001.

———. "Inculturation and Evangelization: Biblical Foundations for Incultura-tion." *Vidyajyoti* 58 (1994) 298–307.

———. "The Parable of the Shrewd Manager (Luke 16:1-13): An Essay in Incultur-ation Hermeneutics." *Semeia* 73 (1995) 189–210.

———. *Sacrifice, African and Biblical: A Comparative Study of Ibibio and Levitical Sacrifices.* Rome: Urbaniana Univ. Press, 1987.

———. "Towards a Renewed Approach to Inculturation Theology." *Journal of Inculturation Theology* 1 (1994) 3–15.

Vaillant, Janet G. *Black, French, and African: A Life of Leopold Sédar Senghor.* Cam-bridge, Mass.: Harvard Univ. Press, 1990.

Vatke, Wilhelm. *Die biblische Theologie wissenschaftlich dargestellt.* Vol. 1, *Die Religion des Alten Testaments nach den Kanonischen Büchern entwickelt.* Berlin: Bethge, 1835.

Veeser, H. Avram. *The New Historicism.* New York: Routledge, 1989.

Vischer, Wilhelm. *Das Christuszeugnis des Alten Testaments.* Zollikon: Evangelis-cher, 1946.

Vriezen, T. C. *An Outline of Old Testament Theology,* 2d ed. Translated by S. Neui-jen. Oxford: Blackwell, 1970.

———. *The Religion of Ancient Israel.* Philadelphia: Westminster, 1967.

Ward, Graham, ed. *The Blackwell Companion to Postmodern Theology.* BCR 4. Oxford: Blackwell, 2001.

———. "Introduction: 'Where We Stand.'" In *The Blackwell Companion to Post-modern Theology,* edited by Graham Ward, xii–xxvii. BCR 4. Oxford: Black-well, 2001.

———. *The Postmodern God.* Oxford: Blackwell, 1998.

Ware, Vron. *Beyond the Pale: White Women, Racism and History.* London: Verso, 1992.

Watson, Francis. *Text, Church and World: Biblical Interpretation in Theological Per-spective.* Edinburgh: T. & T. Clark, 1994.

Weber, Max. *The Protestant Ethic and the Spirit of Capitalism.* Translated by Talcott Parsons. New York: Scribner, 1956.

———. *The Sociology of Religion.* Translated by Ephraim Fischoff. Boston: Bea-con, 1963.

Weems, Renita. *Battered Love: Marriage, Sex, and Violence in the Hebrew Prophets.* OBT. Minneapolis: Fortress Press, 1995.

———. *Just a Sister Away: A Womanist Vision of Women's Relationships in the Bible.* San Diego: LuraMedia, 1988.

———. "Reading Her Way through the Struggle: African American Women and the Bible." In *Stony the Road We Trod: African American Biblical Interpretation,* edited by Cain H. Felder, 57–77. Minneapolis: Fortress Press, 1991.

———. "Song of Songs." In *NIB* 5:363–434. Nashville: Abingdon, 1997.

Weinfeld, Moshe. "Gott als Schöpfer in Genesis 1 und in Deutero-Jesaja." *Tarbiz* 37 (1968) 105–32. [Heb.]

———. "Theological Trends in der Tora-Literatur." *BM* 16 (1971) 10–22. [Heb.]

Weiss, Meir. "Psalm 23: The Psalmist on God's Care." In *Sha'arei Talmon,* edited by Michael Fishbane and Emanuel Tov, 31–40. Winona Lake, Ind.: Eisenbrauns, 1992.

Wellhausen, Julius. *Israelitische und jüdische Geschichte,* 10th ed. Berlin: de Gruyter, 2002.

————. *Prolegomena zur Geschichte Israels*, 5th ed. Berlin: Reimer, 1899. ET= *Prolegomenon to the History of Israel*. New York: Meridian, 1957.

West, Cornel. *Prophesy Deliverance! An Afro-American Revolutionary Christianity*. Philadelphia: Westminster, 1982.

West, Gerald. *The Academy of the Poor: Towards a Dialogical Reading of the Bible*. Sheffield: Sheffield University Press, 1999.

————. *Contextual Bible Study*. Pietermaritzburg: Cluster, 1993.

Westermann, Claus. "Das Verhältnis des Jahweglaubens zu den ausserisraelitischen Religion." In idem, *Forschung am Alten Testament*, 189–218. ThBü 24; Munich: Kaiser, 1964.

Wheelwright, Phillip. *Metaphor and Reality*. Bloomington: Indiana Univ. Press, 1962.

White, Hayden. *Metahistory: The Historical Imagination in Nineteenth-Century Europe*. Baltimore: Johns Hopkins Univ. Press, 1973.

White, Hugh C. "Introduction: Speech Act Theory and Literary Criticism." *Semeia* 41 (1988) 1–24.

————. "The Value of Speech Act Theory for Old Testament Hermeneutics." *Semeia* 41 (1988) 41–63.

Williams, Delores. *Sisters in the Wilderness: The Challenge of Womanist God-Talk*. Maryknoll, N.Y.: Orbis, 1993.

Wimbush, Vincent L., ed. *African Americans and the Bible: Sacred Texts and Sacred Textures*. New York: Continuum, 2000.

————. *The Bible and African Americans: A Brief History*. Facets. Minneapolis: Fortress Press, 2003.

————, ed. *The Bible and the American Myth: A Symposium on the Bible and Constructions of Meaning*. Studies in American Biblical Hermeneutics 16. Macon, Ga.: Mercer Univ. Press, 1999.

————. "Biblical Historical Study as Liberation: Toward an Afro-Christian Hermeneutic." *Journal of Religious Thought* 42 (1985/86) 9–21.

————. "Reading Texts as Reading Ourselves: A Chapter in the History of African-American Biblical Interpretation." In *Reading from This Place*, edited by Fernando Segovia and Mary Ann Tolbert, 1:95–108. Minneapolis: Fortress Press, 1995.

Winter, Gibson. *Liberating Creation: Foundations of Religious Social Ethics*. New York: Crossroad, 1981.

Wolf, Hans Walter, Rolf Rendtorff, and Wolfhart Pannenberg. *Gerhard von Rad: Seine Bedeutung für die Theologie*. Munich: Kaiser, 1973.

Wrede, William. *The Messianic Secret*. Library of Theological Translations. Cambridge: Clarke, 1971.

————. *Über Ausgabe und Methode der sogennanten neutestamentlichen Theologie*. Göttingen: Vandenhoeck & Ruprecht, 1897.

Wright, G. Ernest. *The God Who Acts: Biblical Theology as Recital*. SBT 1/8. London: SCM Press, 1952.

————. *The Old Testament against Its Environment*. SBT 1/2. Naperville, Ill.: Allenson, 1957.

Young, Pamela Dickey. *Feminist Theology/Christian Theology.* Minneapolis: Fortress Press, 1990.

Young, Robert C. *Postcolonialism: An Historical Introduction.* Oxford: Blackwell, 2001.

Zenger, Erich. *Das Erste Testament: Die Jüdische Bibel und die Christen.* Duesseldorf: Patmos, 1992.

Zevit, Ziony. "Jewish Biblical Theology: Whence? Why? and Whither?" SBLAM 2003.

Zimmerli, Walther. "The History of Israelite Religion." In *Tradition and Interpretation,* edited by G. W. Anderson, 351–84. London: Oxford Univ. Press, 1979.

Zwickel, Wolfgang. "Religionsgeschichte Israels: Einführung in den gegenwärtigen Forschungsstand in die deutschsprachigen Ländern." In *Religionsgeschichte Israels: Formale und Materiale Aspekte,* edited by Bernd Janowski und Matthias Köchert. Veröffentlichungen der Wissenschaftlichen Gesellschaft für Theologie 15. Gütersloh: Kaiser, 1999.

Index of Modern Names

Index of Scripture